T0309602

Methods and Innovations for Multimedia Database Content Management

Shu-Ching Chen
Florida International University, USA

Mei-Ling Shyu
University of Miami, USA

Information Science
REFERENCE

Managing Director:	Lindsay Johnston
Senior Editorial Director:	Heather A. Probst
Book Production Manager:	Sean Woznicki
Development Manager:	Joel Gamon
Acquisitions Editor:	Erika Gallagher
Typesetter:	Adrienne Freeland
Cover Design:	Nick Newcomer, Lisandro Gonzalez

Published in the United States of America by
Information Science Reference (an imprint of IGI Global)
701 E. Chocolate Avenue
Hershey PA 17033
Tel: 717-533-8845
Fax: 717-533-8661
E-mail: cust@igi-global.com
Web site: http://www.igi-global.com

Library of Congress Cataloging-in-Publication Data

Methods and innovations for multimedia database content management / Shu-Ching Chen and Mei-Ling Shyu, editors.
    p. cm.
  Includes bibliographical references and index.
  Summary: "This book highlights original research on new theories, algorithms, technologies, system design, and implementation in multimedia data engineering and management with an emphasis on automatic indexing, tagging, high-order ranking, and rule mining"--Provided by publisher.
  ISBN 978-1-4666-1791-9 (hardcover) -- ISBN 978-1-4666-1792-6 (ebook) -- ISBN 978-1-4666-1793-3 (print & perpetual access) 1. Multimedia systems. 2. Database management. I. Chen, Shu-Ching, 1963- II. Shyu, Mei-Ling.
  QA76.575.M48 2012
  006.7--dc23
                          2012002466

British Cataloguing in Publication Data
A Cataloguing in Publication record for this book is available from the British Library.

The views expressed in this book are those of the authors, but not necessarily of the publisher.

Table of Contents

Section 2
Image Classification and Retrieval

Section 3
Video Content Processing and Retrieval

Section 4
Audio Data Processing and Indexing

Section 5
Multimedia Applications: Integration of Multimedia Management and E-Learning Technology

Detailed Table of Contents

Section 1
Multimedia Data Mining and Multimedia Databases

The exponential growth of the technological advancements has resulted in high-resolution devices, such as digital cameras, scanners, monitors, and printers, which enable the capturing and displaying of multimedia data in high-density storage devices. Furthermore, more and more applications need to live with multimedia data. However, the gap between the characteristics of various media types and the application requirements has created the need to develop advanced techniques for multimedia data management and the extraction of relevant information from multimedia databases. Though many research efforts have been devoted to the areas of multimedia databases and data management, it is still far from maturity. The purpose of this article is to discuss how the existing techniques, methodologies, and tools addressed relevant issues and challenges to enable a better understanding in multimedia databases and data management. The focuses include: (1) how to develop a formal structure that can be used to capture the distinguishing content of the media data in a multimedia database (MMDB) and to form an abstract space for the data to be queried; (2) how to develop advanced content analysis and retrieval techniques that can be used to bridge the gaps between the semantic meaning and low-level media characteristics to improve multimedia information retrieval; and (3) how to develop query mechanisms that can handle complex spatial, temporal, and/or spatio-temporal relationships of multimedia data to answer the imprecise and incomplete queries issued to an MMDB.

Semantic knowledge detection of multimedia content has become a very popular research topic in recent years. The association rule mining (ARM) technique has been shown to be an efficient and accurate approach for content-based multimedia retrieval and semantic concept detection in many applications. To further improve the performance of traditional association rule mining technique, a video semantic concept detection framework whose classifier is built upon a new weighted association rule mining (WARM) algorithm is proposed in this article. Our proposed WARM algorithm is able to capture the different significance degrees of the items (feature-value pairs) in generating the association rules for video semantic concept detection. Our proposed WARM-based framework first applies multiple correspondence analysis (MCA) to project the features and classes into a new principle component space and discover the correlation between feature-value pairs and classes. Next, it considers both correlation and percentage information as the measurement to weight the feature-value pairs and to generate the association rules. Finally, it performs classification by using these weighted association rules. To evaluate our WARM-based framework, we compare its performance of video semantic concept detection with several well-known classifiers using the benchmark data available from the 2007 and 2008 TRECVID projects. The results demonstrate that our WARM-based framework achieves promising performance and performs significantly better than those classifiers in the comparison.

Chapter 3

Lin Lin, University of Miami, USA
Mei-Ling Shyu, University of Miami, USA

Motivated by the growing use of multimedia services and the explosion of multimedia collections, efficient retrieval from large-scale multimedia data has become very important in multimedia content analysis and management. In this paper, a novel ranking algorithm is proposed for video retrieval. First, video content is represented by the global and local features and second, multiple correspondence analysis (MCA) is applied to capture the correlation between video content and semantic concepts. Next, video segments are scored by considering the features with high correlations and the transaction weights converted from correlations. Finally, a user interface is implemented in a video retrieval system that allows the user to enter his/her interested concept, searches videos based on the target concept, ranks the retrieved video segments using the proposed ranking algorithm, and then displays the top-ranked video segments to the user. Experimental results on 30 concepts from the TRECVID high-level feature extraction task have demonstrated that the presented video retrieval system assisted by the proposed ranking algorithm is able to retrieve more video segments belonging to the target concepts and to display more relevant results to the users.

Chapter 4

Aiyesha Ma, Oakland University, USA
Ishwar Sethi, Oakland University, USA
Nilesh Patel, Oakland University, USA

Community tagging offers valuable information for media search and retrieval, but new media items are at a disadvantage. Automated tagging may populate media items with few tags, thus enabling their inclusion into search results. In this paper, a multi-label decision tree is proposed and applied to the problem of automated tagging of media data. In addition to binary labels, the proposed Iterative Split Multi-label Decision Tree (IS-MLT) is easily extended to the problem of weighted labels (such as those depicted by tag clouds). Several datasets of differing media types show the effectiveness of the proposed method relative to other multi-label and single label classifier methods and demonstrate its scalability relative to single label approaches.

Section 2
Image Classification and Retrieval

Chapter 5

Chengcui Zhang, University of Alabama at Birmingham, USA
Liping Zhou, University of Alabama at Birmingham, USA
Wen Wan, University of Alabama at Birmingham, USA
Jeffrey Birch, Virginia Polytechnic Institute and State University, USA
Wei-Bang Chen, University of Alabama at Birmingham, USA

Most existing object-based image retrieval systems are based on single object matching, with its main limitation being that one individual image region (object) can hardly represent the user's retrieval target, especially when more than one object of interest is involved in the retrieval. Integrated Region Matching (IRM) has been used to improve the retrieval accuracy by evaluating the overall similarity between images and incorporating the properties of all the regions in the images. However, IRM does not take the user's preferred regions into account and has undesirable time complexity. In this article, we present a Feedback-based Image Clustering and Retrieval Framework (FIRM) using a novel image clustering algorithm and integrating it with Integrated Region Matching (IRM) and Relevance Feedback (RF). The performance of the system is evaluated on a large image database, demonstrating the effectiveness of our framework in catching users' retrieval interests in object-based image retrieval.

Chapter 6

Ramakrishnan Mukundan, University of Canterbury, New Zealand
Anna Hemsley, University of Canterbury, New Zealand

Tissue image classification is a challenging problem due to the fact that the images contain highly irregular shapes in complex spatial arrangement. The multi-fractal formalism has been found useful in characterizing the intensity distribution present in such images, as it can effectively resolve local densities and also represent various structures present in the image. This paper presents a detailed study of feature vectors derived from the distribution of Holder exponents and the geometrical characteristics of the multi-fractal spectra that can be used in applications requiring image classification and retrieval. The paper also gives the results of experimental analysis performed using a tissue image database and demonstrates the effectiveness of the proposed multi-fractal-based descriptors in tissue image classification and retrieval. Implementation aspects that need to be considered for improving classification accuracy and the feature representation capability of the proposed descriptors are also outlined.

Chapter 7

Peter Vajda, Ecole Polytechnique Fédérale de Lausanne – EPFL, Switzerland
Ivan Ivanov, Ecole Polytechnique Fédérale de Lausanne – EPFL, Switzerland
Lutz Goldmann, Ecole Polytechnique Fédérale de Lausanne – EPFL, Switzerland
Jong-Seok Lee, Ecole Polytechnique Fédérale de Lausanne – EPFL, Switzerland
Touradj Ebrahimi, Ecole Polytechnique Fédérale de Lausanne – EPFL, Switzerland

In this paper, the authors analyze their graph-based approach for 2D and 3D object duplicate detection in still images. A graph model is used to represent the 3D spatial information of the object based on the features extracted from training images to avoid explicit and complex 3D object modeling. Therefore, improved performance can be achieved in comparison to existing methods in terms of both robustness and computational complexity. Different limitations of this approach are analyzed by evaluating performance with respect to the number of training images and calculation of optimal parameters in a number of applications. Furthermore, effectiveness of object duplicate detection algorithm is measured over different object classes. The authors' method is shown to be robust in detecting the same objects even when images with objects are taken from different viewpoints or distances.

Section 3
Video Content Processing and Retrieval

Chapter 8
Masaki Takahashi, NHK Science and Technology Research Laboratories, Japan; The Graduate University for Advanced Studies, Japan

Mahito Fujii, NHK Science and Technology Research Laboratories, Japan

Masahiro Shibata, NHK Science and Technology Research Laboratories, Japan

Nobuyuki Yagi, NHK Science and Technology Research Laboratories, Japan

Shin'ichi Satoh, National Institute of Informatics, Japan; The Graduate University for Advanced Studies, Japan

This article describes a system that automatically recognizes individual pitch types like screwballs and sliders in baseball broadcast videos. These decisions are currently made by human specialists in baseball, who are watching the broadcast video of the game. No automatic system has yet been developed for identifying individual pitch types from single view camera images. Techniques using multiple fixed cameras promise highly accurate pitch type identification, but the systems tend to be large. Our system is designed to identify the same pitch types using only the same single-view broadcast baseball videos used by the human specialists, and accordingly we used a number of features, such as the ball's location, ball speed and catcher's stance based on the advice of those specialists. The system identifies the pitch type using a classifier trained with the Random Forests ensemble learning algorithm and achieved about 90% recognition accuracy in experiments.

Chapter 9
Hanif Seddiqui, Toyohashi University of Technology, Japan
Masaki Aono, Toyohashi University of Technology, Japan

Heterogeneous multimedia contents are annotated by a sharable formal conceptualization, often called ontology, and these contents, regardless of their media, become sharable resources/instances. Integration of the sharable resources and acquisition of diverse knowledge is getting researchers' attention at a rapid pace. In this regard, MPEG-7 standard convertible to semantic Resource Description Framework (RDF) evolves for containing structured data and knowledge sources. In this paper, the authors propose an efficient approach to integrate the multimedia resources annotated by the standard of MPEG-7 schema using ontology instance matching techniques. MPEG-7 resources are usually specified explicitly by their surrounding MPEG-7 schema entities, e.g., concepts and properties, in conjunction with other linked resources. Therefore, resource integration needed schema matching as well. In this approach, the authors obtained the schema matching using their scalable ontology alignment algorithm and collected the semantically linked resources, referred to as the Semantic Link Cloud (SLC) collectively for each of the resources. Techniques were addressed to solve several data heterogeneity: value transformation, structural transformation and logical transformation. These experiments show the strength and efficiency of the proposed matching approach.

Chapter 10

Yi Chen, University of Alabama in Huntsville, USA
Ramazan S. Aygün, University of Alabama in Huntsville, USA

Sprite generation is the process of aligning, warping, and blending of pixels that belong to an object in a video. The evaluation of the correctness of a sprite is usually accomplished by a combination of objective and subjective evaluations. Availability of ground-truth image would help mere objective evaluation. In this paper, the authors present video generation from an image based on various camera motion parameters to be used as ground-truth for the sprite evaluation. This paper introduces a framework for evaluation of sprite generation algorithms. Experiments under the proposed framework were performed on the synthetic videos of different camera motion patterns to reveal the components of the sprite generation algorithm to be improved.

Chapter 11

Maia Zaharieva, Vienna University of Technology, Austria
Matthias Zeppelzauer, Vienna University of Technology, Austria
Dalibor Mitrović, Vienna University of Technology, Austria
Christian Breiteneder, Vienna University of Technology, Austria

In this paper, the authors present an approach for video comparison, in which an instantiated framework allows for the easy comparison of different methods that are required at each step of the comparison process. The authors' approach is evaluated based on a real world scenario of challenging video data of archive documentaries. In this paper, the performed experiments aim at the evaluation of the performance of established shot boundary detection algorithms, the influence of keyframe selection, and feature representation.

Section 4
Audio Data Processing and Indexing

Chapter 12

Allan Knight, University of California, Santa Barbara USA
Kevin Almeroth, University of California, Santa Barbara, USA

For large archives of audio media, just as with text archives, indexing is important for allowing quick and accurate searches. Similar to text archives, audio archives can use text for indexing. Generating this text requires using transcripts of the spoken portions of the audio. From them, an alignment can be made that allows users to search for specific content and immediately view the content at the position where the search terms were spoken. Although previous research has addressed this issue, the solutions align the transcripts only in real-time or greater. In this paper, the authors propose AUTOCAP. It is capable of producing accurate audio indexes in faster than real-time for archived audio and in real-time for live audio. In most cases it takes less than one quarter the original duration for archived audio. This paper discusses the architecture and evaluation of the AUTOCAP project as well as two of its applications.

Chapter 13

In popular music information retrieval systems, users have the opportunity to tag musical objects to express their personal preferences, thus providing valuable insights about the formulation of user groups/ communities. In this article, the authors focus on the analysis of social tagging data to reveal coherent groups characterized by their users, tags and music objects (e.g., songs and artists), which allows for the expression of discovered groups in a multi-aspect way. For each group, this study reveals the most prominent users, tags, and music objects using a generalization of the popular web-ranking concept in the social data domain. Experimenting with real data, the authors' results show that each Tag-Aware group corresponds to a specific music topic, and additionally, a three way ranking analysis is performed inside each group. Building Tag-Aware groups is crucial to offer ways to add structure in the unstructured nature of tags.

Section 5
Multimedia Applications: Integration of Multimedia Management and E-Learning Technology

In this paper, the authors present their proposal for adaptation of educational contents of learning objects to a particular mobile device and a specific learner. Content adaptation in mobile learning objects implies user adaptation and device adaptation, and requires additional metadata categories in comparison with SCORM 2004. This learning object content model, ALMA (A Learning content Model Adaptation), inherits from the SCORM standard a subset of metadata categories, and extends it with three top level metadata categories for content adaptation, i.e., Knowledge, Use, and Mobile Device Requirements (Castillo & Ayala, 2008). For user adaptation, the authors developed NORIKO (NOn-monotonic Reasoning for Intelligent Knowledge awareness and recommendations On the move), a belief system based on DLV, a programming system based on Answer Set Programming paradigm. For device adaptation the authors designed CARIME (Content Adapter of Resources In Mobile learning Environments), which uses transcoding and transrating to adapt media content to suit the device characteristics.

Chapter 15

The concept of minimum spanning tree algorithms in data structure is difficult for students to learn and to imagine without practice. Usually, learners need to diagram the spanning trees with pen to realize how the minimum spanning tree algorithm works. In this paper, the authors introduce a competitive board game to motivate students to learn the concept of minimum spanning tree algorithms. They discuss the reasons why it is beneficial to combine graph theories and board game for the Dijkstra and Prim minimum spanning tree theories. In the experimental results, this paper demonstrates the board game and examines the learning feedback for the mentioned two graph theories. Advantages summarizing the benefits of combining the graph theories with board game are discussed.

Chapter 16

Xin Wang, University of Missouri, USA
Borchuluun Yadamsuren, University of Missouri, USA
Anindita Paul, University of Missouri, USA
DeeAnna Adkins, University of Missouri, USA
George C. Laur, University of Missouri, USA
Andrew Tawfik, University of Missouri, USA
Sanda Erdelez, University of Missouri, USA

Online education is a popular paradigm for promoting continuing education for adult learners. However, only a handful of studies have addressed usability issues in the online education environment. Particularly, few studies have integrated the multifaceted usability evaluation into the lifecycle of developing such an environment. This paper will show the integration of usability evaluation into the development process of an online education center. Multifaceted usability evaluation methods were applied at four different stages of the MU Extension web portal's development. These methods were heuristic evaluation, focus group interview and survey, think-aloud interviewing, and multiple-user simultaneous testing. The results of usability studies at each stage enhanced the development team's understanding of users' difficulties, needs, and wants, which served to guide web developers' subsequent decisions.

Chapter 17

Chun-Yi Shen, Tamkang University, Taiwan
Chiung-Sui Chang, Tamkang University, Taiwan

Online teaching is the fastest growing form of delivery in higher education and faculty is expected to integrate technology into their teaching. The purpose of this study is to examine the performance of e-instructors in Taiwan based on the new human performance model. To achieve the purposes, this paper adopted a questionnaire survey and One hundred and six online instructors from 25 universities in Taiwan participated in this study. Correlation and multiple regression are performed to analysis the data. After statistical analysis, the results show that the four factors, advanced skill, basic skill, effort, and self-efficacy, contributed significantly to the model variance of e-instructors' performance in online teaching. The results also provide the evidences of the importance of self-efficacy in online teaching.

Preface

The technological advances on ubiquitous computing, electronic imaging, video devices, storage, and computing power have enabled the generation of huge amounts of multimedia data that are essential in many applications such as education, e-Learning solutions, entertainment, digital libraries, homeland security, health and environmental protection, and adaptive games, to name a few. In addition, the world has also witnessed an unprecedented explosion of multimedia data through the emerging online large-scale social networks such as Flickr, Picasa, Facebook, MySpace, YouTube, and Zooomr. People share personal experiences on these social network websites. For example, people upload home and professional videos on YouTube and digital images on Flickr (more than 350,000 images uploaded each day). Such phenomena involve great challenges in multimedia data management, but they also represent new opportunities for multimedia research in the areas of multimedia databases and multimedia content processing, analysis, mining, and retrieval.

Multimedia data can be of various media types, including text, voice, image, audio, animation, video, et cetera. It is well-acknowledged that the rich semantics and the spatial, temporal, and/or spatio-temporal characteristics of multimedia data make the management and retrieval of such multimedia data more challenging. There is an increasing need in new techniques and tools that can empower the development of the next generation multimedia databases and multimedia information systems. For example, techniques and tools are needed for discovering relationships between objects or segments within images, classifying images based on their content, extracting patterns in sound, categorizing speech and music, discovering patterns within video clips, classifying video semantic concepts based on their content, recognizing objects in video streams, and tracking objects in video streams. Furthermore, many applications can be realized and deployed by taking the advantages of these advanced techniques and tools in multimedia research.

This book consists of seventeen (17) chapters contributed by the researchers, scientists, professionals, software engineers, and graduate/undergraduate students in academia and industry, who present their original research ideas to address the challenges and issues in in-depth content processing, analysis, indexing, learning, mining, searching, management, and retrieval for the collection and distribution of vast amounts of multimedia data. New theories, algorithms, technologies, system designs, and implementations from different aspects in multimedia data engineering and management are included in these chapters. These innovative multimedia techniques and tools can further be deployed to many multimedia applications. One such application included in this book is the effective utilization of multimedia technology for e-learning.

The collection is organized into five (5) sections in the way that each section focuses on a distinct content area and the research ideas are made accessible to the readers who are interested in grasping the basics, as well as to those who would like more technical depth. These five sections are "Multimedia Data Mining and Multimedia Databases," "Image Classification and Retrieval," "Video Content Processing and Retrieval," "Audio Data Processing and Indexing," and "Multimedia Applications: Integration of Multimedia Management and E-Learning Technology."

SECTION 1: MULTIMEDIA DATA MINING AND MULTIMEDIA DATABASES

The first section includes four (4) chapters that present the techniques and tools in multimedia data mining and multimedia databases.

To provide an overview of the current state-of-the-art developments in multimedia databases and data management, the first chapter presents a survey on these areas in "Multimedia Databases and Data Management: A Survey" by Shu-Ching Chen. As indicated by the author, though there have been solutions proposed to address the challenges in the areas of multimedia databases and data management, more research efforts to enable a better understanding in these areas are still in need. This chapter goes into more in-depth discussions on various important aspects. It starts with the discussions on the developments of formal structures that can capture the distinguishing content of the media data in a multimedia database (MMDB) and an abstract space for the data to be queried. Traditional database systems, such as relational database systems, are able to store, manage, and retrieve textual and numerical data. In particular, data retrieval is often based on simple comparisons of text or numerical values, and thus they cannot provide adequate supports for the management, browsing, and searching of multimedia data. Though some attempts have been developed, such as supporting the access to multimedia objects in the forms of pointers to binary large objects (BLOBs) or enabling the definition of the part-of-relationship among objects in an arbitrary structure, the capabilities of accessing various portions of the multimedia objects interactively using BLOBs or managing the spatial, temporal, and/or spatio-temporal relations among the multimedia objects are still limited. Therefore, a formal structure and an abstract space for the multimedia objects in an MMDB are needed. Next, in order to improve multimedia information retrieval in an MMDB, the advanced content analysis and retrieval techniques and tools need to be developed so that the gaps between the semantic meaning and low-level media characteristics can be shortened and bridged. The author conducts the surveys on many research studies contributed to the developments of multimedia content analysis and retrieval that use low-level, mid-level, and/or high-level information in the retrieval process. Finally, after bridging the semantic gap to enable semantic-based information retrieval, it becomes possible to develop effective query mechanisms to handle complex spatial, temporal, and/or spatio-temporal relationships of the multimedia data so that the imprecise and incomplete queries issued to an MMDB can be efficiently answered. Such a detailed survey in these areas provides the insights that are important and beneficial for the researchers in the MMDB research community.

The section chapter is contributed by Lin and Shyu for their paper entitled "Weighted Association Rule Mining for Video Semantic Detection." In this chapter, the authors propose a novel weighted association rule mining (WARM) algorithm for video semantic concept detection. Research in multimedia retrieval and semantic detection has become important in recent years due to the popular applications such as sport highlighters, movie recommenders, image search engines, and music libraries. Supervised content-based multimedia retrieval frameworks typically include the segmentation of the multimedia data, the representation of the multimedia data, the model training process, and the classification for the testing data using the training model. In this chapter, the WARM-based video concept detection framework involves three main steps. In the first step, multiple correspondence analysis (MCA) is applied to project the features and classes into a new principle component space so that the correlation between the 1-feature-value pairs and the classes can be discovered. MCA is a technique that provides the ability to analyze a table containing some measure of correspondence between the rows and columns with more than two variables. In content-based multimedia retrieval, by utilizing MCA, the correspondence between the features and the classes could be captured, which assists the classifier in narrowing the semantic gap between the low-level features and the high-level concepts (class labels) in a multimedia database. The second step calculates the weights for the 1-feature-value pairs by considering both the correlation and percentage information, and uses these weights to generate the association rules. In step 3, these weighted association rules generated in step 2 form the classification rules to check whether a video shot consists of a certain high-level concept of interest (like "outdoor," "road," "walking," etc.). Evaluations are conducted on the TRECVID 2007 and 2008 video corpus to compare the classification performance of 15 selected concepts between their WARM-based framework and seven other well-known classification algorithms. Contributed by the fact that the WARM algorithm is able to capture different significance degrees of the feature-value pairs in generating the association rules, the WARM-based framework outperforms those classifiers in terms of the precision, recall, and F-1 measures.

Chapter 3 presents a novel correlation-based ranking algorithm for information retrieval from the video data in "Correlation-Based Ranking for Large-Scale Video Concept Retrieval" by Lin and Shyu. Efficient searching and retrieval from the huge amount of multimedia data is critical in multimedia data management and multimedia services. It is especially challenging when automatic and accurate concept-based retrieval from the multimedia data is needed. Concept-based retrieval is to detect the existence of objects (like a bus or a hand), the meaning of scenes (like cityscape or nighttime), and the occurrence of events (like airplane flying and people dancing). Hence, effective concept-based multimedia retrieval enables the users to utilize multimedia data for a variety of applications including entertainment, distant education, commerce and business, social communication, navigation, security, surveillance, et cetera. The main idea for their proposed ranking algorithm is to capture the correlation between the video content and the semantic concepts. Their proposed work consists of three stages. In the first stage, the video content is represented by the global and local audio and visual features. Under this way, both the global representation of scenes and local representation of regions are captured. The second stage applies multiple correspondence analysis (MCA) to explore the correlation between video content and semantic concepts. Based on the results generated from MCA, scores are assigned to video segments by considering the features with high correlations and the transaction weights converted from the correlations in the third stage. A user interface is also implemented to facilitate a video retrieval system by displaying the more relevant retrieved video segments to the users. Experiments on the TRECVID data are conducted, and the results demonstrate that their proposed ranking algorithm is able to effectively retrieve more video segments belonging to the target concepts and to display more relevant results to the users.

Chapter 4 is entitled "Multi-Label Classification Method for Multimedia Tagging" by Ma, Sethi, and Patel. Multimedia information retrieval for search queries can be based on two basic approaches, namely (1) similarity of multimedia artifacts and (2) similarity of associated keywords or tags. Though many research studies fall into the first category, providing an example document for the query may be difficult or impossible. On the other hand, the approaches in the second category rely on the association of keywords or tags to the multimedia objects by allowing the search without the need for an example document. Hence, this work is motivated by the fact that only few tags will be associated with new media items (i.e., initially untagged) via automated tagging to help to improve the retrieval of multimedia content, and this enables the inclusion of these media items into the search results. In this context, the authors develop a multi-label decision tree (for binary labels) as well as an Iterative Split Multi-label Decision Tree called IS-MLT (for weighted labels), and apply them to the problem of automated tagging. The idea of their proposed work is to first partition the set of labels into two groups at each node, make a decision using the two groups at a node level and a binary decision method, and then obtain the scores from the leaf node frequencies and assign the labels by thresholding. Evaluations on three data sets of various media types, including a music data set (audio data with binary labels), a photographic scene data set (image data with binary labels), and the data extracted from the Last.FM website (text data with non-binary labels or weighted tags), are conducted and the results demonstrate the effectiveness of their proposed IS-MLT with respect to a variety of performance and loss measures.

SECTION 2: IMAGE CLASSIFICATION AND RETRIEVAL

Section 2 discusses the methodologies in image classification and retrieval in three (03) chapters.

In Chapter 5, Zhang et al. present their proposed Feedback-based Image Clustering and Retrieval Framework (FIRM) in "An Image Clustering and Feedback-based Retrieval Framework" to address the challenges in object-based image retrieval. Object-based image retrieval that retrieves images on the basis of the underlying semantics of the images has become more and more popular. In this area, the semantic content of an image is represented by one or more objects in that image, and the object-based features are considered the user's perceived content of that image. However, such an approach has two main issues. First, most existing systems retrieve images according to a single object/segment of a user's interest. If the user queries require more than one object-of-interest, such systems may not work. In addition, there can be inaccurate image segments due to over-segmentation and/or under-segmentation, which may negatively affect the image retrieval results. Second, most existing systems require a complex user interface to display all the segments (regions) of a query image for the user to choose his/her desirable query region(s) from these segments, which are likely to be cumbersome and confusion due to the large number of segments/objects in each image (7 to 8 images/objects on average). It is claimed by the authors that FIRM includes a novel image clustering algorithm and integrates it with Integrated Region Matching (IRM) and Relevance Feedback (RF). Though IRM can improve the retrieval accuracy by evaluating the overall similarity between images and incorporating the properties of all the regions in the images, it has two disadvantages: (1) it does not take the user's preferred regions into account, and (2) it has undesirable time complexity. FIRM is developed with the attempt to address these two disadvantages. The performance of FIRM is evaluated on a large image database, and the result demonstrates its effectiveness in catching users' retrieval interests in object-based image retrieval.

Chapter 6 is "Tissue Image Classification Using Multi-Fractal Spectra" by Mukundan and Hemsley. It is recognized that automatic image recognition and classification has become more and more popular in biomedical image processing. It is more desirable to have robust classification algorithms for applications involving large-scale image databases with associated operations such as content-based retrieval and analysis. One such application is cell and tissue imaging with large tissue image databases which contain hundreds of specimens and histological types. Tissue diagnostics are important in the screening, treatment, and monitoring of diseases. This chapter is to provide a solution to address the challenges in tissue image classification since the images contain highly irregular shapes in complex spatial arrangement. The authors propose the multi-fractal property of the images. Most of the existing tissue image classification frameworks used techniques such as wavelet transforms and discriminant analysis. The authors approach this problem in a different way. They use two new texture feature descriptors: one constructed from the histogram of Holder exponents in the image, and the second from the geometrical properties of the multi-fractal spectra. Both types of feature descriptors have been found to yield very good results in the classification process. That is, a tissue image can be viewed as a combination of regions with different fractal properties. Experiments on a tissue image database are conducted and the classification and retrieval results, in terms of the sum and iso measures, demonstrate the effectiveness of their proposed descriptors. The authors also indicate that the sum measure is particularly useful since the spectra exhibit excellent intra-class similarity and inter-class variance.

In Chapter 7, Vajda et al. analyze their graph-based approach for 2D and 3D object duplicate detection in still images in their chapter entitled "Robust Duplicate Detection of 2D and 3D Objects." This is an attempt to address the limitations of the features extracted in content-based image retrieval. As more and more images and video sequences are captured and shared in online services, the keyword-based indexing which is very time consuming and inefficient due to linguistic and semantic ambiguities is no longer feasible. This calls for the development of content-based image and video retrieval systems. In general, content-based image retrieval uses different features to describe the image content, such as the global descriptors, feature points, regions, and objects. Given a query image containing an object, an image retrieval system can perform object recognition or object duplicate detection. In this chapter, the authors focus on the object duplicate detection task, which should be robust to changes in position, size, view, illumination, and partial occlusions. That is, the features may change significantly depending on the view point since these features are extracted from images which contain two-dimensional projections of three-dimensional scenes. Such a limitation may lead to the failure of retrieving relevant content for some queries. The authors use a graph model to represent the 3D spatial information of the object based on the features extracted from the training images to avoid explicit and complex 3D object modeling. Their proposed approach combines the efficiency of a bag of words model with the accuracy of a part-based model. In other words, their approach makes an attempt towards 3D modeling, while keeping the efficiency of 2D processing. Experiments on a data set with 850 images are conducted, the advantages and limitations of their proposed approach are discussed, and the set of optimal parameters is obtained. The experimental results demonstrate a considerable performance improvement in comparison with two other representative approaches used in the comparisons.

SECTION 3: VIDEO CONTENT PROCESSING AND RETRIEVAL

In the third section, several techniques to address the challenges and issues in video content processing and retrieval are presented in four (4) chapters.

In Chapter 8, an interesting baseball pitch-type recognition system is discussed in "Automatic Pitch Type Recognition System from Single-View Video Sequences of Baseball Broadcast Videos," by Takahashi et al. The authors develop a system that automatically recognizes individual pitch types (like screwballs and sliders) by using only the information contained in the baseball broadcast videos. A variety of metadata corresponding to different sports have been distributed in real-time. For baseball, the data generated for each pitch is diverse and includes player at bat, the count, ball speed, et cetera.

Though people pay attention to the type of pitch, it is still considered difficult to automatically determine the type of pitch from a baseball broadcast video. The authors utilize the features such as ball trajectory, ball speed, and the catcher's stance just prior to the pitch to train the pitch type classifier based on the Random Forests supervised ensemble-learning algorithm. In their proposed system, one classifier for each pitcher is trained. The ball's location and speed, and the catcher's stance as features are first extracted from the broadcast videos. It obtains the ball locus in every frame by using a ball trajectory visualization system "B-Motion" developed in the authors' previous work, the ball speed can be obtained by automatically recognizing the characters superimposed on the screen just after the pitch, and the catcher's stance can be calculated by detecting the mitt locus just before the pitch. Using these features, the pitch type classifier is created using the Random Forests ensemble-learning algorithm. A large amount of pitch data from previously broadcast baseball videos for each pitcher is collected and used in the experiments to perform the comparisons with several well-known classification algorithms. Analyses of the experimental results are given and some future research directions are also discussed.

In Chapter 9, Seddiqui and Aono discuss how to integrate the multimedia resources annotated by the standard of MPEG-7 schema using ontology instance matching techniques in their chapter entitled "Ontology Instance Matching based MPEG-7 Resource Integration." This is in response to the need for information integration across media due to the proliferation of heterogeneous digital media contents and the popularity of the World Wide Web. Heterogeneous multimedia contents can be annotated by a sharable formal conceptualization, often called ontology, and these contents, regardless of their media types, become sharable resources/instances. Integrating such sharable resources to acquire diverse knowledge has been a very active research. For this purpose, many researchers use the MPEG-7 standard convertible to semantic Resource Description Framework (RDF) for containing the structured data and knowledge sources. MPEG-7 resources are considered since they are usually specified explicitly by their surrounding MPEG-7 schema entities like concepts and properties together with other linked resources. Therefore, there is a need for schema matching in resource integration. To address this issue, in this chapter, the authors use their scalable ontology alignment algorithm and collect the semantically linked resources. The data heterogeneity addressed in this chapter includes value transformation, structural transformation, and logical transformation. Experiments on two types of data sets to evaluate the proposed matching approach are conducted. One of the data sets is for the general purpose instance matching benchmarks; while another data set is a synthetic one based on 10 different images with 10 artificial variants of each of the image data. The experimental results demonstrate the strength and efficiency of their proposed matching approach.

Chapter 10 introduces a new framework for sprite generation evaluation together with new zoom-in, zoom-out, PTZ, and combined patterns for synthetic video generation in "Synthetic Video Generation for Evaluation of Sprite Generation" by Chen and Aygun. Sprite generation is defined as the process of generating sprites for objects in videos, where the term "sprite" refers to the composition of pixels that belong to a video object in a video. Sprite generation is mostly applied to the background in the video because the background scene may not be captured in a single frame of a video, and sprite can be generated by correctly overlapping between sequential frames. In addition, sprite is usually generated when there is a significant global motion and the background regions eventually become visible. The evaluation of the correctness of a sprite is usually composed of subjective and objective evaluations. The subjective evaluation is performed by an expert looking at the sprite and the video, while the objective evaluation typically uses the peak signal-to-noise ratio (PSNR) measure, but the objective evaluation can be enhanced with the help of the ground-truth images. This motivates the authors to present video generation from an image based on various camera motion parameters to be used as the ground-truth for the sprite evaluation. Experiments on synthetic videos of different camera motion patterns are conducted, and the results are able to reveal which components of the sprite generation algorithm can be improved.

Zaharieva, Zeppelzauer, Mitrovic, and Breiteneder present an approach for archive film comparison in Chapter 11, entitled "Archive Film Comparison." The growing video collections have resulted in the need of video copy detection since the capability of detecting video duplicates can facilitate efficient search and retrieval of video content from the video collections. Film and video comparison targets at comparing both reused and unique film material in two video versions that go beyond the boundaries of a single shot. The compared videos can be two versions of the same feature film or two different movies that share a particular amount of film material. It is more challenging in video analysis for archive film due to the loss of the original film versions. In addition, the remaining copies are usually the low-quality backup copies of the film archives. The authors' video comparison approach accounts for the overall video structure at the frame, shot, and video levels, as well as the temporal ordering of corresponding keyframes from matched shots. An additional step to investigate those shots that are labeled as unknown by the system is also included to further increase the performance. Such an approach can select the appropriate hierarchical level for a given task, which can be applied to different application scenarios like the identification of missing shots and the reconstruction of the original film version. Experiments on historical artistic documentaries are conducted, and these films have a distinctive structure characterized by a high number of short and repeating shots with high visual similarity. The experiments focus on evaluating the performance of established shot boundary detection algorithms, the influence of keyframe selection, and the feature representation on the performance of the video comparison process. From the evaluation results, it can be seen that when the SIFT features start to become more universal, the MPEG-7 edge histogram (EHD) features are almost as performant as the SIFT features, which are much more computationally expensive.

SECTION 4: AUDIO DATA PROCESSING AND INDEXING

Section 4 includes two (2) chapters that present the research studies in audio data processing and indexing.

In Chapter 12, Knight and Almeroth present "Fast Caption Alignment for Automatic Indexing of Audio" to discuss the importance of automatic indexing of the audio data in efficient and accurate search from large audio archives. There has been active research work that uses texts for indexing text archives. This suggests that audio archives can also benefit from using texts for indexing. However, it requires the use of transcripts of the spoken portions of the audio to generate the texts from audio archives, and these transcripts further assist in identifying the caption alignments that find the exact time when all the words are spoken in a video and match them with the textual captions in a media file. For example, in closed captions, the aligned text transcripts of audio/video are used. Such alignments enable the users to search for specific content and view the content immediately at the position where the search terms were spoken. The challenge is how to align the transcript of the spoken words with the media itself automatically and accurately since manual alignments are very time consuming and cannot be performed in real-time. Therefore, efficient and automatic approaches to identify such alignments have been an active research. Typically, three technical issues need to be addressed. The first issue is how to align unrecognized utterances since no modern speech recognition system is perfect. The second issue is to decide which techniques to apply if the text does not exactly match the spoken words of the media. The third issue is how to align the caption efficiently. For this purpose, the authors in this chapter propose the AUTOCAP system together with its supporting software components. Experiments on a collection of videos involving a single speaker with good audio quality (172 minutes of audio, 673 captions, and 26,049 words) are conducted and the experimental results demonstrate that AUTOCAP exhibits tolerable error rates for caption alignments and is capable of accurately and efficiently aligning edited transcripts to produce accurate audio indexes for archived audio in faster than real-time and for live audio in real-time.

Chapter 13 is contributed by Rafailidis, Nanopoulos, and Manolopoulos in their chapter, entitled "Building Tag-Aware Groups for Music High-Order Ranking and Topic Discovery," which considers the utilization of tag information to capture users' personal preferences to identify coherent groups/communities in music information retrieval. Recently, social tags have been used widely that allow the users to add metadata in the form of keywords to annotate information/data like images, videos, and music. In music information retrieval, tag clustering has been applied to group similar tags together, and "Tag Radio" and "Tag Cloud" are two of the most popular applications in tag clustering. In "Tag Radio," the users can tune into the tag radio to listen to music that has been tagged with a particular tag such as the artists or songs. On the other hand, "Tag clouds" consist of collective information from the users to provide a visual illustration for these tags. However, it has been shown that tag clustering may not be able to satisfy the listeners' requirements in some applications. Hence, there is a demand for a more powerful way to group and represent information by considering the social tags, users, and music objects. Due to the fact that the ranking of query/search results has become mandatory for the search engines in the general information retrieval field, the "Tag-Aware" groups in which the results are provided in ranked lists and each group refers to a certain music topic have been developed. This is also because that from a user's viewpoint, ranking is extremely useful, especially only the top-k retrieved results are displayed to the user. Towards such a demand, in this chapter, the authors use a generalization of the popular web-ranking concept in the social data domain to analyze how the social tagging data can be used to reveal coherent groups characterized by their users, tags, and music objects (e.g., songs and artists), and to further characterize the most prominent users, tags, and music objects for each group. Experiments on a real data set mined from Last.fm are conducted, and the experimental results demonstrate that their proposed method is effective to achieve a proper division of the data according to the discovered topics. That is, each Tag-Aware group corresponds to a specific music topic and the tags in each group can be very descriptive for the respective songs and artists based on the user preference.

SECTION 5: MULTIMEDIA APPLICATIONS: INTEGRATION OF MULTIMEDIA MANAGEMENT AND E-LEARNING TECHNOLOGY

The advances of network technology and the importance of the ubiquitous learning related topics have made e-learning a popular and widely used method to deliver instructions. The final section discusses the integration of multimedia management and e-learning technology to provide some insights from the position of instructional design to more effectively utilize multimedia technology for e-learning in four (4) chapters.

Castillo and Ayala present their proposed method in "Content Adaptation in Mobile Learning Environments," Chapter 14. In this chapter, the authors propose their frameworks to achieve the adaptation of educational contents of learning objects to a particular mobile device and a specific learner in mobile learning environments. This process of automatically modifying the characteristics of the learning object educational contents in a mobile learning environment is to consider user's interests and specific mobile device in order to enhance the user experience. This process typically involves both user adaptation and device adaptation. For user adaptation, the authors develop the NORIKO (Non-monotonic Reasoning for Intelligent Knowledge awareness and recommendations on the move) framework, which consists of a belief system and a programming system; while for device adaptation, the authors develop the CARIM (Content Adapter of Resources in Mobile learning Environments) framework, which uses transcoding and transrating to adapt media content and the device characteristics. NORIKO allows the users to insert, remove, and consult beliefs, and it performs a beliefs revision process any time a new belief is included or removed to/from the inductive database. A computational model of beliefs is able to include both cognitive and psychological aspects of the learners. CARIM accesses the profile information about diverse mobile devices and some features of the contents of a mobile learning object to acquire the characteristics of the target mobile device and the minimal requirements of the content to be adapted. In addition, to model the contents of mobile learning objects, ALMA (**A L**earning **M**odel content **A**daptation) is proposed by the authors. ALMA is a subset of SCORM 2004 standard metadata categories, and extended SCORM 2004 with three top level categories: Knowledge Metadata, Use Metadata, and Mobile Device Requirements Metadata. The development of this study is to consider the adaptation as a server-side solution and the mobile devices of the learners as the clients, using HTTP User-agent and CC/PP for device characteristics recognition. The evaluation results show that the mobile learning objects selected to be delivered to the learners can be properly adapted to the characteristics of the specific mobile device.

In Chapter 15, Chang, Wang, and Chiu introduce a board game to motivate the students to learn the concept of minimum spanning tree algorithms in "Board Game Supporting Learning Prim's Algorithm and Dijkstra's Algorithm." The motivation of this study is to utilize game-based learning to cultivate learners' ability to apply their knowledge to some specific educational problems. Many researchers found that the most efficient way to combine computer sciences and board game is to demonstrate the network or graph theory on board game. There are many graph theory algorithms that can be combined with games. Among them, the concept of minimum spanning tree is commonly utilized. A spanning tree is defined as an undirected graph that all nodes are connected with no loop or cycle; while a minimum spanning tree is to find the least summation of all the paths' weight assuming each edge is associated with a weight. Therefore, the authors attempt to develop a way to make the students to learn graph theories more efficiently and to motivate their learning interests using a board game. In this chapter, the authors combined the board game "Ticket to Ride" with the well-known Prim's, Dijkstra's, and Kruskal's minimum spanning tree algorithms, and added a considerable amount of rules in the game for its functions. Experiments to evaluate the effectiveness of their proposed system are conducted. The experimental results demonstrate that their proposed system can improve the learner's learning performance, the students are able to use this board game to understand the graph theories more efficiently with higher learning interests, and the feedback of students is quite positive.

Recently, online education has become more and more popular in promoting continuing education or distance learning for adult learners. In Chapter 16, "Iterative Usability Evaluation for an Online Educational Web Portal," Wang et al. describe the design challenges and the usability evaluation that is incorporated into the development process of the online continuing education center at the University of Missouri. This research is conducted due to the fact that most of the studies in this area focused on the design of online learning environments and the potential of online learning to promote collaboration, but very few studies addressed the usability of the online educational environments or integrated the multifaceted usability evaluation into the lifecycle of developing an online educational environment. However, usability evaluation is a critical part of the development efforts since the developers of the online learning system must take into consideration how the major users, such as the educators and learners, navigate the system to help them teach or learn. Hence, the authors in this chapter employ the Multifaceted usability evaluation methods at four different stages of the University of Missouri Extension (MU Extension) web portal's development, namely heuristic evaluation (Phase I: prototype), focus group interview and survey (Phase II: initial design), think-aloud interview (Phase III: detailed website design), and multiple-user simultaneous testing (Phase IV: website build). The results of these studies demonstrate that at each stage, the provision of the first-hand user information to the web development team can actually enhance the development team's understanding of users' difficulties, needs, and wants, which further guides the web developers' subsequent decisions.

The last chapter is by Shen and Chang, who examine the performance of e-instructors in Taiwan based on the new human performance model in their chapter entitled "The Factors that Influence E-Instructors' Performance in Taiwan: A Perspective of New Human Performance Model." It is known that the usage of technology among the faculty members in the university has become more and more critical in higher education, and the faculty members are asked to incorporate technology into their classroom teaching or online teaching. Studies showed that faculty members' self-efficacy is an important factor in their efforts in integrating technology into teaching. Studies also showed that the new human performance model demonstrates that ability, motivation, situational factors, and self-efficacy are the four critical components that impact human performance. Based on such a new human performance model, the authors adopt a questionnaire survey and ask 106 online instructors from 25 universities in Taiwan to participate in the survey so that they can examine the factors which affect e-instructors' performance. Statistical analyses using correlation and multiple regression are performed, and the results demonstrate that advanced skill, basic skill, effort, and self-efficacy are the four major factors contributing to the model variance of the online teaching performance of e-instructors. Basic computer skill has a significant positive effect only on content expertise, while the advanced computer skill has a significant positive effect on technology and negative effects on facilitating learning and content expertise. Effort has a positive effect on performance on the instructional design, administration management, and research development dimensions, while self-efficacy has significant positive effects on all dimensions of performance except facilitating learning, which is consistent with the previous studies. The finding suggests that the university should put more attention to self-efficacy in the training for online teaching.

Shu-Ching Chen
Florida International University, USA

Mei-Ling Shyu
University of Miami, USA

Section 1
Multimedia Data Mining and Multimedia Databases

Chapter 1
Multimedia Databases and Data Management:
A Survey

Shu-Ching Chen
Florida International University, USA

ABSTRACT

The exponential growth of the technological advancements has resulted in high-resolution devices, such as digital cameras, scanners, monitors, and printers, which enable the capturing and displaying of multimedia data in high-density storage devices. Furthermore, more and more applications need to live with multimedia data. However, the gap between the characteristics of various media types and the application requirements has created the need to develop advanced techniques for multimedia data management and the extraction of relevant information from multimedia databases. Though many research efforts have been devoted to the areas of multimedia databases and data management, it is still far from maturity. The purpose of this article is to discuss how the existing techniques, methodologies, and tools addressed relevant issues and challenges to enable a better understanding in multimedia databases and data management. The focuses include: (1) how to develop a formal structure that can be used to capture the distinguishing content of the media data in a multimedia database (MMDB) and to form an abstract space for the data to be queried; (2) how to develop advanced content analysis and retrieval techniques that can be used to bridge the gaps between the semantic meaning and low-level media characteristics to improve multimedia information retrieval; and (3) how to develop query mechanisms that can handle complex spatial, temporal, and/or spatio-temporal relationships of multimedia data to answer the imprecise and incomplete queries issued to an MMDB.

1. INTRODUCTION

Due to the technological advances and widespread adoption of multimedia computing, networking, electronic imaging, video devices, and data storage, a significant amount of multimedia data is being generated across the Internet and elsewhere each day. Multimedia information is ubiquitous and essential in a variety of applications like entertainment, education, digital libraries, manufacturing, marketing, homeland security, medicine, bioinformatics, advertisement, etc. Knowledge of the spatio-temporal phenomena is also of increasing relevance in those applications. Furthermore,

DOI: 10.4018/978-1-4666-1791-9.ch001

the proliferation of social media and the success of many social websites such as Flickr, YouTube, MySpace, Facebook, and Zooomr provide incontrovertible evidence of users' migration to a new Web overwhelmed by multimedia. The availability and popularity of multimedia data, social media, social websites, and their applications have created the needs for multimedia databases (MMDBs) and the supporting methodologies and tools for multimedia data management that make the searching and manipulating the content of such multimedia information a better and more friendly experience in facilitating the multimedia database management systems (MMDBMSs).

Multimedia data come in various media types, including image, video, audio, text, graphics, animation, and a combination of these media types. Conceptually, it seems possible to manage multimedia data in the same manner as the data types such as numbers, dates, and characters in the relational database systems. However, the spatial, temporal, and/or spatio-temporal characteristics of multimedia data have made the design, implementation, and maintenance of multimedia databases more challenging. It is well recognized that the traditional database systems, such as relational database systems, were developed for textual and numerical data, and data retrieval is often based on simple comparisons of text or numerical values. That is, with respect to the management, browsing, and searching of multimedia data, traditional database systems cannot provide adequate supports, since (1) They lack the ability to manage the composition of and the synchronicity among multimedia objects; (2) They lack the facilities to manage the spatio-temporal relations among the multimedia objects; (3) They have limitations in the semantic modeling of time-dependent multimedia data (e.g., video or audio); and (4) They do not cover all features required for multimedia information retrieval (Chen, Kashyap & Ghafoor, 2000; Shyu & Chen, 2005, 2006, 2008). Though there are attempts to support the access to multimedia objects in the forms of pointers to binary large objects (BLOBs) in relational database systems or to enable the definition of the part-of-relationship among objects in an arbitrary structure in object-oriented database systems, their capabilities of accessing the various portions of the multimedia objects interactively using BLOBs or managing the spatio-temporal relations among the multimedia objects using operational transparency are still very limited. Therefore, a new generation of multimedia database systems (MMDBSs) or some kind of multimedia extension to the existing database systems is needed, which must support various media types in addition to providing the facilities for traditional database management system functions like database creation, data modeling, data retrieval, data access and organization, and data independence.

Generally speaking, there have been research studies in the area of multimedia database systems (MMDBSs) since the mid 90s. Some of these MMDBSs relied mainly on the operating system for storing and querying the files and they were all able to handle diverse kinds of data to provide functionalities of querying, retrieval, insertion, and updating of multimedia data. There were MMDBSs that handled multimedia content by providing complex object types for various kinds of media. The object-oriented style provides the facility to define new data types and operators appropriate for the new kinds of media, such as video, image, and audio. Therefore, the broadly used MMDBSs are extensible Object-Relational DBMSs (ORDBMSs). The most advanced solutions are marketed by Oracle 10g, IBM DB2, and IBM Informix. They proposed a similar approach for extending the basic system. For example, a distributed multimedia DBMS called DISIMA is an image database system which enables content-based querying (Oria, Özsu & Iglinski, 2004). Furthermore, some research studies focused on addressing the needs of applications for rich semantic content, which mostly rely on the new MPEG-standards MPEG-7 and MPEG-21 (Kosch, 2003). MPEG-7 is the ISO/IEC 15938 standard for multimedia descriptions and issued in 2002, and it is an XML based multimedia meta data standard, which proposes description elements for the multimedia processing cycle from the capture (e.g., logging descriptors), analysis or filtering (e.g., descriptors of the Multimedia Description Schemes), to the delivery (e.g., media variation descriptors) and interaction (e.g., user preference descriptors). MPEG-21 is the ISO/IEC 21000 standard defining an open multimedia framework, which will enable transparent and augmented use of multimedia resources across a wide range of networks and devices used by different communities. The driving force for MPEG-21 was the current situation that many elements exist to build an infrastructure for the delivery and consumption of multimedia content but not how these elements relate to each others.

From the viewpoint of MMDBSs, there are many open issues and challenges that need to be addressed. One challenge is to deal with the sheer size of the data. For examples, the size of one good quality color image can be up to 6Mb, a five-minute video clip with 30 frames per second of a sequence of such images (called frames) can be up to 54Gb, a sequence of audio will require up to 8Kb in each second, etc. (Dunckley, 2003). The amounts of multimedia data have major influences on the design and development of a multimedia database, since it has to cope up with the huge volume of multimedia data with respect to efficient and effective data processing and management for querying and retrieval of the data. For example, in many video-on-demand (VOD) applications, there is a need to provide services to multiple concurrent requests on real-time large multimedia media objects (Chen, Kashyap & Ghafoor, 2000).

Another challenge is how to manage and model different types of information pertaining to the actual multimedia data as well as to adhere to the real-time and synchronization constraints of the information conveyed. Video and audio data are inherently temporal in nature. The frames of the video must run in the correct sequence and at an acceptance rate to be perceived by the users. For example, the frames of a video have to be presented at the rate of at least 30 frames per second for the eyes to perceive the continuity in the video. When there are interactions of media objects of different media types, periodical synchronization of the media objects will be needed. For example, a video clip of an interview would include audio data and video frames that must be synchronized together to be meaningful. This can be achieved by good multimedia data models and multimedia presentation mechanisms. A multimedia data model must deal with the issue of representing the various media objects to facilitate multimedia data querying and retrieval. Therefore, efficient and effective techniques to support content-based querying and retrieval of the multimedia data are also required.

Searching in MMDBs can be computationally intensive, especially if content-based retrieval is needed for image and video data stored in a compressed or uncompressed form. How to accurately capture the semantic nature of the multimedia data is another challenge. The content of the media objects is analyzed and used to enable content-based information retrieval. Content-based search for image, audio, and video data has been deeply studied in the past years, but it is not yet adopted by the industry sector because of its cost. There are several major research challenges with respect to content-based information retrieval that are noteworthy and of particular importance to the MMDB research community. They are (1) semantic search with emphasis on the detection of concepts in media with complex backgrounds; (2) multimodal analysis and retrieval algorithms especially to exploit the synergy between the various media types, including text and context information; (3) interactive search, emergent semantics, or relevance feedback systems; (4) evaluation with emphasis on representative test sets and usage patterns; to name a few.

This article is organized as follows. Section 2 discusses the research areas in multimedia databases and data management, in particular, the multimedia media abstractions, multimedia content analysis and retrieval, and multimedia query mechanisms. Finally, Section 3 gives the conclusions.

2. MULTIMEDIA DATABASES AND DATA MANAGEMENT

In the early multimedia database systems, the multimedia data such as image or video data was simply files in a directory or entries in an SQL database table. From a computational efficiency perspective, both options exhibited poor performance because most file systems use linear search within directories, and most databases could only perform efficient operations on fixed size elements. Thus, as the size of the multimedia databases or collections grows from hundreds to millions of variable sized data, the response time for information retrieval becomes an issue for a multimedia database (MMDB), which calls for the need of some form of a structure to capture the content composed by various media types. Furthermore, the increasing number of multimedia information systems allows the users to access not only textual or pictorial documents but also video and/or audio data. The various media types involved in an MMDB typically require more advanced automatic analysis techniques to derive high-level descriptions and annotations for retrieval.

2.1 Multimedia Media Abstractions

An MMDB can be represented as a finite set of media abstractions. Media abstractions form the essential parts of an MMDB, since they provide a formal structure used to capture media content, enable a user to determine the distinguishing content of the media data in the MMDB, and form an abstract space for the data to be queried (Megalou

& Hadzilacos, 2003; Subrahmanian, 1998). There can be one or more media types in an MMDB, including video, audio, image, animation, etc. These media types share some common characteristics as well as different properties that distinguish one media type from another. Therefore, the media abstraction should provide a core structure that can describe the common characteristics of the media types and at the same time can be extended to represent the distinct properties of each media type. The shared common characteristics include (1) a set of individual media objects, such as images and video clips, whose content is being described; (2) a certain set of features within each object, such as the dog in the image and the soccer goal occurring in the sports video; (3) one or more attributes for each feature, which may exist some relationships between the different features (e.g., spatial relationships between different objects in an image); and (4) a relation of the states, features, and attributes that may depend upon or independent of the object (Subrahmanian, 1998).

In Subrahmanian (1998), a media abstraction is defined as an 8-tuple (S, fe, $ATTR$, λ, R, F, Var_1, Var_2). In this media abstraction, S is a set of states where a state is the smallest unit of media data to be modeled. For instance, each image may be viewed as a state in an image database, and a state may be any consecutive sequence of frames in a video for a video database. The set of features is fe where each feature is any object in a state that is of interest to a multimedia database application. For example, when the TRECVID video data is considered, the features of interest might be the high-level features/concepts like outdoor, face, etc. $ATTR$ is a set of attribute values, where the attributes (as well as their attribute values) of a feature characterize that feature. For example, the attributes such as grass ratio and volume mean characterize the sports feature in a soccer video, or the attributes such as the date, time, location, and author by which an image was shot can be used for an image. $\lambda: S \rightarrow 2^{fe}$ is a map from states to sets of features, which captures the information of which features occur in which states. R is a set of relations on fe^i x $ATTR^j$ x S, where a relation can be either state-dependent (e.g., the "*left_of*" relation in an image to model one object being on the left of another object in an image) or state-independent (e.g., the "*age*" relation for the "*person*" feature to model the age of a particular person). F is a set of relations of S, where a relation takes two or more states as its input (e.g., the "*before*" relation for two images to model one image being taken before another image). Var_1 is a set of objects ranging over S, and Var_2 is a set of objects ranging over fe.

A combined abstraction of the conceptual and presentational characteristics of multimedia applications was developed in Megalou and Hadzilacos (2003). The authors proposed the Semantic Multimedia Abstractions (SMA) which model both the conceptual structure (modeling the semantics of the real-world media objects by the entities, relationships, and attributes) and the presentational structure (including the media type, logical structure, temporal synchronization, spatial synchronization, and interactive behavior of the media objects). SMA are qualitative abstract descriptions of multimedia applications in terms of their conceptual and presentational properties at multiple and adjustable levels of details. The authors represented SMA's temporal structure using temporal aggregation and temporal grouping constructs to pose certain temporal constraints; and represented SMA's spatial structure using spatial aggregation and spatial-grouping constructs to model the primitives for those objects whose positions in space matters to the multimedia database.

In Chen, Zhao and Shyu (2007), the authors developed a media abstraction called Hierarchical Markov Model Mediator (HMMM) to model various levels of multimedia objects, their temporal relationships, the detected semantic concepts, and the high-level user perceptions. HMMM is defined as an 8-tuple (d, S, F, A, B, Π, O, L), where d is the number of levels in an HMMM, S (S_n) is the set of multimedia objects in each level ($n = 1$ to d), F (F_n) is the set of distinct features or semantic concepts of the multimedia objects in each level ($n = 1$ to d), A (A_n) is the state transition probability matrix in each level ($n = 1$ to d), B (B_n) is the feature/concept matrix in each level ($n = 1$ to d), Π (Π_n) is the initial state probability distribution in each level ($n = 1$ to d), O ($O_{n,n+1} \rightarrow F_{n+1} \times F_n$) is the importance weights for the lower-level features in F_n when describing the higher-level concepts in F_{n+1} ($n = 1$ to d-1), and L ($L_{n, n+1}$) is the link conditions between the higher level states and the lower level states, where $n = 1$ to $d-1$. Here, the value of d is 3, which represents the video shots (d=1), videos (d=2), and video clusters (d=3), respectively. That is, the states represent the video shots and the feature set consists of the low-level or mid-level visual and/or audio features in the first level, the states describe the set of videos and the feature set consists of the semantic events in the second level, and the states represent the set of video clusters and the feature set consists of the user perceptions in the third level. Using HMMM, the authors have shown that it is able to describe various levels of multimedia objects for video database modeling and retrieval.

In multimedia applications, it is critical to be able to reduce the complexity of the search space and hence improve the retrieval performance, due to the huge amounts of multimedia data in an MMDB and the inherent un-structural or semi-structural characteristics of the multimedia data. This is one of the "quantitative" reasons for adopting media abstractions in MMDBs since media abstraction can be used to form an abstract space for queries so as to decrease the complexity in searching. Correspondingly, in order to retrieve multimedia data from an MMDBMS, effective and efficient multimedia content-based analysis, retrieval, and querying techniques and mechanisms must be provided.

2.2 Multimedia Content Analysis and Retrieval

Multimedia information retrieval must be able to meet the complex semantic information needs and therefore require efficient analysis and retrieval mechanisms to extract relevant information. To provide fast response for real-time multimedia applications, information or knowledge needs to be extracted from multimedia data in advance and stored for later retrieval. However, extracting information from multimedia data such as image, video, and audio is time consuming.

It can be seen that most of the current content classification technologies were emerged from the traditional image processing and computer vision, audio analysis and processing, and information retrieval (Dimitrova, 2004). However, unlike in conventional database systems that all data must conform to some predefined structures and constraints in the database schemas and a database query must specify which and where the data objects are to be retrieved and the predicate on which the retrieval is based, multimedia information retrieval typically is based on the content and/or semantics of the media data. To meet such needs, content-based retrieval (CBR) has been widely used to retrieve the desired multimedia objects from a large collection of multimedia data. The traditional approaches for content based image retrieval were by color (such as color histogram, color moments, and color sets), texture (such as structural measures and statistical measures), or shape (such as boundary, region, and matching). However, due to the increasing complexity of the multimedia applications, advanced approaches that provide more powerful searching capabilities are needed.

Many existing multimedia content analysis and information retrieval processes are based on feature analysis and similarity measures, since it is critical to select important features that capture the data characteristics to assist in the content analysis process and to determine suitable similarity measures to assist in the information retrieval process. Furthermore, many approaches focused on the matching of the multimedia objects and their structures by adopting point selection from which the descriptors are derived and addressed. There are many research studies that focus on the low-level feature analysis to provide accesses to the multimedia data based on the properties like color, texture, shape, and etc.; while another direction is to use the mid-level or high-level information in the retrieval process such as using the salient video objects to represent the spatio-temporal characteristics of video clips, using a set of predefined index terms for video annotation and applied traditional information retrieval (IR) techniques for data retrieval, using the high-level video structure or a priori knowledge to assist in extracting video features and semantic meanings, and using the correlations between features and class labels or associations among features with respect to the class labels.

Srivastava, Joshi, Mio and Liu (2005) proposed some learning approaches for shapes. In texture understanding, a new texture feature based on the Radon transform orientation and with the significant advantage of being rotationally invariant was proposed in Jafari-Khouzani and Soltanian-Zadeh (2005). Lowe (2004) developed an efficient object recognition algorithm that constructs a scale space pyramid using difference-of-Gaussian (doG) filters. The doG can be used to obtain an efficient approximation of the Laplacian-of-Gaussian (LoG) function that is used for building the scale space. In Kumar, Ranganath, Huang and Sengupta (2005), Leonardi, Migliorati and Prandini (2004), the high-level video structure or a prior knowledge is used to assist in extracting video features and semantic meanings. The correlation-based or association-based feature analyses for video semantic concept detection were proposed in Lin, Ravitz, Shyu and Chen (2008) and Lin and Shyu (2009). In these studies, the multiple correspondence analysis (MCA) and association rule mining (ARM) techniques are employed to explore the correlation and/or association between different feature-value pairs and class labels (concepts) to generate the classification rules and to bridge the gap between the extracted low-level features and high-level semantic concepts. The authors have also introduced a novel pre-filtering approach which addresses the data imbalance problem in the classifier training step to help reduce the amount of misclassification errors. After feature analyses, the success of an information retrieval approach typically requires a good similarity measure. Cooper, Foote, Girgensohn and Andwilcox (2005) proposed to measure image similarity using time and pictorial content. In Lin and Shyu (2009), the authors developed a new similarity measure of the rules, representing the harmonic mean of inter-similarity and intra-similarity of rules. In this similarity measure, for each rule, the inter-similarity is defined as the similarity between the rule and those multimedia data instances belonging to different classes; while the intra-similarity is the similarity between the rule and those multimedia data instances belonging to the same class.

Semantic understanding of media is another important research direction. One of the main challenges is visual concept detection in the presence of complex backgrounds. There have been existing approaches attempting to classify a whole image or video. However, such granularity is often too coarse to be useful in real-world multimedia applications. For example, for a video surveillance system, it is more desirable to find the human in a video shot or a video clip, rather than the global features. Another limitation is that most of these visual concept detection studies were conducted in laboratory conditions where the background is simple. In the mid-90s, there was a great deal of success in detecting the locations of human faces in grayscale images with complex backgrounds. For near frontal face views in high-quality photographs, the early systems generally performed near 95% accuracy with minimal false positives. However, it is still considered challenging to retrieval non-frontal views or information from

low-quality images. Therefore, the challenge is to detect the high-level features (or semantic) concepts like faces, trees, animals, etc. within an image or a video shot with the emphasis on the presence of complex backgrounds.

To propose a potential solution to address some of these challenges, a subspace-based multimedia data mining framework for video semantic analysis was proposed in Shyu, Xie, Chen and Chen (2008). Their proposed framework consists of novel approaches for (1) multimodal content analysis that extract low-level and middle-level features from audio/visual channels, and (2) the integration of subspace-based distance-based and rule-based data mining techniques that reconstructs and refines the feature dimension automatically as a similarity measure for video semantic detection. In Schneiderman and Kanade (2004), a system for component-based face detection using the statistics of parts was proposed. A multilevel an notation of natural scenes that utilized dominant image components and semantic concepts was developed in Fan, Gao and Luo (2004). In certain contexts, there may be several media type available which allows for multimodal analysis. Amir et al. (2004) proposed a framework for a multimodal system which combined speech recognition and annotated video for video event detection. Another gradient energy directly from the video representation was proposed to detect faces based on the high contrast areas such as the eyes, nose, and mouth (Chua, Zhao & Kankanhalli, 2002). In their article, a rule-based classifier and a neural network were compared and the neural network was found to give the superior accuracy. However, it may be still difficulty to utilize this approach to detect a wider set of concepts other than human faces.

In multimedia information retrieval, the relevance feedback (RF) technique is also widely employed to enhance the retrieval results. RF techniques enable the modeling of user subjective perception from user feedback by showing the user a list of candidate images, asking the user to decide whether each image is relevant or irrelevant, and modifying the parameter space, semantic space, feature space, or classification space to reflect the relevant and irrelevant examples. However, there are some issues when the RF technique is applied. One of them is the heavy human interference in the model training process since it needs the users to provide their feedback on the currently retrieved results to re-train the model with the aim of enhancing the model. Another issue is the size of the training data set. Typically, a user may only want to label a small number of images (say 30) each time; while an effective model training process may need a lot more examples (say 2,000). This issue gets worse if the training data set is too small to training the model. He, King, Ma, Li and Zhang (2003) used both short-term and long term perspectives to infer a semantic space from user's relevance feedback for image retrieval. The short-term perspective was found by marking the top 3 incorrect examples from the results as irrelevant and selecting at most 3 images as relevant examples from the current iteration. The long-term perspective was found by updating the semantic space from the results of the short term perspective. A probabilistic semantic network-based image retrieval framework using the MMM (Markov Model Mediator) mechanism together with relevance feedback to facilitate image retrieval was proposed (Shyu, Chen, Chen, Zhang & Shu, 2006). One of the distinct properties of this framework is that it exploits the structured description of visual contents as well as the relative affinity measurements among the images, which are used to construct the MMM model. The relevance feedback information is then used to enhance the MMM model to improve the retrieval performance.

2.3 Multimedia Query Mechanisms

Due to the facts that multimedia data usually approximates the real-world objects with the multimedia data stored in them and is represented in an imprecise and incomplete ways in an MMDBMS, it has become one of the major challenges as how to handle the imprecise and incomplete queries issued to an MMDBMS to access the multimedia data (Chen, Kashyap & Ghafoor, 2000). In addition, a multimedia query language must also have the abilities to handle complex spatial, temporal, and/or spatio-temporal relationships and to deal with keywords and semantic content of multimedia objects. Therefore, it is essential for an MMDBMS to have a query mechanism that can respond to various types of queries requested by different multimedia applications.

Conventional query languages such as SQL are not adequate for querying an MMDBMS, since their capabilities of handling the unstructured or semi-structured data are limited, especially for fuzzy queries or content-based retrieval queries. There are two main categories of the queries for multimedia data retrieval, namely the visual queries and concept queries (Shyu, Chen, Sun & Yu, 2007). Some visual query approaches are "Query-by-Examples (QBE)" or "Query-by-Pictorial" query languages which focus on retrieval based on low-level or mid-level visual and audio features or the graphic representations of the multimedia objects. In QBE, the video data is considered as a set of images without temporal interrelations, and an image or a video is presented to the system to retrieve similar multimedia objects. In "Query-by-Pictorial" query languages, the steps of submitting a query are (1) a user needs to give the names or labels of the multimedia objects of interest which are then used to import graphic representations of these multimedia objects into a layout editor, (2) the user repositions the multimedia objects spatially based on the desired query, and (3) the layout editor is submitted as a query to the system to retrieve the matched images in some ranked order. The matching is executed via the graphical representations of the multimedia objects and their spatial relationships specified in the layout editor. There are several prototype content based retrieval systems that adopt the QBE or "Query-by-

Pictorial" technique, such as MARVEL, CuVid, and PicQuery. However, such visual queries have some limitations. For examples, when a query requires data from two or more media types that form the content, or when a query requires the analysis and processing of data semantics (such as finding video shots by the presence of specific multimedia objects or events).

To overcome the limitations of visual queries, another ways of representing queries are called "Query-By-Subject/Object" or concept queries. "Query-By-Subject/Object" allows the subjective descriptions of a query to be specified since a keyword can well represent the semantic content; whereas a concept query attempts to query based on the presence of some specified concepts (such as finding video shots with the concept of a goal event). In object retrieval, given a video and a segment of the video, the query mechanism finds all multimedia objects that occurred in either all frames or some frame. An example query will be to find all people who appeared between frames 50 to 75 in a security video. In activity/concept retrieval, given a video and a segment of the video, the query mechanism finds all activities that occurred in either all frames or some frame. An example query will be to find the goal event between frames 50 to 75 in a soccer video.

Another type of query mechanisms is based on media abstractions. In Megalou and Hadzilacos (2003), the authors defined the Semantic Multimedia Abstraction Definition and Query language (SMA-L) which was build based on the Extended Object Modeling Technique (OMT) and uses the BNF notation as its formal syntax. SMA-L is a declarative object-oriented language which is able to provide an integrated representation of the conceptual and presentational structure of their proposed Semantic Multimedia Abstractions (SMAs). The authors have shown that their proposed SMAs and SMA-L provide satisfactory results for the representation and query of the multimedia data at the abstract level for multimedia applications.

3. CONCLUSION

With the explosive growth in the amount of multimedia data, the design and development of advanced techniques for multimedia databases and data management have become important in order to increase our capabilities to utilize the tremendous amounts of multimedia data for a variety of multimedia applications. These multimedia applications have benefited from the effective and efficient data management and information retrieval techniques, methodologies, and tools. However, we have also noticed the open issues and challenges on multimedia databases and data management for multimedia applications, including how to capture the distinguishing content of the media data in an MMDB, how to utilize advanced content analysis techniques for multimedia information retrieval, and how to develop query mechanisms to answer the imprecise and incomplete multimedia queries. In this article, an overview of the current state-of-the-art technologies that addressed the aforementioned open challenges and issues in multimedia databases and data management is presented to provide a better understanding on these important research areas.

REFERENCES

Amir, A., Basu, S., Iyengar, G., Lin, C.-Y., Naphade, M., & Smith, J. R. (2004). A multi-modal system for the retrieval of semantic video events. *Computer Vision and Image Understanding*, *96*, 216–236. doi:10.1016/j.cviu.2004.02.006

Chen, S.-C., Kashyap, R. L., & Ghafoor, A. (2000). *Semantic models for multimedia database searching and browsing*. New York: Springer.

Chen, S.-C., Zhao, N., & Shyu, M.-L. (2007). Modeling semantic concepts and user preferences in content-based video retrieval. *International Journal of Semantic Computing*, *1*(3), 377–402. doi:10.1142/S1793351X07000159

Chua, T. S., Zhao, Y., & Kankanhalli, M. S. (2002). Detection of human faces in a compressed domain for video stratification. *The Visual Computer, 18,* 121–133. doi:10.1007/s003710100137

Cooper, M., Foote, J., Girgensohn, A., & Andwilcox, L. (2005). Temporal event clustering for digital photo collections. *ACM Transactions on Multimedia Computing, Communications, and Applications, 1,* 269–288. doi:10.1145/1083314.1083317

Dimitrova, N. (2004). Context and memory in multimedia content analysis. *IEEE Multimedia, 11*(3), 7-*11.

Dunckley, L. (2003). *Multimedia databases: An object-relational approach.* Reading, MA: Addison-Wesley.

Fan, J., Gao, Y., & Luo, H. (2004), Multi-level annotation of natural scenes using dominant image components and semantic concepts. In *Proceedings of the ACM International Conference on Multimedia* (pp. 540-547).

He, X., King, O., Ma, W.-Y., Li, M., & Zhang, H. J. (2003). Learning a semantic space from user's relevance feedback for image retrieval. *IEEE Transactions on Circuits and Systems for Video Technology, 13,* 39–49. doi:10.1109/TCSVT.2002.808087

Jafari-Khouzani, K., & Soltanian-Zadeh, H. (2005). Radon transform orientation estimation for rotation invariant texture analysis. *IEEE Transactions on Pattern Analysis and Machine Intelligence, 27,* 1004–1008. doi:10.1109/TPAMI.2005.126

Kosch, H. (2003). *Distributed multimedia database technologies supported by MPEG-7 and MPEG-21.* Boca Raton, FL: CRC Press.

Kumar, P., Ranganath, S., Huang, W., & Sengupta, K. (2005). Framework for real time behavior interpretation from traffic video. *IEEE Transactions on Intelligent Transportation Systems, 6,* 43–53. doi:10.1109/TITS.2004.838219

Leonardi, R., Migliorati, P., & Prandini, M. (2004). Semantic indexing of soccer audio-visual sequences: A multimodal approach based on controlled Markov Chains. *IEEE Transactions on Circuits and Systems for Video Technology, 14,* 634–643. doi:10.1109/TCSVT.2004.826751

Lin, L., Ravitz, G., Shyu, M.-L., & Chen, S.-C. (2008). Correlation-based video semantic concept detection using Multiple Correspondence Analysis. In *Proceedings of the IEEE International Symposium on Multimedia (ISM2008)* (pp. 316-321).

Lin, L., & Shyu, M.-L. (2009). Mining high-level features from video using associations and correlations. In *Proceedings of the Third IEEE International Conference on Semantic Computing (IEEE ICSC2009)* (pp. 137-144).

Lowe, D. (2004). Distinctive image features from scale-invariant keypoints. *International Journal of Computer Vision, 60,* 91–110. doi:10.1023/B:VISI.0000029664.99615.94

Megalou, E., & Hadzilacos, T. (2003). Semantic abstractions in the multimedia domain. *IEEE Transactions on Knowledge and Data Engineering, 15*(1), 136–160. doi:10.1109/TKDE.2003.1161587

Oria, V., Özsu, M. T., & Iglinski, P. (2004). VisualMOQL, the DISIMA visual query language. *Multimedia Tools and Applications, 23,* 185–201. doi:10.1023/B:MTAP.0000031756.10332.9d

Schneiderman, H., & Kanade, T. (2004). Object detection using the statistics of parts. *Journal of Computer Vision, 56,* 151–177. doi:10.1023/B:VISI.0000011202.85607.00

Shyu, M.-L., & Chen, S.-C. (2005). Guest editorial: Introduction to the special issue. *Multimedia Tools and Applications*, *26*(2), 151–152. doi:10.1007/s11042-005-0449-1

Shyu, M.-L., & Chen, S.-C. (2006). Guest editorial: Introduction to the special issue on multimedia databases. *Information Systems*, *31*(7), 636–637. doi:10.1016/j.is.2005.12.002

Shyu, M.-L., & Chen, S.-C. (2008). Guest editors' introduction. *International Journal of Semantic Computing*, *2*(2), 161–163. doi:10.1142/S1793351X08000427

Shyu, M.-L., Chen, S.-C., Chen, M., Zhang, C., & Shu, C.-M. (2006). Probabilistic semantic network-based image retrieval using MMM and relevance feedback. *Multimedia Tools and Applications*, *30*, 131–147. doi:10.1007/s11042-006-0023-5

Shyu, M.-L., Chen, S.-C., Sun, Q., & Yu, H. (2007). Overview and future trends of multimedia research for content access and distribution. *International Journal of Semantic Computing*, *1*, 29–66. doi:10.1142/S1793351X07000044

Shyu, M.-L., Xie, Z., Chen, M., & Chen, S.-C. (2008). Video semantic event/concept detection using a subspace-based multimedia data mining framework. *IEEE Transactions on Multimedia, Special Issue on Multimedia Data Mining*, *10*(2), 252–259.

Srivastava, A., Joshi, S. H., Mio, W., & Liu, X. (2005). Statistical shape analysis: Clustering, learning, and testing. *IEEE Transactions on Pattern Analysis and Machine Intelligence*, *27*, 590–602. doi:10.1109/TPAMI.2005.86

Subrahmanian, V. S. (1998). *Principles of multimedia database systems*. San Francisco: Morgan Kaufmann.

This work was previously published in the International Journal of Multimedia Data Engineering and Management, Volume 1, Issue 1, edited by Shu-Ching Chen, pp. 1-11, copyright 2010 by IGI Publishing (an imprint of IGI Global).

Chapter 2
Weighted Association Rule Mining for Video Semantic Detection

Lin Lin
University of Miami, USA

Mei-Ling Shyu
University of Miami, USA

ABSTRACT

Semantic knowledge detection of multimedia content has become a very popular research topic in recent years. The association rule mining (ARM) technique has been shown to be an efficient and accurate approach for content-based multimedia retrieval and semantic concept detection in many applications. To further improve the performance of traditional association rule mining technique, a video semantic concept detection framework whose classifier is built upon a new weighted association rule mining (WARM) algorithm is proposed in this article. Our proposed WARM algorithm is able to capture the different significance degrees of the items (feature-value pairs) in generating the association rules for video semantic concept detection. Our proposed WARM-based framework first applies multiple correspondence analysis (MCA) to project the features and classes into a new principle component space and discover the correlation between feature-value pairs and classes. Next, it considers both correlation and percentage information as the measurement to weight the feature-value pairs and to generate the association rules. Finally, it performs classification by using these weighted association rules. To evaluate our WARM-based framework, we compare its performance of video semantic concept detection with several well-known classifiers using the benchmark data available from the 2007 and 2008 TRECVID projects. The results demonstrate that our WARM-based framework achieves promising performance and performs significantly better than those classifiers in the comparison.

DOI: 10.4018/978-1-4666-1791-9.ch002

1. INTRODUCTION

Managing multimedia databases requires the ability to retrieve meaningful information from the digital data, in order to help users find relevant multimedia data more effectively and to facilitate better ways of entertainment. Motivated by a large number of requirements and applications such as sport highlighters, movie recommenders, image search engines, and music libraries, multimedia retrieval and semantic detection have become very popular research topics in recent years (Lew, Sebe, Djeraba & Jain, 2006; Shyu, Chen, Sun & Yu, 2007; Snoek & Worring, 2008). The general steps for supervised content-based multimedia retrieval consist of the segmentation of the multimedia data (i.e., detecting the basic units for processing), the representation of the multimedia data (i.e., extracting low-level features per unit), the model training using the low level features, and the classification of the testing data using the trained model.

The most frequently used features for image retrieval are low-level features such as color, texture, and shape (Datta, Joshi, Li & Wang, 2008); while for video retrieval, the features are these visual features as well as some low-level audio and motion features (Lew, Sebe, Djeraba & Jain, 2006). One of the biggest challenges of multimedia retrieval is that it is hard to bridge the semantic gaps between the low-level features and the high-level features/concepts. Traditionally, these low-level features are considered contributing equally to the models, and the models are trained by using all the features they are provided. Later, the models are required to have the ability to select the features that better represent a certain concept class. In this manner, the features are selected before the model training process, and hence the models do not necessary benefit from the feature selection process (Lin, Ravitz, Shyu, & Chen, 2008; Liu & Motoda, 1998). From another point of view, the importance of the features is not considered

equally anymore, but is considered as "good" or "bad" while performing the feature selection.

1.1 Weighted Features

The feature weighting gets more and more attentions from the researchers recently, since the contributions of different features may not be the same and it is very limited to discriminate the features as either selected ones or non-selected ones. The simplest method for feature weighting is manually set the weight values to various features. In Vadivel, Majumdar and Sural (2004), the fixed weights were given to the color and texture features on a large database of images. Different weights were experimented to 28,000 images and the best results appeared when the texture feature's weight was from 0.1 to 0.2. Some other methods based on the mutual information, gain ratio, odds ratio, and term strength were reviewed in Pekar, Kakoska and Staab (2004). In addition, the authors proposed a feature weighting strategy for word retrieval, which combined the discriminative weights of a feature with each of its characteristic weights. The improved results showed that feature weighting before classification reflected how much the particular feature revealed about class membership of the instances.

An image retrieval model with weighted features based on relevance feedback was proposed by Kim et al. (2008). The annotation of an image was first done by using keywords, and then the confidence level of the keywords was modified in response to the user's feedback. The discrimination power was used to represent how well the positive and negative images were distinguished when the images were re-ranked according to the visual features. The weight of a visual feature was simply calculated as the normalized discrimination power of that feature. In Ziou, Hamri and Boutemedjet (2009), a content-based image retrieval model with probability-based feature weighting was presented. A hybrid probabilistic framework adopted the generalized Dirichlet mixture and maximum likelihood to accurately estimate the statistical model of the data. The idea was under the assumptions that the relevance of different features is not the same for a given node, and a relative relevance of the features is sufficient to discriminate between nodes. Therefore, if a feature is irrelevant, then its weight should be small and its contribution in the indexing and retrieval should be weak. Another statistical measure based feature weighting method was introduced in Wakabayashi, Pal, Kimura and Miyake (2009). The Fisher ratio (F-ratio) was defined as the ratio of the between-class variance and the within-class variance and was used as the weight of the shape character. The higher the F-ratio is, the more useful information is to discriminate the similar classes the feature is contained. The experimental results of similar shape characters of different scripts showed the ability of the weighting scheme to (i) enhance the feature elements that belonged to the distinguishable portions of the similar shape characters and (ii) reduce the feature elements of the common portion of the characters. In Sun, Song and Wu (2009), a Support Vector Machine classifier based on weighted features was presented to show that feature weighting could assist the classifier. The proposed framework first defined the deviation between two random variables and then the weight of each feature was determined via the principle of maximizing deviations between two categories. The experimental results demonstrated that with these weighed features not only the accuracy of the SVM classifier could be improved but also the numbers of support vectors could be decreased.

1.2 Weighted Association Rule Mining (WARM)

Association rule mining (ARM) has been developed to automatically detect semantics from a multimedia database taking the advantages of its good performance and ability to handle large databases (Anwar & Naftel, 2008; Bouzouita & Elloumi, 2007; Lin, Ravitz, Shyu & Chen, 2007).

Given a database B of transactions $T_i \in B$, where i=1 to I and I is total number of transactions/instances in the database, a rule in the form of $A \Rightarrow C$ indicates that when a transaction T_i has item A in it, it most probably also contains item C as well (Ceglar & Roddick, 2006). In order to create association rules from a list of itemsets, two measures are considered in the traditional association rule mining algorithms. One of the measures is "support", defined as $P(A \cap C)$, which is the proportion of the transactions in a database that have both items A and C; while the other one is "confidence", defined as $P(C \mid A)$, which measures the accuracy of the rule. The Apriori algorithm (Agrawal & Srikant, 1994) is one of the most commonly used algorithms. It first finds the frequent itemsets satisfying the minimum support threshold and then generates the strong rules from the frequent itemsets which satisfy the minimum confidence threshold.

Weighed association rule mining (WARM) is a new extension to ARM by allowing a weight to be associated with each item (feature-value pair) in the itemset in the resulting association rules. The rationale behind this extension is to capture the various importance degrees of the feature-value pairs so that the applicability of ARM could be improved. There are several strategies to assign such weights. The simplest way is to use the average weight which is the sum of the weights of all the feature-value pairs in one association rule divided by the number of the feature-value pairs in that rule. When there is only one single feature-value pair in an association rule, for example $A \Rightarrow C$, then the weight of the association rule is the same as the weight of that feature-value pair.

One of the first weighted association rule mining models was provided by Cai et al. (1998). Both the support and the importance ratio factor were considered as the weighted support of a rule to distinguish different features. A corresponding algorithm to mine the weighted binary association rules was also given in that article. Several efficient methods were developed for mining the weighted association rules (WAR). In (Wang, Yang & Yu, 2000), the WAR were generated by satisfying the support, confidence, and density thresholds for each frequent itemset. The weighted downward closure property was exploited in Tao, Murtagh and Farid (2003) to improve the model of weighted support measurement. In Jiang, Zhao and Dong (2008), a framework for mining the positive and negative weighted association rules (PNWAR), which the interest measure method was combined with the algorithm for mining the association rules based on the weighted support was presented. An ALlocation Pattern (ALP) model was introduced in Wang, Zheng, Coenen, and Li (2008). In this model, a weighing score between 0 and 1 was associated with each feature item. This method was also called one-sum because the sum of all feature item scores was 1. The ALP indicated the implicative co-occurring relationship between two disjoint itemsets and captured the allocating relationships among the feature items. For example, in the marketing application, ALP could show the individual customer's habit of allocating an amount of money to various goods. In Ge, Qiu, Chen and Yin (2008), association rule mining was applied into information push technique to improve the recommendation based on quantitative computation of relative information. The mixed weights integrated the analyzed users' behaviors and the Google's PageRank algorithm. In Balasubramamian and Duraiswamy (2009), a temporal mining algorithm was applied to assist the Bayesian classification. The temporal mining with priority items involved the mining based on the weights assigned to the items according to their importance and the time at which the transaction took place. Sun and Bai (2008) described a w-support measure of itemsets based on the assumption that good transactions consist of good items. The weights were derived from the internal structure of the database so that the

weights were not assigned to the support as in most of the existing frameworks.

Though ARM has been applied in the areas of multimedia retrieval and semantic detection and WARM has been developed in the area of data mining, very few algorithms utilized WARM in multimedia retrieval. Note that the term weight/score of a rule is used in some existing multimedia retrieval algorithms, but the weighted rules usually represent the generated rules with certain score values which are used for rule selection and rule evaluation. Therefore, in such cases, each feature item is still considered contributing equally. On the other hand, in WARM, the focus is to assign different weights to different feature items based on their degrees of significance, and therefore each feature item is considered contributing unequally to rule generation.

In our previous studies (Lin, Ravitz, Shyu & Chen, 2008; Lin, Shyu, Ravitz & Chen, 2009), we have utilized the Multiple Correspondence Analysis (MCA) methodology as the association rule generation mechanism. Considering a multimedia database, the columns represent the features and classes, and the rows represent the instances. Using MCA, the correspondence between the features and classes could be captured, and it was shown that our proposed approach helped the classifiers detect more positive instances in the testing data set without misclassifying too many negative instances of the investigated concepts. However, it did not consider the discrimination of the feature-value pairs, and therefore, the feature-value pairs were considered equally important to the association rules.

In this article, we propose one of the first weighted association rule mining (WARM) algorithms for video semantic concept detection. Our proposed WARM-based framework consists of (1) applying multiple correspondence analysis (MCA) to features and classes to discover the correlation information between feature-value pairs and classes, (2) considering both correlation and percentage information as the measurement to assign the weights to feature-value pairs and thus generating weighted association rules, and (3) performing classification by using these weighted association rules. To evaluate the proposed WARM-based framework, its semantic concept detection performance is compared with that of several well-known classifiers on the benchmark data available from the 2007 and 2008 TRECVID project. The results demonstrate that our proposed WARM-based framework achieves promising performance and performs significantly better than those classifiers in the comparison.

The article is organized as follows. Section 2 discusses the architecture of the proposed framework as well as the details of each component. The implementations and observations of experimental results are described in Section 3. Finally, Section 4 gives the conclusions.

2. THE PROPOSED FRAMEWORK

The system architecture of our proposed WARM-based video semantic concept detection framework is shown in Figure 1. Since the shot boundary information is provided by TRECVID (Smeaton, Over & Kraaij, 2006), video segmentation is beyond the scope of this article. We adopt "shots" as the basic unit for processing in this study.

The twenty-eight shot-based audio and visual features that were used in (Lin, Ravitz, Shyu & Chen, 2008) are extracted from the TRECIVD videos. The numerical feature values are normalized to lie in a range [0, 1] using the method introduced in (Witten & Frank 2005) by subtracting the minimum value and dividing by the difference between the maximum and the minimum values per video. The data instances for each concept class are characterized by $F+1$ features (columns), i.e., F normalized numerical features A_f (where $f = 1$ to F and F is 28 in this article) and 1 nominal class label C whose values are C_p or C_n (where C_p is the target concept class and C_n

is the non-target concept class). The example normalized data instances are shown in Table 1. The data instances labeled with the target concept class C_p are called positive instances and the data instances labeled with the non-concept class C_n are called negative instances. Then the normalized data is split into two parts, where two-third of the data is used for training and one-third of the data is used for testing.

Due to the fact that ARM requires the input data to be nominal, all the features are discretized adopting the discretization method used in (Lin, Ravitz, Shyu & Chen, 2008). This discretization method uses the information gain for the disparity measure to give various numbers of partitions for each feature (Fayyad & Irani, 1992). If there

Figure 1. The proposed video semantic concept detection framework

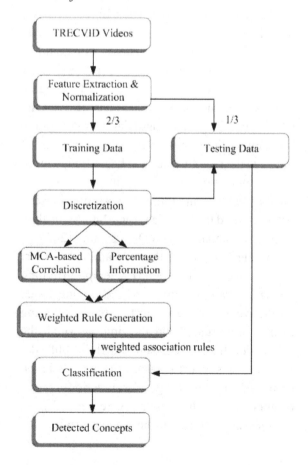

Table 1. Example data instances in the database after normalization

A_1	A_2	...	A_{28}	Class Label C
0.23	0.78	...	0.05	C_p
0.17	0.67	...	0.02	C_p
...	...	...	...	...
0.10	0.59	...	0.21	C_n

is only one partition for a feature by using the aforementioned discretization method, then the discretizaton is done by using the average value of that feature, which results in two partitions. The training data is discretized and these partition ranges are used to discretize the testing data. These partitions generated by the discretization process are called items in the traditional ARM algorithm, but they were called feature-value pairs in this study.

After discretization, each feature A_f has K_f nominal feature-value pairs A_f^k (where $f = 1$ to F and $k=1$ to K_f). Let K be the sum of the total number of nominal feature-value pairs (i.e., $\sum_{f=1}^{28} K_f$) and the total number of class labels in $\boldsymbol{C}$. For example, in the multimedia database, A_{17} represents the feature of the pixel changes and is discretized to 3 partitions. Hence, $K_{17} =3$ and A_{17}^1, A_{17}^2 and A_{17}^3 represent the partitions of the feature value ranges [0, 0.32865], (0.32865, 0.5044], and (0.5044, 1], respectively. In this manner, each data instance is represented by twenty-eight 1-feature-value pairs and one of the class labels in $\boldsymbol{C}$. Take the example discretized data instances in Table 2. The first data instance (i.e., the second row) in this table is represented by the 1-feature-value pairs ($A_1 = A_1^2$), ($A_2 = A_2^3$), ..., ($A_{28} = A_{28}^1$), and the class label ($\boldsymbol{C}=C_p$), which means that its A_1 value falls into the second par-

tition, its A_2 value falls into the third partition, etc. To generate the weighted association rules (WARM), the correlation information between each 1-feature-value pair ($A_f = A_f^k$) and the class label $\boldsymbol{C}$ (C_p or C_n) is calculated by applying MCA to the discretized training data set.

2.1. Multiple Correspondence Analysis (MCA)

Multiple correspondence analysis (MCA) is an extension of the standard Correspondence Analysis (CA) by providing the ability to analyze a table containing some measure of correspondence between the rows and columns with more than two variables (Salkind, 2007). In a multimedia database, the columns contain the low-level audio and visual features (or attributes) as well as the class labels for concepts/events, and the data instances are the rows in the database. By utilizing MCA, the correspondence between the features and the classes could be captured, which assists the classifier in narrowing the semantic gap between the low-level features and the high-level concepts (class labels) in a multimedia database.

As mentioned earlier, our TRECVID database consists of I data instances which are characterized by $F =28$ discretized low-level features A_f^k ($f=1$ to F and $k=1$ to K_f) and 1 class label $\boldsymbol{C}$ (C_p or C_n), and there are totally K nominal feature-

Table 2. Example data instances in the database after discretization

A_1	A_2	...	A_{28}	Class Label
A_1^2	A_2^3	...	A_{28}^1	C_p
A_1^1	A_2^3	...	A_{28}^2	C_p
...	...	...	...	...
A_1^1	A_2^3	...	A_{28}^4	C_n

value pairs and class labels in the database. Therefore, the MCA table with *I* rows and *F* + 1 columns is available to be utilized later, and part of the MCA table is presented in Table 3.

MCA scans these nominal data in the table to generate the indicator matrix. The indicator matrix (*X*) is a binary representation of the different categorical values, where each column represents a level (feature-value pair) generated during the data discretization process and each row represents a data instance. The indicator matrix indicates the appearance of the feature-value pairs using the value 1. That is, only one feature-value pair can be present for each feature, and therefore each feature can only have one value of 1 in the indicator matrix for each data instance. An example of the indicator matrix is shown in Table 4, and the size of the indicator matrix is $I \times K$.

Standard CA analyzes the indicator matrix; while MCA calculates the inner product of the indicator matrix, which generates the Burt matrix $Y = X^T X$. An example of the Burt matrix is shown in Table 5 where the size of the Burt matrix is $K \times K$. Let the grand total of the Burt matrix be G and the probability matrix be $Z = Y/G$. The vector of the column totals of Z is a $1 \times K$ mass matrix M, and $D = diag(M)$.

Calculating the chi-square distance among tabulations of the Burt table, MCA will provide the principle components using singular value decomposition (SVD) as follows.

Table 3. Example of the MCA table

A_1	A_2	$\cdots$	A_{28}	C_p / C_n
A_1^2	A_2^3	...	A_{28}^1	C_p
A_1^1	A_2^3	...	A_{28}^2	C_p
...	...	...	...	...
A_1^1	A_2^3	...	A_{28}^4	C_n

Table 4. Example of the indicator matrix

$$X = \begin{matrix} & A_1^1 & A_1^2 & A_2^1 & .. & A_{28}^4 & C_p & C_n \\ & 1 & 0 & 0 & .. & 1 & 1 & 0 \\ & ... & ... & ... & & ... & ... & ... \\ & 0 & 1 & 0 & .. & 0 & 0 & 1 \end{matrix}$$

$$\left(D\right)^{1/2}\left(Z - MM^T\right)\left(D^T\right)^{-1/2} = P\Delta Q^T, \qquad (1)$$

Where Δ is the diagonal matrix of the singular values, the columns of P is the left singular vectors (gene coefficient vectors), and the rows of Q^T is the right singular vectors (expression level vectors) in the singular value decomposition (SVD) theorem.

Therefore, the multimedia data could be projected into a new space by using the first and the second principle components discovered using Equation (1). The correlation between the different feature-value pairs and the different class labels can be used as an indication of their similarity. Such similarity could be calculated as the inner product of each feature-value pair and each class label, i.e., the cosine of the angle between each feature-value pair and each class label.

The higher correlated the feature-value pair and the class label would be the pairs that project to the new space with a smaller angel between them. For instance, for the concept "face" in the TRECVID 2007 data, the feature "center to corner ratio" has three feature-value pairs (A_{24}^1, A_{24}^2 and A_{24}^3) after discretization. The projection of that feature and its corresponding three feature-value pairs are shown in Figure 2. The absolute values of the angles between each feature-value pair and the positive class label for the face concept (class) are 126.59, 24.12, and 122.34 degrees, respectively. As we discussed above, the second feature-value pair (A_{24}^2) appears to be a better representation for the positive class label (C_p), and the feature-value pairs (A_{24}^1 and A_{24}^3) seem to

Table 5. Example of the Burt matrix

$$Y = \begin{array}{c|ccccc} & A_1^1 & A_1^2 & \ldots & C_p & C_n \\ \hline A_1^1 & 1 & 0 & \ldots & 1 & 0 \\ A_1^2 & 0 & \ldots & & \ldots & \ldots \\ \ldots & \ldots & \ldots & & \ldots & \ldots \\ C_p & 1 & \ldots & & \ldots & \ldots \\ C_n & 0 & \ldots & & \ldots & \ldots \end{array}$$

be good representations for the negative class label (C_n) in this example.

2.2 Weighted Association Rule Mining (WARM)

The weight of each feature-value pair consists of two parts. One is the correlation information from MCA and the other is the percentage information from the frequency count. After extracting the angle value of each feature-value pair (A_f^k, where $f = 1$ to F and $k = 1$ to K_f) from MCA, the weight from the correlation information is calculated using Equation (2).

$$weight\_ang_f^k = \pm\left(180 - angle_f^k\right)/90, \qquad (2)$$

where $angle_f^k \in [0, 90]$, and the positive sign or negative sign is determined by whether the corresponding feature-value pair is a good representation for the positive or negative class label. In the special case when $angle_f^k$ is 90 degrees, the value of $weight\_ang_f^k$ is 0.

The pseudo-code for the calculation of the percentage information is presented in Table 6. It can be seen from Table 6 that the pseudo code is iterated for all the features $f = 1$ to F. From Lines 2 to 11, the iteration covers all the feature-value pairs for each feature $k = 1$ to K_f. First, from Line 3 to 8, the $item\_count_f^k$ for each feature-value pair is calculated, and next, from Lines 9 to 10, the positive and negative percentage information

for each feature is captured. From Lines 12 to 34, four conditions are checked to assign the weight $weight\_per_f^k$ to each feature-value pair, where the first check is from Lines 12 to 20, the second one is from Lines 21 to 25, the third one is from Lines 26 to 30, and the last one is from Lines 31 to 34.

Based on our empirical study, $thred1 = 0.25$ and $thred2 = 0.4$ are used in this article. The final weight for each feature-value pair is calculated using Equation (3). Each weighted 1-feature-value pair association rule for A_f^k is generated if its $weight_f^k$ passes a certain threshold, and this rule is included in the final rule set for classification. This threshold is determined by applying different threshold values to the training data set, and the one yielded the best F1-score value is kept as the threshold.

$$weigh_f^h = weight\_ang_f^k \times weight\_per_f^k. \qquad (3)$$

Then classification by using these weighted association rules is performed for semantic detection. First, each testing data instance in the testing data set is checked to see if it includes any of the feature-value pairs. Second, for those feature-value pairs that exist in the testing data instance, the sum of the weights of the matched feature-value pair rules is considered as a score to determine the class label assigned to the testing data instance. If the score is larger than or equal to zero, the testing data instance is predicted as a concept instance; otherwise, the non-concept class label is assigned to the testing data instance.

3. EXPERIMENTS AND RESULTS

Our proposed WARM-based video semantic concept detection framework is evaluated by testing fifteen concepts from the TRECVID videos available for the high-level feature extraction task in 2007 and 2008, and comparing the results

Figure 2. Projection with the first and the second principle components

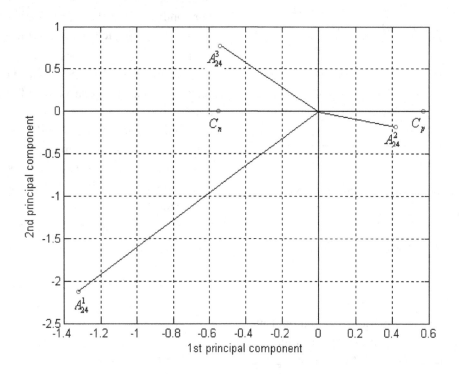

with seven well-known classifiers to show its effectiveness and robustness. The fifteen high-level features (concept classes) are two people (c7), outdoor (c8), building (c9), vegetation (c11), street (c12), road (c13), sky (c14), hand (c15), urban (c16), waterscape (c17), crowd (c18), face (c19), person (c20), animal (c26), and walking (c34). The detailed descriptions of these concepts can be found in Smeaton, Over, and Kraaij (2006). Seven commonly used classifiers in multimedia retrieval, namely Decision Tree (C4.5 algorithm from the trees category), Support Vector Machine (Sequential Minimal Optimization (SMO) algorithm from the function category), Neural Network classifier (MultilayerPerception algorithm from the function category), Naive Bayesian (NaiveBayes algorithm from the Bayes category), AdaBoost classifier (AdaBoostM1 algorithm with C4.5 classifier from the meta category), Kth Nearest Neighbor classifier (Ibk algorithm from the lazy category), and one rule based (JRip algorithm from the rules category) classifier are used in the evaluation

comparison. These classifiers are available in WEKA (Witten & Frank, 2005) and their default parameters are adopted in our performance evaluation. The precision, recall, and F1-score measures are calculated as the performance metrics from the 3-fold cross-validation approach in the experiments. In order to ensure that each data instance in the data set would be tested at least once in the 3-fold cross-validation, the positive data instances and negative data instances are split into three equal parts separately in our experiments. Two parts of the positive data instances and two parts of the negative data instances are combined as the training set, and the remaining part of the positive data instances and the remaining part of the negative data instances are used for testing.

The results of the average precision (Pre), recall (Rec), and F1-score (F1) values from the three folds for the fifteen concepts in the evaluation comparison are demonstrated in Table 7, Table 8, and Table 9 (each with five concept classes). The performance of Decision Tree (DT), Support

Table 6. Pseudo-code for calculating the weight from the percentage information

1	for $f \leftarrow 1$ to F
2	for $k \leftarrow 1$ to K_f
3	for $i \leftarrow 1$ to I
4	if A_f^k and C_p exist in data instance i and $weight\_ang_f^k > 0$ or
5	if A_f^k and C_n exist in data instance i and $weight\_ang_f^k < 0$ then
6	$item\_count_f^k \leftarrow item\_count_f^k + 1$;
7	else $item\_count_f^k \leftarrow 0$;
8	end
9	if $weight\_ang_f^k > 0$ then $pos\_per_f \leftarrow item\_count_f^k /$ (no. of positive data instances);
10	elseif $weight\_ang_f^k < 0$ then $neg\_per_f \leftarrow item\_count_f^k /$ (no. of negative data instances);
11	end
12	if $pos\_per_f > thred1$ and $neg\_per_f > thred1$ then
13	for $k \leftarrow 1$ to K_f
14	if $weight\_ang_f^k > 0$ then
15	if $pos\_per_f < thred2$ then $weight\_per_f^k \leftarrow 1 + pos\_per_f$;

continued in following column

Table 6. Continued

16	else $weight\_per_f^k \leftarrow 1 + pos\_per_f / 2$;
17	else if $weight\_ang_f^k < 0$ then
18	if $neg\_per_f < thred2$ then $weight\_per_f^k \leftarrow 1 + neg\_per_f$;
19	else $weight\_per_f^k \leftarrow 1 + neg\_per_f / 2$;
20	end
21	else if $pos\_per_f > thred1$ and $neg\_per_f = 0$ then
22	for $k \leftarrow 1$ to K_f
23	if $weight\_ang_f^k > 0$ then $weight\_per_f^k \leftarrow 1 + pos\_per_f$;
24	else $weight\_per_f^k \leftarrow 1$;
25	end
26	else if $neg\_per_f > thred1$ and $pos\_per_f = 0$ then
27	for $k \leftarrow 1$ to K_f
28	if $weight\_ang_f^k < 0$ then $weight\_per_f^k \leftarrow 1 + neg\_per_f$;
29	else $weight\_per_f^k \leftarrow 1$;
30	end
31	else then
32	for $k \leftarrow 1$ to K_f
33	$weight\_per_f^k \leftarrow 1$;
34	end
35	end

Table 7. Performance evaluation for five high-level concept classes

two-people	DT	SVM	NN	NB	ADA	KNN	JR	WARM
Pre	0.51	0.00	0.44	0.43	0.40	0.40	0.52	0.36
Rec	0.19	0.00	0.25	0.28	0.36	0.47	0.19	0.92
F1	0.27	0.00	0.32	0.34	0.38	0.43	0.26	0.52
outdoor	DT	SVM	NN	NB	ADA	KNN	JR	WARM
Pre	0.59	0.59	0.53	0.51	0.52	0.51	0.58	0.47
Rec	0.39	0.37	0.48	0.51	0.51	0.53	0.46	0.75
F1	0.47	0.46	0.50	0.51	0.51	0.52	0.51	0.57
building	DT	SVM	NN	NB	ADA	KNN	JR	WARM
Pre	0.57	0.55	0.50	0.50	0.51	0.47	0.53	0.45
Rec	0.34	0.27	0.42	0.50	0.46	0.54	0.44	0.81
F1	0.42	0.36	0.46	0.50	0.48	0.50	0.48	0.58
vegetation	DT	SVM	NN	NB	ADA	KNN	JR	WARM
Pre	0.51	0.54	0.45	0.51	0.46	0.44	0.53	0.45
Rec	0.35	0.14	0.46	0.41	0.42	0.49	0.34	0.71
F1	0.42	0.21	0.45	0.46	0.44	0.46	0.41	0.55
street	DT	SVM	NN	NB	ADA	KNN	JR	WARM
Pre	0.55	0.58	0.49	0.54	0.55	0.47	0.54	0.51
Rec	0.50	0.47	0.49	0.60	0.48	0.58	0.53	0.74
F1	0.52	0.52	0.49	0.57	0.51	0.52	0.54	0.60

Vector Machine (SVM), Neural Network (NN), Naive Bayesian (NB), Adaboost (ADA), Kth Nearest Neighbor (KNN), and Rule based JRip classifier (JR) obtained from WEKA are given in columns two to eight, respectively; while the performance of our proposed framework (WARM) is shown in the last column.

As can be clearly observed from Tables 7 to 9, our proposed framework always achieves the highest recall and F1-score values for all the concepts. The higher average recall values are considered as performing the higher accuracy of detecting the high-level concepts. The recall values from our proposed framework are 70% or higher, and in average 20% higher than the recall values achieved by the seven classifiers in the comparison. In other words, more good weighed association rules for the positive classes could be generated from our proposed framework, and at

the same time, the different weights of the feature-value pairs could indicate the various importance degrees of the feature-value pairs with respect to the classes. In addition, the higher average F1-socers are considered as the better results since it takes into account for both recall and precision values. Although there is a little bit trade-off between the precision and recall values, the overall F1-scores have been improved 5% in average when using our proposed WARM-based framework.

Furthermore, it can be seen that, except our proposed WARM-based framework, the other classifiers in the comparison are not robust enough to be able to work well for all the concept classes. For example, for the concepts "two people" and "outdoor", the Kth Nearest Neighbors classifier gives the second best F1-scores; for the concept "crowd", the Neural Network classifier gives

Table 8. Performance evaluation for five high-level concept classes

road	DT	SVM	NN	NB	ADA	KNN	JR	WARM
Pre	0.58	0.59	0.50	0.51	0.54	0.49	0.57	0.46
Rec	0.34	0.35	0.47	0.55	0.49	0.58	0.44	0.79
F1	0.42	0.44	0.48	0.53	0.51	0.53	0.49	0.59
sky	DT	SVM	NN	NB	ADA	KNN	JR	WARM
Pre	0.62	0.64	0.56	0.57	0.55	0.53	0.67	0.53
Rec	0.48	0.45	0.51	0.57	0.52	0.56	0.45	0.70
F1	0.54	0.52	0.54	0.57	0.54	0.54	0.52	0.60
hand	DT	SVM	NN	NB	ADA	KNN	JR	WARM
Pre	0.46	0.33	0.42	0.49	0.42	0.39	0.54	0.43
Rec	0.31	0.06	0.40	0.42	0.39	0.45	0.35	0.77
F1	0.37	0.10	0.41	0.45	0.40	0.42	0.42	0.55
urban	DT	SVM	NN	NB	ADA	KNN	JR	WARM
Pre	0.51	0.53	0.47	0.52	0.48	0.44	0.53	0.48
Rec	0.41	0.25	0.45	0.54	0.45	0.50	0.44	0.72
F1	0.46	0.34	0.46	0.53	0.46	0.47	0.48	0.58
waterscape	DT	SVM	NN	NB	ADA	KNN	JR	WARM
Pre	0.58	0.65	0.53	0.55	0.55	0.54	0.62	0.51
Rec	0.49	0.47	0.52	0.58	0.49	0.59	0.49	0.77
F1	0.53	0.54	0.52	0.56	0.52	0.56	0.55	0.61

Figure 3. The recall results

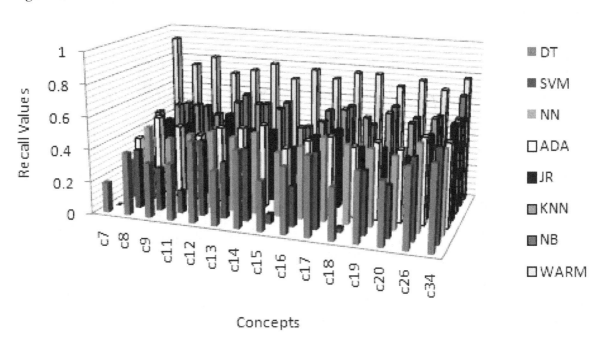

Table 9. Performance evaluation for five high-level concept classes

crowd	DT	SVM	NN	NB	ADA	KNN	JR	WARM
Pre	0.54	0.78	0.50	0.49	0.50	0.45	0.52	0.43
Rec	0.32	0.03	0.49	0.47	0.44	0.55	0.39	0.77
F1	0.40	0.06	0.50	0.48	0.47	0.49	0.45	0.55
face	DT	SVM	NN	NB	ADA	KNN	JR	WARM
Pre	0.60	0.68	0.55	0.52	0.53	0.48	0.61	0.47
Rec	0.43	0.39	0.48	0.60	0.48	0.59	0.40	0.70
F1	0.50	0.50	0.51	0.56	0.51	0.53	0.49	0.57
person	DT	SVM	NN	NB	ADA	KNN	JR	WARM
Pre	0.54	0.61	0.48	0.51	0.49	0.51	0.54	0.45
Rec	0.39	0.32	0.45	0.54	0.45	0.54	0.36	0.75
F1	0.45	0.42	0.47	0.53	0.47	0.53	0.43	0.56
animal	DT	SVM	NN	NB	ADA	KNN	JR	WARM
Pre	0.62	0.66	0.57	0.55	0.59	0.54	0.66	0.55
Rec	0.49	0.50	0.54	0.56	0.54	0.58	0.51	0.70
F1	0.54	0.57	0.55	0.55	0.56	0.56	0.57	0.61
walking	DT	SVM	NN	NB	ADA	KNN	JR	WARM
Pre	0.56	0.59	0.53	0.56	0.53	0.51	0.58	0.55
Rec	0.52	0.57	0.52	0.70	0.52	0.59	0.59	0.78
F1	0.54	0.57	0.52	0.62	0.53	0.55	0.58	0.64

Figure 4. The F1-score results

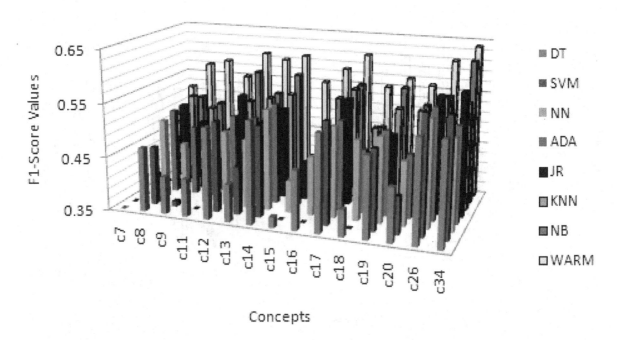

the second best F1-scores; and for the concept "animal", the Support Vector Machine classifier and Rule based JRip classifier give the second best F1-scores. This observation demonstrates that some of the classifiers in the comparison only perform well for some of the concepts, but on the other hand, our proposed framework outperforms all the other seven classifiers in all the investigated high-level concept classes.

More directly to present the performance comparison, the recall values and F1-scores are further plotted in Figure 3 and Figure 4, respectively. From these two figures, it can be clearly seen that our proposed framework improves the results for the positive classes, since the recall values have been significantly increased. This demonstrates that our proposed framework is able to achieve promising results by extracting the high-level concepts from the video data using the association information from WARM together with the correlation information among the feature-value pairs and target concept class from MCA.

4. CONCLUSION

A video semantic concept detection framework via weighted association rule mining (WARM) is proposed in this article. First, we utilize the functionality of MCA to measure the correlation between different 1-feature value pairs and the classes to infer the high-level concepts from the extracted low-level audio-visual features. Next, the association rules are generated by using the weighted 1-feature-value pairs, where the correlation information and the percentage information are integrated as the final weight measurement. Classification is performed directly by using those weighted 1-feature-value pair rules. Data for fifteen target concepts taken from the TRECVID 2007 and 2008 video corpus is tested to validate the detection performance of our proposed framework. The experimental results demonstrate that our proposed framework performs well in de-

tecting all the selected fifteen concepts from the TRECVID benchmark data with higher overall recall and F1-score performance over the well-known Decision Tree, Support Vector Machine, Naive Bayesian, Neural Network, AdaBoost, Kth Nearest Neighbor, and rule based JRip classifiers.

REFERENCES

Agrawal, R., & Srikant, R. (1994). Fast algorithms for mining association rules in large databases, *In Proceedings of the International Conference on Very Large Data Bases (VLDB94)*, (pp. 487-499).

Anwar, F., & Naftel, A. (2008). Video event modeling and association rule mining in multimedia surveillance systems. In *Proceedings of the International Conference on Visual Information Engineering (VIE08)* (pp. 426-431).

Balasubramanian, C., & Duraiswamy, K. (2009). An application of Bayesian classification to interval encoded temporal mining with prioritized items. *International Journal of Computer Science and Information Security, 3*(1), 9250–9259.

Bouzouitz, I., & Elloumi, S. (2007). Integrated generic association rule based classifier. In *Proceedings of the IEEE International Conference on Database and Expert Systems Applications (DEXA07)* (pp. 514-518).

Cai, C. H., Fu, A. W. C., Cheng, C. H., & Kwong, W. W. (1998). Mining association rules with weighted items. *In Proceedings of the IEEE International Conference on Database Engineering and Applications Symposium (IDEAS98)* (pp. 68-77).

Ceglar, A., & Roddick, J. F. (2006). Association mining. *ACM Computing Surveys, 38*(5), 5. doi:10.1145/1132956.1132958

Datta, R., Joshi, D., Li, J., & Wang, J. Z. (2008). Image retrieval: Ideas, influences, and trends of the new age. *ACM Computing Surveys, 40*(2), 1–60. doi:10.1145/1348246.1348248

Fayyad, U. M., & Irani, K. B. (1992). On the handling of continuous-value attributes in decision tree generation. *Machine Learning, 8*(1), 87–102.

Ge, J., Qiu, Y., Chen, Z., & Yin, S. (2008). Technology of information push based on weighted association rules mining. In *Proceedings of the IEEE International Conference on Fuzzy Systems and Knowledge Discovery (FSKD08)* (pp. 615-619).

Jiang, H., Zhao, Y., & Dong, X. (2008). Mining positive and negative weighted association rules from frequent itemsets based on interest. In *Proceedings of the IEEE International Symposium on Computational Intelligence and Design (ISCID08)* (pp. 242-245).

Kim, W.-C., Song, J.-Y., Kim, S.-W., & Park, S. (2008). Image retrieval model based on weighted visual features determined by relevance feedback. *Information Sciences, 178*(22), 4301–4313. doi:10.1016/j.ins.2008.06.025

Lew, M. S., Sebe, N., Djeraba, C., & Jain, R. (2006). Content-based multimedia information retrieval: State of art and challenges. *ACM Transactions on Multimedia Computing, Communications and Applications, 2*(1), 1–19.

Lin, L., & Ravitz, G. Shyu, M.-L., & Chen, S.-C. (2008). Effective feature space reduction with imbalanced data for semantic concept detection. In *Proceedings of the IEEE International Conference on Sensor Networks, Ubiquitous, and Trustworthy Computing (SUTC08)* (pp. 262-269).

Lin, L., Ravitz, G., Shyu, M.-L., & Chen, S.-C. (2007). Video semantic concept discovery using multimodel-based association classification. In *Proceedings of the IEEE International Conference on Multimedia and Expo (ICME07)* (pp. 859-862).

Lin, L., Ravitz, G., Shyu, M.-L., & Chen, S.-C. (2008). Correlation-based video semantic concept detection using multiple correspondence analysis. In *Proceedings of the IEEE International Symposium on Multimedia (ISM08)* (pp. 316-321).

Lin, L., Shyu, M.-L., Ravitz, G., & Chen, S.-C. (2009). Video semantic concept detection via associative classification. In *Proceedings of the IEEE International Conference on Multimedia and Expo (ICME09)* (pp. 418-421).

Liu, H., & Motada, H. (1998). *Feature selection for knowledge discovery and data mining*. Dordrecht, The Netherlands: Kluwer Academic Publishers.

Pekar, V., Krkoska, M., & Staab, S. (2004). Feature weighting for co-occurrence-based classification of words. In *Proceedings of the International Conference on Computational Linguistics (COLING04)* (no. 799).

Salkind, N. J. (Ed.). (2007). *Encyclopedia of measurement and statistics*. Newbury Park, CA: SAGE Publications.

Shyu, M.-L., Chen, S.-C., Sun, Q., & Yu, H. (2007). Overview and future trends of multimedia research for content access and distribution. *International Journal of Semantic Computing, 1*(1), 29–66. doi:10.1142/S1793351X07000044

Smeaton, A. F., Over, P., & Kraaij, W. (2006). Evaluation campaigns and TRECVid. In *Proceedings of the ACM International Workshop on Multimedia Information Retrieval (MIR06)* (pp. 321-330).

Snoek, C. G. M., & Worring, M. (2008). Concept-based video retrieval. *Foundations and Trends in Information Retrieval, 2*(4), 215–322. doi:10.1561/1500000014

Sun, B., Song, S.-J., & Wu, C. (2009). A new algorithm of support vector machine based on weighted feature. In *Proceedings of the IEEE International Conference on Machine Learning and Cybernetics* (pp. 1616-1620).

Sun, K., & Bai, F. (2008). Mining weighted association rules without preassigned weights. *IEEE Transactions on Knowledge and Data Engineering, 20*(4), 489–495. doi:10.1109/TKDE.2007.190723

Tao, F., Murtagh, F., & Farid, M. (2003). Weighted association rule mining using weighted support and significance framework. In *Proceedings of ACM SIGKDD International Conference on Knowledge Discovery and Data Mining (KDD03)* (pp. 661-666).

Vadivel, A., Majumdar, A. K., & Sural, S. (2004). Characteristics of weighted feature vector in content-based image retrieval applications. In *Proceedings of the IEEE International Conference on Intelligent Sensing and Information Processing (ICISIP04)* (pp. 127-132).

Wakabayashi, T., Pal, U., Kimura, F., & Miyake, Y. (2009). F-ratio based weighted feature extraction for similar shape character recognition. In *Proceedings of the IEEE International Conference on Document Analysis and Recognition (ICDAR09)* (pp. 196-200).

Wang, W., Yang, J., & Yu, P. S. (2000). Efficient mining of weighted association rules (WAR). In *Proceedings of the ACM SIGKDD International Conference on Knowledge Discovery and Data Mining (KDD00)* (pp. 270-274).

Wang, Y. J., Zheng, X., Coenen, F., & Li, C. Y. (2008). Mining allocating patterns in one-sum weighted items. In *Proceedings of the IEEE International Conference on Data Mining Workshops (ICDMW08)* (pp. 592-598).

Witten, I. H., & Frank, E. (2005). *Data mining: Practical machine learning tools and techniques* (2nd ed.). San Francisco: Morgan Kaufmann.

Ziou, D., Hamria, T., & Boutemedjeta, S. (2009). A hybrid probabilistic framework for content-based image retrieval with feature weighting. *Pattern Recognition, 42*(7), 1511–1519. doi:10.1016/j.patcog.2008.11.025

This work was previously published in the International Journal of Multimedia Data Engineering and Management, Volume 1, Issue 1, edited by Shu-Ching Chen, pp. 37-54, copyright 2010 by IGI Publishing (an imprint of IGI Global).

Chapter 3
Correlation–Based Ranking for Large–Scale Video Concept Retrieval

Lin Lin
University of Miami, USA

Mei-Ling Shyu
University of Miami, USA

ABSTRACT

Motivated by the growing use of multimedia services and the explosion of multimedia collections, efficient retrieval from large-scale multimedia data has become very important in multimedia content analysis and management. In this paper, a novel ranking algorithm is proposed for video retrieval. First, video content is represented by the global and local features and second, multiple correspondence analysis (MCA) is applied to capture the correlation between video content and semantic concepts. Next, video segments are scored by considering the features with high correlations and the transaction weights converted from correlations. Finally, a user interface is implemented in a video retrieval system that allows the user to enter his/her interested concept, searches videos based on the target concept, ranks the retrieved video segments using the proposed ranking algorithm, and then displays the top-ranked video segments to the user. Experimental results on 30 concepts from the TRECVID high-level feature extraction task have demonstrated that the presented video retrieval system assisted by the proposed ranking algorithm is able to retrieve more video segments belonging to the target concepts and to display more relevant results to the users.

INTRODUCTION

Multimedia retrieval has become a popular research area due to the explosive growth of digital image and video collections and the widespread accessibility of media in social networks and internet. The demand for solutions and tools to search and retrieve the interesting information effectively and efficiently is increasing. Meanwhile, the capacity of multimedia data grows larger and faster. For instance, it has become more suitable to measure the sizes of videos in TB (terabytes) rather than in GB (gigabytes) now. Hence, how to manage and retrieve the desired information

DOI: 10.4018/978-1-4666-1791-9.ch003

from the huge amounts of multimedia data has challenged researchers in the multimedia area (Chen, 2010).

Concept-based retrieval (Snoek & Worring, 2008) is to detect the existence of objects (such as bus and hand), the meaning of scenes (such as cityscape and nighttime), and the occurrence of events (such as airplane flying and people dancing). It enables the users to utilize multimedia data for entertainment, distant education, commerce and business, social communication, navigation, security, surveillance, and etc. For example, a user may enjoy watching the segments of videos with singing if she/he loves music, or may seek news videos with protest content if she/he is interested in politics. Correctly detecting the classroom setting from the videos would help information search for educational applications, and retrieving the bridge and mountain would assist the users who are planning a trip. The high-level concepts such as doorway and street from video games could be used for navigation, while emergency vehicle and traffic intersection from video surveillance and security cameras could be used for tracking.

Most of the existing search and retrieval approaches are restricted to textual information which is metadata such as surrounding text and closed caption, or are dependent on an interactive framework which requires users' feedback and log files. The advances of database and data warehouse technologies provide us a proper way to manage these textual data and they seem to be efficient tools that are able to facilitate the users to access the data on demand. However, challenges arise when heavy human efforts are demanded for annotation, correcting the textual information, as well as performance evaluation of the retrieved results. To address these issues, content-based multimedia retrieval has emerged in recent years. Most of the content-based frameworks utilize support vector machine (SVM) detectors trained on scale-invariant feature transform (SIFT) descriptors and rank the retrieved results based on the scores obtained from the classifiers. However,

SVM is very time consuming with a huge demand in space. Moreover, the classification-based ranking methods suffer from the ad-hoc mechanism to determine the threshold for class labels. Therefore, they cannot be used for real-time online searching.

In addition to efficiency, another important consideration of a retrieval system is effectiveness. The overall retrieval performance is usually evaluated through the mean average precision (MAP) of the retrieved results obtained from the ranking algorithm. To make a fair comparison on the effectiveness of the approaches, the benchmarked video concepts provided by the TREC Video Retrieval Evaluation (TRECVID) community (Smeaton, Over, & Kraaij, 2006) are the most commonly used testbed for evaluating large-scale standardizing data sets. In 2008 and 2009, there are totally 30 concepts for high-level feature extraction task and 219 videos with annotations for the training purpose (Divakaran, 2009).

In this paper, a novel correlation-based ranking algorithm is proposed to assist in video concept retrieval from large-scale video collections. There are three stages in our video retrieval system. First, video content is represented by the global and local low-level audio and visual features rather than the point SIFT descriptors, and thus both the global representation of scenes and local representation of regions are captured. Second, multiple correspondence analysis (MCA) is applied to explore the correlation between video content and semantic concepts rather than between video context and semantic concepts, thus without the effort for extracting the textual information from the videos. In our previous work, MCA-based correlation information has been investigated and used as transaction weights for data pruning (Lin, Shyu, & Chen, 2009) and feature weights for generating weighted association rules (Lin & Shyu, 2010). Moreover, MCA technique has been used for low-level feature selection in event detection (Shirahama, Sugihara, Matsuoka, & Uehara, 2009) and concept detection (Zhu, Lin, Shyu, & Chen, 2010). In this paper, MCA has been utilized in the third stage to perform ranking scores by considering the features with high correlations and the transaction weights converted from correlations. The experimental results demonstrate that the proposed ranking algorithm performs comparably with the top-ranked results submitted to TRECVID. Finally, a user interface is implemented in our video retrieval system to display the top-ranked video segments based on the user's interested target concept and their corresponding scores, which shows the effectiveness of our proposed correlation-based ranking algorithm.

This paper is organized as follows. Related work in video concept retrieval and ranking is presented, especially for those using TRECVID benchmark data sets in their performance evaluation. Our video retrieval system and the detailed discussion on the proposed ranking algorithm are then presented and Experimental results for video search are given. Finally, the paper is concluded.

RELATED WORK

The approaches in video concept retrieval and ranking can be broadly categorized into several categories. First category is the context-based methods. In (Jiang, Ngo, & Chang, 2009), the semantic context across heterogeneous sources was transferred to adaptively refine the detector similarity for video retrieval. The Flickr context similarity which reflected the co-occurrence statistics of words in image context was used to transfer semantic context and to improve concept detector accuracy tested on TRECVID 2005 to TRECVID 2008 benchmarks. Another context based framework was introduced in (Wei, Jiang, & Ngo, 2009), including the construction of a context space considering the concept relationship and the exploration of the space for cross-domain context-based concept fusion. Experiment on TRECVID 2005 to TRECVID 2008 datasets, the improvement of concept detection was observed when context space was used.

Next category is the content-based methods integrating with context information. In Natsev, Haubold, Tevsic, Xie, and Yan (2007), several retrieval approaches based on lexical rule-based ontology mapping and statistical correlation analysis were presented. Given the co-occurrence counts, a likelihood ratio statistical significance test was applied to measure whether the correlations were significant. The experimental results showed that it achieved 77% improvement over a text-based retrieval baseline method when evaluated on TRECVID 2006 benchmark. A video retrieval framework using semantic word similarity and visual co-occurrence was proposed in Aytar, Shah, and Jiebo (2008). Based on the assumption that certain concepts tend to occur together, the context between high-level concepts was exploited by point-wise mutual information and the visual co-occurrence relations between concepts were obtained. Evaluating the concepts from TRECVID 2006 and 2007 data sets, the visual content based semantic retrieval performed 81% better than the text-based retrieval method. Most of the methods in this category are query-dependent, which target at identifying whether a video segment is relevant or irrelevant to a given query. In Liu, Mei, Wu, and Hua (2009), a query-independent model (MG-OIL) for video search was introduced. MG-OIL constructed multiple graphs where queries and video segments were connected by relational similarity and semantic similarity, and their experimental results over TRECVID 2005 to 2007 benchmark data showed that MG-OIL achieved significant improvement over a text search baseline method.

In the third category, the methods were based on SVM learning. In Yanagawa, Chang, Kennedy, and Hsu (2007), SVM models with RBF kernels were trained separately using three visual features (color, texture, and edge). A simple late fusion scheme that averages the scores resulting from each classifier was applied to obtain the final score. The baseline models achieved very good performance in the TRECVID 2006 concept detection benchmark data and provided a strong baseline platform for researchers to expand upon. In Jiang, Yang, Ngo, and Hauptmann (2010), SVM models with RBF kernels were trained using keypoint based representation bag-of-visual-words (BoW). Keypoints refer to local interest points defined as salient patches containing rich local information. The BoW representation consists of the following steps. First, the keypoints are detected automatically and described by the descriptors (e.g., SIFT descriptor). Next, vector quantization is adopted to cluster the keypoint descriptors using clustering algorithms (e.g., k-means algorithm). Last, a visual word vocabulary is generated that describes local patterns shared by keypoints in different clusters. Using TRECVID 2008 data, their proposed method ranked top 10 out of 200 submissions. Later in Cao, Jing, Ngo, and Zhang (2009), utilizing the combined scores of Yanagawa, Chang, Kennedy, and Hsu (2007) and Jiang, Yang, Ngo, and Hauptmann (2010), a distribution-based concept selection (DBCS) algorithm was introduced to select the most discriminative concepts and considered the variance of ranking scores. A cross-domain SVM (CDSVM) was developed in Jiang, Zavesky, Chang, and Loui (2008) to help detect concepts in a new domain for adapting previously learned support vectors from the old domain. In other words, extra source data in the old domain whose distribution was different from the target data set in the new domain was used for training models.

The approaches in the forth category focus on the ranking methods, instead of using classification-based scores. The ranking algorithm we proposed in this paper can be considered as one in this category. In Yang and Hsu (2008), an ordinal re-ranking approach was proposed, which re-ranks an initial text-based search list by utilizing the co-occurrence patterns via the ranking function ``ListNet.'' ListNet was a listwise approach which transformed the initial scores and the re-ranked scores into probability distributions, and used cross-entropy to measure

the distance between these two distributions. Their experiments on TRECVID 2005 concepts presented that the ordinal re-ranking approach offered 35.6% improvement over the text-based search. A Bayesian re-ranking framework was discussed in Tian, Yang, Wang, Yang, Wu, and Hua (2008). It maximized the ranking score consistency among visually similar video segments by maximizing the product of conditional prior and the likelihood, while minimizing the ranking distance between the objective ranking list and the initial text-based list by minimizing the hinge distance and preference strength distance. Evaluation on TRECVID 2007 concepts, there was 61% improvement relative to the text search baseline. Merler et al. (2009) proposed a rank learning algorithm called Imbalanced RankBoost. RankBoost was a famous method in computer vision that could automatically select and combine a pool of weak ranking features into a composite ranking function. Their imbalanced RankBoost algorithm merged the RankBoost method and an iterative threshold scheme into a unified loss optimization framework which achieved an improvement over the RankBoost method in terms of both ranking accuracy and efficiency in the experiments on TRECVID 2008 concepts.

VIDEO CONCEPT RETRIEVAL

In this section, a video retrieval system supported by our proposed novel correlation-based ranking algorithm is introduced. As discussed, there are three important stages in our proposed video retrieval system, namely *video content representation*, *MCA-based correlation*, and *correlation-based ranking strategy*.

A. Video Content Representation

The basic logical interconnected units for video processing and demonstration in most of the retrieval approaches are shots and keyframes. A shot is defined as a sequence of frames that appear to be continuously captured from the same camera. For ease of analysis and computation, a segmented video shot could be represented by one or more frames, the so-called keyframes. Audio and motion features are usually shot-based, while visual features are usually keyframe-based extracted from global, local, and/or keypoint levels. The video content can be represented by low-level, mid-level, and high-level features. The low-level features are raw visual (such as color and texture) and audio (such as volume and energy) features. The mid-level features, such as object category, audio category, bag-of-visual-words, and features obtained from face detection, can help extract the high-level features which are semantic concepts in video retrieval.

Based on the provided shot boundary and keyframe information, some shot-based and keyframe-based low-level and mid-level features are captured in this paper. In our shot-based feature set, there are 16 audio features, 11 visual features, and 1 meta feature. The meta feature is the length of shots, i.e., the number of frames of each shot. The low-level audio features are exploited in time-frequency domain, which are divided into volume-related, energy-related, and spectrum-flux-related features. Furthermore, the average zero crossing rate is added. The low-level shot-based visual features are pixel change, pixel histogram change, background mean, background variance, dominant color values. The mid-level shot-based visual feature is grass ratio and motion features are to estimate the motion intensity of the video shot, such as center to corner pixel change ratio, and etc. In the keyframe-based feature set, 16-dimensional features representing color dominant in RGB space, 51-d features for color histogram in HSV space, 108-d local features for color moment in YCbCr space, 47-d features for edge histogram, 36-d features for texture co-occurrence, 219-d features for texture wavelet, 3-d features for Tamura texture, 24-d features for Gabor texture, and 1 feature representing the

local binary patterns are extracted. In addition, 8 more mid-level keyframe-based features from face detection are captured, such as the number of faces.

All the 28 shot-based features are used and 20 key-frame based features are selected from 513 features for each high-level concept using the chi-squared attribute evaluation algorithm in WEKA (Witten & Frank, 2005). In other words, based on our previous studies, 48 features for each concept have been extracted. There are no specific reasons of the number of the shot-based and keyframe-based features. The main reasons of using two different sets of features are as follows. (1) shot-based visual features are not good enough for different video types, and therefore, more keyframe-based visual features are considered. On the other side, if only keyframe-based features are used, the audio and motion information of each shot are missing; (2) in the real world, different representations of the same video can be accessed from different sources. Therefore, synchronization of different representations is very important and can also show the adaption and robustness of a framework.

Once extracted, these numerical features for each video are normalized to reduce the effects caused by the fact that different videos were broadcasted differently. Two different normalization methods are applied (Witten & Frank, 2005). One is min-max method used to normalize shot-based features which is to subtract the minimum value and divide by the distance between the maximum and the minimum values for each feature. The other is z-score normalization used for keyframe-based features, which gives the range between the raw feature and the population mean in units of the standard deviation. Synchronization is carried out after feature extraction and normalization that converts all features to a shot-based segmentation scheme by averaging keyframe-based features per shot. The aforementioned content representation process maps the raw video segmentations/shots to numerical feature instances.

B. MCA-Based Correlation

Multiple Correspondence Analysis (MCA) provides the ability to analyze tables containing some measure of correspondence between rows and columns with more than two variables (Salkind, 2007). From our previous studies (Lin, Shyu, & Chen, 2009; Lin & Shyu, 2010), for multimedia data sets storing feature values and concept labels (i.e., classes) per video segment, if considering the instances as the rows and features and classes as the columns in an MCA table, the correspondence between features and classes can be captured. That is, the significance of the features with respect to the classes can be learned by the MCA-based correlation, which helps bridge the semantic gap between low-level features and high-level concepts.

Since MCA takes only nominal data as its input, all the extracted numerical feature values need to be converted via discretization. The goal of discretization of the training data set is to discover a set of breakpoints to partition the range of a feature into a small number of intervals that have good class coherence, which is usually measured by an evaluation function. In addition to maximizing interdependence between classes and feature values, an ideal discretization method should have a secondary goal to minimize the number of intervals without significant loss of class-feature mutual dependence. A typical discretization process for the training data consists of four steps: sorting the numerical values of the feature to be discretized, identifying all potential breakpoints using certain evaluation measures, splitting an interval into two intervals or merging adjacent intervals into one interval based on each breakpoint, and finally stopping the whole process based on a preset criterion.

Minimal Description Length (MDL) principle is used to determine a stopping criterion for a recursive discretization process introduced in Witten

and Frank (2005). Due to the fact that it considers one big interval containing all known values of a feature and then recursively partitions this interval into smaller subintervals until some stopping criterion, it may result in only one partition. This can be solved by adding the Information Entropy Maximization (IEM) criterion which obtains the maximum information gain as the stopping point to improve MDL. This is achieved as follows. If the MDL criterion is accepted, then the boundary is determined. Otherwise, if no boundary can be determined, the IEM criterion is used. Once discretized, for each numeric feature, its values are converted to several categorical vales which are called *feature-value pairs* in our studies. For instance, the normalized shot-based feature of *pixel changes* (feature values in the range of [0,1]) is converted to three partitions by applying discretization. Two breakpoints from the MDL criterion are 0.32865 and 0.5044. Therefore, three nominal feature-value pairs are generated to represent the partitions of the *pixel changes* feature, namely [0, 0.32865], (0.32865, 0.5044], and (0.5044, 1], respectively.

The process of MCA calculation is shown in Figure 1. MCA is applied to scan the discretized training data and to create an indicator matrix (I). Each column in the indicator matrix indicates the appearance of a feature-value pair and each row represents a data instance. In other words, only one feature-value pair can be presented for each feature per shot. Therefore, for a data instance, each feature can only have one value of 1 in the indicator matrix. Then, the inner product of the indicator matrix, named Burt matrix (B), is generated for the analysis. Let $B(m,n)$ be each element of Burt matrix. The chi-square distance among the tabulations of the Burt table is applied by calculating the differences between Probability matrix (Z) and inter product of the Mess matrix (M) normalized by $\left(DD^T \right)^{\frac{1}{2}}$, and then principle components are captured by using singular value decomposition (SVD). Therefore, the data instances for a video concept could be projected into a new subspace by using the first principal component (i.e., the eigenvector with the largest eigenvalue) and the second principle component (i.e., the eigenvector with the second largest eigenvalue).

Let A_i^j represent a feature-value pair, where i=1 to total number of features (i.e., 48 in this study) and j=1 to the total number of partitions for the i-th feature. The MCA-based correlation between a feature-value pair A_j^i and a class (target concept C_p or non-target concept C_n) is represented by the feature-value pair weight $weight_i^j$, which indicates the similarity between them, and is calculated using Equation (1).

if $\frac{A_i^j \cdot C_p}{|A_i^j||C_p|} > 0$, $weight_i^j = +1 + \frac{A_i^j \cdot C_p}{|A_i^j||C_p|}$

else if

$\frac{A_i^j \cdot C_n}{|A_i^j||C_n|} > 0$, $weight_i^j = -1 - \frac{A_i^j \cdot C_n}{|A_i^j||C_n|}$ (1)

else, $weight_i^j = 0$

From this definition, the larger positive value of the feature-value pair weight, the higher correlation between a feature-value pair and a target concept class; while the smaller negative value of the feature-value pair weight, the higher correlation between a feature-value pair and a non-concept class. In most of the existing retrieval frameworks, the features in each data instance

Figure 1. The process of MCA calculation

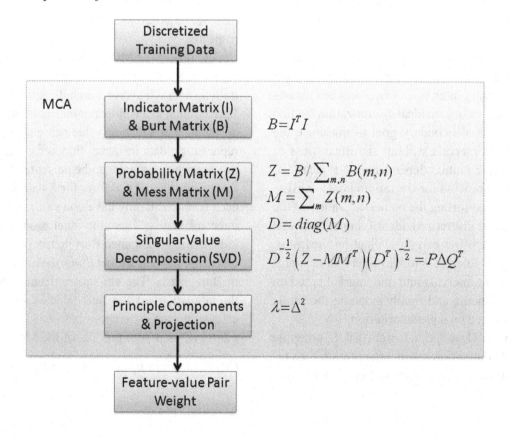

are considered equally important with respect to the class labels. However, by utilizing MCA, the feature-value pairs can be weighted differently based on their correlation to various classes.

Hence, each feature-value pair is assigned with a weight value. These feature-value pair weights are utilized in two ways in the following proposed ranking algorithm. These weights horizontally represent different contributions to each data instance and vertically demonstrate different degrees of significance of the features.

C. Correlation-Based Ranking Strategy

For a data instance (i.e., a video shot in this study) in the multimedia database, the content is represented by the low-level and mid-level features (as discussed in Section III.A). Here, a data instance consisting of the feature-value pairs but excluding the class label is defined as a transaction. An example of a transaction is shown in Table 1. Then the discretization process is applied to the training data to obtain a set of breakpoints which are then used to discretize the evaluation data instances. An example of a transaction after discretization is demonstrated in Table 2. Table 3 shows the example of the MCA-based feature-value pair

Table 1. An example of a transaction

A_1	A_2	...	A_{48}
0.78	-0.23	...	0.05

Table 2. An example of a transaction after discretization

A_1	A_2	...	A_{48}
A_1^3	A_2^2	...	A_{48}^1

Table 3. An example of MCA-based feature-value pair weights of a transaction

A_1	A_2	...	A_{28}
1.02	1.92	...	-1.05

weights (from Section III.B) of all the features in a transaction.

Based on the correlation values from MCA and the MCA-based feature-value pair weights, a novel correlation-based ranking strategy is proposed (shown in Figure 2).

As can be seen from this figure, one score contributing to the final score is the transaction-based score which is the sum of all the MCA-based feature-value pair weights in a transaction. The transaction weight of the k-th evaluation data instance is $score_{tw}^{(k)}$ shown in Equation (2).

$$score_{tw}^{(k)} = \sum_{i=1}^{48} weight_i^j \qquad (2)$$

where $weight_i^j$ is the weight of the j-th feature-value pair for the i-th feature in the k-th evaluation data instance. In other words, the transaction-based score considers the contributions of the feature-value pairs that constitute each data instance. As discussed in Section III.B, a larger positive feature-value pair weight indicates a higher correlation between the feature-value pair and a target concept class. Therefore, a larger $score_{tw}^{(k)}$ implies a higher chance to retrieve the k-th evaluation data instance as a target-concept class.

The other score is the distance-based scores in which the feature-value pair weights are used for representing the significance of each feature. First, utilizing the MCA-based feature-value pair weights, the best two features are selected. If the absolute value of a feature-value pair weight is the largest, that feature is selected. The feature with the next largest absolute value of a feature-

Figure 2. The proposed ranking strategy

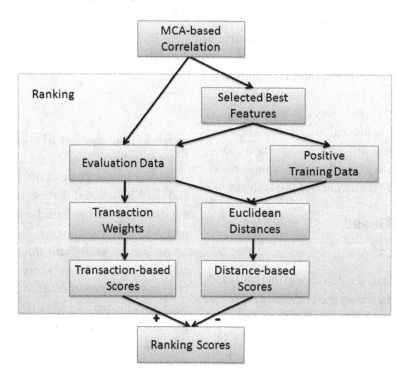

value pair weight and different from the first selected feature is kept as the second one. For example, the two features selected for the "person-playing-musical-instrument" concept are A_{35} (the ratio of the number of frames whose feature value are less than 50% of the average feature value for the first sub band) and A_{29} (the shot spectral flux range). Next, considering the positive data instances (i.e., instances labeled with the target concept) in the training set as the positive set, the average value of the distances (e.g., Euclidean distances) of the two selected features between each evaluation data instance and the positive set are calculated. Assume that there are N_p positive instances (i.e., N_p =280 for concept "person-playing-musical-instrument") in the training data. Let x_k and y_k be the values of A_{35} and A_{29} of the k-th evaluation data instance, and x_p and y_p be the values of A_{35} and A_{29} of the p-th data instance in the positive set. The distance-based score of the k-th evaluation data instance

is defined as in Equation (3), where a smaller value indicates that the evaluation data instance is closer to the positive set.

$$score_{fd}^{(k)} = \frac{1}{N_p} \sum_{p=1}^{N_p} \sqrt{\left(x_k - x_p\right)^2 + \left(y_k - y_p\right)^2}$$

(3)

The final ranking score for the k-th evaluation data instance is $score_{tw}^{(k)} - score_{fd}^{(k)}$, which does not rely on the classification-based scores and therefore independent of the classifiers. A larger ranking score indicates that the evaluation data instance is more likely on the top of the retrieved results.

EXPERIMENTS AND RESULTS

The video concepts considered in our experiments are from the TRECVID 2008 and 2009 benchmark data. The detailed descriptions of these high-level semantic concepts could be found in (Smeaton, Over, & Kraaij, 2006), while the concept names and some statistics information of the data are shown in Figure 3.

A 3-fold stratified cross-validation is adopted to ensure each data instance is evaluated. Stratification is applied to randomly split two-thirds of total data as the training data (to generate the MCA-based feature-value pair weights) and the remaining one-third as the evaluation data (to evaluate the retrieval performance). This ensures that each class is properly represented in both training and evaluation sets. Afterward, the 3 fold-cross validation can make sure that each instance would be selected once as a testing instance. To evaluate the performance of our video retrieval system with the proposed correlation-based ranking strategy, a conventional measure called mean average precision (MAP) is adopted. The mean of the 3-fold average precision (AP) values considers not only precision and recall, but also the order in which the retrieved results are presented. Let r be the ranked data instances and N_{pos} be the total number of retrieved positive data instances. $\mathrm{Pr}\,ecision\left(r\right)$ is the precision of the retrieved data instance r, which is 1 or 0 replying on whether the relevance of data instance r ($\mathrm{Re}\,levance\left(r\right)$) is true or false, respectively. N_{ret} is the total number of the retrieved data instances, usually being a fixed number such as 10, 20, ..., and may up to 200.

$$AP = \frac{1}{N_{ret}} \sum_{r=1}^{N_{pos}} \mathrm{Pr}\,ecision\left(r\right) \times \mathrm{Re}\,levance\left(r\right)$$

(4)

A. Result Discussions

The average MAP values from the 3-fold cross-validation over 26 concepts for the first 10, 20, 30, 50, 70, 100, 150, and 200 retrieved results

are shown in columns 2 to 9 in Table 4. Here, the second, third, and fourth rows of Table 4 present the results from the Columbia University team (denoted by CU) in Yanagawa, Chang, Kennedy, and Hsu (2007), the results from City University of Hong Kong team (denoted by CUHK) in Jiang, Yang, Ngo, and Hauptmann (2010), and our proposed MCA-based ranking strategy (denoted by MCA), respectively. The ranking scores from CU are the strong baseline scores, and the ranking scores from CUHK are the top-ranked ones submitted to TRECVID. Please note that the MAP values for four concepts (5: "two-people," 12: "chair," 15: "doorway," and 17: "person-playing-musical-instrument") are not provided by CU and CUHK, thus not included in this table.

Furthermore, the MAP values of the top 20 retrieved results for all 30 concepts are presented in Figure 4, where the results for the four aforementioned concepts for CU and CUHK are 0 in this figure. It can be seen from Figure 4 that the MAP values for 5 concepts are over 90% (3: "dog," 14: "traffic-intersection," 17: "person-playing-musical-instrument," 21: "person-riding-bicycle," and 23: "person-eating"). As shown in Figure 3, the ratios (numbers of positive vs negative data instances) of these five concepts are less than 5%, which means that for every 100 negative data instances, there are fewer than 5 positive data instances in the evaluation set (i.e., imbalanced data). In other words, our ranking algorithm performs comparably well for balanced data sets and achieves promising performance for imbalanced data sets, in comparison with the other two methods.

Take two concepts for example (concept 17:"person-playing-musical-instrument" and concept 21:"person-riding-a-bicycle"), where the description for concept 17 is "both player and instrument visible" and for concept 21 is "a bicycle has two wheels, while riding, both feet are off the ground and the bicycle wheels are in motion". The reasons why the ranking component achieves such good results for these concepts are

Figure 3. Ratios (\# of positive vs \# of negative data instances) for 30 concepts

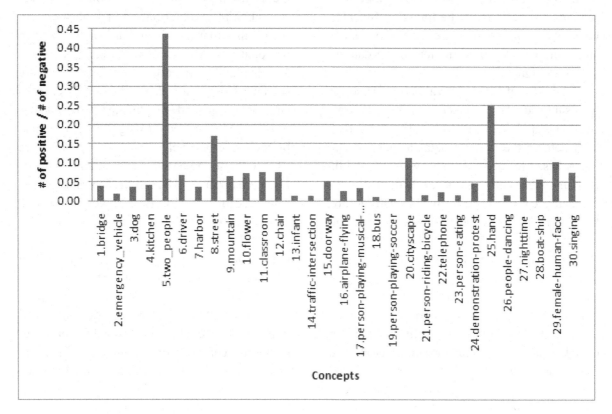

Figure 4. Mean average precision for 30 concepts for the top 20 retrieved results

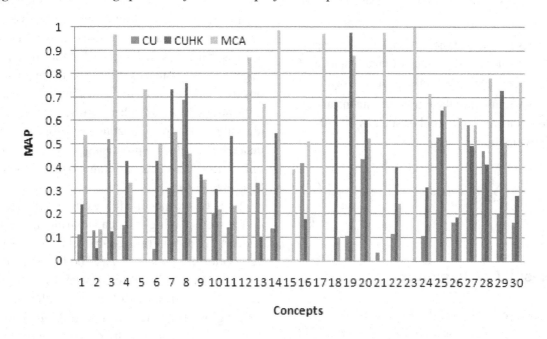

Table 4. Mean Average Precision for all 26 concepts

	10	20	30	50	70	100	150	200
CU	0.27	0.25	0.22	0.20	0.18	0.17	0.15	0.14
CU HK	0.44	0.40	0.40	0.38	0.36	0.34	0.32	0.31
MCA	0.59	0.54	0.51	0.48	0.45	0.42	0.39	0.37

given as follows. By utilizing MCA and calculating from Equation (1), the feature-value pairs that have higher absolute values of weights indicate the higher correlation with the positive or negative class. In other words, weights from these feature-value pairs present key roles in the final scores for ranking the retrieved results. For the concept "person-playing-musical-instrument", the feature-value pairs that have large weight values are: (1) color features that indicate the "indoor" scene (e.g., max values of red, green and blue channels and location of the maximum bin in the brightness histogram); (2) texture features that help detect the "instrument" (e.g., different edge directions using Sobel filter on different blocks); (3) features from face detection to help identify the "person" (e.g., the pixel histogram of the largest face); (4) audio features that represent the audio part and help detect the corresponding "music" (e.g., zero crossing rate to detect pure speech and energy-lowrate of the third sub-band).

For concept "person-riding-a-bicycle", some feature-value pairs with higher correlation with positive class are as below and the corresponding weights are all 1:999, such as (1) the third interval (values in the range of (3.6475, ∞)) of variance of 12 high frequency coefficients of Haar wavelet with 4 decomposition levels of block1; (2) the third interval (values within (-0:272405, 0:271495]) of variance of 12 high frequency coefficients of Haar wavelet with 4 decomposition levels of block2; (3) the sixth interval (values in the range of (2:3449,∞)) of the size of the largest face (the size is represented as half of the diagonal length). Some feature-value pairs with higher correlation with negative class are as follows and the corre-

sponding weights are -2 and -1:978, respectively. (1) The first interval (values in the range of (-∞, -0:376955]) of variance of 12 high frequency coefficients of Haar wavelet with 4 decomposition levels of block2 and (2) the second interval (values in the range of (0:007418, 0:49206]) of intra-frame pixel difference of center area. It can be explained that feature-value pairs from texture features can assist to detect the "bicycle", from face detection can help extract the "person" and from features that estimate the motion intensity of the video shot can help capture the action of "riding". Without a doubt, all audio features do not contribute as many as the previous listed features for concept "person-riding-a-bicycle". This also prove that MCA is a very useful and important analysis technique that can demonstrate the correlation between feature-value pair and class, especially to the positive class with very little instances, and can merge the semantic gap between them.

B. User Interface

The proposed video retrieval system is based on the structure of the DMMManager system in our previous work (Chen, Shyu, & Zhao, 2003). It consists of three parts, namely *database-side*, *server-side*, and *client-side*, distributed and connected in IP networks.

The database-side employs PostgreSQL database management system for TRECVID multimedia database, which stores the source data, processed data, and result data. PostgreSQL is a open source and an object-relational database management system that also provides related

Cygwin interface. Therefore, the database-side can be installed on both Windows and Linux platforms. The source data refer to raw multimedia data including textual, image, audio and video data. The processed data include extracted features, segmented shots, and any temporary results produced during video retrieval. The result data are final results obtained from classification. When a video retrieval is performed, the results are saved in the database so that users can directly view the results in the client-side next time if the same query is requested.

The server-side consists of the Ranking Module which is implemented in C++ language. C++ is adopted by considering its high speed performance which is crucial to online system. It can be performed in both Windows and Linux operation systems. Its request handling interface uses the multi-thread mechanism to handle the requests from the client-side and speed up the service; while

its database handling interface provides database access function. Moreover, the ranking module can perform a real-time application.

The client-side is developed using Java language and runs in Windows operation system. Java is used because it is more flexible and suitable to develop network software. With this characteristic, the client-side is easy to run on any computer connected to IP networks. It provides a convenient platform for the users to manage a large amount of multimedia data. The client-side consists of two main interfaces: user interface and request handling interface. The user interface provides a channel for the users to interact with the whole system; while the request handling interface handles the communications between the client-side and the server-side.

In the user interface, the video retrieval component is responsible for retrieving the videos based on the user's interested concepts. Figure 5 shows

Figure 5. User interface for "person-playing-musical-instrument" retrieval with top ranked results

the user interface of the retrieved videos for the concept "person-playing-musical-instrument". Users can choose his/her interested concept on the list of concepts in the upper right corner of Figure 5 and the corresponding details of each concept is shown in the next box. After retrieval, for each concept, its keyframe images of the corresponding result shots are displayed so that they can choose to play the shots to determine whether the shots contain the target concept or not. In an alternative way, the results can be shown in a table listing the video identifier, shot identifier and corresponding starting frame number and end frame number.

CONCLUSION

In this paper, a novel ranking algorithm based on MCA-based correlations is proposed to address one of the main challenges in large dimension concept-based retrieval and to provide efficient search ability. Each feature-value pair is assigned with a MCA-based weight which horizontally represents different contributions to each data instance and vertically demonstrates different levels of significance of the features. The final ranking score takes advantage of both transaction weight score and feature distance-based score, and eliminate the classification-based scores so that they are independent of classifiers and the proposed ranking algorithm can be integrated in any retrieval system. Experimental results on TRECVID 2008 and 2009 benchmark concepts demonstrate promising results for both balanced and imbalanced data and the mean average precision is comparable with other two top-ranked results submitted to TRECVID. Moreover, an interface is implemented so that the ranking algorithm is executable when there is a retrieval request and the video shots are listed to the user based on their corresponding ranking scores.

REFERENCES

Aytar, Y., Shah, M., & Jiebo, L. (2008). Utilizing semantic word similarity measures for video retrieval. In *Proceedings of the IEEE International Conference on Computer Vision and Pattern Recognition (CVPR08)* (pp. 1-8).

Cao, J., Jing, H., Ngo, C.-W., & Zhang, Y. (2009). Distribution-based concept selection for concept-based video retrieval. In *Proceedings of the ACM International Conference on Multimedia (MM09)* (pp. 645-648).

Chen, S.-C. (2010). Multimedia databases and data management: a survey. *International Journal of Multimedia Data Engineering and Management*, *1*(1), 1–11.

Chen, S.-C., Shyu, M.-L., & Zhao, N. (2003). Mediamanager: A distributed multimedia management system for content based retrieval, authoring and presentation. In *Proceedings of the International Conference on Distributed Multimedia Systems* (pp. 17-22).

Divakaran, A. (Ed.). (2009). *Multimedia content analysis, theory and applications*. Berlin: Springer Verlag.

Jiang, W., Zavesky, E., Chang, S.-F., & Loui, A. (2008). Cross-domain learning methods for high-level visual concept classification. In *Proceedings of the IEEE International Conference on Image Processing (ICIP08)* (pp. 161-164).

Jiang, Y.-G., Ngo, C.-W., & Chang, S.-F. (2009). Semantic context transfer across heterogeneous sources for domain adaptive video search. In *Proceedings of the ACM International Conference on Multimedia (MM09)* (pp. 155-164).

Jiang, Y.-G., Yang, J., Ngo, C.-W., & Hauptmann, A. G. (2010). Representations of keypoint-based semantic concept detection: a comprehensive study. *IEEE Transactions on Multimedia*, *12*(1), 42–53. doi:10.1109/TMM.2009.2036235

Lin, L., & Shyu, M.-L. (2010). Weighted association rule mining for video semantic detection. *International Journal of Multimedia Data Engineering and Management, 1*(1), 37–54.

Lin, L., Shyu, M.-L., & Chen, S.-C. (2009). Enhancing concept detection by pruning data with MCA-based transaction weights. In *Proceedings of the IEEE International Symposium on Multimedia (ISM09)* (pp. 304-311).

Liu, Y., Mei, T., Wu, X., & Hua, X.-S. (2009). Multigraph-based query-independent learning for video search. *IEEE Transactions on Circuits and Systems for Video Technology, 19*(12), 1841–1850. doi:10.1109/TCSVT.2009.2026951

Merler, M., Rong, Y., & Smith, J. R. (2009). Imbalanced RankBoost for efficiently ranking large-scale image/video collections. In *Proceedings of the IEEE International Conference on Computer Vision and Pattern Recognition (CVPR09)* (pp. 2607-2614).

Natsev, A., Haubold, A., Tevsic, J., Xie, L., & Yan, R. (2007). Semantic concept-based query expansion and re-ranking for multimedia retrieval. In *Proceedings of the ACM International Conference on Multimedia (MM07)* (pp. 991-1000).

Salkind, N. J. (Ed.). (2007). *Encyclopedia of Measurement and Statistics*. Thousand Oaks, CA: Sage.

Shirahama, K., Sugihara, C., Matsuoka, Y., & Uehara, K. (2009). Query-based video event definition using rough set theory. In *Proceedings of the ACM international Workshop on Events in Multimedia* (pp. 9-16).

Smeaton, A. F., Over, P., & Kraaij, W. (2006). Evaluation campaigns and TRECVid. In *Proceedings of the ACM International Workshop on Multimedia Information Retrieval (MIR06)* (pp. 321-330).

Snoek, C. G. M., & Worring, M. (2008). Concept-based video retrieval. *Foundations and Trends in Information Retrieval, 2*(4), 215–322. doi:10.1561/1500000014

Tian, X., Yang, L., Wang, J., Yang, Y., Wu, X., & Hua, X.-S. (2008). Bayesian video search reranking. In *Proceedings of the ACM International Conference on Multimedia (MM08)* (pp. 131-140).

Wei, X.-Y., Jiang, Y.-G., & Ngo, C.-W. (2009). Exploring inter-concept relationship with context space for semantic video indexing. In *Proceedings of the ACM International Conference on Image and Video Retrieval (CIVR09)* (pp. 1-8).

Witten, I. H., & Frank, E. (2005). *Data mining: practical machine learning tools and techniques* (2nd ed.). San Francisco: Morgan Kaufmann.

Yanagawa, A., Chang, S.-F., Kennedy, L., & Hsu, W. (2007). *Columbia University's baseline detectors for 374 LSCOM semantic visual concepts* (Tech. Rep. No. 222-2006-8). New York: Columbia University, ADVENT.

Yang, Y.-H., & Hsu, W. H. (2008). Video search reranking via online ordinal reranking. In *Proceedings of the IEEE International Conference on Multimedia and Expo (ICME08)* (pp. 285-288).

Zhu, Q., Lin, L., Shyu, M.-L., & Chen, S.-C. (2010). A novel metric integrating correlation and reliability for feature selection. In *Proceedings of the IEEE International Conference on Semantic Computing (ICSC10)*.

This work was previously published in the International Journal of Multimedia Data Engineering and Management, Volume 1, Issue 4, edited by Shu-Ching Chen, pp. 60-74, copyright 2010 by IGI Publishing (an imprint of IGI Global).

Chapter 4
·Multi–Label Classification Method for Multimedia Tagging

Aiyesha Ma
Oakland University, USA

Ishwar Sethi
Oakland University, USA

Nilesh Patel
Oakland University, USA

ABSTRACT

Community tagging offers valuable information for media search and retrieval, but new media items are at a disadvantage. Automated tagging may populate media items with few tags, thus enabling their inclusion into search results. In this paper, a multi-label decision tree is proposed and applied to the problem of automated tagging of media data. In addition to binary labels, the proposed Iterative Split Multi-label Decision Tree (IS-MLT) is easily extended to the problem of weighted labels (such as those depicted by tag clouds). Several datasets of differing media types show the effectiveness of the proposed method relative to other multi-label and single label classifier methods and demonstrate its scalability relative to single label approaches.

INTRODUCTION

The retrieval of multimedia information for search queries can be based on two basic approaches: similarity of multimedia artifacts, and similarity of associated keywords or tags. Although the bulk of content-based retrieval work falls within the first category, providing an example document for the query may be difficult or impossible. Thus

DOI: 10.4018/978-1-4666-1791-9.ch004

the second approach allows the search to proceed without an example document, but relies upon the association of keywords or tags to the multimedia item. Many websites allow the user community to supply these tags, thus enabling easier retrieval. For example, a YouTube user may add tags when adding a video, while the entire community may manually specify content tags on Flickr. Not all users or communities are equally ambitious with their tagging, however. Thus, automatic assignment or suggestions of tags for new or untagged multimedia documents may help to improve the retrieval of multimedia content.

Existing tag data can be used for training classifiers to enable the automatic assignment of keywords or tags (Snoek & Worring, 2009). A multimedia document is likely to have many tags associated with it, but traditional classifiers make assignments to disjoint categories. Although a classifier could be created for each potential label, this approach does not scale to large numbers of tags. Multi-label classifiers, however, assign a set of labels using a single classifier. These classifiers exploit data similarities between tags, such that a single multi-label classifier may perform better than a set of single label classifiers, (Ueda & Saito, 2003; Rousu et al., 2004; Blockeel et al., 2006; Vens et al., 2008), in addition to being more scalable.

To this end, we developed a multi-label decision tree and applied it to the problem of automated tagging. The basic idea consists of partitioning the set of labels into two groups at each node. Using the two groups a node level decision is created using a binary decision method such as SVM or Information Gain. After constructing the tree, the leaf node frequencies are considered scores and labels are assigned by thresholding. The proposed method was applied to the problem of tagging emotions in music sound clips; this paper slightly expands the results in our earlier work, (Ma et al., 2009), by varying the training-validation ratios as well as comparing the multi-label classifier methods to single-label classifiers. This paper further demonstrates the proposed multi-label decision tree by applying it to the problem of tagging photographs with scene descriptors.

Some websites with community tagging depict tag clouds (see Figure 1). Thus, instead of the binary input of inclusion and exclusion of a tag, each tag has a weight associated with it that generally indicates the proportion of users who included that particular label when tagging the content. Although these weighted tags could be converted to the binary problem of inclusion and exclusion, these weights may provide additional information to the classifier. To the best of our knowledge no multi-label classifier methods have addressed this weighted labeling problem.

Since the premise of our multi-label decision tree is to partition the set of labels into two groups, it is easily extended to this weighted multi-label problem: rather than using a binary distance measure in the partition clustering, a real valued distance measure is used, and the performance measure used to determine the amount of pruning is similarly changed from a binary evaluation

Figure 1. Example of a Tag Cloud: The Beach Boys, from Last.FM

approach to a rank based evaluation approach. The proposed modified multi-label decision tree is then applied to the problem of predicting tags applied to musicians and bands based on textual summaries.

General background information is presented in the following section, including a review of existing multi-label classifier approaches and a discussion of performance measures applicable to multi-label classifiers. The proposed multi-label decision tree is described in *Methodology*. *Application* describes the datasets, and then presents experimental results and comparisons to alternative approaches. Finally, a conclusion is presented in the last section.

BACKGROUND

Multi-Label Classifier Design

Early multi-label problems were identified in the area of text categorization (Joachims, 1998; McCallum, 1999; Schapire & Singer, 2000), and many multi-label methods since then were developed or used for text categorization (Gao et al., 2004; Cesa-Bianchi et al., 2006; Yu et al., 2005; Rousu et al., 2004, 2006; Zhang & Zhou, 2007a; Ueda & Saito, 2003). Multi-label classification techniques, however, are also applicable to a wide range of other areas such as: patent classification (Rousu et al., 2005, 2006), speech categorization (Schapire & Singer, 2000), semantic scene classification (Boutell et al., 2003; Hardoon et al., 2006; Yan et al., 2007; Tsoumakas & Vlahavas, 2007; Zhang & Zhou, 2007a), and functional genomics (Clare & King, 2002; Struyf et al., 2005; Barutcuoglu et al., 2006; Blockeel et al., 2006; Tsoumakas & Vlahavas, 2007; Vens et al., 2008).

Multi-label classification approaches have ranged from sets of single label classifier systems with methods of joining the classifiers or outputs (Joachims, 1998; Boutell et al., 2003, 2004; Gao et al., 2004; Cesa-Bianchi et al., 2006; Barutcuoglu

et al., 2006; Yan et al., 2007; Vens et al., 2008), to a single classifier that decides multiple labels, and to ensemble approaches with sets of multiple label classifiers (Tsoumakas & Vlahavas, 2007; Kocev et al., 2007). Traditional learning techniques are often used as a basis for single multi-label classifier methods (Zhang & Zhou, 2007b). Suzuki et al. (2001), Clare and King (2002), Kim and Lee (2003), Struyf et al. (2005), Blockeel et al. (2006), and Vens et al. (2008) all used decision trees with modifications to account for the multi-label nature. Zhang and Zhou (2007a) used a nearest neighbor approach; McCallum (1999) and Ueda and Saito (2003) derived their methods from mixture models; and Rousu et al. (2004, 2005, 2006) developed multi-label maximum margin Markov networks.

Since the method presented in this paper is a multi-label decision tree, those methods are discussed further. A classic single label decision tree is C4.5 (Quinlan, 1993). C4.5 is a top-down induction method in which the split criterion is selected using information gain. To modify such a method for multi-label classification, either the information gain function can be modified for multiple labels (as by Suzuki et al. (2001), Clare and King (2002), and Kim and Lee (2003)), the classes over which the entropy is calculated can be some function of the labels, or the split mechanism can be replaced (as by Struyf et al. (2005) and Blockeel et al. (2006)). Also discussed are the single label classifier combination approach taken by Boutell et al. (2004) and RAKEL proposed by Tsoumakas and Vlahavas (2007), both of which are later used for comparison.

Boutell et al. (2004) use a one-vs-all SVM for each base class. They compare three labeling options: P-Criterion, where the corresponding labels are applied for all positive scores, and a test case is labeled as 'unknown' if there are no positive scores; T-Criterion, which is the same as P-Criterion except the test case is labeled to correspond with the top score if all scores are negative; and C-Criterion, where the corresponding labels are applied for the top M scores that are close enough. The maximum a posteriori (MAP) principle is used to determine the threshold for judging closeness in the C-Criterion method. As mentioned in the introduction, this approach of building a classifier for each class suffers the problem of scalability.

An ensemble based approach called RAKEL is presented by Tsoumakas and Vlahavas (2007). In RAKEL (Random K-Labelsets) k size label-subsets are iteratively selected from the powerset of the label space. These k-labelsets are selected without replacement, and an LP (Label Powerset) classifier is constructed on this label subspace. In an LP classifier, each member of the powerset is considered a distinct class, and a set of SVM's are constructed using a one-against-one strategy. Although this method takes into account label correlations (as opposed to single label classifiers), it still suffers from scalability for large numbers of labels. Also, the sparsity of sets of labels will be a problem, albeit it clearly improves upon the single powerset-classifier approach.

The number of class dimensions is reduced during the traversal of a decision tree presented by Suzuki et al. (2001). This reduction is accomplished in their Bloomy decision tree by using internal 'flower' nodes; flower nodes consist of a set of petals, and each petal assigns a label to a particular class dimension. For the decision nodes of the tree, a summation of the gain ratios for each class is used as the evaluation criterion; the gain ratio is the mutual entropy between an attribute and a class. After each decision node is constructed, the tree is pruned by using Cramér's V for each class dimension.

Clare and King (2002) use an information function instead of the entropy function in C4.5; this information function describes the number of bits needed to represent the set of classes an example belongs to. Their objective, however, was to create accurate rules for labeling. Thus, bootstrapping was used to create a large number of training sets. Rulesets were extracted from the created decision trees, and then the rules were tabulated to select those that were stable and reliable.

Three splitting criteria are compared by Kim and Lee (2003). All three quantify homogeneity for data containing multiple response variables. For the first approach the joint frequency distributions of the response variables are used to extend the entropy and Gini criteria. A weighted sum of node homogeneities is used for the second approach, but this approach has the limitation that the weights must be accurately supplied. The third approach attempts to minimize the expected loss.

A predictive clustering tree (PCT) approach is used by Struyf et al. (2005). Node splitting is accomplished by minimizing intra-cluster variation in PCTs, where the intra-cluster variation is defined as the sum of squared distances between a cluster prototype and the cluster members. A weighted Euclidean distance between vector representations of the class labels, where the weights exponentially decrease by hierarchy depth, is used to describe the distance between two sets of labels. A majority class is required at the leaf nodes for positive labeling.

Blockeel et al. (2006) present a variant on the PCT approach by Struyf et al. (2005), which Blockeel et al. call 'Clus-HMC'. Rather than requiring a majority at a leaf node, a threshold is used to determine all categories to which an instance belongs. Since leaf nodes contain probabilities of the likelihood of all labels, the threshold of the parent label will be greater than or equal to the threshold of the child label to ensure parent classes are included when a child class is included.

In the approach presented by Vens et al. (2008), a set of single label decision trees are built on the edges of the label hierarchy; they call their method CLUS-HSC. Their objective was to develop an approach applicable to hierarchical multi-label classification when the labels have multiple parents, and thus are organized by directed acyclic graphs. In CLUS-HSC a classifier is built for each label-parent (label) combination and the final prediction is made using the product rule, F_1. This is in contrast to the top down fashion of label hierarchy classifiers used by Cesa-Bianchi et al. (2006). Vens et al. compare CLUS-HSC to the previously mentioned CLUS-HMC and to a set of single label decision trees built on each label (CLUS-SC); they find CLUS-HMC to perform the best when considering predictive accuracy, model size, and induction time.

Multi-Label Performance Measurements

Two types of performance analysis methods can be used when evaluating a multi-label classifier: micro-label and macro-label methods. When the measure looks at the label-instance pairs, thus providing a measure that takes into account the frequency of the labels, it is considered a *micro-label* method. If the frequency of a particular label is ignored, and the performance is averaged over the labels, then it is considered a *macro-label* method. Several common performance measures exist within these two broad groupings, and usages often depend on the area of application or the objective of the classifier. Three evaluation methods based on contingency matrices are described in this section, followed by brief summaries of loss based and rank based evaluation measures since details of these methods can be found in the paper by Zhang and Zhou (2007a). The end of this section discusses rank correlation for the evaluation of weighted multi-label classifiers.

The Receiver Operating Characteristic (ROC) curve is often used in the health and medical fields as a performance measure. It is formed by $1 - specificity$ (false positive rate) on the x-axis versus *sensitivity* (true positive rate) on the y-axis, for a range of sensitivity values. The area under this curve, referred to as the AUROC or C-statistic, is one method of reporting the overall performance of a classifier without regards to a specific threshold. Yu et al. (2005) used the AU-ROC values averaged over the output dimensions to provide a macro-averaged evaluation.

Precision is related to the correctness of the predicted positives, and recall is related to the predictability of the actual positives. In the area of text categorization and semantic scene analysis, these two measures are often reported in pairs to describe the performance. Precision, $TP/(TP+FP)$, and recall, $TP/(TP+FN)$, are adapted to report the micro-label performance in multi-label applications by computing TP as the number of correctly predicted labels overall, FP as the number of incorrectly predicted labels overall, and $(TP+FN)$ as the total number of positive labels. Rousu et al. (2005, 2006), Hardoon et al. (2006), Blockeel et al. (2006), and Vens et al. (2008) use the micro-label precision and recall for reporting performance. Blockeel et al. (2006) and Vens et al. (2008) avoid commitment to a particular threshold by constructing a precision-recall curve and using the area under the curve as their performance measure.

Since precision and recall are inversely related, it may be difficult to directly compare two pairs of precision-recall values, thus the F-measure provides a single quantitative value of the performance which considers both precision and recall.

$$F_\beta = \frac{(1 + \beta^2)(precision \cdot recall)}{\beta^2 \cdot precision + recall} = \frac{(1 + \beta^2)TP}{(1 + \beta^2)TP + \beta^2 FP + FN}$$

The importance of recall relative to precision can be specified by the $\hat{a}$ parameter: in the F_1 measure, $\hat{a} = 1$, precision and recall are weighted equally; in the F_2 measure, $\hat{a} = 2$, recall is twice as important as precision; and in the $F_{0.5}$ measure, $\hat{a} = 0.5$, precision is twice as important as recall.

The micro-label F-measure is computed by the same changes mentioned for precision and recall, and was used for reporting performance by Yang (1999), Ueda and Saito (2003), Gao et al.(2004), Ghamrawi and McCallum (2005), Yu et al. (2005), Zhu et al. (2005), Rousu et al. (2005, 2006), and Tsoumakas and Vlahavas (2007).

To compute the macro-label F-measure, the F-measure values for each label are averaged. Let $F_{\hat{a}}(l)$ be the $F_{\hat{a}}$ value for label l over the dataset, then the macro-label F-measure over the set of all labels L is,

$$F_{\hat{a}}^{Macro} = \frac{1}{size(L)} \sum_{l \in L} F_{\hat{a}}(l)$$

Ghamrawi and McCallum (2005) and Yu et al. (2005) both use the macro-label F_1, while Gao et al. (2004) provide a different formulation of the macro-label F_1 to the same effect.

The Hamming, or symmetric difference, loss counts the number of misclassified labels, and is perhaps the most commonly used loss function. Cesa-Bianchi et al. (2006), however, also describe and use hierarchically aware loss functions.

Ranking loss, one error, coverage, and average precision are all based on the idea of rank. Given a list of ranked labels, ranking loss evaluates the number of label pairs that are reversely ordered, while coverage considers the point in the list where all the actual labels are included. The number of times the top ranked label is not in the actual label set is called the one-error measure. Average precision is the precision, the percentage of true labels that lie above a threshold in the ranked list, averaged over all possible thresholds. Cesa-Bianchi et al. (2006), Rousu et al. (2005), Zhang and Zhou (2007a, 2007b), Tsoumakas and Katakis (2007), Tsoumakas and Vlahavas (2007), and Grodzicki et al. (2008) all used these methods of evaluation.

All these performances measures are defined for binary labels, however. Furthermore, for the purposes of tagging, relative ranks are perhaps of more interest than the absolute predicted weight. For example, "Are more people going to tag this item with this label, or this other label?" would be the relative rank question, while "What percent of people labeling this item will use this tag?" would become a regression problem. Two rank correlation methods are used for evaluation: Spearman's correlation coefficient and Kendall's Tau.

Let x_1 and x_2 be two actual ranks, and y_1 and y_2 be two predicted ranks, then Spearman's correlation coefficient is,

$$\tilde{n} = \frac{\sum_i (x_i - \overline{x})(y_i - \overline{y})}{\sqrt{\sum_i (x_i - \overline{x})^2 \sum (y_i - \overline{y})^2}}$$

Kendall's Tau is,

$$\hat{o} = \frac{n_c - n_d}{\frac{1}{2}n(n-1)}$$

where n_c is the number of concordant pairs, $sgn(x_1 - x_2) = sgn(y_1 - y_2)$; n_d is the number of discordant pairs, $sgn(x_1 - x_2) = -sgn(y_1 - y_2)$; and n is the total number of pairs.

Let $L_i(l)$ be the actual label weight and $W_i(l)$ be the predicted label weight of a data instance, i, for a particular label l. Then, either the ranks of labels for a particular instance could be compared, $Rank(L_i(l))$ relative to $Rank(L_i(k))$ and $Rank(W_i(l))$ relative to $Rank(W_i(k))$, and averaged over all the instances in the dataset, or the ranks of instances for a particular label could be compared, $Rank(L_i(l))$ relative to $Rank(L_j(l))$ and $Rank(W_i(l))$ relative to $Rank(W_j(l))$, and averaged over the labels. This second comparison will be referred to as the macro, or macro-label, performance ($\tilde{n}_M$ and $\hat{o}_M$), and the first will be referred to as the average instance rank correlation ($\tilde{n}_I$ and $\hat{o}_I$).

METHODOLOGY

This section describes the multi-label decision tree model developed. The tree building follows a top-down induction approach, where at each node in the tree a 'best' split is obtained. Section

Iterative Split Decision describes the iterative process by which a binary split is obtained in the presence of multiple labels. Classification using the tree model is discussed in Section *Classification*, followed by a discussion on pruning the tree in Section *Pruning*.

Iterative Split Decision

To determine a binary split in the presence of multiple labels, a clustering approach is used to initially separate the labels into two groups. After which an iterative process selectively adjusts the label clusters according to influence from the data points. This process is outlined in Figure 2, with specific details of the steps following.

First, the process is initialized by clustering the label vectors into two groups, G_1 and G_2 (Cluster(L) is described further in Section *Initial Label Clustering*). Then the iterative portion begins by using the two groups to form decision targets, G', data points associated with labels in the first group are targeted to be in the left child of the split, and data points associated with labels in the second group are targeted to be in the right child of the split (Assign(G') in Section *Assignment of G'*). Using the decision targets, a split, S, is formed (Section *Split Methods*). Using this split, two new target groups, G_1 and G_2, are formed based on the frequency of labels on each side of the split (Section *Redefining G_1 and G_2*), and a new split decision S is found. The iterative process continues until S is unchanged or the maximum iteration limit is reached.

Occasionally the iterative adjustment of G may cause a worse split, where 'worse' is considered to be an increase in the impurity of either G or S. In this case, slight changes are made to G with the intent of improving the resulting split. The calculation of Impurity(G) and Impurity(S), along with the adjustment to G (Perturb(G)) are described further in Section *Perturbing G*.

Figure 2. Overview of iterative split process

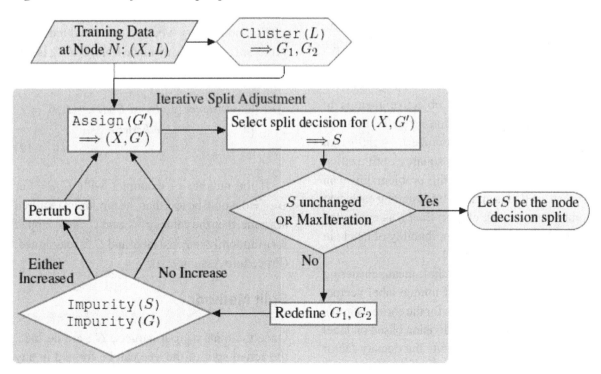

Initial Label Clustering

A label vector L_i can be formed for each data example X_i, where the length of L_i is equal to the number of labels. In the case of binary labels, $L_i(l)$ contains zero, or false, for each label l the data example doesn't have, and one, or true, for each label l that is associated with the example. When weighted labels are of interest in the model building, L_i will be a real valued vector, most likely ranging in value from 0 to 1 (if normalized). In the development of this multi-label decision tree two clustering methods have been used, although virtually any appropriate to the type of vector could be used. K-means clustering with Euclidean distance is used for weighted label clustering, and block-diagonal clustering, (Li, 2005), is used for binary vector clustering.

In block diagonal clustering, (Li, 2005), the clustering problem is modeled as an assignment of data into clusters, A, as well as an assignment of features (here, labels) into clusters, B. Thus,

$$LX = ABT + E$$

where L_X is the set of label vectors to be clustered, A is a binary matrix of size $|X| \times 2$ mapping data points (here, label vectors) to clusters, and B is a binary matrix of size $|l| \times 2$ mapping features (labels) to clusters. The objective then is to minimize the approximation error, E; thus the objective criterion is to minimize $L_X - AB^{T2}$. An iterative alternating least squares optimization procedure is used to solve this problem: given an estimate of B, A is updated by assigning each data point to the nearest cluster; then B is computed by assigning $b_{lk} = 1$ if the probability of label l in cluster k is greater than 1/2.

To reduce computation, the k-means clustering is performed on the set of unique label vectors (instead of the label vectors for the entire dataset). Although this results in a division based on label vector similarity, it discounts the density factor for the label vectors.

Once two clusters have been formed from the clustering algorithm, G_1 and G_2 are vectors of length equal to the number of labels and assigned based on the cluster results. Block-diagonal clustering returns two vectors, where one vector designates the labels in that particular cluster, and the other vector is the complement; let one of these vectors be G_1 and set the other as G_2. K-means clustering also returns two centroids, C_1 and C_2. For binary label vectors, let $G_1(l) = 1$ if $C_1(l) > C_2(l)$, then set G_2 to be the complement. For non-binary label vectors, set one cluster centroid as G_1 and the other as G_2.

Assignment of G'

The target group G' is based on whether the data example i should be associated with G_1 or G_2. For binary vectors, G' is positive if the data example has more positive labels in G_1 than in G_2.

$$G' = \begin{cases} 1 & Count\{l \mid (L_i(l) = 1) \wedge (G_1(l) = 1)\} > Count\{l \mid (L_i(l) = 1) \wedge (G_2(l) = 1)\} \\ 0 & otherwise \end{cases}$$

(1)

For non-binary vectors, or weighted label vectors, $G' = 1$ if the distance from L_i to G_1 is less than the distance to G_2.

$$G_i' = \begin{cases} 1 & \textbf{\textit{Distance}}\left(\textbf{\textit{L}}_i, \textbf{\textit{G}}_1\right) < Distance(\textbf{\textit{L}}_i, \textbf{\textit{G}}_2) \\ 0 & \textbf{\textit{otherwise}} \end{cases}$$

(2)

If the number of examples with $G'(i)=1$ or $G'(i)=0$ would be less than the minimum required at a node, then the values of G_1 and G_2 are swapped for a randomly selected label and G' is reassigned, (Procedure Assign(G')).

Split Methods

Once the binary group targets, G', are defined, the actual split of the tree can be formed in any number of ways; we have, depending on the application, considered Information Gain, Naïve Bayes, and Support Vector Machine (SVM), for example. For this paper we focus on using SVMs. An SVM split tries to form the best separating hyperplane relative to the binary target groups G'.

Redefining G_1 and G_2

After selection, the split criterion is applied to the data X, dividing (X, G') into two subgroups S_1 and S_2. This subdivision then defines the new target objectives. For binary labels, a label $l \in L$ is positive in the new objective target G if the frequency of label l in S_1 is greater than the frequency of l in S_2.

$$G_1(l) = \begin{cases} 1 & \dfrac{Count\{i \mid (L_i(l) = 1) \wedge (i \in S_1)\}}{size(S_1)} > \dfrac{Count\{i \mid (L_i(l) = 1) \wedge (i \in S_2)\}}{size(S_2)} \\ 0 & otherwise \end{cases}$$

For non-binary labels, G_1 is the centroid or mean of the label vector of all instances in the left split, and G_2 is the centroid of those in the right split.

$$G_1 = mean\left(\{L_i \mid i \in S_1\}\right)$$

$$G_2 = mean(\{L_i \mid i \in S_2\})$$

Perturbing G

Occasionally the split S is worse than the prior splits produced during the iterative process. At this point a forced change to a better split is attempted by modifying the target groups G_1 and G_2. The split S is considered worse if the summed entropy of the labels relative to either S or G increases.

Let $freq(l > 0, S_1)$ be the frequency of label l in S_1, meaning

$$freq(l > 0, S_1) = Count\{i \mid i \in S_1, L_i(l) > 0\} / size(S_1)$$

and $freq(l = 0, S_1)$ be the frequency of the absence of label l in S_1, meaning

$$freq(l = 0, S_1) = Count\{i \mid i \in S_1, L_i(l) = 0\} / size(S_1) = 1 - freq(l = 1, S_1)$$

Similarly, let $freq(l > 0, S_2)$ be the frequency of label l in S_2, and $freq(l = 0, S_2)$ be the frequency of the absence of label l in S_2. Then the entropy of a label l relative to the split S is calculated as shown in Equation 3, and the impurity of S is defined as the sum of these label entropies (Equation 4). The impurity of G is defined in the same manner.

$$Entropy(l|S) =$$
$$\sum_{s \in \{1,2\}} \left(-\frac{|S_s|}{|S|} \sum_{c \in \{0,1\}} freq(l = c, S_s) \log\left(freq(l = c, S_s)\right) \right) \tag{3}$$

$$Impurity(S) = \sum_{l \in L} Entropy(l|S) \tag{4}$$

The label with the smallest difference in frequency between G_1 and G_2 is swapped with the opposite target group if either *Impurity*(*S*) or *Impurity*(*G*) increases over the corresponding prior best impurity. The member with the next smallest difference is chosen if this swap would cause either G_1 or G_2 to form a trivial target objective, where a trivial target object is $G'(i) = 1$ $\forall i$, or $G'(i) = 0$ $\forall i$.

Should there be no label that can be swapped without causing G' to be a trivial target objective, then the original G_1 and G_2 are kept. Let $freq(l|S_s) = Count\{i | i \in S_s, L_i(l) = 1\} / size(S_s)$, then the frequency differences are calculated as shown in Equation 5.

$$FrequencyDifference(l) = \left| freq(l|S_1) - freq(l|S_2) \right| \tag{5}$$

Classification

Rather than classifying by majority rule at the leaf nodes, a score is assigned based on the training set labels at the leaf nodes and a function is then applied to the score to obtain the classification or labeling. The assigned score is the frequency of a label at the leaf node when the problem contains binary labels, and $mean\left(L_{\forall i}(l)\right)$ when the problem contains weighted labels. Then for binary label classification, a threshold is chosen for the tree so that any instance is positively labeled if its score is above the threshold. In the case of multiple labels, either a single threshold can be assigned regardless of label, or a threshold can be assigned for each label. In most cases a single threshold is determined for all labels, but a separate threshold for each label is determined when evaluating the performance of the final tree using the macro-F_1 and macro-AUROC measures. When the objective is the prediction of weighted labels, the scores are used to provide a ranking of the labels or items.

Pruning

To prevent over-fitting of the model to the training data pre-pruning was used after the third node in the tree. A leaf node was immediately created if the node had fewer training examples than a specified minimum, *MpN* (*MpN* was set equal to 5), otherwise the pair of potential child nodes was obtained. These child nodes were added only if the overall performance of the validation set was improved, otherwise the node became a leaf node.

$$KeepChildren = \quad \left(size(S_1) > MpN\right) \wedge \left(size(S_2) > MpN\right) \\ \wedge \left(PerfEval\left(T_{\{N+S_1+S_2\}}\right) > PerfEval(T_N)\right)$$

Tree T_N indicates the current tree, and tree T_{N+L+R} indicates the tree when the two child nodes of N, S_1 and S_2, are added to the current tree.

The number of data examples that would be passed to either child node is denoted by $size(S_s)$, and $PerfEval(T)$ is the performance of the validation set for the specified tree, T.

Performance can be determined using any one of the measures described in Section *Multi-label Performance Measurements*; for the datasets presented in this paper, three were used: the micro-F measure result for a single specified beta value, the micro-F measure result for a set of beta values (averaged), and the instance averaged Spearman correlation, $\tilde{n}_I$, for non-binary labels.

APPLICATION

The described tree induction method (IS-MLT) is applied to three datasets. In the first dataset, the objective is to label audio music clips with the perceived emotions. The second dataset looks at labeling photographic images with scene information. For the third dataset, IS-MLT is used to tag music artists and bands based on textual descriptions extracted from the web. Section *Datasets* describes these three datasets in further detail, and Section *Results* presents and compares the results.

Datasets

Trohidis et al. (2008) created a music dataset from 223 music albums in 7 genres and obtained a set of 6 emotion labels. From each album, 8 rhythmic and 64 timbre features were extracted from a 30-second clip to form the attributes. A set of 6 main emotion clusters were selected based on the Tellegen-Watson-Clark model of mood: 'amazed-surprised', 'happy-pleased', 'relaxing-calm', 'quiet-still', 'sad-lonely', and 'angry-fearful'. These were applied as labels to the dataset. Examples of co-occurring labels in the dataset included amazed-surprised with happy-pleased, happy-pleased with relaxing-calm, and quiet-still with both sad-lonely and relaxing-calm.

The dataset was divided into a training set (391 entries) and testing set (202 entries) by Trohidis et al.

The photographic scene dataset was that used by Boutell et al. (2004). Four hundred images for each of six classes were selected from personal photos and a Corel stock photo library, to obtain a dataset of 2400 photos. Half of the images for each class were placed in the training set, and the other half in the testing set. These images were then re-labeled by three human observers to form a multi-label dataset using six labels: beach, sunset, fall foliage, field, mountain, and urban. Multiple labels applied to 7.4% of the dataset. The images were divided into 49 blocks, and the first and second moments of each band in the LUV color space were used as features, resulting in a 249-dimension feature vector.

The third dataset used for demonstration was constructed from data extracted from the Last.FM website. The names of 487 bands, musicians, and composers were selected from a personal music collection. Each artist or band was looked up on Last.FM and the textual summary description and the user community tags were extracted. Stopwords were removed from the text summaries, as well as words occurring in only one description. Then the relative term frequencies (TF-IDF) were used as the features, resulting in 4282 attributes. The user community tags were extracted as weighted labels, where the font size used to display the label was the weight (these were scaled relative to the maximum font size used in the full dataset). Tags that were only used once were discarded, resulting in 1689 labels. The dataset was then formed into 10 folds, with an attempt to evenly distribute labels with more than 10 occurrences across the folds. For the purposes of training only those labels with at least one example in every fold were used during training (163 labels).

RESULTS

Labeling Emotions in Music

For the emotions in music dataset, the ISMLT method was applied with Block-Diagonal clustering to initialize the iterative split method and SVMs for the node level decision splits. Several IS-MLTrees were built and each was pruned using a different beta value for the F-measure evaluation ($\beta = \{0.1, 0.5, 1, 2, 10\}$).

Then by maximizing the micro-F_1 value of the validation set, a single threshold was found for each tree. Using the micro-F_1 performance, the single model with the best validation performance was selected from the set of IS-MLT trees, and this model was used to classify the testing data. Several other performance measures mentioned in Section *Multi-label Performance Measurements* were also calculated on the classification of the test set. For the macro-F_1 and Hamming-Loss measures separate thresholds for each label were used; these were obtained by maximizing the F_1 measure for the label on the validation set.

Since the original dataset does not specify a validation set (only a training and testing set), a portion of the training data was used as the validation data. Table 1 shows the performance results for various percentages of the training data used for training. This shows that a 60% training split and a 75% training split performed similarly, although the 60% split was slightly better. The 90% training split was clearly worse; this is probably because the resulting validation set (~39 entries) is an insufficient sample of the dataset for accurately pruning the tree and setting the final threshold.

The performance of the proposed IS-MLT method is compared to two other multi-label classifier methods, CLUS (Blockeel et al., 2006; Vens et al., 2008) and RAKEL (Tsoumakas & Vlahavas, 2007), and to single label SVMs in Table 2. For

Table 1. Effect of changing the percent of validation examples, for IS-MLT. ↑ indicates a larger value is better; ↓ indicates a smaller value is better

	60% Train	75% Train	90% Train
Micro F_1 ↑	**0.8242**	0.8019	0.7913
Macro F_1 ↑	**0.8223**	0.8009	0.7782
Macro AUROC ↑	0.8022	**0.8041**	0.7532
Hamming Loss ↓	**0.0767**	0.0858	0.0965
One Error ↓	**0.5000**	0.6667	0.6667
Coverage ↓	1.6667	**1.5000**	2.3333
Ranking Loss ↓	0.1750	**0.1417**	0.2875
Average Precision ↑	**0.7993**	0.7831	0.7480

the single label SVMs, SVMLight (Joachims, 1999) was used with both the linear kernel option and the polynomial kernel option on each label. The CLUS version 2.7 software was downloaded from http://www.cs.kuleuven.be/~dtai/clus. The training data was again divided into a training set and a validation set, then using the classification

scores output by the program, the thresholds for the model were selected in the same manner as described for IS-MLT. After testing at various ratios of training and validation data, the 70% training level was found to perform slightly better than the other ratios; these results are shown in the Table 2. Trohidis et al. (2008) apply RAKEL to the Emotions dataset; the performance results listed here were taken from that paper. The proposed IS-MLT method clearly outperforms the other approaches overall.

Tagging Photographs with Scene Labels

For the photographic scene dataset, a set of nine trees were built using the F-measure performance evaluation method for pruning, with $\hat{a} = 1$. The best performing model for the validation data, with respect to the micro-F_1 measure, was selected and used with the same threshold to classify the testing data. Again the trees used Block-Diagonal clustering to initialize the iterative splitting process and SVMs were used for the decision making at each node. Also, since a validation set was not pre-specified, 75% of the

Figure 3. Comparison of individual label F_1 measure performance, scene dataset

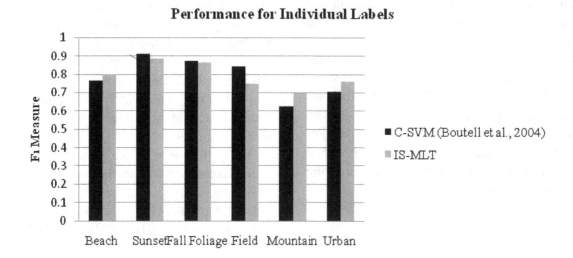

Table 2. Comparison of Performance Measures, Emotions Dataset. ↑ indicates a larger value is better; ↓ indicates a smaller value is better.

	Single Label SVMs		Multi-label Classifier Methods		
	Linear	**Polynomial**	**IS-MLT**	**CLUS**	**RAKEL**
Micro F_1 ↑	0.8121	0.8005	**0.8242**	0.7614	0.7002
Macro F_1 ↑	0.8150	0.7992	**0.8223**	0.7628	0.6766
Macro AUROC ↑	**0.8220**	0.8039	0.8022	0.7490	---
Hamming Loss ↓	0.0825	0.0833	**0.0767**	0.1304	0.1845
One Error ↓	0.3020	0.3861	0.5000	0.3333	**0.2669**
Coverage ↓	1.9753	2.0198	**1.6667**	2.3614	1.9974
Ranking Loss ↓	0.1809	0.1986	**0.1750**	0.2664	0.2635
Average Precision ↑	0.7860	0.7568	**0.7993**	0.7291	0.7954

training data was used for training and the remaining 25% was used for validation purposes.

Table 3 and Figure 3 compare the results of the IS-MLT model to the results published by Boutell et al. (2004) (referred to as C-SVM here, for C-Criterion SVM). Also shown are results of RAKEL from graphs published by Tsoumakas and Vlahavas (2007); these, however, depict the result when selecting the optimal threshold value for the test set. This table shows that IS-MLT and C-SVM perform comparably. The Micro-F_1 from (Boutell et al., 2004) is slightly better than that obtained using IS-MLT, while the Macro-F_1 performance was slightly better using the proposed IS-MLT. IS-MLT is again better than RAKEL. Figure 3 compares the performance for individual labels. Again the IS-MLT and C-SVM results are comparable: for half of the labels the performance is better when using the IS-MLT model.

Tagging Musical Artists and Bands

The performance of IS-MLT on the Last.FM band textual summary data is compared with both CLUS

and individual label classifiers. The IS-MLT ree again uses an SVM decision split at each node, but the initial clustering method is K-Means with a Euclidean distance measure, and the evaluation for pruning was $\tilde{n}_l$ (rather than the micro-F_1). Individual label classifiers were built using both an SVM approach and a discrete Naïve Bayesian

Table 3. Comparison of Performance Measures, Scene Dataset. ↑ indicates a larger value is better; ↓ indicates a smaller value is better.

	IS-MLT	**C-SVM**	**RAKEL**
Micro F_1 ↑	0.7887	**0.791**	~0.735
Macro F_1 ↑	**0.7945**	0.789	
Hamming Loss ↓	0.0530		~0.093
One Error ↓	0.3737		
Coverage ↓	0.8763		
Ranking Loss ↓	0.1561		
Average Precision ↑	0.7685		

Table 4. Comparison of timing. average across folds, in seconds

	Indv. Label		Multi-label	
	Naïve Bayes	**SVM**	**0/1 IS-MLT**	**IS-MLT**
Training Time	2097	4374	1569	470
Classification Time	---	11495	210	181

model. Both these and the CLUS models were trained using binary labels (inclusion/exclusion), where the label was considered to be included if $L_i(l) > 0$. IS-MLT trained using binary labels is also considered (0/1 IS-MLT); for this block-diagonal clustering is used for the initialization and micro-F_1 is used during the pruning evaluation. For binary label evaluation for all the methods, the same inclusion threshold of zero was used. For the Ranking Correlation evaluations, the output scores were used for ranking in the same manner as for IS-MLT.

As mentioned in the introduction, one of the issues with a single label classifier approach is the problem of scalability. Table 4 compares the training and classification time for each method. Thus, while the proposed IS-MLT method took approximately 8 minutes to train a classifier for each fold, the individual label Naïve Bayes method took almost 4 times longer at approximately 35 minutes for each fold, and the individual label SVM method took almost 8 times longer at approximately 1 hour and 13 minutes for each fold. On the classification side, the weighted label

Table 5. Comparison of performance measures, Last.FM band summary dataset, label subset

	Indv. Label		Multi-label		
	Naïve Bayes	**SVM**	**CLUS**	**0/1 IS-MLT**	**IS-MLT**
Micro F_1 ↑	0.502	**0.716**	0.680	0.598	*0.683*
Macro F_1 ↑	0.411	**0.525**	0.446	0.431	*0.480*
Average Precision ↑	0.131	**0.570**	0.524	0.436	*0.528*
Hamming Loss ↓	0.149	**0.118**	0.161	0.168	*0.157*
One Error ↓	0.973	**0.162**	*0.173*	0.367	0.197
Coverage ↓	158.8	**131.6**	145.1	146.9	*134.5*
Ranking Loss ↓	0.785	**0.187**	0.235	0.421	*0.221*
$\tilde{n}_I$ ↑	0.405	**0.422**	0.377	0.251	*0.384*
$\tilde{n}_M$ ↑	0.155	**0.244**	0.121	0.035	*0.169*
$\hat{\delta}_I$ ↑	0.197	**0.205**	0.183	0.111	*0.186*
$\hat{\delta}_M$ ↑	0.077	**0.112**	0.057	0.015	*0.079*

Figure 4. Performance of individual labels relative to their frequency, last.fm band summary dataset

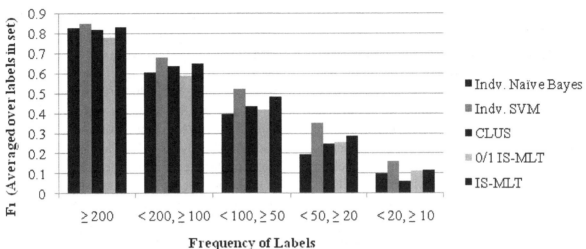

IS-MLT method was only slightly faster than the binary label IS-MLT; the average resulting tree size was 10 nodes for the binary IS-MLT method, and 10.6 nodes for weighted label IS-MLT method. The individual label SVM method was substantially slower, taking over 3 hours to classify the training, validation, and test sets, but the IS-MLT method only took about 3 minutes to classify the three subsets of data.

Table 5 shows a comparison of the test performance for the 163 labels used in training; binary evaluation measures are shown in the upper portion of the table and the ranking correlation methods in the lower portion. The best method overall is noted by the bold font, while the best

Table 6. Comparison of F_1-Measure Performance for 10 most frequent labels

	Indv. Label		Multi-label		
Label	Naive Bayes	SVM	CLUS	0/1 IS-MLT	IS-MLT
rock	0.9505	**0.9534**	0.9211	0.8853	0.9367
pop	0.9305	**0.9406**	0.9031	0.8921	0.9199
classic+rock	0.8990	**0.9079**	0.8959	0.8451	0.9067
indie	0.8883	**0.8982**	0.8684	0.8467	0.8834
alternative	**0.8901**	0.8892	0.8776	0.8340	0.8780
favorites	0.8652	**0.8753**	0.8507	0.7970	0.8552
80s	0.8590	**0.8839**	0.8475	0.8047	0.8638
american	0.8548	**0.8916**	0.7782	0.8043	0.8341
singer-songwriter	**0.8379**	0.8220	0.7591	0.7681	0.8218
folk	0.8239	**0.8338**	0.7849	0.7843	0.8045

of the multi-label approaches is marked in italics. The single label classifier SVM approach is a clear winner for overall performance, but IS-MLT generally comes in second best for over half the performance measures. Thus, because of the lack of scalability of the individual SVM approach, IS-MLT is the best alternative among those tested. Also note that none of the results are particularly good; in particular, the ranking correlation evaluations indicate almost no correlation between the relative ranks of the predicted labels and those of the actual labels. Since the number of examples relative to the number of labels is small, a larger training set would be likely to improve the results, as evidenced by the F_1 performance of the more frequent labels.

Figure 4 shows the F_1 performance of labels, macro-averaged across groups corresponding to the frequency of those labels. For each classifier method the macro-average performance decreased with fewer examples. Again the best performance was obtained by the individual classifier SVM approach and the second best was obtained by the IS-MLT approach. For the 20 labels with over 200 examples total in the dataset, the average F_1 performance was 0.8301 using IS-MLT; for the 35 labels with 100 to 200 examples, the average F_1 performance dropped to 0.6520 using IS-MLT.

Table 6 shows the individual F_1 performance of the 10 most frequent labels. For these common labels the individual label classifier approaches perform best.

CONCLUSION

This paper presented a multi-label decision tree method, capable of handling both binary and non-binary labels. The proposed decision tree was applied to the problem of automated tagging for three datasets of differing media: music (audio), photographs, and text. Two of these datasets con-sisted of binary labels and the third of non-binary labels or weighted tags. Also, two of these datasets had few labels (six), while the other had many tags (163). For all of these datasets the proposed IS-MLTree performed noticeably better than other pre-existing multi-label approaches for a variety of performance and loss measures. When comparing IS-MLT to single label classifiers, IS-MLT was found to be better than a single label Naïve Bayes approach, but the results were mixed when a single label SVM approach was considered. The IS-MLTree method was substantially faster than the single label approaches for both training and classification (a couple hours to train and classify all portions of a 10-fold dataset, versus a couple days) and is therefore far more scalable to datasets with large numbers of tags. Thus, the proposed multi-label tree method seems applicable to a variety of datasets.

Although the focus on this work is on tagging of multimedia and in particular on those applications where the tags may be weighted by usage, only one of the three presented datasets had weighted labels. We intend to create additional datasets from the audio and image domains that use weighted tag representations, and further test the proposed method on its predictive tagging abilities.

REFERENCES

Barutcuoglu, Z., Schapire, R. E., & Troyanskaya, O. G. (2006). Hierarchical multi-label prediction of gene function. *Bioinformatics (Oxford, England)*, *22*(7), 830–836. doi:10.1093/bioinformatics/btk048

Blockeel, H., Schietgat, L., Struyf, J., Džeroski, S., & Clare, A. (2006). Decision trees for hierarchical multilabel classification: A case study in functional genomics. In *Principle and Practice of Knowledge Discovery in Databases*.

Boutell, M., Shen, X., Luo, J., & Brown, C. (2003). *Multi-label semantic scene classification (Tech. Rep.)*. Rochester, NY: University of Rochester, Department of Computer Science.

Boutell, M. R., Luo, J., Shen, X., & Brown, C. M. (2004). Learning multi-label scene classification. *Pattern Recognition, 37*(9), 1757–1771. doi:10.1016/j.patcog.2004.03.009

Cesa-Bianchi, N., Gentile, C., & Zaniboni, L. (2006). Incremental algorithms for hierarchical classification. *Journal of Machine Learning Research, 7*, 31–54.

Clare, A., & King, R. D. (2002). Machine learning of functional class from phenotype data. *Bioinformatics (Oxford, England), 18*(1), 160–166. doi:10.1093/bioinformatics/18.1.160

Gao, S., Wu, W., Lee, C.-H., & Chua, T.-S. (2004). A MFoM learning approach to robust multiclass multi-label text categorization. In *Proceedings of the International Conference on Machine Learning* (p. 42). New York: ACM Press.

Ghamrawi, N., & McCallum, A. (2005). Collective multi-label classification. In *Proceedings of the ACM International Conference on Information and Knowledge Management* (pp. 195-200). New York: ACM Press.

Grodzicki, R., Mańdziuk, J., & Wang, L. (2008). Improved multilabel classification with neural networks. In *Parallel Problem Solving from Nature* (LNCS 5199, pp. 409-416).

Hardoon, D., Saunders, C., Szedmak, S., & Shawe-Taylor, J. (2006). A correlation approach for automatic image annotation. In *International Conference ADMA* (LNCS 4093).

Joachims, T. (1998). Text categorization with support vector machines: learning with many relevant features. In C. N'edellec & C. Rouveirol (Eds.), *European Conference on Machine Learning* (pp. 137-142). New York: Springer.

Joachims, T. (1999). *Kernel Methods - Support Vector Learning*. Cambridge, MA: MIT-Press.

Kim, S.-J., & Lee, K. B. (2003). Constructing decision trees with multiple response variables. *International Journal of Management and Decision Making, 4*(4), 337–353. doi:10.1504/IJMDM.2003.003998

Kocev, D., Vens, C., & Struyf, J. (2007). Ensembles of multi-objective decision trees. In *Proceedings of the European Conference on Machine Learning* (LNCS 4701, pp. 624-631). New York: Springer.

Li, T. (2005). A general model for clustering binary data. In *Proceedings of the ACM SIGKDD International Conference on Knowledge Discovery in Data Mining* (pp. 188-197).

Ma, A., Sethi, I. K., & Patel, N. (2009). Multimedia content tagging using multilabel decision tree. In *Proceedings of the IEEE Intl. Workshop on Multimedia Information Processing and Retrieval (MIPR)*.

McCallum, A. (1999). Multi-label text classification with a mixture model trained by EM. In *Proceedings of the AAAI99 Workshop on Text Learning*.

Quinlan, J. (1993). *C4.5: Programs for Machine Learning*. San Francisco, CA: Morgan Kaufmann Publishers.

Rousu, J., Saunders, C., Szedmak, S., & Shawe-Taylor, J. (2004). On maximum margin hierarchical classification. In *Proceedings of the NIPS 2004 Workshop on Learning With Structured Outputs*.

Rousu, J., Saunders, C., Szedmak, S., & Shawe-Taylor, J. (2005). Learning hierarchical multicategory text classification models. In *Proceedings of the International Conference on Machine Learning*.

Rousu, J., Saunders, C., Szedmak, S., & Shawe-Taylor, J. (2006). Kernel-based learning of hierarchical multilabel classification models. *Journal of Machine Learning Research*, 7, 1601–1626.

Schapire, R. E., & Singer, Y. (2000). Boostexter: A boosting-based system for text categorization. *Machine Learning*, *39*(2-3), 135–168. doi:10.1023/A:1007649029923

Snoek, C. G. M., & Worring, M. (2009). Concept-based video retrieval. *Foundations and Trends in Information Retrieval*, *4*(2), 215–322.

Struyf, J., Dzeroski, S., Blockeel, H., & Clare, A. (2005). Hierarchical multi-classification with predictive clustering trees in functional genomics. In *Proceedings of the Workshop on Computational Methods in Bioinformatics at the 12th Portuguese Conf. on AI*.

Suzuki, E., Gotoh, M., & Choki, Y. (2001). Bloomy decision tree for multi-objective classification. In *Proceedings of the European Conference on Principles of Data Mining and Knowledge Discovery* (pp. 436-447).

Trohidis, K., Tsoumakas, G., Kalliris, G., & Vlahavas, I. (2008). Multilabel classification of music into emotions. In *Proceedings of the International Conference on Music Information Retrieval*.

Tsoumakas, G., & Katakis, I. (2007). Multi label classification: An overview. *International Journal of Data Warehousing and Mining*, *3*(3), 1–13.

Tsoumakas, G., & Vlahavas, I. (2007). Random k-labelsets: An ensemble method for multilabel classification. In J. Kok, J. Koronacki, R. de Mantaras, S. Matwin, D. Mladenic, & A. Skowron (Eds.), *Proceedings of the European Conference on Machine Learning* (LNAI 4701, pp. 406-417). Berlin: Springer Verlag.

Ueda, N., & Saito, K. (2003). Parametric mixture models for multi-labeled text. In Becker, S., Thrun, S., & Obermayer, K. (Eds.), *Advances in Neural Information Processing Systems* (*Vol. 15*). Cambridge, MA: MIT Press.

Vens, C., Struyf, J., Schietgat, L., D˘zeroski, S., & Blockeel, H. (2008). Decision trees for hierarchical multi-label classification. *Machine Learning*, *73*(2), 185–214. doi:10.1007/s10994-008-5077-3

Yan, R., Tesic, J., & Smith, J. R. (2007). Model-shared subspace boosting for multi-label classification. In *Proceedings of the ACM SIGKDD International Conference on Knowledge Discovery and Data Mining* (pp. 834-843). New York: ACM Press.

Yang, Y. (1999). An evaluation of statistical approaches to text categorization. *Information Retrieval*, *1*(1-2), 69–90. doi:10.1023/A:1009982220290

Yu, K., Yu, S., & Tresp, V. (2005). Multi-label informed latent semantic indexing. In *Proceedings of the International ACM SIGIR Conference on Research and Development in Information Retrieval* (pp. 258-265). New York: ACM Press.

Zhang, M.-L., & Zhou, Z.-H. (2007a). ML-KNN: A lazy learning approach to multi-label learning. *Pattern Recognition*, *40*(7), 2038–2048. doi:10.1016/j.patcog.2006.12.019

Zhang, M.-L., & Zhou, Z.-H. (2007b). Multi-label learning by instance differentiation. In *Proceedings of the AAAI Conference on Artificial Intelligence* (p. 669).

Zhu, S., Ji, X., Xu, W., & Gong, Y. (2005). Multi-labelled classification using maximum entropy method. In *Proceedings of the International ACM SIGIR Conference on Research and Development in Information Retrieval* (pp. 274-281). New York: ACM Press.

This work was previously published in the International Journal of Multimedia Data Engineering and Management, Volume 1, Issue 3, edited by Shu-Ching Chen, pp. 57-75, copyright 2010 by IGI Publishing (an imprint of IGI Global).

Section 2
Image Classification and Retrieval

Chapter 5

An Image Clustering and Feedback–Based Retrieval Framework

Chengcui Zhang
University of Alabama at Birmingham, USA

Liping Zhou
University of Alabama at Birmingham, USA

Wen Wan
University of Alabama at Birmingham, USA

Jeffrey Birch
Virginia Polytechnic Institute and State University, USA

Wei-Bang Chen
University of Alabama at Birmingham, USA

ABSTRACT

Most existing object-based image retrieval systems are based on single object matching, with its main limitation being that one individual image region (object) can hardly represent the user's retrieval target, especially when more than one object of interest is involved in the retrieval. Integrated Region Matching (IRM) has been used to improve the retrieval accuracy by evaluating the overall similarity between images and incorporating the properties of all the regions in the images. However, IRM does not take the user's preferred regions into account and has undesirable time complexity. In this article, we present a Feedback-based Image Clustering and Retrieval Framework (FIRM) using a novel image clustering algorithm and integrating it with Integrated Region Matching (IRM) and Relevance Feedback (RF). The performance of the system is evaluated on a large image database, demonstrating the effectiveness of our framework in catching users' retrieval interests in object-based image retrieval.

DOI: 10.4018/978-1-4666-1791-9.ch005

INTRODUCTION

Object-based image retrieval has recently become an important research issue in retrieving images on the basis of the underlying semantics of images. Within the context of object-based image retrieval, the semantic content of an image is represented by one or more of the objects present in that image, where object-based features are used to describe the user's perceived content of that image. However, two critical issues exist in existing object-based image retrieval systems. First, most existing systems retrieve images according to a single object/segment of a user's interest, which cannot meet the requirement of those user queries where more than one object-of-interest is involved. In addition, image segmentation, known as an extremely difficult process, may produce inaccurate segmentation resulting from over-segmentation and/or under-segmentation. Consequently, the inaccurate segments may negatively affect the image retrieval results. Secondly, most existing systems require a complex user interface which is capable of displaying all the segments (regions) of a query image so that users can choose desirable query region(s) from these segments. Such an interface can be cumbersome and confusing, mostly due to the inaccurate segmentation results by over- and under-segmentation, but also partly due to the fact that there are usually 7~8 segments/objects on average in each image.

Integrated Region Matching (IRM) (Carson, Thomas, & Belongie, 1999) has been proposed to alleviate the above two problems to some degree. IRM measures overall similarity between two images with the following two advantages. First, IRM effectively reduces the side effect of inaccurate segmentation by incorporating properties of all the regions in the images into one region matching scheme. Moreover, unlike other existing object-based image retrieval systems, IRM does not require a complex user interface to display all the segments/objects in the query image because IRM adopts an overall image-to-image similarity measure based on the similarity of two sets of objects/segments. Therefore, users only need to specify a query image without having to specify particular objects of interest through a complex user interface. However, several challenges remain in IRM, including: (1) how to efficiently index and search in a large-scale image segment/object database, and (2) how to bridge the "semantic gap" between low level object features and high level perceptions of image content consisting of a set of objects. As an unsupervised similarity measure, the original IRM ranks the retrieved images based on the overall similarity between two sets of image segments without any input of user guidance/knowledge, where the significance of each image segment is fully determined by low level object features such as region/object size. The significance score is then used to calculate the pair-wise segment similarity score between a segment of the query image and a segment from an image in the database. The overall similarity score is the sum of pair-wise segment similarity scores between two images. However, this matching scheme failed to capture the user's preferences such as the relative importance of certain objects according to the user's subjective perception, and a selected few regions that form the profile of the user's search interest in a query image. In other words, the original IRM scheme does not reflect the relative importance of individual regions/objects in the query image according to the user's own preferences. This article aims to design an object-based image clustering and retrieval framework with feedback-based integrated region matching to address the challenges aforementioned.

In order to support integrated region-based image retrieval, we need to divide each image into several semantic regions. Instead of viewing each image as a whole, we examine integrated region similarity during image retrieval. However, this further increases the search space by a factor of 7~8 when compared with single-region based image retrieval which is already one magnitude more complex than non-object based image retrieval. Clustering is a process of grouping a set of physical or abstract objects into classes based on some similarity criteria. In this study, objects correspond to image regions. Given the huge amount of regions/segments in this problem, we first preprocess image regions by grouping them into clusters. In this way the search space can be reduced to a few clusters that are relevant to the regions/objects in the query image. K-means is a traditional clustering method and has been widely used in image clustering. However, it is incapable of finding non-convex clusters and tends to fall into local optimum especially when the number of data objects is large. In contrast, Genetic Algorithm is known for its robustness and ability to approximate global optimum. In this article, we propose a new Genetic Algorithm based clustering algorithm for image region clustering which is more robust compared to the state-of-the-art.

To fill the semantic gap between low level region/object features (e.g., color, texture, and shape) and high-level user perceptions, relevance feedback is used as a powerful technique in the field of information retrieval and has been an active research area for the past decade. In this article, we proposed a Feedback-based Integrated Region Matching (FIRM) scheme to address this issue. With the proposed scheme, we consider each image as a set of regions, and the entire image database can be viewed as a large collection of regions. According to the region distance measured based on the similarity of region features, image regions are grouped into clusters. Each cluster represents a specific semantically meaningful concept. In the initial retrieval, the user provides a query image, and the system performs retrieval on the set of image clusters (reduced search space) that include the regions in the query image using the original IRM scheme. After the initial retrieval results are returned to the user, the user is asked to provide feedback (positive/relevant or negative/irrelevant) for each returned image among the top 20-40 returned images. To capture the user's high-level perception on the query image (search target), we integrate the user's relevance feedback with the integrated region-matching scheme, i.e., the so-named FIRM scheme. In brief, we assume that the regions in the query image are not equally important to the user query. Some regions capture more of the user's attention during retrieval than the others. This is modeled in our matching scheme through assigning different weights to individual regions. The region weights are then used in the calculation of the similarity between the query image and an image in the database. A learning component is designed and implemented to automatically calculate and adjust the weights of query regions according to the user's feedback. We take the set of region weights as our hypothesis of the user's search interest and continue with the feedback-retrieval process using the proposed FIRM scheme. Through several iterations, the user's preferences are captured through gradual refinement of region weights.

The arguments for our framework start with a brief discussion on image clustering and retrieval framework. Next, an overview of our system is presented. Thirdly, the implementation of proposed framework is described, followed by the discussion of the processing, clustering, relevance feedback, and the retrieval components. Finally, the evaluation of system performance with experimental results is presented, followed by the summary and conclusion.

RELATED WORKS

Several image clustering and retrieval frameworks have been proposed in the literature. Most of the object-based image retrieval systems are based on a single object matching. In order to support region-based image retrieval, systems need to divide each image into several semantic regions and examine region similarity during the image retrieval (Zhang & Chen, 2005; Babu & Nagesh, 2008). In our framework, instead of retrieving images based on a single object matching, we consider all the regions in an image as an entirety and examine the overall similarity between images based on the IRM measure (Wang, Li, & Wiederhold, 2001; Babu & Nagesh, 2008). One well-known system, the SIMPLIcity (Semantics-Sensitive Integrated Matching for Picture Libraries), adopts IRM to measure the overall similarity between images; however, no interactive learning mechanism is used in this retrieval scheme. The drawback is that the retrieval system has no clue about which regions/objects in the query image the user is interested in, and therefore, the retrieval system cannot adjust similarity measures to accommodate individual users' search interest. In order to alleviate this problem, in this study, we propose a Feedback-based Integrated Region Matching (FIRM) scheme by learning from the user's relevance feedback. Using the user feedback, we can refine the retrieval results with a more sophisticated learning algorithm. The proposed scheme can be categorized as region-based image retrieval with interactive learning capabilities. Several other works in this category can be found in (Ji, Yao, & Liang, 2008; Bradshaw, 2000).

Genetic Algorithm for Image Data

Genetic Algorithm (GA) (Haupt & Haupt, 2004) is a search technique in providing exact or approximate solutions to optimization and search problems. The concept of this type of algorithms is borrowed from the Darwin's theory – "survival of the fittest". The original GA which was developed by Holland in 1975 simulates an evolutionary process of a living species, using genetic operators such as "selection", "mutation", "crossover", and "reproduction". GAs have been broadly applied to a variety of fields, including ecology, biology, and statistics (Ding & Gasvoda, 2005; Tomassini, 1998). In GA, problems are solved by an evolutionary process, which results in a fittest (optimal) solution, i.e., the survivor. In our research, a Modified GA (MGA) is proposed and

serves as a clustering algorithm for grouping image regions according to their object visual features.

In general, the objective of all clustering algorithms is to divide a set of data points into subgroups so that the objects within a subgroup are similar to each other whereas objects in different subgroups have diverse qualities. In this study, the main purpose of clustering is to reduce the search space by grouping a set of similar image regions into clusters based on some similarity criteria, and therefore reduce the time-complexity in the subsequent retrieval.

There are some related works in this research area. Ding and Gasvoda (2005) address the application of GAs for clustering image dataset. It is common that the running time for most GAs will dramatically increase when the number of data points in the input set or the number of clusters desired grows. Ding and Gasvoda (2005) try to solve this problem by reducing the input dataset of GA.

Another problem is that traditional GA tends to fall into local optima especially when clustering discretely represented data such as image data in this study. The CMA-ES (Covariance Matrix Adaptation Evolution Strategy) (Hansen, 2008) is an attractive option for non-linear optimization when general search methods failed due to a discontinue search landscape or sharp bends. In this article, we introduce an innovative Genetic Algorithm, i.e., Modified Genetic Algorithm (MGA) to cluster image regions. The performance of the proposed MGA has been compared to that of CMA-ES and proved to be more robust when applied to real world problems where discrete data such as image data is involved.

Relevance Feedback Methods

Relevance feedback is a powerful technique in content-based image retrieval (CBIR). In CBIR systems, there exists inherently "semantic gap" between high level concepts and low level features. Human perception of image similarity is always subjective and task-dependent, and the retrieval systems based on the similarities of pure visual features are not necessarily perceptually or semantically meaningful. Relevance Feedback (RF) is a supervised learning technique used to improve the effectiveness of information retrieval systems. It helps to establish the link between high level concepts and low level features and thus bridges the semantic gap.

Most of the relevance feedback methods can be classified into two categories: query point movement (Su, Zhang, & Ma, 2000) and query re-weighting. In the proposed method, the weights of image regions are updated automatically and therefore it falls into the second category. Several other existing works belong to this category. For example, Ji, Yao, and Liang (2008) proposed a Dynamic Region Matching (DRM) which adopts a probabilistic fuzzy region matching algorithm to retrieve and match images at the object level. In the matching algorithm, the weights of regions in the query image are updated through relevance feedback. However, the problem with this algorithm is that for all matched regions in the query image, their weights are either increased or decreased by a fixed factor, making the performance gain obtained through RF rather limited.

Some other works also attempt to incorporate Support Vector Machines (SVM) (Su et al., 2000) into the learning process based on relevance feedback. However, SVM is not directly suitable for the relevance feedback because the training data set is too small to be representatives of the true distributions. In (Wang et al., 2001; Zhang & Chen, 2005), One-Class SVM is transformed to model the non-linear distribution of image regions and to separate positive regions from negative ones.

In this article, we propose a relevance feedback algorithm integrated into an innovative region-matching scheme. Each region of the query image is assigned an equal initial weight, and the weight is updated gradually based on its distances to the matched regions in positive images. Therefore, a smaller distance indicates a higher similar-

ity between the matched pair of regions. A new integrated region matching scheme is proposed which calculates the overall similarity between two images as weighted region similarities. The region weights are automatically and gradually refined through iterations of the feedback-retrieval process.

FRAMEWORK OVERVIEW

The system architecture of the proposed framework is illustrated in Figure 1. The proposed framework consists of three major modules, including the preprocessing module, the clustering module, and the relevance feedback and retrieval module. In the preprocessing module, images are segmented into semantic regions. Then, object-level features are extracted for each image region. In our study, 8 features are used – 3 color features, 3 texture features, and 2 shape features. We use the proposed Genetic Algorithm as the clustering method to group image regions into clusters. In this way, an image can belong to more than one cluster if its containing regions are grouped to different clusters. At the time of retrieval, all the image clusters that involve the regions in the query image form the candidate image pool (reduced search space) for subsequent retrieval and user feedback.

In the initial query, since there is no user feedback yet available, the original IRM scheme is used to rank all the images in the candidate pool. After the initial retrieval, the user can label all the positive images that he thinks relevant to the query image according to his own preferences (e.g., preferred query region(s)). In our current implementation, only the top 30 ranked images are returned to the user for feedback because a larger set may undermine the user experience for feedback-retrieval. Using the proposed matching scheme that integrates relevance feedback, the retrieval system is able to learn automatically the user's preferences from the user's feedback and

Figure 1. The system architecture

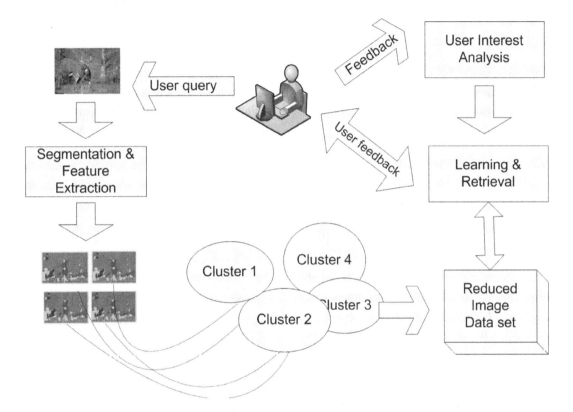

predict the significance/weights of individual regions in the query image. The similarity between two images is thus evaluated over weighted integrated region similarities. The predicted weights are used in the next round of retrieval, followed by another round of user relevance feedback. It is expected that though multiple iterations, the region weights can be gradually refined so that the user's preferences in the case of region-based retrieval can be captured.

PREPROCESSING

Region Segmentation

In our framework, we employ a fast yet effective image segmentation method called WavSeg as proposed in our previous work (Zhang, Chen, Shyu, & Peeta, 2003) to partition images instead

of manually dividing each image into a couple of regions (Yang & Lozano-Prez, 2000). In Wavseg, a wavelet analysis in concert with the SPCPE algorithm (Chen, Sista, Shyu, & Kashyap, 2000) is used to segment an image into regions.

By using wavelet transform and choosing proper wavelets (Daubechies wavelets), the high-frequency components will disappear in larger scale sub bands and therefore, the region areas will become more evident. In our implementation, images are pre-processed by Daubechies wavelet transform because it is proven to be suitable for image analysis. The decomposition level is 1. Then by grouping the salient points from each channel, an initial coarse partition can be obtained and passed as the input to the SPCPE segmentation algorithm. In fact, even the coarse initial partition generated by wavelet transform approximates more closely to some global minima in SPCPE than a random initial partition. In other words, a better initial partition will lead to better segmentation results. Based on our experimental results, the wavelet based SPCPE segmentation framework (WavSeg) outperforms the random initial partition based SPCPE algorithm on average. It is worth pointing out that WavSeg is fast. The processing time for a 240×384 image is only about 0.33 s on average.

Region Feature Extraction

Region feature extraction is a built-in component in the proposed framework, which is used to extract low-level, object-based visual features that can be used to describe image content. In this article, we extract eight visual features as adopted in Blobworld (Carson, Belongie, & Greenspan, 2002) for each region. The eight visual features include 3 color features, 3 texture features, and 2 shape features for each extracted image region.

CLUSTERING OF IMAGE REGIONS

In this section, we present an innovative image region clustering algorithm named Modified Genetic Algorithm (MGA). Clustering is especially important when performing image retrieval on a large-scale dataset since the increase of dataset size significantly degrades the searching efficiency. After clustering, the original image dataset is reduced to a few image clusters related to the query image so that the search scope can be narrowed down. Here, we adopt MGA to approximate the global optimal solution, where a solution, within the context of image region clustering, consists of a set of cluster centroids in a non-convex and discontinued search space. In the remaining sections of this article, our experimental results show that the proposed clustering algorithm alleviates a problem in traditional GAs where they could easily fall into a local optimum.

Overview of Genetic Algorithms

Genetic Algorithms (Ortiz, Simpson, Pignatiello, & Heredia-Langner, 2004) are iterative optimization procedures that repeatedly apply GA operations (such as selection, crossover, and mutation) to a group of solutions until some criteria of convergence are satisfied. In a GA, a search point, a setting in the search space, is coded into a string which is analogous to a chromosome in biological systems. The string (chromosome) is composed of characters which are analogous to genes. In a statistical application, the chromosome corresponds to a particular setting of k factors (or regressors), denoted by $X=[x_1, x_2, ..., x_k]$ in the design space and i^{th} gene in the chromosome corresponds to x_i, the value of the ith regressor. A set of multiple concurrent search points or a set of chromosomes (or individuals) is called a population. Each iterative step where a new population is obtained is called a generation.

In general, the procedure of a GA consists of the following steps:

1. Define an objective/fitness function and its variables. Configure GA operations (such as population size, parent/offspring ratio, selection method, number of crossovers and the mutation rate).
2. Randomly generate the initial population.
3. Evaluate each individual (or chromosome) in the initial population by the objective function.
4. Generate an offspring population by GA operations (such as selection/mating, crossover, and mutation).
5. Evaluate each individual in the offspring population by the objective function.
6. Decide which individuals to include in the next population. This step is referred to as "replacement" in that individuals from the current parent population are "replaced" by

a new population, whose individuals come from the offspring and/or parent population.

7. If a stopping criterion is satisfied, then the procedure stops. Otherwise, go to Step 4.

The Proposed Modified Genetic Algorithm (MGA)

GAs are a large family of algorithms that have the same basic concept but differ from one another with respect to several strategies such as stopping rules and operations which control the search process. Based on previous experiences, in this study, the type of selection we utilize is random pairing. The blending crossover is utilized, and the number of crossover points depends on the number of dimensions of a specific objective function and is set to 2. Random uniform mutation is utilized and the mutation rate is set to 0.04. The type of replacement over both parent and offspring populations is ranking (Hamada, Martz, Reese, & Wilson, 2001; Myers & Montgomery, 2002).

The GA itself does not utilize any directional search explicitly. In order to improve the computational efficiency of the GA, we modify the GA by incorporating local search into the GA process, namely MGA (Wan, 2007). The method of Steepest Descent (SD) (Haupt & Haupt, 2004) and the Newton-Raphson method (NR) are two kinds of well-known local search methods, both of which require the partial derivatives of an objective function f. It is not expected that SD or NR can always find a proper direction from the current point since an objective function may not be simple or unimodal, but very complicated, locally rough and unsmoothed. Thus, we developed a new local directional search method which is derivative-free and denoted by "DFDS".

The local search approach has the same main idea: utilizing numerical information from a GA process to find some appropriate local directions by only requiring a few extra function evaluations so that the GA process may be guided to further possible improvement. The numerical information we utilize in our study is focused on the best offspring among both the current parent and offspring populations.

When the best offspring among both the offspring and the parent populations is found, we can trace back to find its parents. These parents then can be considered as two different starting points. Both of them go to the same point: the current best offspring. Therefore, two directions are established: one is from the first parent to the current best offspring; the other is from the second parent to the same offspring. Both directions have obtained improvement, since the best offspring of interest is an improvement over both of its parents in terms of values of an objective function. We individually project the two directions to n axis for an n-dimension space and compare the components of parent directions in i^{th} axis, if both parent directions are consistent on i^{th} axis (either both positive or both negative), the third direction is the common direction; otherwise, the third direction is zero which means the searching point will not move on i^{th} axis for the third direction.

Figure 2 illustrates the three defined directions in a 2-dimension space. The original point before performing our local search method is represented as "O", its optimal point is denoted by "Θ". P_1 and P_2 are its parent's points from a GA process. It is easy to see the two parents directions P_{1O} and P_{2O}, expressed as $\delta_{P1O}=[\delta_{11}, \delta_{12}]$ and $\delta_{P2O}=[\delta_{21}, \delta_{22}]$, respectively. It is obvious that in the third direction $\delta_3=[\delta_{31}, \delta_{32}]$, $\delta_{31}>0$ since both $\delta_{11}>0$ and $\delta_{21}>0$. This indicates that the common direction in this case is positive along the x_1 axis. In addition, $\delta_{32}=0$ since $\delta_{12}>0$ and $\delta_{22}<0$, which indicates that the common direction has no relative movement along the x_2 axis.

MGA Application on Image Region Clustering

In our application, one image is defined as a set of image regions, and each image region is represented as an 8-dimension data point in the dataset.

Figure 2. Three defined directions in a 2-dimension space

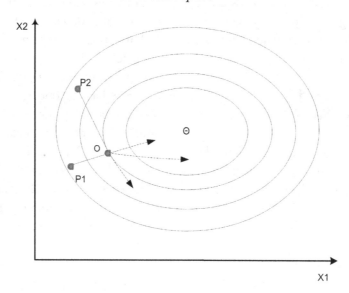

Therefore, the image region clustering problem is defined as the task of dividing an original image region dataset into a desired number of groups so that the Euclidean distance between each data point and its corresponding cluster centroid is minimized, which is a commonly used method for clustering images. The total distance of each point to its cluster centroid, known as the total distance measurement of the clustering, is calculated as in Equation 1. We use the Euclidean distance to calculate the distance between two images as in Equation 2.

$$F(C) = \sum_{j=1}^{k} \sum_{p_i \in C_j} D(p_i, C_j) \qquad (1)$$

$$D(I, J) = \left(\sum_t \left| f_t(I) - f_t(J) \right|^2 \right)^{1/2} \qquad (2)$$

In Equation 1, C_j is the jth cluster centroid of input dataset (the set of regions); p_i represents the ith data point (image region) in cluster j; each data point (region) is described as an 8-feature vector. C_j is an existing data point (image region) in the dataset chosen as the centroid for cluster j. Equation 2 is used to calculate the distance $D(I,$ J) between region I and region J, where $f_t(I)$ is the tth feature of region I (t=1…8).

It is very common to have as many as 50,000~60,000 fitness evaluations during one single run of a GA. The impact that the fitness function has on the execution time of the GA is obvious. The complexity of the fitness function cannot be too high for any GA that is to be used to perform clustering on a very large dataset. In our research, fitness function is defined as the inverse value of the total distance which is calculated as shown in Equation 3. Our MGA aims at approximating the maximum of the fitness function.

$$fit = \frac{1}{F(C)} \qquad (3)$$

In order to apply the proposed MGA to the clustering of image regions, a chromosome encoding scheme is proposed. In the proposed encoding scheme, the cluster centroids are encoded as genes into the chromosome and the length of each chromosome is the number of cluster centroids and also the number of desired clusters. In our test image database, there are 8,900 images which are further segmented into 82,556 regions. Therefore, the value of each gene in a chromosome is its index in the set of regions which ranges from 1 to 8,900, and the values of genes in the same chromosome must be unique. One limitation of many clustering algorithms is that they assume the number of clusters is known. However, in practice, the number of clusters may not be known in priori. This problem is called unsupervised clustering. In this study, we use an approach to achieve pseudo-unsupervised clustering which aims at determining an appropriate number of clusters $|C|$, without any prior knowledge about it. In particular, we proceed by repeating the clustering for several $|C|$ values, and choosing the best partition. Since this is done off-line, the high computational cost can be afforded. For scalability, whenever there is a significant growth of the image database, new clusters can be discovered by comparing the distance between each newly added image region and the existing cluster centroids – if the distance value is too large for any existing cluster, the newly added region will form a new cluster of its own, without the need to completely re-cluster all the image regions in the database.

Using this approach, through several runs on the dataset, we finally decide to divide the whole set of image regions into 1,000 clusters since it results in a good balance between good fitness and efficiency. In other words, the original image dataset is represented with a dataset which contains 82,556 points (image regions) centered around 1,000 cluster centroids. Initially, the 1,000 cluster centroids are randomly selected. By several iterative optimization procedures of MGA, the solution chromosome is a set of encoded cluster centroids, which produces the minimum sum of the distances of each point to its cluster centroid (maximum fitness value) through those iterations. Also, the total distance is used to measure the quality of the clustering results.

Comparison between MGA and CMA-ES

In order to evaluate the performance of the proposed MGA, we compare it with Covariance Matrix Adaptation Evolution Strategy (CMA-ES) (Hansen, 2008) in solving the image region clustering problem. The quality of clustering is evaluated in terms of the total distance measure as mentioned in previous section, and a smaller total distance value indicates better clustering quality. The CMA-ES is considered as an attractive option for non-linear optimization in a discontinuous search landscape. In our application, the data points (image regions) are scattered in a multi-dimensional space and therefore are discrete. For an input dataset with 82,556 data points (regions), our goal is to cluster these points into 1,000 groups where the total distance of each point to its corresponding cluster centroid is minimized. Table 1 demonstrates the comparison results of MGA and CMA-ES. The comparison is based on 2,400 evaluations of the fitness function. The results presented in the next section are also based on the same number of evaluations. This particular number is chosen because both algorithms start to converge at around 2,000 evaluations for this particular dataset. We can see that MGA has a better performance than CMA-ES based on the total distance measure. We also tested on different numbers of evaluations of the fitness function and the same trend persists.

Table 1. Results of comparison between MGA and CMA-ES

		The total distance
100 Groups	MGA	100,451.0
	CMA-ES	110,950.0
1000 Groups	MGA	67,872.1
	CMA-ES	69,926.4

RELEVANCE FEEDBACK AND RETRIEVAL

The Proposed Region-matching Scheme

In our proposed retrieval framework, an innovative region-matching scheme using feedback-based IRM for measuring the similarity of two images is proposed. Compared with the original IRM scheme, our region-matching scheme improves the retrieval accuracy by incorporating the relevance feedback into the IRM scheme. Therefore, the overall similarity of two images is computed as a weighted sum of the region similarity between two images. An advantage of using an integrated region similarity measure is that it is robust against poor segmentation by incorporating the properties of all the regions in the images. In designing the integrated similarity measure, we first attempt to match regions in two images. The principle of matching is that the most similar region pair is matched first. The matching allows one region of an image to be matched to several regions of another image. The distance between two regions can be easily calculated as the Euclidean distance in terms of the features extracted. During the matching process, the similarities of region pairs are calculated, and proper weights are assigned to them. The overall integrated similarity score between two images is computed as a weighted sum of the similarity between region pairs. We define the overall distance of two images using Equation 4, where I_1 is the query image and I_2 represents an image in the database; i and j denotes the ith region of I_1 and the jth region of I_2. s_{ij} represents the weight assigned to the region pair i and j from the two images. d_{ij} is the Euclidean distance between two regions i and j. w_i is the weight of region i in the query image (I_1). The initial value of w_i is set to 1, and w_i is automatically updated through relevance feedback learning process.

$$D(I_1, I_2) = \sum_{i=1}^{m} w_i \sum_{j=1}^{n} s_{ij} d_{ij} \qquad (4)$$

The matrix S is referred to as the significance matrix, in which s_{ij} indicates the significance of the matched region pair i and j for determining the similarity between images. D is referred to as the distance matrix in which d_{ij} represents the distance of the matched region pairs.

$$D_{1,2} = \begin{bmatrix} d_{11} & d_{12} & \cdots & d_{1n} \\ d_{21} & d_{22} & \cdots & d_{2n} \\ \vdots & \vdots & \ddots & \vdots \\ d_{m1} & d_{m2} & \cdots & d_{mn} \end{bmatrix} S_{1,2} = \begin{bmatrix} s_{11} & s_{12} & \cdots & s_{1n} \\ s_{21} & s_{22} & \cdots & s_{2n} \\ \vdots & \vdots & \ddots & \vdots \\ s_{m1} & s_{m2} & \cdots & s_{mn} \end{bmatrix}$$

For each image in the candidate pool, a significance matrix S and a distance matrix D will be constructed in order to calculate the integrated region similarity between the query image and that candidate image. Considering that the size of the matrix will increase polynomially with the number of regions in an image, we choose to use the six biggest regions (or less if there are no more than six regions) in the query image for retrieval and ignore the other smaller regions. It is not uncommon that one image may have more than ten regions due to over-segmentation, which leads to significant increase of the time-complexity in calculating the overall distance. Another reason is that some regions are relatively less meaningful due to over-segmentation and cannot carry a concrete semantic concept. For example, some region resulting from poor segmentation covers only a small part of a concrete object and cannot be used to represent one complete semantic object in that image. In this case, ignoring these smaller regions in the retrieval actually reduces noise in the dataset.

The number of regions (<=6) in the query image determines the number of rows in S and D which is fixed for each S and D. For each candidate image, the maximum number of regions used in similarity comparison is also confined to six which determines the number of columns in its corresponding S and D. Since the number of regions in each candidate image may not be the same, the number of columns in its corresponding S and D varies accordingly. In the initial query, the distance between the query image and a candidate image is calculated using the original IRM scheme, meaning that the initial weights of regions in the query image are all set to 1 (see Equation 4). The construction of S and D matrices is detailed in the next subsection. The top 30 ranked images are returned to the user for feedback. Through the learning via relevance feedback, the weights of regions in the query image are refined automatically and gradually.

Learning through Relevance Feedback

In the proposed relevance feedback framework, we collect the user's positive feedback as samples to construct the training dataset. Through feedback, an image labeled as positive indicates that it has regions that match the target regions in the query image according to the user's preferences. This information is used to update the weights of the regions in the query image. The weight of a region in the query image represents the significance of that region for calculating the integrated similarity between the two images, where the significance of a region in the query image can be reflected by the degree of matching between the region and the matched region in the candidate image. The degree of matching between a pair of regions can be determined by the distance between them. The less the distance is, the better matched they are. Equation 5 formulates the re-weighting scheme.

$$w_i = w_i^{'} \times \Pi_p \frac{1}{\min_k(d_{ik})} \quad (5)$$

where $w_i^{'}$ is the current weight of ith region in the query image; d_{ik} is the distance between region i in the query image and region k in a positive

image (p) labeled by the user. Assume one query image I_1 has m regions, represented by a region set $R_1 = \{r_1^1, r_2^1, ..., r_m^1\}$, and a candidate image I_2 has n regions represented by $R_2 = \{r_1^2, r_2^2, ..., r_n^2\}$. We denote d_{ij} as the distance of r_i^1 and r_j^2, and use s_{ij} to represent the significance value for the pair r_i^1 and r_j^2. The significance of r_i^1 and r_j^2 in I_1 and I_2 are denoted as s_i^1 and s_j^2, respectively. We initiate the significance value of a region as the area percentage of that region in a given image, assuming that important objects in an image tend to occupy larger areas. Therefore, s_i^1 is actually the area percentage of region i in image I_1. s_{ij} can be derived from s_i^1 and s_j^2, subject to the following constraint as given in Equation 6.

$$\sum_{j=1}^{n} s_{ij} = s_i^1 \quad \sum_{i=1}^{m} s_{ij} = s_j^2 \quad (6)$$

To find the first pair of best matched regions, we locate the minimum distance value in D matrix and obtain the corresponding row and column indices i and j. The significance values of regions i and j are then updated with Eqs.7 and 8 which make sure that the best matched region pair has the highest significance value. If $s_i^1 < s_j^2$, s_i^1 becomes 0, and region i in image I_1 will be removed from the next round of 'finding the best matched pair'. This is because we have already found the best matched region for r_i^1 in I_2. Similarly, if $s_j^2 < s_i^1$, s_j^2 becomes 0, and region j in I_2 will be removed from the next round.

$$s_i^1 = s_i^1 - \min(s_i^1, s_j^2) \quad (7)$$

$$s_j^2 = s_j^2 - \min(s_i^1, s_j^2) \quad (8)$$

We detail the construction procedure for S and D matrices as follows:

1. Initialize a $m \times n$ matrix $S_{1,2}$ for images I_1 (the query image) and I_2 (a candidate image) with its components being set to zeros.

2. Calculate the distance matrix $D_{1,2}$ for all region pairs in images I_1 and I_2.

3. Choose the minimum d_{ij}, and obtain the best matched region pair (r_i^1, r_j^2). $\min(s_i^1, s_j^2)$ is assigned to the corresponding element s_{ij} in the matrix $S_{1,2}$.

4. Update the significance values of regions s_i^1 and s_j^2 with Equation 7 and Equation 8. Eliminate those distance values from $D_{1,2}$ matrix that are associated with the region that should be removed according to the discussion aforementioned.

5. If $\sum_{i=1}^{m} s_i^1 \neq 0$ and $\sum_{j=1}^{n} s_j^2 \neq 0$, go to Step 3. Otherwise, go to Step 6, which indicates that we have finished the construction of the matrix $S_{1,2}$.

6. Calculate the integrated similarity score with Equation 4, return the top 30 most similar images from the ranked list for user feedback.

The initial weights of regions in the query image I_1 are all set to 1s, and therefore, the initial query results will be the same as that of the original IRM scheme. However, by incorporating users' feedback into the retrieval and integrated region matching, we can dynamically update the significance (weight) of each query region as follows:

For the query image I_1 and its region set $R_1 = \{r_1^1, r_2^1, ..., r_m^1\}$, a positive image I_{P1} with l regions is represented by a region set $R_{P1} = \{r_1^P1, r_2^P1, ..., r_l^P1\}$.

1. Construct the distance matrix $D_{1,P1}$ according to Equation 2.

2. For each row of $D_{1,P1}$, i.e., for each region in the query image, locate $\min(d_{ik})_{k=1,..., n}$ and calculate the inverse of $\min(d_{ik})$. Repeat the above calculation for each positive image labeled by the user and compute the updated weight of region i with Equation 5.

3. The updated weights of regions in the query image are recorded and will be used in the next round of retrieval for computing updated integrated similarity scores.

4. This feedback-retrieval process will run for several iterations until the user is satisfied with the returned results.

PERFORMANCE EVALUATION

In this section, we evaluate the performance of the proposed system by applying the proposed method on a Corel image database consisting of 8,900 images from 100 categories. After segmentation, there are in total 82,556 image segments. The number of clusters is selected to be 1,000 according to the discussion in the previous section. For each region in the query image, the cluster that contains that region is located. All segments in that cluster share similar semantic meaning since the extracted object features from them are similar. A set of such clusters forms the reduced search space for the subsequent retrieval based on IRM. In our case, the size of each region cluster ranges from 14 to 294 (regions). As aforementioned, an image can belong to more than one cluster if its regions are grouped into different clusters. By utilizing the clustering results, we are able to significantly reduce the search space, and the size of which is between 50 and 1,700 (images). The proposed feedback-retrieval framework is based on the candidate images in the reduced image set. Compared with the full image database search, the use of MGA effectively reduces the search space to about 10% of the original search space (8,900 images) on average, and thus, can reduce the time complexity significantly in the subsequent retrieval process.

Performance Evaluation Measures

In our experiments, we randomly select 50 images from 12 categories as query images. In addition, we adopt the Average Retrieval Rank (AVR), Average Normalized Modified Retrieval Rank (ANMRR)

(Cieplinski, 2001), and Accuracy as the standard performance measures for this dataset. The AVR and ANMRR measures are defined in Equations 9-10, respectively.

$$AVR(q) = \frac{1}{NG(q)} \sum_{k=1}^{NG(q)} Rank^*(k) \qquad (9)$$

In Equation 9, q is the current query; $NG(q)$ is the number of positive images in the top 30 returned images in our case; $\sum_{k=1}^{NG(q)} Rank^*(k)$ is the retrieval rank capped by the $Rank^{max}$ which is defined as the upper limit of the retrieval rank (30 in our case). However, AVR mainly focuses on the quality of ranking in the retrieval and is not very indicative of the total number of positive images returned by the retrieval system. Therefore, we use another measure called ANMRR measure which is the averaged MPEG-7 Normalized Modified Retrieval Rank (NMRR) over the query set, as defined in Equation 10.

$$NMRR(q) = \frac{AVR(q) - 0.5 * [1 + NG(q)]}{Rank^{max} - 0.5 * [1 + NG(q)]} \qquad (10)$$

In our retrieval system, the proposed system returns the top 30 images with the highest similarity scores as a short check-list to the user. The Accuracy is defined as the percentage of relevant images out of the returned short list, which is commonly and widely used as a criterion for performance measure in content-based image retrieval (Zhang & Chen, 2005). However, as a disadvantage, using Accuracy to measure retrieval performance cannot faithfully reflect the rank of the returned images.

In this article, the rank of a target image is defined as the ordinal position of a relevant/positive image in the retrieved image list. It is obviously that a good retrieval system should return all the relevant images at the top of the list, i.e., a lower value in rank. For example, the

lowest (or best) rank is 1, and the highest rank is 30. A true positive image becomes a missed hit or false negative if it does not appear in the short list. Therefore, it is important to consider the rank of the retrieved relevant image since it directly reflects the retrieval performance. We adopt not only the Accuracy measure to demonstrate the effectiveness of the retrieval results, but also the AVR and ANMRR measures to evaluate the rank of the retrieved relevant image.

The AVR measure fairly ranks the retrieval results if the numbers of target images retrieved from different results are the same. However, problem occurs when comparing results with different number of relevant images returned. For instance, the AVR measure is 1 if only one relevant image is retrieved at the top 1 ordinal position. Similarly, the AVR measure is 1.5 if only two target images are retrieved at the top 2 ordinal positions. In the above example, the performance of the latter is better than that of the former; however, the AVR measure does not reflect this fact directly. Therefore, in this article, we evaluate the performance mainly using the ANMRR and Accuracy measures although we list all the three measures in the experimental results.

In our experimental setting, five rounds of relevance feedback are performed for each query image - Initial with no feedback, First, Second, Third, and Fourth. AVR, Accuracy, and ANMRR (Cieplinski, 2001) are individually calculated for the top 30 retrieved images.

The Effectiveness of MGA in Reducing the Search Scope

In this experiment, we study the performance of the proposed FIRM scheme with and without the use of MGA in reducing the search scope. The motivation of this experiment is to show that without significantly sacrificing the performance of image retrieval, MGA can effectively narrow down the search scope, and therefore, reduce the time complexity. We present the experimental results in Table 2 which compares the performance in terms of AVR, ANMRR, and Accuracy measures.

In Table 2, FIRM indicates that MGA is used in the proposed scheme, while FULL indicates that MGA is not used in the proposed matching scheme, i.e., a full database search is performed. Through this comparison, the lower AVR and ANMRR values indicate better performance. On the contrary, higher accuracy indicates better retrieval results.

In general, full search (FULL) should have a better retrieval performance than that of FIRM which is performed on a much reduced search space, and this is evidenced by ANMRR and Accuracy measures in Table 2. The AVR, as mentioned earlier in the previous subsection, cannot faithfully reflect the retrieval performance when the numbers of target images retrieved are different. However, it is still worth noting that FIRM with MGA demonstrates a better performance than FULL in terms of AVR (see Table 2).

It is worth noting that as a trade off, full-scope search achieves better retrieval accuracy at the cost of significantly higher time complexity, while FIRM trades accuracy for efficiency, which is essential for a practical integrated region-based image retrieval system. In our current implementation, with full search, it takes about 4 minutes to perform one single iteration of query for one query image (there are 5 iterations involved in our experiments), while it only takes about 20 seconds to perform the same query with FIRM and

MGA. This indicates that the full search becomes impractical when the size of the image database rapidly grows. Besides, we can observe from Table 2 that the performance of both FIRM and FULL are gradually improved through iterations, owing to the use of relevance feedback. It is also worth noting that at the end of the fourth round of retrieval, the performance of FIRM with MGA is very close to that of FULL.

The Effectiveness of Relevance Feedback

We further compare the proposed framework (FIRM), i.e., feedback-based integrated region matching, with the traditional IRM (IRM) by using the above three evaluation criteria. We illustrate the comparison results in Figure 3 which shows the AVR, ANMRR, and Accuracy of tradition IRM and that of the proposed framework (FIRM) with four iterations of feedback and retrieval.

In Figure 3, lower AVR and ANMRR scores indicate better performance. On the contrary, higher accuracy indicates better retrieval performance. The AVR, ANMRR, and Accuracy values of the proposed framework (FIRM) are 12.07, 0.23, and 0.41, respectively, while those of the traditional IRM (IRM) are 12.64, 0.26, and 0.39, respectively. The experimental results indicate that the proposed framework (FIRM) outperforms the tradition IRM (IRM) scheme, which also show the effectiveness of integrating IRM with rele-

Table 2. The effectiveness of MGA

#	AVR		ANMRR		Accuracy	
	FIRM	*FULL*	*FIRM*	*FULL*	*FIRM*	*FULL*
1	12.64	14.69	0.325	0.255	0.395	0.436
2	12.39	14.56	0.318	0.247	0.399	0.441
3	11.90	17.71	0.320	0.235	0.392	0.451
4	11.98	14.20	0.300	0.230	0.400	0.445
5	12.07	14.16	0.299	0.229	0.408	0.446

#: 1: Initial; 2: First; 3: Second; 4: Third; 5: Fourth

Figure 3. Comparison of IRM with FIRM

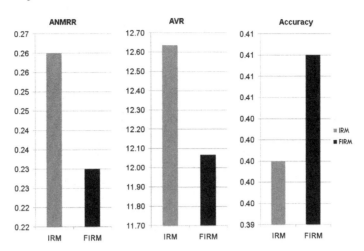

Figure 4. Comparison of FIRM, DRM, and SVM based on AVR measure

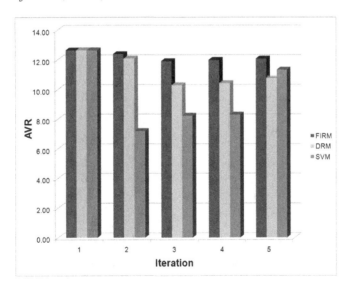

vance feedback. It is worth pointing out that the retrieval is performed on a much reduced search space with at most 1,700 images in the candidate pool. The noise level is significantly lower than that in a full image database. It is our expectation that the superiority of the proposed method over the original IRM will be more evident if the retrieval is performed on the full image database. However, due to the time consuming nature of full search, the related experiments will be included in our future work.

Compare the Proposed Framework FIRM with DRM and SVM

In this experiment, we compare the performance of FIRM with two other existing approaches, including Dynamic Region Matching (DRM) and Support Vector Machine (SVM). This experiment aims to evaluate the learning algorithms used in the relevance feedback process. We apply the above three methods on the same test images and compare their performance with the three evalua-

Figure 5. Comparison of FIRM, DRM, and SVM based on ANMRR measure

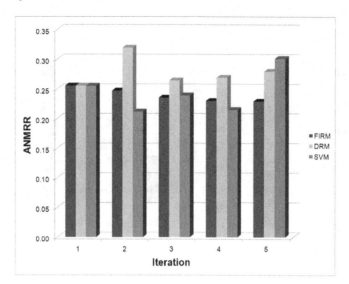

Figure 6. Comparison of FIRM, DRM, and SVM based on Accuracy measure

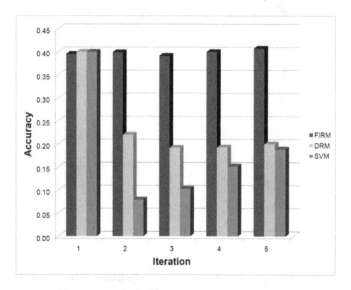

tion measures. Figures 4-6 show the comparison results in terms of the AVR, ANMRR, and Accuracy measures, respectively.

According to our experimental results, the overall results of SVM and DRM are not as good as that of FIRM in terms of the ANMRR and Accuracy measures. In constructing the SVM for comparison, each positive image is used as a training data sample. And each input dimension of the One-Class SVM corresponds to a region in the query image, and its input value is calculated as $\sum_{j=1}^{n} s_{ij} d_{ij}$ for each region i in the query image. Through the learning of SVM using user feedback, a reasonably good combination of all query regions can be gradually discovered and used for future retrieval. In this study, we used a non-linear kernel (Radial Basis Function) for One-Class SVM learning.

The reason that DRM performs worse than FIRM is that the weights of regions in the query image are either increased or decreased by a fixed factor through relevance feedback, and therefore, some regions in the query image may quickly overpower the others through iterations of feedback-retrieval. Consequently, the performance gain obtained through feedback is limited.

In addition, we can observe from these three figures that the proposed framework (FIRM) has the best performance in terms of ANMRR and Accuracy values. However, the AVR measure does not second this observation. The reason is due to the problem of AVR as mentioned in the first subsection of this section.

CONCLUSION

In this article, we present a Feedback-based Image Clustering and Retrieval Framework (FIRM) which improves the region-based image retrieval accuracy and efficiency by using a novel image clustering algorithm and integrating it with Integrated Region Matching (IRM) and relevance feedback. In our framework, images are first segmented into regions, then the Modified Genetic Algorithm (MGA) is applied to cluster image regions, resulting clusters of images with similar regions. This process effectively narrows down the search scope and, therefore, reduces the time-complexity in the subsequent retrieval step. IRM is then adopted with a new region-matching scheme that is suitable for relevance feedback, which measures the overall similarity between two images based on overall weighted region similarities. In addition, relevance feedback is adopted in this framework to reduce the semantic gap, which helps to progressively learn the user's preferred query regions based on the user selected positive images from the query results.

The performance of the system is evaluated on a large image database containing 8,900 general-purpose images with 82,556 image regions. Our experimental results demonstrate that MGA can effectively reduce the search space by 90%. In addition, the results in Figure 3 show significant improvement in Accuracy, Average Retrieval Rank (AVR), and Normalized Modified Retrieval Rank (NMRR), when compared with IRM without feedback. By comparing the proposed method with dynamic region matching (DRM) and support vector machines (SVM), we also demonstrate that the proposed learning algorithm outperforms both DRM and SVM.

REFERENCES

Babu, K. S., & Nagesh, V. (2008, March 9). Optimal solution for image retrieval using integrated region matching. In *Proceedings of the 2ⁿᵈ National Conference on Challenges & Opportunities in Information Technology (COIT-2008),* Mandi Gobindgarh, India (pp. 223 226).

Bradshaw, B. (2000, October 30-November 3). Semantic based image retrieval: A probabilistic approach. In *Proceedings of ACM Multimedia 2000*, Marina del Rey, CA (pp. 167-176).

Carson, C., Belongie, S., Greenspan, H., & Malik, J. (2002). Blobworld: image segmentation using expectation-maximization and its application to image querying. *IEEE Transactions on Pattern Analysis and Machine Intelligence, 24*(8), 1026–1038. doi:10.1109/TPAMI.2002.1023800

Carson, C., Thomas, M., & Belongie, E. A. S. (1999). Blobworld: A system for region based image indexing and retrieval. In *Proceedings of the 3ʳᵈ International Conference on Visual Information System*, Amsterdam, The Netherlands (pp. 509-516).

Chen, S.-C., Sista, S., Shyu, M.-L., & Kashyap, R. L. (2000, January). An indexing and searching structure for multimedia database systems. In *Proceedings of the IS&T/SPIE Conference on Storage and Retrieval for Media Databases*, Santa Clara, CA (pp. 262-270).

Cieplinski, L. (2001). MPEG-7 color descriptors and their applications. In *Computer analysis of images and patterns* (pp. 11-20). Heidelberg, Germany: Springer Berlin.

Ding, Q., & Gasvoda, J. (2005). A genetic algorithm for clustering on image data. *International Journal of Computational Intelligence, 1*(1), 75–80.

Hamada, M., Martz, H. F., Reese, C. S., & Wilson, A. G. (2001). Statistical practice: finding near-optimal bayesian experimental designs via genetic algorithms. *The American Statistician, 55*(3), 175–181. doi:10.1198/000313001317098121

Hansen, N. (2008). *The CMA evolution strategy: A tutorial*. Retrieved April 2008, from http://lautaro.fb10.tu-berlin.de/user/niko/cmatutorial.pdf

Haupt, R. L., & Haupt, S. E. (2004). *Practical genetic algorithms*. New York: John Wiley & Sons.

Ji, R. R., Yao, H. X., & Liang, D. W. (2008). DRM: dynamic region matching for image retrieval using probabilistic fuzzy matching and boosting feature selection. *Signal, Image and Video Processing, 2*(1), 59–71. doi:10.1007/s11760-007-0037-0

Myers, R. H., & Montgomery, D. C. (2002). *Response surface methodology: Process and product optimization using designed experiments*. New York: John Wiley & Sons.

Ortiz, F., Simpson, J. R., Pignatiello, J. J., & Heredia-Langner, A. (2004). A genetic algorithm approach to multiple-response optimization. *Journal of Quality Technology, 36*(4), 432–450.

Su, Z., Zhang, H. J., & Ma, S. P. (2000, November 13-15). Using bayesian classifier in relevant feedback of image retrieval. In *Proceedings of the IEEE International Conference on Tools with Artifitial Intelligence*, Vancouver, BC, Canada (pp. 258-261).

Tomassini, M. (1998). A survey of genetic algorithm. *Annual Reviews of Computational. Physics, 3*, 87–118.

Wan, W. (2007). *Semi-parametric techniques for multi-oesponse optimization*. Doctoral dissertation, Virginia Polytechnic Institute and State University.

Wang, J. Z., Li, J., & Wiederhold, G. (2001). SIMPLIcity: Semantics-sensitive integrated matching for picture libraries. *IEEE Transactions on Pattern Analysis and Machine Intelligence, 23*, 947–963. doi:10.1109/34.955109

Yang, C., & Lozano-Prez, T. (2000, February 28-March 3). Image database retrieval with multiple-instance learning techniques. In *Proceedings of the 16th International Conference on Data Engineering,* San Diego, CA (pp. 233-243).

Zhang, C., Chen, S.-C., Shyu, M.-L., & Peeta, S. (2003, December 15-18). Adaptive background learning for vehicle detection and spatio-temporal tracking. In *Proceedings of the 4th IEEE Pacific-Rim Conference on Multimedia*, Singapore (pp. 1-5).

Zhang, C., & Chen, X. (2005, August 21-24). OCRS: An interactive object-based image clustering and retrieval system. In *Proceedings of the 4th International Workshop on Multimedia Data Mining (MDM/KDD2005), ACM SIGKDD International Conference on Knowledge Discovery & Data Mining,* Chicago (pp. 71-78).

Zhang, C., & Chen, X. (2005, July 20-22). Region-based image clustering and retrieval using multiple instance learning. In *Proceedings of the International Conference on Image and Video Retrieval*, Singapore (pp. 194-204).

This work was previously published in the International Journal of Multimedia Data Engineering and Management, Volume 1, Issue 1, edited by Shu-Ching Chen, pp. 55-74, copyright 2010 by IGI Publishing (an imprint of IGI Global).

Chapter 6
Tissue Image Classification Using Multi-Fractal Spectra

Ramakrishnan Mukundan
University of Canterbury, New Zealand

Anna Hemsley
University of Canterbury, New Zealand

ABSTRACT

Tissue image classification is a challenging problem due to the fact that the images contain highly irregular shapes in complex spatial arrangement. The multi-fractal formalism has been found useful in characterizing the intensity distribution present in such images, as it can effectively resolve local densities and also represent various structures present in the image. This paper presents a detailed study of feature vectors derived from the distribution of Holder exponents and the geometrical characteristics of the multi-fractal spectra that can be used in applications requiring image classification and retrieval. The paper also gives the results of experimental analysis performed using a tissue image database and demonstrates the effectiveness of the proposed multi-fractal-based descriptors in tissue image classification and retrieval. Implementation aspects that need to be considered for improving classification accuracy and the feature representation capability of the proposed descriptors are also outlined.

INTRODUCTION

Automatic methods for image recognition and classification are increasingly being used in the field of biomedical image processing (Maree, 2005; Esgiar & Chakravorty, 2007). Robust classification algorithms are particularly useful in

applications involving large-scale image databases with associated operations such as content based retrieval and analysis. In recent years, there has been a rapid growth in the availability and use of new techniques and systems for cell and tissue imaging. Tissue diagnostics play a key role in the screening, treatment and monitoring of diseases. Large tissue image databases containing hundreds of specimens and histological types are com-

DOI: 10.4018/978-1-4666-1791-9.ch006

monly used in diagnostic services and research in the areas of tissue engineering and telemedicine (Filippas et al., 2003). Further, online databases containing tissue microarray images are now publicly available for research groups. Therefore, there is a renewed interest in methods for tissue image classification, indexing and mining (Gholap et al., 2005). In this paper we present a framework based on multi-fractal formalism for the construction of efficient feature descriptors for tissue image classification and retrieval. The primary motivation for our work is the need for robust algorithms for classifying tissue images based on spatial relationships between various structures present in each tissue class. Such algorithms could be further extended to complement histological techniques for identifying/indexing regions of pathological interest.

Tissue and cell images can be categorized into a broad class of irregularly shaped statistically self-similar objects, suggesting the application fractal based methods for their classification. Shapes with statistical self-similarity are characterized by the property that they have certain statistical properties or measures that are preserved across various scales. Several examples can be found in nature, such as trees, mountainous terrains, clouds and blood vessels (Mandelbrot, 1982). Fractal structures can be classified using a numerical measure called the fractal dimension. Such a classification of tissue images into normal and cancerous, purely on the basis of fractal dimension computed from the image, can be found in (Esgiar & Chakravorty, 2007). It has been shown that tissue images contain a collection of several fractal structures with varying dimension at varying strengths (Reljin, Reljin, & Pavlovic, 2000; Reljin & Reljin, 2002). The composition of several fractal dimensions is called multi-fractality (Falconer, 2003; Arbeiter & Patzschke, 1996). The multi-fractal theory and the associated multi-fractal spectrum are useful for describing the irregularities of biomedical images (Uma, Ramakrishnan, & Anathakrishna, 1996; Qi & Yu, 2008). Methods based on multi-

fractal spectra have been recently developed for the analysis of retinal images (Stosic & Stosic, 2006), digital mammograms (Stojic, Reljin, & Reljin, 2006), brain MRI images (Ruan & Bloyet, 2000) and DNA sequences (Kinsner & Zhang, 2009). Multi-fractal geometry has also been used for the analysis of various other phenomena such as sleep EEGs (Song et al., 2007), human gait (Munoz-Diasdado, 2005), and facial expressions (Yap et al., 2009).

The intensity distribution in tissue and cell images does not permit a straightforward definition of shape parameters using geometrical descriptors. In singular fractals (Musgrave, 2004), the local intensity distribution at each pixel, within a particular region, scales with the region size, and the structure obeys such a scaling law where the exponent is a function of the fractal dimension. Multi-fractal images, on the other hand, consist of several such structures with different fractal dimensions, coexisting simultaneously. Multi-fractal analysis is based on the assumption that one can define measures of local intensity distribution that scale according to a power law; in this case each different exponent represents a different fractal structure with its own fractal dimension. The scaling exponents also called coarse Holder exponents, together with the multi-fractal spectrum can be used as a statistical characterization of the overall image structure. Multi-fractal analysis can also be used to provide local information, and to isolate regions of a particular fractal dimension (Reljin, Reljin, & Pavlovic, 2000).

This paper introduces a novel framework for tissue image classification and retrieval that uses the multi-fractal property of the images. Tissue image classification has been previously attempted using techniques such as wavelet transforms and discriminant analysis (Hwang et al., 2005; Aksoy et al., 2002). Our paper proposes a completely different approach, and presents two new texture feature descriptors: one constructed from the histogram of Holder exponents in the image, and the second from the geometrical properties of the multi-fractal spectra. Theoretical as well as implementation aspects related to the multi-fractal-based system for classification and retrieval is detailed. A database of tissue images is used in the experimental analysis, and the results of both classification and retrieval tasks show the efficiency and discriminating power of the proposed features.

The paper is organized as follows: The next section gives an outline of common intensity-based measures used in multi-fractal analysis, and a brief overview of the process of computing the multi-fractal spectrum of an image. The section "Feature vectors and similarity computation" introduces two different types of feature vectors and the associated similarity functions that can be used to construct feature descriptors for tissue image classification and retrieval. The experimental analysis section gives a comparison of multi-fractal features for different classes of a tissue image database, and presents the results of classification and retrieval tasks. The section on implementation aspects details some of the intensity transformations that are useful in the computation of the feature descriptors. Finally, the paper concludes with a summary of the work reported, and an outline of future work.

MULTI-FRACTAL MEASURES AND SPECTRA

Tissue images contain several regions of abrupt changes in intensity values. An intensity- based measure is commonly used to represent the degree of intensity variation at each pixel position. Tissue images also contain an internal structure formed by several statistically self-similar patterns. In other words, a tissue image can be viewed as a combination of regions with different fractal properties. The multi-fractal spectrum characterizes this structure in terms of fractal dimensions of patterns that

have similar local intensity gradients (Falconer, 2003; Blunt, 1989). The multi-fractal spectrum computed from an image therefore depends on an intensity- based measure that represents local variations of intensity values. This variation at a pixel P is measured in the neighborhood of P using a small window W of size r, centered at P. We denote the measure function as $\mu_p(r)$. A valid measure must satisfy the following properties:

$\mu_P(r) > 0$, for all P, and $r>0$.

$\mu_P(r) = 0$, only if $r=0$.

$$\mu_P(r) \geq \mu_P(s) \text{ if } r > s, \text{ for all } P. \tag{1}$$

We also require that $\mu_p(r)$ scales with r according to the power law:

$$\mu_P(r) = C\, r^{\alpha_P} \tag{2}$$

where C is a constant of proportionality. The term α_p, the coarse Holder exponent, is an important term in characterizing the variation of intensity (or the local regularity) at point P (Arbeiter, 1996; Falconer, 2003; Riedi, 1999). A few commonly used definitions for $\mu_p(r)$ are outlined below. A detailed analysis of these measures can be found in a previous publication (Hemsley & Mukundan, 2009).

Sum Measure

The Sum measure is perhaps the most commonly used for multi-fractal analysis, and is defined as the sum of intensity values within W. This measure satisfies the conditions in (1) and (2).

A. Normalized Sum Measure

This measure normalizes the above sum measure to the range [0,1] by defining

$$\mu_P(r) = \frac{\sum\limits_{(i,j)\in W} g(i,j)}{\sum\limits_{(i,j)\in I} g(i,j)} \qquad (3)$$

where $g(i,j)$ is the grayscale intensity at pixel (i,j), and I is the set of all pixels within the image.

B. Maximum Intensity Measure

The Maximum intensity measure defines $\mu_p(r)$ to be equal to the maximum intensity value within the window W. Although this measure satisfies the required conditions in (1), the variation of μ with r may not strictly obey the power law in (2). Should a local maximum intensity be encountered within a window, the measure will remain constant for all subsequent windows of increasing size r, and the estimate of α may be inaccurate.

C. Inverse Minimum Measure

A minimum intensity measure, where $\mu_p(r)$ is equal to the minimum intensity value in each window W (Liu & Li, 1997; Reljin et al., 2000; Stojic et al., 2006) will result in negative α values, as the measure obeys an inverse power law, and thus is unsuitable. As an alternative, we can invert the computed minimum value, with respect to global maximum intensity I_{MAX}, to define an "Inverse Minimum" measure that has the required scaling property in (1):

$$\mu_P(r) = I_{MAX} - W_{MIN} \qquad (4)$$

where W_{MIN} is the minimum grayscale intensity inside the window W. However, like the Maximum measure, this Inverse Minimum measure will not always obey the power law in (2).

D. Iso Measure

The Iso measure provides a representation of a two-dimensional isosurface in the window, and

is equal to the number of pixels with intensity same as that of the centre pixel P. A modified Iso measure has also been proposed (Stojic, Reljin, & Reljin, 2006), where intensities are compared within a degree of accuracy, such as ± 2% of the intensity range.

E. Sum of Absolute Differences: SAD Measure

A SAD measure can also be defined where $\mu_p(r)$ is equal to the sum of absolute intensity differences between P and the remaining pixels in the window W:

$$\mu_P(r) = \sum_{(i,j)\in W} |g_P - g(i,j)| \qquad (5)$$

where g_p is the intensity at P, and $g(i,j)$ the intensity at location (i,j).

There are a number of methods available for computing the multi-fractal spectrum of an image with a chosen measure (Chhabra & Jensen, 1989; Renyi, 1970; Tricot, 1993; Dansereau & Kinsner, 2001). For our analysis, we consider a method based on direct estimation of the Holder exponent at each pixel position (Levy-Vehel, Mignot, & Berroir, 1992; Reljin & Reljin, 2002). This method is particularly suited for image analysis applications (Stosic & Stosic, 2006) and uses a two-pass algorithm. In the first pass, the Holder exponents are estimated, and in the second pass, the fractal dimensions corresponding to different ranges of exponent values are computed (Figure 1). The value of $\mu_p(r)$ is first computed on m concentric square windows surrounding each pixel P, where the size of each square is given by

$$r = 2k+1, \ k = 0, 1, 2, ..., m-1. \qquad (6)$$

In the above equation, m denotes the total number of windows used. The value of α_p at P is then estimated as the slope of the linear regression line through points on a log-log plot where $\log(r)$

Figure 1. Computation of the multi-fractal spectrum using a direct estimation of the Holder exponent α at each pixel position, and box-counting method for computing the fractal dimensions corresponding to each α value

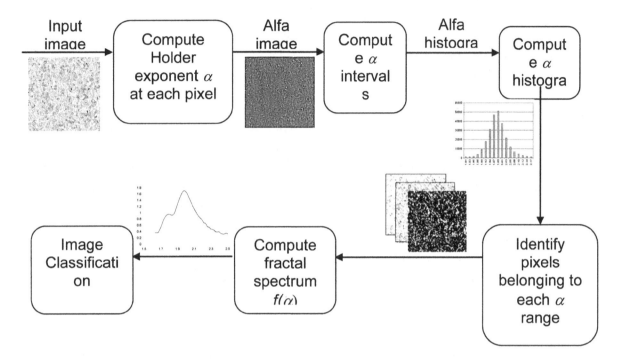

is plotted along the *x*-axis, and $\log(\mu_p(r))$ along the *y*-axis.

The exponent α_p also establishes a mapping from the original intensity image to an *α*-image where the intensity at *P* represents the exponent at that point. The range of *α* values is further subdivided into a set of *n* small discrete intervals $\alpha_0, \alpha_1, \alpha_2 \ldots \alpha_n$. The *α* histogram gives the number of points with *α* values falling within each of these intervals.

For each α_i, only those pixels containing *α* values belonging to the interval $[\alpha_i, \alpha_{i+1}]$, $i=0..n-1$ are considered, and the collection of these pixels form a binary sub-image that can be considered as an "*α*-slice" of the original image. The fractal dimension of the resulting image can be computed using the box-counting method (Falconer, 2003). The computed value defines the spectral component $f(\alpha)$ corresponding to the range $[\alpha_i, \alpha_{i+1}]$. The values $f(\alpha)$ collectively give the multi-fractal spectrum of the original image. If the image has *N*x*N* pixels, the computation of the *α*-image takes $O(N^2(2m+1)^2)$ time. The estimation of the box-counting dimension for each sub-interval of the *α*-range requires on an average $O((N^2/2)\log N)$ time.

FEATURE VECTORS AND SIMILARITY COMPUTATION

Classification and retrieval operations on image databases require a feature descriptor comprising of a feature vector and a similarity computation to identify the best matching image class. Robust classifiers need to take into account important characteristics of images present in the database. Tissue images are characterized by a collection of highly irregular patterns, and therefore we use the multi-fractal formalism to construct feature vectors. A feature vector based on the Holder exponent α would be invariant to scale variations in the measure function $\mu_p(r)$. We propose two different types of feature vectors for classification and retrieval of tissue images – one based on alpha-histogram, and the other based on the multi-fractal spectra.

A. Feature Vector Based on Alpha-Histogram

Color histograms are commonly used as image descriptors in content based indexing and retrieval. We could use the histogram hist(α), computed from the α-image (Figure 1) to form a feature vector. As described in the previous section, the range of values of computed Holder exponents at each pixel $[\alpha_{MIN}, \alpha_{MAX}]$ is divided into 100 intervals $\alpha_0(= \alpha_{MIN})$, α_1, α_2,...$\alpha_{100}(=\alpha_{MAX})$, and for each α_i, the number of pixels h_i with α values in the range $[\alpha_i, \alpha_{i+1}]$ gives the alpha-histogram. The feature vector $\{ h_i \mid i = 0,...99 \}$ can be directly used with an L1-distance (Manhattan distance) function for classification. An alpha-histogram generally has a bell-shape, with variations mainly in the values of α_{MIN}, α_{MAX}, and max($h(\alpha)$). The dimension of the feature vector can therefore be greatly reduced by storing only the primary geometrical shape features of the histogram, as outlined in the next section on experimental analysis. The main advantage of using the alpha-histogram is that the second pass of computation for extracting the multi-fractal spectrum need not be performed for any of the images.

B. Feature Vector Based on Multi-Fractal Spectrum

Compared to the alpha-histogram, the multi-fractal spectrum contains the additional information of the degree of statistical self similarity of structures within the image that are formed by pixels where the Holder exponents are nearly equal. As in the case of the alpha-histogram, the values of

$f(\alpha)$ could also be stored as a vector $\{ f(\alpha_i) \mid i = 0,...99 \}$, and then compared using L1-distance function. Unlike the alpha-histogram, the multi-fractal spectrum contains several shape features that need to be accounted for while trying to reduce the dimension of the feature vector. The spectrum also exhibits high frequency variations at both ends of the α-range (Figure 2a). We propose below a method based on piece-wise cubic polynomial approximation for the construction of a reduced feature set.

We subdivide the multi-fractal spectrum into four or five sections based on the location of sharp changes in tangent directions. Given a set of points (x_i, y_i) in a section, we use least square error method to find the coefficients c_i of the cubic polynomial $y = c_0 + c_1 x + c_2 x^2$ that closely approximates the graph within each section. Alternatively we could also use Bernstein cubic polynomials using just four control points per section. The cubic polynomial approximation is found to capture essential geometrical characteristics of the spectrum (Figure 2b). The feature vector consists of the number of sections, the α values at section boundaries, and the polynomial coefficients for each section:

$$V = \{ n, \alpha_0, \alpha_1,..., \alpha_n, c_{00}, c_{10}, c_{20}, c_{01}, c_{11}, c_{21}, ..., c_{0(n-1)}, c_{1(n-1)}, c_{2(n-1)} \}. \quad (7)$$

The similarity computation between two curves with different ranges of α values normally requires linear interpolation for each point of the test data. This problem is eliminated by the use of approximating functions, and the L1 distance at any point $(\alpha, f(\alpha))$ of a test data is easily obtained as $|f(\alpha) - (c_{0i} + c_{1i} \alpha + c_{2i} \alpha^2)|$ where $\alpha_i \leq \alpha \leq \alpha_{i+1}$.

EXPERIMENTAL ANALYSIS

In this section, we present the results of classification and retrieval using a database consisting of six different classes of images (Figure 3). Each image

Figure 2. (a) A multi-fractal spectrum subdivided into 5 sections (b) Piecewise cubic polynomial curve approximation of the multi-fractal spectrum

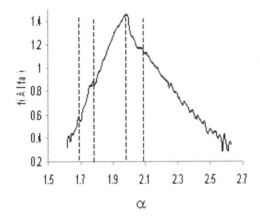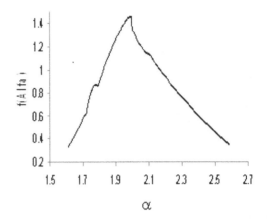

consists of 256x256 grayscale values derived from images in Stanford Tissue Microarray Database.

For a successful multi-fractal spectra-based classification scheme, the feature vector must exhibit minimum intra-class variation and good inter-class variance. This property holds for both types of feature vectors introduced in the previous section. A detailed comparative analysis of the inter- and intra-class variation of multi-fractal

Figure 3. The database of 54 grayscale images of size 256x256 pixels, used for spectra calculations and classification experiments

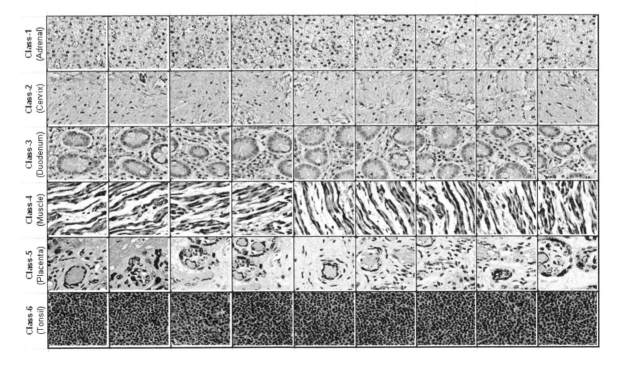

Figure 4. Alpha-histograms of each class used in the classification experiment. The x-axis represents the values of the Holder exponent α, and the y-axis denotes the number of pixels in the image that have a given value within a small interval around α.

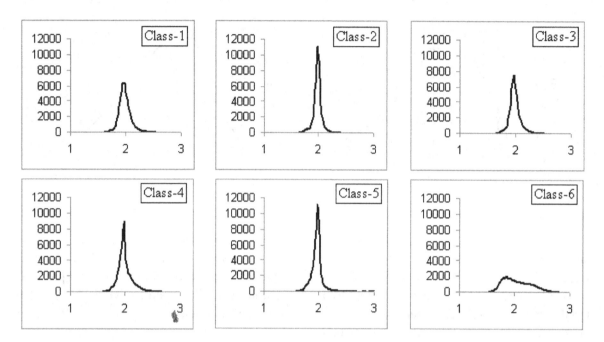

spectra for different measures can be found in (Hemsley & Mukundan, 2009).

We first consider the use of a feature vector based on the alpha-histogram. The feature set for each class is obtained as the average of features derived from three randomly chosen images belonging to the class. The Holder exponents were computed using the sum measure, and the alpha-histograms for each class are shown in Figure 4. For the purpose of comparison, the axes have uniform scales. Note that classes 2 and 5 have very similar alpha-histograms.

The feature vector consisted of 100 values $\{h_i|$ $i=0...99\}$, where the α-range is quantized into 100 intervals as follows:

$$i = \text{trunc}(25\alpha + 0.5), \quad h_i = \text{hist}(\alpha), \quad \alpha < 4.0. \quad (8)$$

The classification results obtained using the above scheme are shown in Figure 5a, as a confusion matrix. In order to reduce the dimension of

the feature vector, we take note of the fact that the maximum value of the histogram occurs at $\alpha=2.0$, and this corresponds to h_{49} when the α range from 0 to 4 is quantized into 100 integer values according to (8). We used 5 values around the peak of the histogram to construct the reduced feature vector as follows,

$$V = \{h_{41}, h_{45}, h_{49}, h_{53}, h_{57}\} \quad (9)$$

and the smallest sum of absolute differences between corresponding elements as the similarity metric for classification. The reduced feature vectors for each image class, derived from the histograms in Figure 4 are given in Table 1. The classification results obtained using this set are given in Figure 5b.

Figure 5a shows accurate results for classes 3, 4, and 6, and acceptable results for other classes, given that the alfa-histograms have similar shapes for classes 1 and 3, and classes 2

Figure 5. Confusion matrices obtained using (A) full, and (B) reduced feature vectors constructed from alpha-histograms. The entries show percentages of images classified.

(A)
Predicted

Actual	c1	c2	c3	c4	c5	c6
c1	67	0	33	0	0	0
c2	0	89	11	0	0	0
c3	0	0	100	0	0	0
c4	0	0	0	100	0	0
c5	0	22	0	0	78	0
c6	0	0	0	0	0	100

(B)
Predicted

Actual	c1	c2	c3	c4	c5	c6
c1	78	0	22	0	0	0
c2	0	56	11	0	33	0
c3	0	0	100	0	0	0
c4	0	0	11	89	0	0
c5	0	78	11	0	11	0
c6	0	0	0	0	0	100

and 5. Figure 5b shows that classification error has increased with the reduction of the length of the feature vector from 100 to 5. This is particularly noticeable for class-5, where 78% of the images were misclassified as belonging to class-2. Alfa-histograms, though simple to construct, do not have sufficient inter-class variation.

Multi-fractal spectra show excellent intra-class invariance (Hemsley & Mukundan, 2009). However, the desired property of discriminating power or good inter-class variation can be obtained only with the selection of appropriate intensity measures used for computing the Holder exponents. It has been shown that sum and inverse-minimum measures give good inter-class variance. We present below the results for the sum and iso measures. The multi-fractal spectra with the sum measure,

Table 1. Reduced feature set derived from the alpha-histograms in Figure 4

	h_{41}	h_{45}	h_{49}	h_{53}	h_{57}
Class-1	163	1545	11951	2421	515
Class-2	105	1019	19833	1210	167
Class-3	112	1260	14745	2271	454
Class-4	180	1906	14289	2801	848
Class-5	186	1961	17895	977	364
Class-6	999	4233	3609	2836	2448

computed from the first image of each class are shown in Figure 6. For the analysis reported in the previous paragraph, we had used the average of three alpha-histograms for each class. However, for constructing the feature vector using multi-fractal spectra, we use only one image as representing the whole class, and piecewise cubic polynomial curves (Figure 2b) for a smooth approximation of the spectrum. The feature vector in all the cases discussed below have the form given in (7).

The multi-fractal spectra computed using the iso measure are given in Figure 7. As can be seen from the figure, the iso surface gives poor inter-class variation compared to the sum measure. Further, the iso measure gives a maximum value in windows with constant intensity distribution. In this case, the measure value increases as the square of the window size. Thus the maximum value of the Holder exponent α can only be 2. The confusion matrices obtained from the classification experiment using sum and iso measures are given in Figure 8. While the sum measure gave the overall best result, the iso measure was able to discriminate images in class 1 and 3 effectively. Ways of further improving the classification accuracy are discussed in the next section on implementation aspects.

Figure 6. Multi-fractal spectra computed using the sum measure from a single image selected from each class. Each spectrum is then converted into a set of cubic polynomial curves, and the polynomials coefficients are used in the similarity computation.

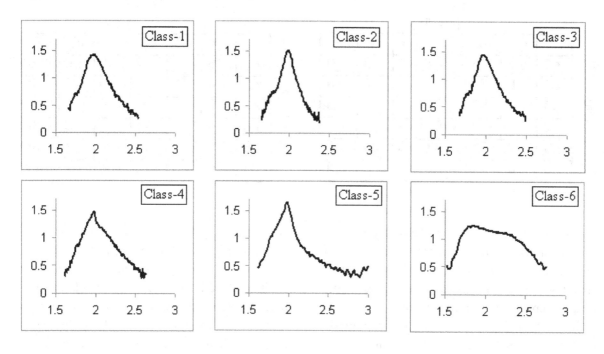

Figure 7. Multi-fractal spectra computed using the iso measure from a single image selected from each class

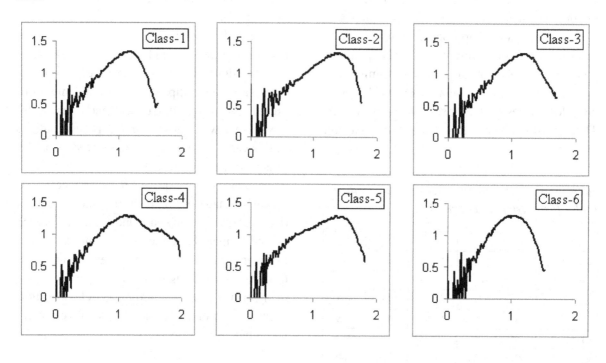

We now explore the suitability of the multi-fractal approach in an image retrieval algorithm. The framework used is different to that of classification in the following aspects:

- The database consists of not only tissue images but also several other images including synthetic images and images of natural objects such as clouds, water leaves and trees.
- One of the images from the class of tissue images is selected randomly, and used as the query image.
- The feature vectors of the classes (Figures 4 and 6) are not used. The cubic polynomial approximations of multi-fractal spectra which were pre-computed for each class are also there not used. In fact, none of the class specific information is available to the system.
- The features of the images in the database are compared directly with features of the query image. Feature descriptors are derived from the multi-fractal spectra of the query image and the test image, and then compared. Details of the feature vector used are given below.

The feature vector for the retrieval system consisted of 100 values $\{f_i | i = 0 \ldots 99\}$, where the α-range is quantized into 100 intervals, similar to (8).

$$i = \text{trunc}(25\alpha + 0.5), f_i = f(\alpha), \alpha < 4.0. \tag{10}$$

where $f(\alpha)$ denotes valued of the multi-fractal spectrum. The uniform quantized α-scale is useful for a direct one-to-one comparison of the multi-fractal spectra of the query and test images, without the need for any interpolation. For similarity computation, metrics like sum of absolute differences and sum of squared differences could be considered, but we prefer a point-wise similarity of the multi-fractal spectra rather than similarity in an average sense. We count the number of points n where the spectrum magnitude is greater than 0.4, and the absolute difference is greater than a pre-defined threshold T, i.e.,

$$n = \#\{i: |f_i - f_i''| > T, f_i > 0.4 \} \tag{11}$$

If n is less than 10% of the total number of points with $f_i > 0.4$, the image is retrieved. The threshold 0.4 for the spectrum magnitude is used to compare only significant values, and not the noisy region at both ends of the spectrum (see Figures 5 and 6). The second threshold T used

Figure 8. Classification results based on multi-fractal spectra computed using (A) sum measure, and (B) iso measure. The entries show percentages of images classified.

(A)

Predicted

		c1	c2	c3	c4	c5	c6
Actual	c1	67	0	33	0	0	0
	c2	0	100	0	0	0	0
	c3	0	0	100	0	0	0
	c4	0	0	0	100	0	0
	c5	0	11	0	0	89	0
	c6	0	0	0	0	0	100

(B)

Predicted

		c1	c2	c3	c4	c5	c6
Actual	c1	100	0	0	0	0	0
	c2	0	89	11	0	0	0
	c3	0	0	100	0	0	0
	c4	0	0	22	78	0	0
	c5	0	11	0	0	89	0
	c6	0	0	0	0	0	100

in the comparison affects the retrieval accuracy. Experiments were done with values between 0.5 and 1.5, and a threshold value of $T = 1.0$ gave the overall best results when the sum measure was used. Figure 9 gives the precision-recall graphs, showing the performance of the retrieval algorithm for three different threshold values: 1.0, 1.2, 1.5. Each chart gives the results of the retrieval algorithm when a specific image from one of the six tissue image classes was used as the query image. The caption "C1[3]" means that the third image from class-1 was used as the query image. Images in class-6 are distinctly different from the rest of the images, and returned a precision value of 1.0. For other images, the proposed method returned fairly accurate results.

IMPLEMENTATION ASPECTS

In order to obtain an accurate multi-fractal spectrum and therefore a robust classification system, there are a number of important implementation aspects to be considered. Some of the factors that affect the performance of the algorithm such as the number of windows used for α estimation, the update of alpha-histogram removing α values that are represented only by very few pixels in the image, image padding in regions where the sliding window crosses the image boundary, etc. have been discussed previously in literature (Hemsley & Mukundan, 2009). Additional variable parameters that affect the classification accuracy are now discussed.

Figure 9. Precision-recall graphs showing retrieval accuracy for query images from each class. The dashed line gives the graph for T = 0.1, the solid line T = 0.12, and the dotted line T = 0.15.

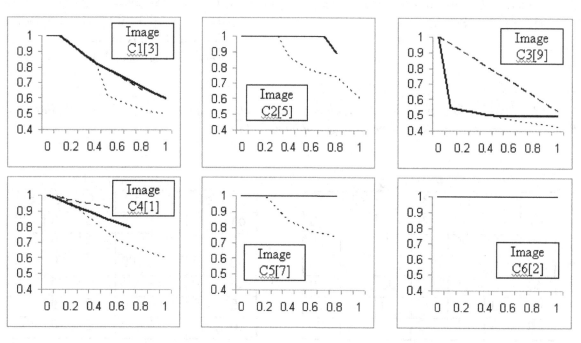

A. Intensity Transformations and the Multi-fractal Spectrum

A general linear transformation of the gray-level intensity levels $g(i,j)$, at pixels (i,j) can be written as

$$g(i,j)' = C_1 g(i,j) + C_2 \qquad (12)$$

where $g(i,j)'$ is the transformed intensity and C_1 and C_2 are constants. A pure scale transformation with $C_1 > 0, C_2 = 0$, does not affect the multi-fractal spectrum. However a shift of the image intensity values ($C_2 \neq 0$) results in a shift of the multi-fractal spectrum computed using the sum measure, but this shift is negligible for $C_2 < 10$. We could therefore remap the gray-level intensity range from [0-255] to [5-260] before the multi-fractal spectrum is computed, so that problems associated with log(0) can be eliminated. The results presented in the experimental analysis section were all generated after using this transformation.

B. Image Classification Using Iso Measure

We have seen that the Iso measure generates multi-fractal spectra with lower than desired level of inter-class variance. We also saw that the range of α values in this case is limited to [0, 2]. We could get improved results in the classification accuracy by using a weighted Iso measure. Here we assign a weight that depends on the window size to the number of pixels that matches the current pixel, for computing the Holder exponent. For the smallest window of size 1x1 (with only the current pixel in the window), the weight is 1, and for the next window of size 3x3, the weight is 2, and so on. The range of the α values is also extended by this method.

C. Spectrum Threshold

It is clear from Figures 6 and 7 that the multi-fractal spectra below the value of 0.5 contains high frequency components and noise that affect classification and retrieval accuracy. A threshold of 0.4 was therefore used in the retrieval system. A similar threshold could also be used in the classification system. It has been experimentally verified that considering only values greater than 0.5 improves the classification accuracy.

CONCLUSION AND FURTHER WORK

The paper has presented the details of a framework based on multi-fractal spectrum for the classification and retrieval of tissue images. It has proposed the use of texture feature descriptors constructed using the alpha-histogram and the multi-fractal spectrum. Both types of feature descriptors have been found to yield very good results in the classification process. The dimension of the feature vector could be significantly reduced in both cases, by using only a few points around $\alpha=2$ in the histogram, and by using piecewise cubic polynomials for approximating the multi-fractal spectrum. Experimental analysis of classification and retrieval accuracy have been presented with the multi-fractal spectra computed using the sum and iso measures. The sum measure is particularly found to be useful in the analysis as the spectra exhibited excellent intra-class similarity and inter-class variance. The results have been summarized as confusion matrices and precision-recall graphs. A few implementation aspects to further improve the accuracy of results have also been outlined.

Further work is being done to compare the performance of the feature descriptors proposed in this paper with other commonly used texture descriptors such as Homogeneous Texture Descriptor (Wu et al., 2000) and Gradient Indexing (Tao & Dickson, 2000). Robust feature descriptors could be designed by combining the information from alpha-histograms or multi-fractal spectra obtained using two different measures. Research in this area is currently directed towards the development of multi-fractal-based techniques for content-based tissue image indexing and mining, where different histological types can be effectively classified and retrieved.

REFERENCES

Aksoy, S., Marchisio, G., Tusk, C., & Koperski, K. (2002). Interactive classification and content-based retrieval of Tissue Images. In *Proceedings of the SPIE Annual Meeting, Applications of Digital Image Processing Session* (Vol. 4790, pp. 71-81).

Arbeiter, M., & Patzschke, N. (1996). Random Self-Similar. Multi-fractals. *Mathematische Nachrichten, 181*, 5–42.

Blunt, M. (1989). Geometry of Multi-fractal Systems. *Physical Review A., 39*(5), 2780–2782. doi:10.1103/PhysRevA.39.2780

Chhabra, A., & Jensen, R. (1989). Direct determination of the f(α) singularity spectrum. *Physical Review Letters, 62*(12), 1327–1330. doi:10.1103/PhysRevLett.62.1327

Esgiar, A. N., & Chakravorty, P. K. (2007). Fractal based classification of colon cancer tissue images. In *Proceedings of the International Symposium on Signal Processing and its Applications* (pp. 1-4).

Falconer, K. (2003). *Fractal Geometry - Mathematical Foundations and Applications* (2nd ed.). London: Wiley.

Filippas, J., Arochena, H., Amin, S. A., Naguib, R. N. G., & Bennett, M. K. (2003). Comparison of two AI methods for colonic tissue image classification. In *Proceedings of the IEEE Conference of Engineering in Medicine and Biology, 2*, 1323–1326.

Gholap, A., Naik, G., Joshi, A., & Rao, C. V. K. (2005). Content based tissue image mining. In *Proceedings of the IEEE Computational Systems Bioinformatics Conference* (pp. 359-363).

Hemsley, A., & Mukundan, R. (2009). Multi-fractal measures for tissue image classification and retrieval, In *Proceedings of the IEEE International Symposium on Multimedia* (pp. 618-623).

Hwang, H., Choi, H., Kang, B., Yoon, H., Kim, H., Kim, S., & Choi, H. (2005). Classification of breast tissue images based on wavelet transform using discriminant analysis, neural network and SVM. In *Proceedings of the International Workshop on Enterprise Networking and Computing in Healthcare Industry* (pp. 345-349).

Kinsner, W., & Zhang, H. (2009). Multi-fractal analysis and feature extraction of DNA sequences. In *Proeedings of the IEEE Intlernational Conference on Cognitive Informatics* (pp. 29-36).

Levy-Vehel, J., Mignot, P., & Berroir, J. (1992). *Texture and Multi-fractals: New Tools for Image Analysis* (Tech. Rep. No. 1706). France: INRIA.

Liu, Y., & Li, Y. (1997). New Approaches of multi-fractal analysis. In *Proceedings of the IEEE International Conference on Information, Communication and Signal Processing* (Vol. 2, pp. 970-974).

Mandelbrot, B. B. (1982). *The Fractal Geometry of Nature*. New York: W. H. Freeman and Company.

Maree, R., Geurts, P., Piater, J., & Wehenkel, L. (2005). Biomedical Image Classification with Random Subwindows and Decision Trees. In *Proceedings of the ICCV workshop on Computer Vision for Biomedical Image Applications (CVIBA 2005)* (Vol. 3765, pp. 220-229).

Munoz-Diosdado, A. (2005). A non linear analysis of human gait time series based on multi-fractal analysis and cross correlations. *Journal of Physics: Conference Series, 23*, 87–95. doi:10.1088/1742-6596/23/1/010

Musgrave, F. K. (2004). Fractal Forgeries of Nature. *Symposia Pure Mathematics, 72*(2).

Qi, D., & Yu, L. (2008). Multi-fractal Spectrum theory used to medical image from CT testing. In *Proceedings IEEE International Conference on Advanced Intelligent Mechatronics* (pp. 68-73).

Reljin, I., & Reljin, B. (2002). Fractal Geometry and Multi-fractals in Analyzing and Processing Medical Data and Images. *Archive of Oncology, 10*(4), 283–293. doi:10.2298/AOO0204283R

Reljin, I., Reljin, B., & Pavlovic, I. (2000). Multi-fractal analysis of grayscale images. In *Proceedings of the Mediterranean Electro-technical Conference, 2*, 490–493.

Renyi, A. (1970). *Probability Theory*. New York: North-Holland.

Riedi, R. H. (1999). *Introduction to Multi-fractals*. Houston, Texas: Rice University, Department of ECE.

Ruan, S., & Bloyet, D. (2000). MRF models and multi-fractal analysis for MRI segmentation. In *Proceedings IEEE International Conference on Signal Processing* (Vol. 2, pp. 1259-1262).

Song, I. H., et al. (2007). Multi-fractal analysis of sleep EEG dynamics in humans. In *Proceedings of the IEEE/EMBS International Conference on Neural Engineering* (pp. 546-549).

Stanford Tissue Microarray Corsortium Web Portal. (n.d.). Retrieved November 2009, from http://smd.stanford.edu/resources/databases.shtml

Stojic, T., Reljin, I., & Reljin, B. (2006). Adaptation of multi-fractal analysis to segmentation of micro-calcifications in digital mammograms. *Physica A, 367*, 494–508. doi:10.1016/j.physa.2005.11.030

Stosic, T., & Stosic, B. D. (2006). Multi-fractal analysis of human retinal vessels. *IEEE Transactions on Medical Imaging, 25*(8), 1101–1107. doi:10.1109/TMI.2006.879316

Tao, B., & Dickson, B. W. (2000). Texture recognition and image retrieval using gradient indexing. *Journal of Visual Communication and Image Representation, 11*(3), 327–342. doi:10.1006/jvci.2000.0448

Tricot, C. (1993). *Curves and Fractal Dimension*. Berlin: Springer.

Uma, K., & Ramakrishnan, K. R. (1996). Image analysis using multi-fractals. In *Proceedings of the IEEE International Conference on Acoustics, Speech, and Signal Processing, 4*, 2188–2190.

Wu, P. (2000). A texture descriptor for browsing and similarity retrieval. *Signal Processing Image Communication, 16*(1-2), 33–43. doi:10.1016/S0923-5965(00)00016-3

Yap, M. H., et al. (2009). A short review of methods for face detection and multi-fractal analysis. In *Proceedings of the IEEE International Conference on Cyber Worlds* (pp. 231-236).

This work was previously published in the International Journal of Multimedia Data Engineering and Management, Volume 1, Issue 2, edited by Shu-Ching Chen, pp. 62-75, copyright 2010 by IGI Publishing (an imprint of IGI Global).

Chapter 7
Robust Duplicate Detection of 2D and 3D Objects

Peter Vajda
Ecole Polytechnique Fédérale de Lausanne – EPFL, Switzerland

Ivan Ivanov
Ecole Polytechnique Fédérale de Lausanne – EPFL, Switzerland

Lutz Goldmann
Ecole Polytechnique Fédérale de Lausanne – EPFL, Switzerland

Jong-Seok Lee
Ecole Polytechnique Fédérale de Lausanne – EPFL, Switzerland

Touradj Ebrahimi
Ecole Polytechnique Fédérale de Lausanne – EPFL, Switzerland

ABSTRACT

In this paper, the authors analyze their graph-based approach for 2D and 3D object duplicate detection in still images. A graph model is used to represent the 3D spatial information of the object based on the features extracted from training images to avoid explicit and complex 3D object modeling. Therefore, improved performance can be achieved in comparison to existing methods in terms of both robustness and computational complexity. Different limitations of this approach are analyzed by evaluating performance with respect to the number of training images and calculation of optimal parameters in a number of applications. Furthermore, effectiveness of object duplicate detection algorithm is measured over different object classes. The authors' method is shown to be robust in detecting the same objects even when images with objects are taken from different viewpoints or distances.

DOI: 10.4018/978-1-4666-1791-9.ch007

INTRODUCTION

With the technological evolution of digital acquisition and storage technologies, millions of images and video sequences are captured every day and shared in online services such as Facebook, Flickr, and Picasa. As keyword-based indexing is very time consuming and inefficient due to linguistic and semantic ambiguities, content-based image and video retrieval systems have been proposed (Vajda, Dufaux, Minh, & Ebrahimi, 2009), which search and retrieve documents based on visual features. Within such systems, a query document is compared to all the documents in the database by making use of content-based features extracted from it. However, since the features are extracted from images which contain two-dimensional projections of three-dimensional scenes, the features may change significantly depending on the view point. Thus, systems often fail to retrieve relevant content in response to some queries.

In general, content-based image retrieval can utilize different representations for describing the image content, including global descriptors, feature points, or regions. Recently, interest has turned towards higher-level representations such as objects. Given a query image containing an object, an image retrieval system can perform two tasks: object recognition or object duplicate detection. Object recognition aims at finding all the instances of a certain object class (such as cars, or shoes), while object duplicate detection represents a more specific task of finding only a particular sample of that object class (such as "red Citroen C3 car" or "white Converse sneakers"). Figure 1 illustrates the relationship between object duplicate detection and object recognition problems. Therefore, within a complete system object recognition is usually applied first to detect a relevant class of objects (e.g., faces, cars) and then object duplicate detection is used to find a specific instance of that object class. Our object

Figure 1. Illustration of relationship between object recognition and object duplicate detection. While the former groups objects into different classes such as cars and shoes, the latter distinguishes between specific shoes or cars

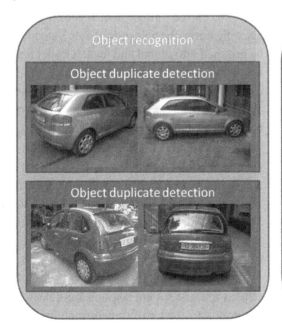 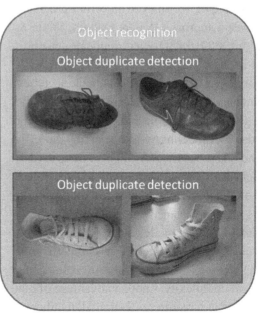

duplicate detection system is able to fulfill both tasks together.

In this paper, we are focusing on the object duplicate detection task. The general goal is to detect the presence of a target object in a set of images based on an object model created from a small set of training images. Duplicate objects may vary in their perspective, have different sizes, or be modified versions of the original object after minor manipulations, which do not change their identity. Therefore, object duplicate detection should be robust to changes in position, size, view, illumination, and partial occlusions.

A large number of applications can benefit from object duplicate detection. For example, in the popular photo sharing websites, untagged images can be automatically annotated based on the detection of the same objects from a smaller set of images with associated tags. Also, object duplicate detection may be used to search a specific object in a large collection, such as a suspect car in a video surveillance database. Moreover, when a user takes a picture of an object with his/her mobile phone, additional information about the object can be retrieved from the web, such as the price of a product, or the name and location of a monument.

In this paper, we analyze an earlier proposed graph-based approach (Vajda, Dufaux, Minh, & Ebrahimi, 2009) for 3D object duplicate detection in still images. This approach combines the efficiency of a bag of words model with the accuracy of a part-based model, which are described in the Related work section, i.e., we make an attempt towards 3D modeling, while keeping the efficiency of 2D processing. A graph model is used to represent the 3D spatial information of the object based on the features extracted from the training images so that we can avoid explicitly making a complex 3D object model. Therefore, improved performance can be achieved in comparison to existing methods in terms of robustness and computational complexity. Another advantage of our method is that it requires only a small number of

training images in order to build a robust model for the target object. Several images from different views are needed to create 3D model. However in our approach, just few common features are necessary to link spatial graphs from different views; therefore fewer training images are needed for the model creation. The method is evaluated through a comprehensive set of experiments, in which an in-depth analysis of its advantages and limitations is performed and optimal parameters are derived from such an analysis. A comparison with two representative methods shows its considerable performance improvement.

The remaining sections of this paper are organized as follows. We introduce related work in the next section. Then, we describe our approach for object duplicate detection in more detail. Next, experiments and results are shown. Finally, we conclude the paper with a summary and perspectives for future work.

RELATED WORK

Feature Extraction

The first important step of object duplicate detection is to extract salient features from given images. Features for object duplicate detection can be grouped into global and local. Global features usually describe an object as a whole, while local features are extracted from special parts of the object, such as salient regions. One of the best global features is the Histogram of Oriented Gradient (HOG) (Felzenszwalb, Mcallester, & Ramanan, 2008). Global features usually require an exhaustive search of the whole image over various scales and sizes to localize the target object. Thus, it is more time consuming when compared to a search using local features, which are typically scale and rotation invariant. The extraction of these local features usually consists of two steps. First, the salient regions are detected in a way robust to geometric transformations. Second, a region description for each of the detected region is generated to make them distinguishable. Reliable region detectors robust to illumination and viewpoint changes consider affine covariant regions (Mikolajczyk et al., 2003) known to be scale, rotation and translation invariant. Among the most commonly used region descriptors is the Scale Invariant Feature Transform (SIFT) (Lowe, 2004), which is based on an approximation of the human perception. A faster version of SIFT descriptor with comparable accuracy, called Speeded Up Robust Features (SURF), is proposed in (Bay, Tuytelaars, & Gool, 2006).

Object Representation

Regarding object representation, one can generally distinguish between spatial and non-spatial approaches. The latter does not consider any spatial information with respect to the object and its individual parts, such as the Bag of Words (BoW) model, which is based on a histogram of local features (Fei-Fei & Perona, 2005). Zhang et al. (Zhang, Marszalek, Lazebnik, & Schmid, 2007) presented a comparative study on different local features on texture and object recognition tasks based on global histogram of features. This method gives a robust, simple, and efficient solution for recognition without considering the spatial information of the object. The advantage of our object representation over the BoW model is that spatial information from the object is considered using a graph representation. However, the graph modeling adds to the complexity.

On the other hand, spatial models such as the Part-Based Model also consider the spatial information of objects for improved performance. Connections between different parts of an object can be achieved using different structures. A star structure has been used to represent objects based on HOG features (Felzenszwalb, Mcallester, & Ramanan, 2008). Another common way for considering spatial relationships between individual parts is to employ graph models often referred

to as structural pattern recognition (Neuhaus & Bunke, 2006). These graph matching approaches have been successfully applied to handwriting, character, and contour-line recognition. A generative model based on graph matching is the Random Attributed Relational Graph (RARG), which is able to capture the structural and appearance characteristics of parts extracted from objects (Zhang & Chang, 2006). However these methods are more suitable for object recognition and they need several training images for training the object model.

Most of the object representations consider the objects in the 2D image space only. However, since real-world objects are inherently 3D a higher performance can be achieved using 3D models. However, the creation of complete 3D models requires a large number of images from all possible angles, which may not be available in real applications. However, some interesting solutions have been proposed for multi-view retrieval of objects from a set of images or video. An approach described in Sivic, Schaffalitzky, and Zisserman (2006) uses tracking to retrieve different views of the same object and to group video shots based on object appearance. The model is then used to recognize objects more reliably. In (Rothganger, Lazebnik, Schmid, & Ponce, 2004) a full 3D model of the object is used for the detection of objects and model creation from video sequences. Our approach makes an attempt towards 3D modeling, while keeping the efficiency of 2D processing, using a graph model to represent the 3D spatial information so that we can avoid explicitly making a complex 3D object model.

Object Duplicate Detection

Typically, any object duplicate detection method contains the following tasks: feature extraction, object representation, similarity measurement and searching tasks. In this section we review representative object duplicate detection methods based on the previously described tasks.

Local features are used for object duplicate detection in (Lowe, 2004). The General Hough Transformation is then applied for object localization. Furthermore, pose is estimated using the RANSAC algorithm. Our object duplicates detection method is based on this algorithm and the detection accuracy is improved by using our spatial graph matching method. Our method is also extended by considering more training images. Therefore, 3D objects can be detected with more accuracy.

In (Sivic & Zisserman, 2006), descriptors are extracted from local affine-invariant regions and quantized into visual words, reducing the noise sensitivity of the matching. Inverted files are used to match the video frames to a query object and retrieve those which are likely to contain the same object. However, this work considers only 2D objects, such as posters, signs, ties, and does not take into account real 3D objects. In this paper an analysis of this method for real 3D objects is provided.

An extension (Sivic, Schaffalitzky, & Zisserman, 2006) of this approach uses key-point tracking to retrieve different views of the same object and to group video shots based on the objects appearance. The tracked object is then used as an implicit representation of the 3D structure of the objects to improve the reliability of the object duplicate detection. This method has proven to be more effective than a query with a single image, but it requires that all the relevant aspects of the desired object are present in the query shot, which limits its applicability.

A useful application of object duplicate detection is presented in (Gool, Breitenstein, Gammeter, Grabner, & Quack, 2009). Images coming from webcams on large database are automatically annotated with bounding boxes on object level. They also deal with searching in large database.

Detecting buildings in a large database is presented in (Philbin, Chum, Isard, Sivic, & Zisserman, 2007). The BoW method is applied for preselecting images from the large database

and an efficient spatial verification is considered for further analysis. The database contains up to one million images. To resolve the problem of large database they use a forest of 8 randomized k-d trees as a data structure for storing and searching features.

OBJECT DUPLICATE DETECTION ALGORITHM

In this section, the 3D object duplicate detection algorithm, which was first introduced in (Vajda, Dufaux, Minh, & Ebrahimi, 2009), will be described in more detail. The goal of this algorithm is to detect the presence of target objects and to predict their location in a set of images based on an object model created from training images. In this method, SIFT features are used to increase the detection speed in large databases thanks to existence of efficient search methods for local features. We target 3D object duplicate detection by using a graph model, which imposes spatial constraints between features and between the different viewpoints of the whole object to improve the accuracy of the object duplicate detection.

Since objects are considered as 3D objects, in principle more than one training image is needed to create a reliable 3D model for an object. However, as the spatial graph model is only an approximation of a 3D model with multiple 2D models (views) linked with each other, fewer training images (including only one image) are sufficient for model creation. In fact, we will show in the experimental section that only very few images are needed to create a reliable model for 3D object detection.

The system architecture is shown in Figure 2. In the training phase, an object model is created from a set of images containing this object. In the testing phase, this object model is used to detect objects and to predict their locations and sizes in test images. Each of the two phases starts with the same feature extraction step, which is shown

Figure 2. Overview of the object duplicate detection approach with the individual training and testing stages, and the commonly used feature extraction step

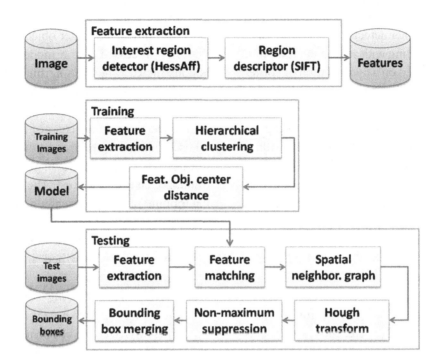

separately. In the following sections, the feature extraction, the training, and the testing phases are explained in detail.

Feature Extraction

There are mainly two kinds of features: global and local. Global features represent the whole object and usually require an exhaustive search of the whole image over various scales and sizes to localize the target object. Thus, it is more time consuming when compared to a search using local features, which are typically scale and rotation invariant.

The extraction of these local features usually consists of two steps. First, the salient regions are detected in a way robust to geometric transformations. Second, a region description for each of the detected region is generated to make them distinguishable. In our case, these steps are also separated as shown in the pseudo code of the feature extraction (see Exhibit 1)

1. Sparse local features are used to resolve the object localization problem more efficiently.

Exhibit 1.

F = **Feature extraction**(i:image)
IR:= **Hessian affine detector** (i); IR_i:(p:position, o:orientation, s:scale), interest region on image i.   F:= **SIFT**(IR);   where F_i: (IR_i, f:feature descriptor), feature.

Interesting regions are extracted using the Hessian affine detector (Mikolajczyk & Schmid, 2002), as it has been shown to outperform other detectors (Mikolajczyk et al., 2005) dealing with scale and view point changes. Based on a combination of corner points detected by an Hessian matrix, multi-scale analysis through the Gaussian scale-space, and affine normalization using an iterative affine shape adaptation algorithm, the Hessian affine detector finds regions which are stable across different scales, rotations, translations, as well as changes in illumination and viewpoint. The position, scale and orientation are computed for each of the regions and will be used within the graph model.

2. To *describe* the detected regions, features based on the Scale Invariant Feature Transform (SIFT) (Lowe, 2004) are extracted, as they remain robust to arbitrary changes in viewpoints. The idea of this algorithm is to approximate the human visual perception mechanism through features that share similar properties with the neurons in the inferior temporal cortex used for object recognition in primate vision systems (Serre, Kouh, Cadieu, Knoblich, Kreiman, & Poggio, 2005). High contrast candidate points and edge response points are processed for each region and dominant orientations are considered as in the inferior temporal cortex. These steps ensure that region descriptors are more stable for matching.

Training

During the training phase, a set of training images containing the target object from different views is processed, and a model for the object is constructed. The training images correspond to a single object filling up the whole field of view. Therefore, we assume that the object is positioned around the center of training images, whose boundaries are used as the bounding box of that object. In the following, each step of the training phase is described. The pseudo code of the training phase is presented in Exhibit 2.

1. *Features are extracted* from the training images, as described in the previous subsection.

2. *Hierarchical clustering* is applied to the features, to group them based on their similarity. This improves the efficiency of the feature matching by adopting a fast approximation for the nearest neighbor search. More specifically, hierarchical k-means clustering (MacQueen, 1967) is used to derive the vocabulary tree, similar to that described in (Nister & Stewenius, 2006). It is a balanced tree whose inner nodes correspond to the feature of the cluster centers derived from all its children. The balanced tree is a tree where there are no big differences between the depths of the leaves. The computational complexity of finding a nearest neighbor for a given feature in this tree structure is significantly less than an exhaustive nearest

Exhibit 2.

Model = **Training**(I:images)
F:= **Feature extraction** (I); Storage:= **Hierarchical clustering**(F); Model:= **Spatial neighborhood graph creation**(F); where Model:(G:Graph, A:Graph attributes) G:(V:feature nodes, E: edges), edges are between the close features in spatial domain. A(E): (d:distance, o:orientation), attributes of the edges. A(V):(p:position, o:orientation, s:scale), relative position, orientation and scale to the object center and object scale.

neighbor search. However, it is important to mention that this approximation may occasionally cause erroneous matches, which are discarded by the further validation process.

3. Finally, the *spatial graph model is constructed* from the features and their positions. The nodes of the graph are the features of the training images. Each node also stores the scale, and orientation of the corresponding region of the feature and the relative position from the object center, normalized by the size of the object. The edges of the graph are the spatial nearest neighbors of two features. The attributes of edges are the distance and orientation of the neighboring nodes. These attributes are important for the matching step in the testing phase.

Testing

In the testing phase, the graph model derived from a small set of training images is used to detect similar objects in other test images and to predict their bounding boxes. The whole testing phase is illustrated in Figure 3 and its individual steps will be described in more detail below. The pseudo code of the training phase is presented in Exhibit 3.

1. *Features are extracted* from the query image, as described before, which results in several robust region descriptors.

2. These features are matched to those in the graph model derived from the training images using a one to one nearest neighbor *matching* which is illustrated in Figure 4. First, for every feature from the test images the nearest neighbors in the graph model are determined based on the Euclidean distance. Then, for each feature from the graph model the best matching feature in the test image is searched back. If it leads to the original feature in the test image then this match is a one to one match, otherwise the matching features are not corresponding to each other and they are discarded. Furthermore, matches with a distance larger than a predefined threshold T_d are also discarded. This procedure ensures the selection of very reliable matching features. Due to the tree representation of features as described before, the complexity of this matching step is $O(N \log N)$, where N is related to the number of features.

3. A *spatial graph is constructed* from the features and their positions from the query image applying the same method as the graph creation in the training phase. Graph match-

Exhibit 3.

Bounding boxes = **Testing**(i:image, Model)
F:= **Feature extraction** (i); Matches$_{feature}$:= **Feature matching**(F, Model.G.V) ∩ **Feature matching**(Model.G.V, F); Matches:{(f$_{query}$:feature, f$_{model}$:feature)} one to one matching using Storage. Query:= **Spatial neighborhood graph creation**(F); Query:(G:Graph, A:Graph attributes) G:(V:feature nodes, E: edges), edges are between the close features in spatial domain. A(E): (d:distance, o:orientation), attributes of the edges. A(V):(p:position, o:orientation, s:scale) Matches$_{graph}$:= **Graph matching**(Query, Model, Matches$_{feature}$) Matches$_{graph}$ = {(V$_{query}$xV$_{model}$:feature matches, E$_{query}$xE$_{model}$:edge matches)} Bounding boxes:= **General Hough Transformation**(Query, Model, Matches$_{graph}$) Bounding boxes = {(c:coordinates, F$_{query}$:Features)} Bounding boxes:= **Non-maximum Supression**(Bounding boxes) Bounding boxes:= **Bounding box merging**(Bounding boxes, Matches$_{graph}$)

ing is applied between the graph model derived from training images and the graph created from the query image. Figure 5 shows the graph matching step. The graph contains spatial information from the potentially matching objects, hence making the algorithm more robust. The previous feature-matching step creates the connections between these two graphs, as shown with red and blue lines in Figure 5. First, on the graphs we match the edges. To avoid wrong connections, only those edges which have similar properties relative to the object size are matched, as shown with a red line in Figure 5. An edge on the query graph is matched with an edge on the model graph, if the normalized scales of both end of the edge are similar. More precisely, the edges are matched if the ratio between normalized scales is between T_R and $1/T_R$, where the threshold T_R is set manually. The scale values are obtained in the feature extraction step as described in subsection Feature extraction. The normalized scale is the scale of the feature divided by the scale of the matched feature. Second, the number of edges that go out from each node is examined and only the nodes having at least T_{outdeg} edges are accepted. This produces a rather robust graph of objects. An expected property of this graph is that, ideally, nodes of a given edge should not be part of two different objects (i.e., each edge is a part of only one object). However, it is possible to have more than one graph per object. With this method, several mismatched features can be discarded, thanks to the spatial position in the object and the normalized scale of features.

4. To estimate the bounding boxes of the detected objects, the *General Hough Transform* is applied on the nodes of the matched graph (Ballard, 1981). Each node in this graph votes for the center and the size of the bound-

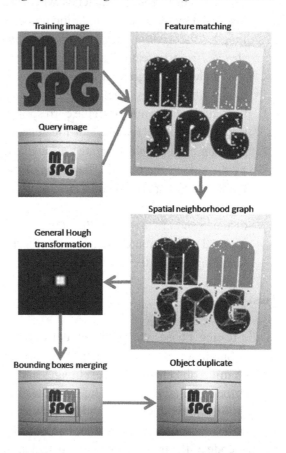

Figure 3. Illustration of the different steps of the testing stage with individual feature matching, spatial graph matching and bounding box estimation

ing box in the query image, using the orientation and scale of the extracted features. The weight of each vote corresponds to the number of edges connected to the node. This creates a histogram of the object's center and its scale. Then, the local maxima are searched for in the obtained histogram. A general threshold T is then applied on these local maxima.

5. As the above described procedure may return several bounding boxes with spatial overlaps, *non-maximum suppression* is applied to discard duplicate bounding boxes (Neubeck & Van Gool, 2006). This method leads to good results when using one training image; however if different views of

Figure 4. One to one feature matching

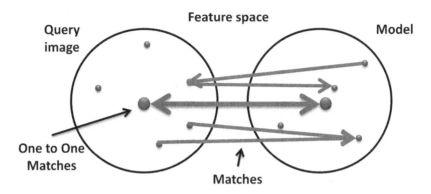

the same object in training images are used, then more separate bounding boxes can be obtained for that object.

6.   Bounding boxes obtained due to the different views of an object in training images are *merged based on graph intersection* as shown in Figure 6. This is done by considering the number of edges of the graphs intersecting two bounding boxes. The ratio between the number of intersected edges and the number of edges in both bounding boxes are threshold by a parameter T_{bb}. Thus, if a sufficient number of edges intersect, the two bounding boxes are merged (Warshall, 1962). Finally, each bounding box represents a target object in the test image. This graph based method solves the problem of multi-view images in

which separate bounding boxes may be obtained for the same object. Even if more than one target object is present in the test image, our algorithm still successfully detects them, as each object produces a separate graph.

EXPERIMENTAL SETUP

In this section the evaluation environments are assessed.

The parameter settings of our algorithm are set based on several experiments and heuristics. The number of clusters in the vocabulary tree was set to 128, as this provided a good tradeoff between complexity and accuracy. For the feature match-

Figure 5. Spatial neighborhood graph matching between the model graph and the query graph.

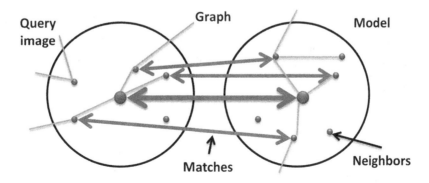

Figure 6. Bounding box merging based on graph intersection

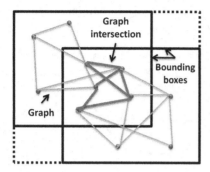

ing, the distance threshold was selected to be $T_d = 10^5$. In the spatial neighborhood graph $T_{outdeg} = 4$, to accept robust matching features. The normalized scale ratio was set to $T_R = 2$. Finally, the threshold $T_{bb} = 0.1$ was chosen to merge bounding boxes. The optimal detection threshold T for the algorithm was derived based on various experiments as summarized below.

The considered dataset is described in subsection Database. Finally in subsection Evaluation the evaluation methodologies are presented.

Database

A dataset including 850 images was created in order to evaluate the object duplicate detection method described in this paper. It consists of ten 3D and five 2D object classes as shown in Figure 7: bag, bicycle, body, face, shoes, stone, can, car, building, motor, poster, logo, newspaper, book and workbook.

Each of the 15 classes contains at least 3 samples. Figure 8 provides 3 images for 2 selected classes: building and shoes. As it can be seen from these samples, images with a large variety of view points and sizes are included in each class.

Angles and relative size of image point of views are calculated for each image in 3D dataset for further analysis on full, 360° duplicate detection as shown in Results section.

Evaluation

The detection task (Fawcett, 2006) can be evaluated using correspondences between a set of predicted objects which are represented by their bounding boxes, and a set of ground truth objects. A pair-wise comparison of ground truth and predicted objects is performed in order to see if they are the same or not. The results are used to obtain the values of true positives (*TP*), true negatives (*TN*), false positives (*FP*) and false negatives (*FN*). This confusion matrix serves as a basis on which two curves can be derived.

First, the receiver operating characteristic (ROC) curve represents the true positive rate (*TPR*) versus the false positive rate (*FPR*), with:

$$TPR = \frac{TP}{TP + FN}$$

$$FPR = \frac{FP}{FP + TN}$$

Second, the precision recall (PR) curve plots the precision (*P*) versus the recall (*R*) with:

$$P = \frac{TP}{TP + FP}$$

$$R = \frac{TP}{TP + FN}$$

This curve does not consider *TN* which is not uniquely defined for detection problems.

In order to determine the optimum thresholds for object detection, the F-measure is calculated as the harmonic mean of *P* and *R* values, given by:

$$F = \frac{2 \cdot P \cdot R}{P + R}$$

which considers *P* and *R* equally weighted. The more general definition of the F-measure consid-

Figure 7. Samples of the different 2D and 3D object classes within the dataset used in evaluations

Figure 8. Samples for two objects under diverse viewing conditions within the dataset used in evaluations

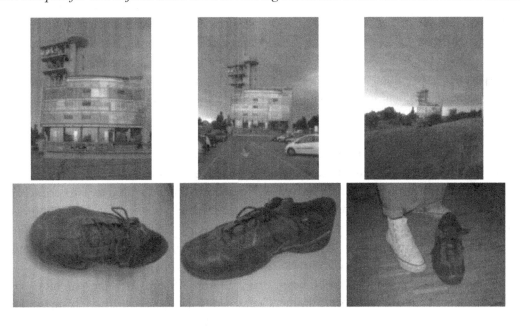

ers the weighted values of *P* and *R*, and measures the effectiveness of the object duplicate detection algorithm with respect to a user who gives β times the importance to *P* when compared to *R*:

$$F_{\hat{a}} = \frac{(1 + \hat{a}^2) \cdot P \cdot R}{\hat{a}^2 \cdot P + R}$$

RESULTS AND ANALYSIS

In this section we present the evaluation results of our graph-based object duplicate detection algorithm and analyze them in order to answer the following important questions:

1. What is the impact of the number of training images on the accuracy of our algorithm?
2. What are the optimal parameter settings?
3. How does the detection performance depend on the object class?
4. How does its performance compare to the state of the art?
5. How can object duplicate detection be performed reliably for any point of view?

Influence of the Number of Training Images

In a first experiment, we trained our system with one, two or three images, and tested it with the remaining images in order to analyze the performance of the object duplicate detection as a function of the number of training images. Negative images are all images which do not contain the ground truth object. In our experiments we define as negative images all different images from the same class of the object and several not related images.

Figure 9 plots the corresponding ROC curves. The results show that the performance of the algorithm varies according to the number of training images. One can notice that using more than one training image can significantly improve the

performance because it makes the object model robust against different points of views. As an example, the results show that for $FPR = 0.10$ a $TPR = 0.85, 0.92, 0.97$ is achieved when the system is trained with one, two and three images, respectively.

The object duplicate detection algorithm was also evaluated using PR curves as shown in Figure 9. These curves complement the previously discussed results and provide a better visualization of the opposing effects (high precision vs. high recall) which are inherent to any detection task. For instance, the results show that for $R = 0.90$ a then $P = 0.28, 0.67, 0.78$ is achieved when the system is trained with one, two and three images, respectively. For a high recall value greater than 0.8, higher precision values are obtained when more than one training image are used.

Optimal Parameter Selection

In a second experiment, we estimated the optimal parameter settings of our system. The F-measure is calculated in order to determine the optimal threshold values for different applications.

First, the F-measures obtained for the different thresholds in the object duplicate detection approach are calculated to determine the optimal threshold value. The results are shown in Figure 10. For each of the cases where one, two and three training images are used, the maximum F-measure is found and shown with a marker in this figure. According to the results in this figure, F-measures of 0.80, 0.82 and 0.84 can be reached with thresholds equal to 51, 140 and 288, if our system is trained with one, two or three images respectively. Therefore, the optimal threshold is highly correlated with the number of training images. The optimal threshold increases significantly if more training images are used.

Figure 10 provides the parameter β of the general F-measure over different threshold values. Using the general F-measure, the importance of the precision and recall can be balanced according

Figure 9. Receiver operating characteristic (ROC) curves for different numbers of training images (1, 2 and 3) per object is shown on the left. A larger number of training images leads to an increased TPR for a fixed FP value. Recall versus precision curves for different number of training images (1, 2 and 3) per object is shown on the right

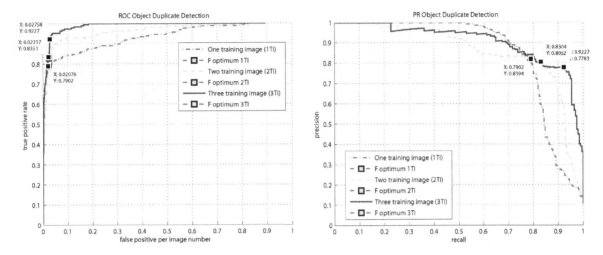

to the requirement of a given application using the object duplicate detection. If the β parameter is equal to one, the precision is as much important as the recall. Two other commonly used F-measures are the $F_{0.5}$ measure, which weights the precision twice as much as the recall, and the F_2 measure, which weights the recall twice as much as the precision. The optimal F-measure parameter settings, for which the precision and the recall are equally weighted, are also shown as markers in Figure 10.

Figure 10. F-measure versus detection threshold for different number of training images (1, 2 and 3) is shown on the left. Both the F-measure and the detection thresholds increase with a larger number of training images. Detection threshold versus â parameter of the general F-measure for different number of training images is shown on the right

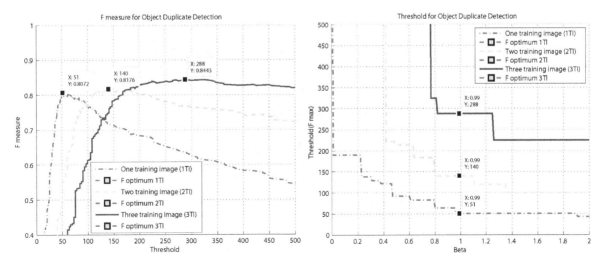

Performance Across Different Classes

The goal of a third experiment was to measure the performance of the object duplicate detection algorithm as a function of different object classes. The F-measure is computed for each of the 2D and 3D object classes and different classes are compared with each other.

The results are shown in Figure 11. According to these results, there are big differences in detection performance between different classes, which are caused by various factors such as reflection properties, amount and presence of textures, or number of salient features. The object duplicate detection algorithm performs well with newspapers, thanks to the large number of pictures and textures in such objects. Duplicate detection of human bodies considers only the texture of the clothes and not their shape, which gives a surprisingly good result. Face identification is also a possible application, although its performance should be compared to those of state of the art face detection algorithms. Shiny objects, such as motor bicycles and cars, are hard to detect due to the changing reflections depending on lighting condition. Books are also among the classes showing the worst performance due to large illumination variations during the image acquisition of our dataset, which was not the case for newspapers.

Finally, an interesting example is shown in Figure 12. The object duplicate detection algorithm is performed on the class of cars. Interestingly, even the opposite side of a car can be correctly recognized when only one training image is used, which is the case in this example. This is due to the fact that the license plate of a car is the most salient region on both the front and the back side of the car. Nevertheless, the location of the car is shifted upwards due to the different position of the license plate with respect to the overall object.

Comparison with State of the Art

The goal of the fourth experiment was to assess the quality of proposed method for object duplicate

Figure 11. Performance of the object duplicates detection in F-measure for each object class. The difference between classes is caused by various factors such as reflection properties, amount and presence of textures, or number of salient features

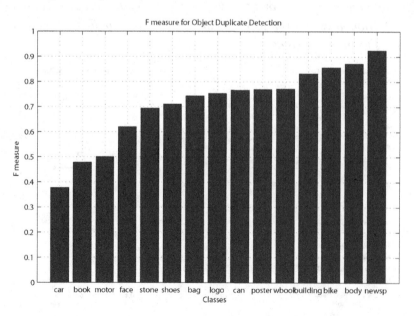

Figure 12. An example where our object duplicate detection algorithm detects the back side of a car thanks to its license plate. The training image is shown in the bottom left corner

detection in relation to the state of the art. We have compared it to the BoW method (Fei-Fei & Perona, 2005) and to Lowe's object duplicate detection (Lowe, 2004).

The general drawback of the BoW method is that it does not consider any spatial information from the object; hence it creates a general histogram from local features. The resulted histograms are then compared by Euclidean, L_1 and histogram intersection distance (Swain & Ballard, 1991). Histogram intersection distance performed the best among them; therefore in this paper this result is presented

Lowe's object duplicate detection (Lowe, 2004) algorithm is considering the spatial information by using General Hough Transformation similar to our approach. However our method improves the quality of the matched features, due to the graph matching.

In Figure 13, ROC curves and PR curves are shown for the three methods. The results show significant differences between these algorithms. The BoW method performs worst, since it does not consider any spatial information. Lowe's method shows improved performance by considering

this information. However, our method provides another considerable performance gain due to the graph matching.

For a more detailed analysis we compared the performance of the methods across the different classes shown in Figure 14. The advantage of our algorithm is observable for most of the classes. However, there are some cases where our method does not perform as good as the other methods. The BoW method works well on "cars" and "bags" compared to the other methods, since it is more robust to the spatial information changes caused by varying view point and distance. In these objects there are just a few features and the available spatial information is not very reliable. However, for objects where the spatial information is crucial such as "books", "shoes", "posters", "buildings", "bodies", "newspapers", the BoW method shows very bad results.

Towards Omnidirectional Detection

Imagine a scenario where you take a picture of an object with your mobile phone and you would like to get information about the object from an

Figure 13. Comparison of our method with BoW method and Lowe's object duplicate detection algorithm (Lowe, 2004). On the left side, ROC curve and on the right side PR curve are shown

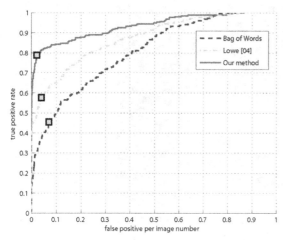
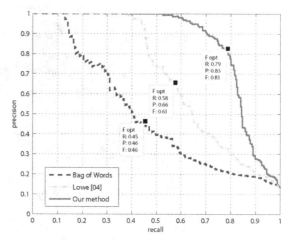

online application. To recognize the object in your picture, you would need an omnidirectional duplicate detection algorithm that works well (e.g., a recall of 80%) even if the picture was taken from an arbitrary direction.

In this section, we examine the experimental results shown above further in order to obtain requirements for omnidirectional object duplicate detection. We analyze the recall of our algorithm with respect to the viewing angle difference between the object appeared in the training and test images and the distance measured as the object size relative to the original objects in the training images.

The results of the analysis are shown in Figure 15. It shows that the recall starts to decrease when the object size in the test image is less than 75% the original size or the viewing angle differs by more than 40° from that of the training image. If the viewing angle differs by 90°, the recall drops down to 0.45. In contrast to previous works, this shows that real objects have to treat as convex 3D objects instead of planar 2D objects which may be detected for up to 180° angle difference between training and test images.

Based on these results, it is possible to drive the requirements on the number of training im-

ages and the angles and distances of the objects in the images in order to achieve a certain overall recall value. If we want to detect at least 80% of the test objects by using an object model trained with only one training image, the test images may differ from the training image in angle only up to ±47° and in size up to 65%. Therefore, if we want to detect at least 80% of the test objects for all possible rotations around a single axis, four training images are enough because one image can cover 94° among 360° as shown in Figure 16. There is no need to take pictures from different distances, because a simple rescaling to 65% is enough.

If we consider omnidirectional object duplicate detection in the 3D space, it is necessary to solve the problem of positioning circles (or, equivalently, cameras) to cover a sphere. More precisely, the problem is to find the minimum number of congruent circles to cover a sphere for a given radius of the circles, or conversely, to find the minimum radius of the circles to cover a sphere for a given number of circles so that every point of the sphere belongs to at least one circle. Although a general solution of the problem for an arbitrary number of circles is not available, the solutions for some numbers of circles were given

Figure 14. Comparison is shown between our method, BOW and Lowe's object duplicate detection algorithm through different classes of objects

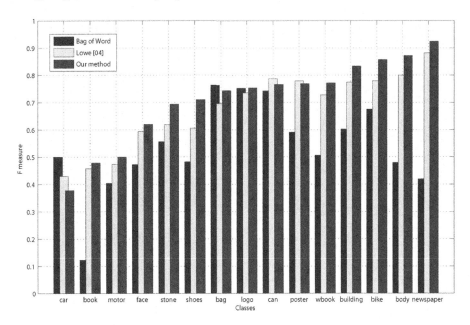

Figure 15. Recall measurement vs. relative size of the object in the test image (left) and recall measurement vs. viewing angle difference between the training and test images (right)

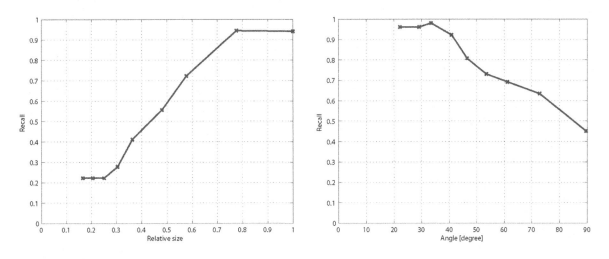

Table 1. Solutions for the problem of covering a sphere with "#cameras" congruent, overlapping circles. The second row shows the radius of the circles in degree, where the centers of the circles are the cameras and the radius of the circles is the covering angle of a camera

#cameras	4	5	6	7	8	9	10	11	12	13	14	15	16
radius	70.53	63.43	54.74	51.03	48.14	45.88	42.31	41.43	37.38	37.07	34.94	34.04	32.90

Figure 16. Ordering of cameras for planar detection in the 3D space. The positions of the cameras are the centers of the circles and the detection area of each camera is shown as a gray disk

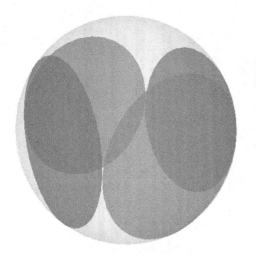

Figure 17. Ordering of cameras for omnidirectional detection in the 3D space. The positions of the cameras are the centers of the circles and the detection area of each camera is shown as a gray disk

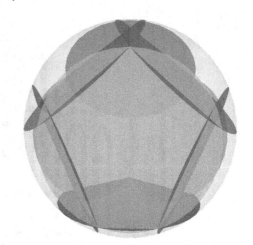

by Fejes Tóth (Fejes Tóth, 1972). For different numbers of cameras, the required covering radius of the cameras is shown in Table 1 (Hardin, Sloane, & Smith, 1997).

Therefore, to cover a sphere with circles having a radius of 47°, 9 training images are enough, if the ordering of the cameras is done as shown in Figure 17. The positions of the cameras in this case are shown in Table 2. If we want to detect at least 90% of the test objects contained in images taken from any direction, it is allowed to have angle difference up to 40° (Figure 15) and thus it is sufficient to use 12 images for training as shown in Table 1.

CONCLUSION

Image and video retrieval systems are becoming increasingly important in many applications. Automatic video and image tag propagation, video surveillance, and high level image or video search are among some of the applications which require accurate and efficient object duplicate detection methods. In this work, we have analyzed a robust graph-based object duplicate detection algorithm for 2D and 3D objects. The experiments are performed on various classes of objects. The main conclusions that can be drawn from our experiments are:

Table 2. Nine 3D coordinates of the centers of the circles which covers a unit sphere when the radii of the circles are 47°

Axis/Cam	1	2	3	4	5	6	7	8	9
x	-0.039	0.870	-0.013	-0.673	-0.577	0.057	-0.858	0.664	0.568
y	-0.078	0.266	-0.637	-0.726	0.344	0.992	0.372	0.268	-0.802
z	0.996	0.415	-0.771	0.145	-0.741	0.110	0.356	-0.698	0.187

- The performance of our object duplicate detection algorithm shows that more than one training image can significantly improve the detection accuracy.

- Considering F-measure and F_z-measure values, the optimal threshold was determined and found to vary with the requirement of specific applications.

- The comparison of performance between various classes of objects shows that our algorithm performs well with textured objects, while shiny object are most difficult to detect.

- We showed that our method works significantly better than Bag of Words method and Lowe's object duplicate detection method (Lowe, 2004) on our dataset, due to way the spatial information is considered through graph matching.

- Four training images are enough for 3D object duplicate detection from planar point of view and 9 training images for full detection.

Furthermore, the our method has shown to be robust in detecting the same objects even if the images with objects are taken from very different viewpoints or distances.

As future work, we will explore automatic geotag propagation in social networks based on our object duplicate detection method. We will also consider extension of the method to deal with duplicate object detection in video.

ACKNOWLEDGMENT

This work was supported by the Swiss National Science Foundation Grant "Multimedia Security" (number 200020-113709), the Swiss National Foundation for Scientific Research in the framework of NCCR Interactive Multimodal Information Management (IM2), and partially supported by the European Network of Excellence PetaMedia (FP7/2007-2011).

REFERENCES

Ballard, D. H. (1981). Generalizing the hough transform to detect arbitrary shapes. *Pattern Recognition, 13*(2), 111–122. doi:10.1016/0031-3203(81)90009-1

Bay, H., Tuytelaars, T., & Gool, L. V. (2006, May). Surf: Speeded up robust features. In *Proceedings of the 9th European Conference on Computer Vision.*

Fawcett, T. (2006). An introduction to ROC analysis. *Pattern Recognition Letters*, 861–874. doi:10.1016/j.patrec.2005.10.010

Fei-Fei, L., & Perona, P. (2005). A Bayesian hierarchical model for learning natural scene categories. In *Proceedings of Computer Vision and Pattern Recognition, 2*, 524–531.

Fejes Tóth, L. (1972). *Lagerungen in der Ebene auf der Kugel und im Raum* (2nd ed.). Berlin: Springer Verlang.

Felzenszwalb, P., Mcallester, D., & Ramanan, D. (2008, June). A discriminatively trained, multi-scale, deformable part model. In *Proceedings of the IEEE International Conference on Computer Vision and Pattern Recognition.*

Gool, L. V., Breitenstein, M. D., Gammeter, S., Grabner, H., & Quack, T. (2009). Mining from Large Image Sets. In *Proceedings of the ACM Int. Conference on Image and Video Retrieval.*

Hardin, R. H., Sloane, N. J., & Smith, W. D. (1997, May 30). *Spherical Coverings*. Retrieved from http://www.sphopt.com/math/question/covering.html

Leibe, B., Leonardis, A., & Schiele, B. (2008). Robust object detection with interleaved categorization and segmentation. *International Journal of Computer Vision, 77,* 259–289. doi:10.1007/s11263-007-0095-3

Lowe, D. G. (2004). Distinctive image features from scale-invariant keypoints. *International Journal of Computer Vision, 60*(2), 91–110. doi:10.1023/B:VISI.0000029664.99615.94

MacQueen, J. B. (1967). Some Methods for classification and Analysis of Multivariate Observations. In *Proceedings of 5th Berkeley Symposium on Mathematical Statistics and Probability* (pp. 281-297).

Mikolajczyk, K., & Schmid, D. (2002). An affine invariant interest point detector. In *Proceedings of the 7th European Conference on Computer Vision,* Copenhagen, Denmark (pp. 128-142). New York: Springer.

Mikolajczyk, K., Tuytelaars, T., Schmid, C., Zisserman, A., Matas, J., & Schaffalitzky, F. (2005). A comparison of affine region detectors. *International Journal of Computer Vision, 65,* 43–72. doi:10.1007/s11263-005-3848-x

Neubeck, A., & Van Gool, L. (2006). Efficient non-maximum suppression. In *Proceedings of the International Conference on Pattern Recognition* (pp. 850-855).

Neuhaus, M., & Bunke, H. (2006). Edit distance based kernel functions for structural pattern classification. *Pattern Recognition, 39,* 1852–1863. doi:10.1016/j.patcog.2006.04.012

Nister, D., & Stewenius, H. (2006). Robust scalable recognition with a vocabulary tree. In *Proceedings of the IEEE Computer Society Conference on Computer Vision and Pattern Recognition* (pp. 2161-2168).

Philbin, J., Chum, O., Isard, M., Sivic, J., & Zisserman, A. (2007). Object retrieval with large vocabularies and fast spatial matching. In *Proceedings of the IEEE Conference on Computer Vision and Pattern Recognition.*

Rothganger, F., Lazebnik, S., Schmid, C., & Ponce, J. (2004). 3D Object Modeling and Recognition Using Local Affine-Invariant Image Descriptors and Multi-View Spatial Constraints. *International Journal of Computer Vision, 66*(3), 231–259. doi:10.1007/s11263-005-3674-1

Rothganger, F., Lazebnik, S., Schmid, C., & Ponce, J. (2004). Segmenting, modeling, and matching video clips containing multiple moving objects. In *Proceedings of the Conference on Computer Vision and Pattern Recognition* (pp. 914-921).

Serre, T., Kouh, M., Cadieu, C., Knoblich, U., Kreiman, G., & Poggio, T. (2005). *A theory of object recognition: computations and circuits in the feedforward path of the ventral stream in primate visual cortex.* Cambridge, MA: MIT.

Sivic, J., Schaffalitzky, F., & Zisserman, A. (2006). Object level grouping for video shots. *International Journal of Computer Vision, 67*(2), 189–210. doi:10.1007/s11263-005-4264-y

Sivic, J., & Zisserman, A. (2006). Video Google: Efficient visual search of videos. *Toward Category-Level Object Recognition* (LNCS, pp. 127-144). New York: Springer.

Swain, M. J., & Ballard, D. H. (1991). Color indexing. *International Journal of Computer Vision.*

Vajda, P., Dufaux, F., Minh, T. H., & Ebrahimi, T. (2009). Graph-based approach for 3d object duplicate detection. In *Proceedings of the International Workshop on Image Analysis for Multimedia Interactive Services.*

Warshall, S. (1962). A theorem on boolean matrices. *Journal of the ACM, 9*(1), 11–12. doi:10.1145/321105.321107

Zhang, D., & Chang, S.-F. (2006). A generative-discriminative hybrid method for multi-view object detection. In *Proceedings of the IEEE International Conference on Computer Vision and Pattern Recognition.*

Zhang, J., Marszalek, M., Lazebnik, S., & Schmid, C. (2007). Local features and kernels for classification of texture and object categories: A comprehensive study. *International Journal of Computer Vision, 73*(2), 213–238. doi:10.1007/s11263-006-9794-4

This work was previously published in the International Journal of Multimedia Data Engineering and Management, Volume 1, Issue 3, edited by Shu-Ching Chen, pp. 19-40, copyright 2010 by IGI Publishing (an imprint of IGI Global).

Section 3
Video Content Processing and Retrieval

Chapter 8

Automatic Pitch Type Recognition System from Single-View Video Sequences of Baseball Broadcast Videos

Masaki Takahashi
NHK Science and Technology Research Laboratories, Japan; The Graduate University for Advanced Studies, Japan

Mahito Fujii
NHK Science and Technology Research Laboratories, Japan

Masahiro Shibata
NHK Science and Technology Research Laboratories, Japan

Nobuyuki Yagi
NHK Science and Technology Research Laboratories, Japan

Shin'ichi Satoh
National Institute of Informatics, Japan; The Graduate University for Advanced Studies, Japan

ABSTRACT

This article describes a system that automatically recognizes individual pitch types like screwballs and sliders in baseball broadcast videos. These decisions are currently made by human specialists in baseball, who are watching the broadcast video of the game. No automatic system has yet been developed for identifying individual pitch types from single view camera images. Techniques using multiple fixed cameras promise highly accurate pitch type identification, but the systems tend to be large. Our system is designed to identify the same pitch types using only the same single-view broadcast baseball videos used by the human specialists, and accordingly we used a number of features, such as the ball's location, ball speed and catcher's stance based on the advice of those specialists. The system identifies the pitch type using a classifier trained with the Random Forests ensemble learning algorithm and achieved about 90% recognition accuracy in experiments.

DOI: 10.4018/978-1-4666-1791-9.ch008

1. INTRODUCTION

Many kinds of metadata on various sports are being distributed in real time via data broadcasting and the Internet (Kon'ya, Kuwano, Yamada, Kawamori, & Kawazoe, 2005; Liddy et al., 2002). For baseball in particular, the data generated for each pitch is diverse and includes player at bat, the count, ball speed, etc. A lot of research has gone into scene analysis in baseball videos (Chan, Han, & Gong, 2002; Ando, Shinoda, Furui, & Mochizuki, 2007; Lien, Chiang, & Lee, 2007).

Even though baseball spectators pay a lot of attention to the type of pitch, it is difficult to determine the pitch type automatically from a baseball broadcast video, and so far, human specialists are needed to make the decision from single-view pitching sequences (Hoshikawa, 2006; Shibata, 2007).

To make this work less costly, we developed a system that automatically recognizes the type of pitch by using only the information contained in the baseball broadcast video. We selected features such as ball trajectory, ball speed, and the catcher's stance just prior to the pitch after referring to the opinions of expert judges of the pitch type.

Various methods of analyzing baseball broadcast video images to display the pitch trajectory or segment the baseball events have been researched (Chen, 2006; Chen, Chen, Tsai, Lee, & Yu, 2007; Shum & Komura, 2004), but no method until now has been established for identifying pitch type. A method that shows the ball speed and changes in breaking balls by analyzing their trajectory has been presented (Chu, Wang, & Wu, 2006), but it goes no further than deciding whether it is a straight ball or breaking ball. Thus, we aimed at developing a new system that can automatically classify the same kinds of individual pitch types with the accuracy of human specialists.

Data on pitch types for all professional baseball games in Japan is available from metadata distributors such as Data Stadium Inc. (n.d.). Although there are various pitch types in professional base-

ball, human specialists in Data Stadium classify pitches into nine types: straight balls, screwballs, curveballs, sliders, cutballs, forkballs, change-ups, sinkers, and other. Our system classifies pitches into nine types, as in Data Stadium's method.

Techniques using multiple fixed cameras to obtain the 3-D position of a ball have been developed (Gueziec, 2002; Rander, 1998); one method creates three-dimensional ball trajectories by using multiple stereo cameras (Theobalt, Albrecht, Haber, Magnor, & Seidel, 2004). These techniques can reproduce the curve of a breaking ball. 3-D ball position measurements promise highly accurate pitch identification, but the systems incorporating them tend to be large. Japan Broadcasting Corporation (NHK), which the authors belong to, broadcasts more than 100 live professional baseball programs a year. If we used multi-cameras for each game, the amount of setting up and adjustment required would be large. Considering operability and the need to get results quickly, determining the type of pitch only from broadcast video is a more desirable method for us.

In addition, our system can be used for video searches of previous baseball broadcast videos because it only needs broadcast video as input. In contrast, techniques using multiple fixed cameras cannot be used for video searches because they don't work on broadcast video. The system has the advantage that can annotate the type of pitch in previous broadcasts.

Moreover, the number of pitch types, ball speed, and the degree of changes in trajectory vary depending on the pitcher. Hence, we need to create a classifier or decide thresholds for each pitcher even if the 3-D positions of ball data are measured.

Another study analyzed changes in trajectory by considering the aerodynamics of breaking balls (Alaways, 1998). However, the special sensor cameras are needed to measure the roll of a ball. It is difficult to measure it from a broadcast image because the ball in the image appears small and has motion blur.

Our system extracts the ball's location and speed, and the catcher's stance as features from broadcast videos. It obtains the ball locus in every frame by using a ball trajectory visualization system "B-Motion" that we had previously developed (Takahashi, Misu, Tadenuma, & Yagi, 2005). B-Motion draws a CG trajectory of the ball thrown by the pitcher on the broadcasting image. The ball's locus is measured by tracking the ball in the image. The ball speed is obtained by automatically recognizing the characters superimposed on the screen just after the pitch, and catcher's stance is calculated by detecting the mitt locus just before the pitch.

The pitch type classifier is created using the Random Forests ensemble-learning algorithm from these features. Random Forests is suitable for this task because it creates high accuracy classifier in high speed, is robust against noise, and can compute the importance of each feature.

Our system has the following advantages.

- It can accurately identify the pitch type
- It can judge the same kinds of individual pitch types as well as human specialists judge
- It identifies the pitches only from single-view video sequences of baseball broadcast videos
- It does not require any additional cameras
- It can show the result immediately
- It can annotate the type of pitch for previous baseball broadcast videos

Our system is novel because it can identify nine kinds of individual pitches only from baseball broadcast video. The system is also effective; it obtained almost 90% recognition accuracy in experiments.

We describe the ball trajectory visualization "B-Motion" in section 2, and the automatic pitch type recognition system in section 3. In sections 4 and 5, we describe the features for automatic recognition from broadcast image sequences and the learning algorithm for creating the classifier. We discuss the results of the experiment in sections 6 and conclude in section 7.

2. "B-MOTION" BALL TRAJECTORY VISUALIZATION SYSTEM

2.1. System

"B-Motion" is a ball trajectory visualization system that we developed in 2004. B-Motion extracts the ball region from each frame of professional baseball broadcast video and tracks the region frame by frame automatically. The detected ball locus is used to compose a computer-generated locus image. It is capable of real-time processing, and the trajectory can be displayed immediately after the pitch. Another feature of the system is that the ordinary broadcast camera video can be used as the input.

The system has been used for the past six years by the Japanese broadcaster NHK. In these games, composited trajectory images are recorded to VTR for every pitch, and the image is replayed slowly from the VTR when it is broadcasted. The image is shown just after a pitch and between innings. The system has been admired by viewers for making it easy to understand the course of the pitch and the difference in breaking balls. The image is also useful for sports commentators, and it has been highly evaluated by commentators and producers.

Figure 1 presents a broadcast video image that is displayed by B-Motion.

2.2. Ball Tracking

The ball tracking process is shown in Figure 2. First, the ball release position is specified on the broadcast video image and the search region is set. The search region is a rectangle as shown in the example of Figure 3, and ball extraction

Figure 1. Example display of the ball trajectory

Figure 2. Extraction and tracking process

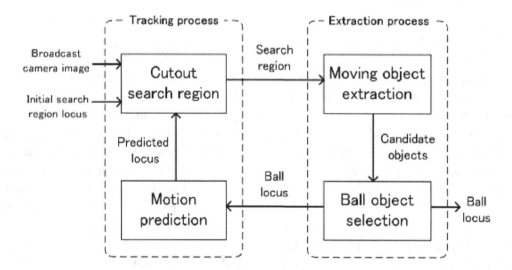

processing is performed only in that region. Limiting the processing to within the search region is intended to expedite the processing and reduce extraction errors.

During a pitch, the camera image does not move. This enables frame difference processing to be performed within the search region and moving objects to be extracted as ball candidates.

Figure 3. Initial ball search region

The frame difference images are created by calculating the difference in luminance of pixels in the search area. Then, two frame difference images are generated from three images in a frame interval.

The pixel values that are at the same locus of frame difference images 1 and 2 are the investigated. If there is a region in which the sign of the pixel differs between images 1 and 2, and both absolute values are beyond the specified threshold, it is considered as a candidate "ball object." The system creates a candidate object image that shows ball candidate regions in binary.

Figure 4 shows an example of finding a candidate ball object. The gray regions in (a) and (b) mean that the difference is 0, the white regions mean a positive difference, and the black regions mean a negative difference. The white regions in (c) show candidate objects, and the black region is the background.

The candidate object image may include false objects produced by player movements. Therefore, the candidate object in the region that is judged to be the most like a ball according to features such as color, size, and shape is selected. The center of gravity is obtained by calculating an average position vertically and horizontally in the selected ball candidate region and is output as the ball position.

This approach, however, does not necessarily give the ball position in every frame. Extractions can fail when the ball passes through background regions that are close to the ball in their brightness and color, such as when the ball moves close to or past a left-handed batter or billboards.

Figure 4. Generation of the candidate object image

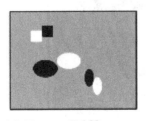 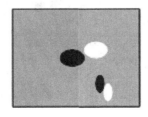 

(a) Frame Difference Image 1   (b) Frame Difference Image 2   (c) Candidate Object Image

For that reason, we supplemented the "B-Motion" with a prediction-based re-track function and an interpolation function. Once a ball is extracted, a Kalman filter (Yu, Xu, Tian, & Leong, 2003) is used to predict the ball position and range for the next frame. The prediction continues even after an extraction failure, so it is possible to pick up the ball again after it passes through background where extraction is difficult, as shown in Figure 5.

A Kalman filter, which assumes uniform straight-line motion, is used for prediction. It predicts the vectors **X** and **P** for each frame by using the following equations.

$$\mathbf{X}_t = \mathbf{FX}_{t-1}$$

$$\mathbf{P}_t = \mathbf{FP}_{t-1}\mathbf{F}^T + \mathbf{Q}$$

Here, t is frame number, **X** is the state estimation vector that consists of location coordinates, and **P** is the covariance matrix of the prediction error. **F** is the state propagator matrix whose elements express uniform straight-line motion for the linear prediction. $\mathbf{F}^T$ means the transposition of **F**. **Q** is the covariance matrix of the process noise.

If the system succeeds in extraction, **X**, **P**, and the Kalman gain **K** are updated using the following equations.

$$\mathbf{X'} = \mathbf{X} + \mathbf{K}(\mathbf{Y} - \mathbf{HX})$$

$$\mathbf{P'} = (\mathbf{I} - \mathbf{KH})\mathbf{P}$$

$$\mathbf{K} = \mathbf{PH}^T(\mathbf{HPH}^T + \mathbf{R})^{-1}$$

Y is the measurement state (extracted location), and **X'** and **P'** are updated values of **X** and **P**. **H** is the matrix that converts a state vector into a measurement vector. **R** is the covariance matrix of the measurement error.

When the extraction fails, the diagonal elements of **P** become large, and when it succeeds, the elements become small. Therefore, the size of the search area is controlled according to the values of **P**.

Furthermore, the ball position in the region where extraction failed can be determined by interpolation, so complete, gapless locus data can be obtained regardless of the extraction failures along the way.

Figure 5. Example of automatic ball tracking

3. PITCH TYPE RECOGNITION SYSTEM

The shape of the ball trajectory varies with the pitch type, so we expect the ball trajectory to be useful in pitch recognition. However, the pitch type is not necessarily determined by the locus shape alone. According to experts that judge pitch types, the process of determining pitch type by eyesight is as follows.

- The types of pitch in the pitcher's repertoire and the relative frequency of their use are confirmed in advance of the judging.
- Just prior to the pitch, the catcher's stance is observed to narrow the pitch candidates down to two or three types.
- During the pitch, the shape of the ball locus and the ball's speed are observed.
- After the pitch, the final decision on the pitch type is made from the ball speed displayed on the screen.

There are thus a number of factors other than trajectory shape that determine pitch type. They vary in subtle ways from pitcher to pitcher, so it is difficult to manually set a uniform threshold value. Therefore, we chose to extract multiple features that would serve as the factors of pitch type recognition from broadcast video images and use a machine-learning algorithm to create classifiers in our system.

In selecting the features, we referred to the decision method used by the expert judges. First, the repertoire of pitches and ball speeds, and the curve of breaking balls vary among pitchers, so we chose to make a classifier for each pitcher. The catcher's stance just prior to the pitch is measured using the histograms of oriented gradients (HOG) algorithm to detect the catcher's mitt region on the video. The ball trajectory is obtained with B-Motion. The ball speed is obtained by character recognition processing of the text display region in the video. All these features can be obtained only from broadcast video images of professional baseball.

The training and recognition process is shown in Figure 6. In the training phase, the features for each pitch are extracted from previously broadcast professional baseball video. To create a pitch-type classifier, those features are presented to a supervised learning algorithm along with pitch-type metadata produced by Data Stadium, which serves as the correct data.

In the recognition phase, the system requires only a regular broadcast camera video shot from the deep center for input and extracts the same features as were used in the training phase. The classifier automatically recognizes the type of pitch from these features.

The system can be operated without other sensor cameras or live broadcasting equipment. The processing hardware comprises only a personal computer and a video capture board. Furthermore, the processing is almost fully automatic, so the pitch type can be displayed immediately after the pitch. The only manual operations are setting the markers for specifying the rough location of the catcher region and billboard region that is used to calibrate the catcher's position (see Section 4) and setting the rough position of the initial search region of B-Motion. Those operations need only be performed once just before the game begins. When a pitcher is replaced or the camera angle changes, the initial search region should be reset.

4. FEATURES

4.1. Ball's Location

The system extracts the ball's location by using B-Motion. As described above, B-Motion can detect the ball's position at frame intervals without gaps from baseball broadcast images. Some examples of ball trajectory data produced by "B-Motion" are shown in Figure 7. Even though the position information is in the form of two-dimensional

Figure 6. Flow of training and recognition

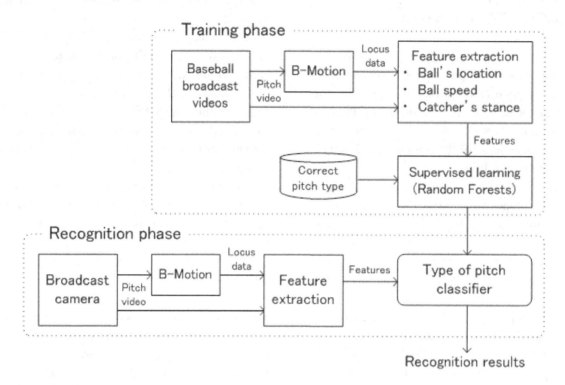

image coordinates, the shape features can be seen, especially in curveballs.

The camera angle changes somewhat in each pitching scene. Therefore, the system has to extract features that reduce the effect of the changing camera angle. The following thirty features are extracted from the ball trajectory data.

- Locus slope (4)
- Locus curvature (4)
- Average motion vectors (12)
- Speed ratio (9)
- Tracking time (1)

The numbers in parentheses show numbers of dimensions. Locus slope is a first-order differential coefficient that is calculated by a straight-line approximation. It is calculated for the entire, first part, center part, and last part of locus data; therefore, it has 4 dimensions. Locus curvature is a second-order differential coefficient that is calculated by a 2-dimensional curve approximation. It has 4 dimensions as well. Average motion vectors are calculated for the first part, center part, and last part of the trajectory in total length, horizontal length, and vertical length, respectively, so this feature has 12 dimensions. Speed ratio

Figure 7. Example of ball trajectory data

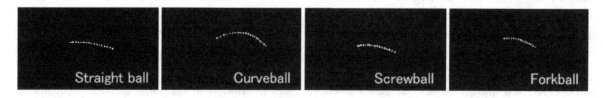

is the ratio of motion vectors, calculated for the first part over the center part, the center part over the last part, and the last part over the first part. Each ratio is calculated for total, horizontal and vertical elements, respectively, so the feature has 9 dimensions. Tracking time is the number of frames from the time tracking started to the time it finished. As described above, the system extracts 30-dimensional features in total from the ball trajectory data.

Figure 8 illustrates some features obtained from the ball trajectory. The curved line shows the trajectory curvature of entire; the straight lines are the slopes of the first part, center part, and last part of the trajectory; the arrows represent the motion vectors.

The speed ratio is calculated from the average motion vectors, and tracking time is represented by the number of extracted ball's locations.

4.2. Ball Speed

The speed at which the ball moves varies with the type of pitch, so we can expect ball speed to be effective in identifying the type of pitch. While it is possible to calculate the ball speed from the ball trajectory data, it is difficult to get stable measurements of high enough accuracy because of extraction errors.

In professional baseball broadcasts, the ball speed measured by a speed gun is displayed as text superimposed on the video. It is measured at a single point, so it is not possible to obtain the initial speed or the final speed. Nevertheless, the accuracy is high and the speed is displayed immediately after the pitch. We therefore chose to obtain the ball speed by using character recognition technology to read the superimposed characters.

Character recognition is generally divided into the following two tasks.

- Delineating the character region
- Performing character recognition within that region

Although the position of the character display region does not vary much from program to program, the system delineates the character regions in an effort to enhance generality.

Figure 8. Features obtained from the ball trajectory

An example of the superimposed character display is shown in Figure 9. The character display area generally has the features listed below, so we used these features to search for the display area.

- Strong edges
- High brightness
- Uniform color
- Displayed for a fixed amount of time
- Constant position within the image coordinate system
- Text is aligned either vertically or horizontally

The process to obtain the ball speed is shown in Figure 10. First, an edge image E is created for each of the images from the current frame (I_t) to the frame before frame m. The Prewitt operator is used in the processing. Almost all superimposed characters have strong edges, so a threshold can be set high without auto-configuration. The edge-detecting threshold was determined experimentally. An example edge image is shown in Figure 11. Next, a search is made in the edge images from frame t to frame t-m for pixels whose values (edge strengths) are large and change little. Pixels that meet these criteria are given the binary value True, and the others are given the binary value False in order to obtain the binary image S.

The True pixels in image S are counted in the horizontal and vertical directions. Lines are drawn for the rows and columns that have high pixel counts, and the largest rectangular area enclosed by the lines is taken to be the character display region, as shown in Figure 12.

Finally, the character display area that has been digitized with the brightness threshold is input to

Figure 9. Ball speed display

the OCR program, which automatically recognizes the letters and numerals in the image to obtain the ball speed. For character recognition, we use the Panasonic color OCR library, a highly accurate commercial product (Panasonic, n.d.).

The ball speed is displayed in numerals, so misrecognitions are rare, unlike for the various characters in player names. In scenes where the ball speed display is turned off immediately because of a hit ball, it may not be possible to extract the display region, but the correct ball speed is obtained for over 90% of the pitches.

4.3. Catcher's Stance

4.3.1. Catcher's Mitt Locus

Usually, the catcher gives a sign before the pitch to specify the ball's course and type of pitch, and then assumes a stance that gives the pitcher a target to aim at. By analyzing the catcher's stance, it is possible to narrow down the range of the type of pitch to some extent. For example, when the catcher holds the mitt low, the probability of a forkball is high; if the mitt is held to the right of a right-handed pitcher's viewpoint, the probability of a curveball is low. We therefore chose to detect the catcher's mitt region and use the locus as a feature.

4.3.2. Measuring the Mitt Position

We used the histograms of oriented gradients (HOG) algorithm (Yamauchi, Fujiyoshi, Hwang, & Kanade, 2008), which employs the luminance gradient as a feature to detect the mitt region. HOG describes the feature over the given region. It can represent the rough shape of the object. The algorithm is suitable for mitt detection because the mitt region is a blob and its appearance slightly changes in each pitching scene.

The HOG descriptor is calculated as follows. First, the magnitude and orientation of the gra-

Figure 10. Ball speed recognition process

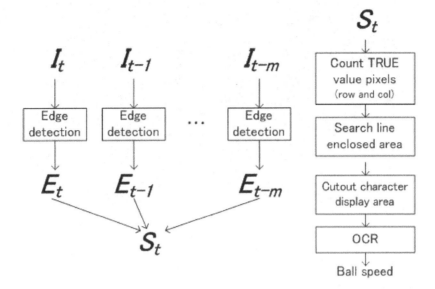

dients are computed. The target region is divided into cells of 5×5 pixels and each group of 3×3 cells is integrated into a block in a sliding fashion, as shown in Figure 13. Each cell consists of a 9-bin histogram of HOG features. Each block contains a concatenated vector of all its cells. The feature vectors, which are called the HOG descriptor, are normalized in each block.

We created a mitt region discriminator by using support vector machine (SVM) (Chen, Lin, & Schölkopf, 2005; Schölkopf, Platt, Shawe-Taylor, Smola, & Williamson, 2001). SVM is a set of related supervised learning methods used for classification and regression. SVM performs classification by constructing an N-dimensional hyper plane that optimally separates the data into two categories.

Figure 14 shows the way of measuring the mitt region. In the training phase, mitt region discriminator is created from HOG descriptors calculated from learning data. We used about 100 mitt region images for positive samples and about 800 other region images for negative samples as learning data (Figure 15 and 16).

Just before each pitch in a game, the mitt search area is cutout from broadcast video and the system searches for a mitt region only in that area. The mitt search area is manually determined to be around the catcher before the game (Figure 17). Target regions of 50×35 pixels of in the mitt search area are cutout and HOG descriptors are calculated for each target region. SVM discriminates a mitt region from the HOG descriptors.

The small rectangle in Figure 17 shows a detected mitt region in a broadcast image. A comparison of the automatically acquired mitt position with the manually plotted position reveals a difference of about 3.33 pixels.

Figure 11. Edge image (Ball speed display in lower center)

Figure 12. Detection of the ball speed display region

Figure 13. Cells and blocks

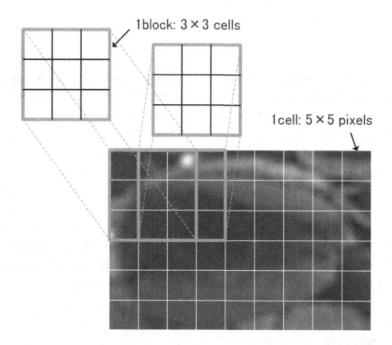

4.3.3. Extracting the Billboard Region

In baseball broadcasting, the camera position and camera angle may vary slightly between pitches, so the catcher's mitt position cannot be represented as absolute position coordinates within the image. We therefore chose to represent the mitt position by coordinates that are relative to the center of an advertising billboard that is in the background near the center of the image (Figure 18). The billboard region generally has strong edges, a feature that is easily detected and is thus suitable for extraction.

SIFT features (Lowe, 2004) are used to detect the feature point. SIFT is an algorithm to detect feature points on the image and describe 128-dimensional gradient-based characteristics at each feature point. SIFT is able to deal with expansion, reduction, and rotation of the target region and changes in illumination, so it is a suitable for situations where there is camera movement or changes in brightness.

SIFT describes similar features to those of HOG. The difference is that SIFT describes a feature at the candidate locus (keypoint), while HOG describes the feature over the given region. SIFT is suitable for detecting sharply defined regions such as billboards.

An example of SIFT features in a pitching scene is shown in Figure 19. The starting point of each arrow in the figure is the position of a feature point, the direction indicates the orientation, and the length indicates the gradient scale.

First, the billboard region is manually specified before the game by two points on the screen, $\rho_1 = (x_1, y_1)$ and $\rho_2 = (x_2, y_2)$. Then the position midway between these two points ρ_c, and the size l are obtained. At the same time, SIFT features within the billboard region are obtained and saved as a SIFT feature template W_{temp}.

For each pitching scene, a SIFT feature S_t is obtained near the center of the screen, and its corresponding points with W_{temp} are obtained. If M feature points are extracted from the current frame image of time t and there are N feature points in the template billboard region image, the feature points for the two images can be expressed by the following equation.

$$S_t^M = \left(S_1^M, S_2^M, \cdots, S_{128}^M \right)$$

$$W_{temp}^N = \left(W_1^N, W_2^N, \cdots, W_{128}^N \right)$$

The corresponding points n' between the features in the current frame (m[th]) and features in the template image are detected with the following equation.

$$n' = \arg\min_{n \in N} \sum_{i=1}^{128} \sqrt{\left(S_i^m - W_i^n \right)^2}$$

The billboard region template image and a matching result are shown in Figure 20. Although some errors exist in the image, several corresponding points of high similarity are used in the actual processing, so the billboard region can be detected correctly.

Next, an affine matrix for expansion, reduction, and translation is calculated from the positional relations of corresponding points (Gray, 1997). The obtained matrix is used to determine the center ρ_c' and size l' of the billboard region in the current pitching scene.

The mitt locus is obtained as a distance and angle relative to the center of the billboard region. The distance is normalized to the size of the billboard region l'.

4.4. List of Features

As described above, the system extracts the 33-dimensional features from ball's location, ball speed, and catcher's stance, listed in Figure 21. In Figure 21 the characters 'E', 'F', 'C', and 'L' mean entire, first part, center part, last part of trajectory. 'T', 'H', and 'V' mean total, horizontal, and vertical. 'F-C', 'C-L', and 'L-F' mean ratio of the motion vector of the first part over that of the center part, the center part over the last part, and the last part over the first part. The system extracts all features only from a single-view video sequence of baseball broadcast videos.

5. CREATING THE CLASSIFIER

To create a classifier for identifying the type of pitch, we used the Random Forests supervised ensemble-learning algorithm (Breiman, 2001; Jin & Masakatsu, 2007). This algorithm quickly creates a high accuracy classifier, and is robust against noise in the training data. The ball locus data is particularly susceptible to noise due to extraction errors, so Random Forests is a suitable algorithm for this task. In addition, the features

Figure 14. Flow for measuring the mitt position

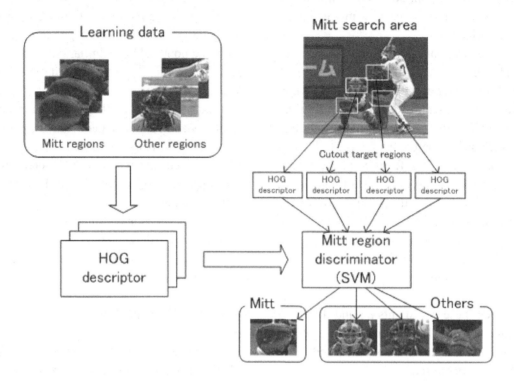

need not be narrowed down beforehand, because Random Forests computes feature importance and selects the important features automatically.

The flow of training and identification of Random Forests is shown in Figure 22. Pitch data is created for each pitch. The pitch data includes 33-dimensional features and a correct pitch type. The correct pitch types are reliable because they are made by two or more experts at Data Stadium Inc., which distributes sports metadata in Japan.

We created a large amount of pitch data from previously broadcast baseball videos for each

Figure 15. Positive samples

 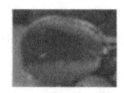 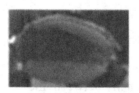 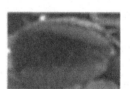

Figure 16. Negative samples

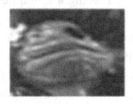   

Figure 17. Mitt search area (large rectangle) and detected mitt region (small rectangle)

Figure 18. Billboard region and mitt position

pitcher, because the number of pitch types, ball speed, and trajectory vary depending on the pitcher.

A large number of data subsets are created from the population of pitch data by using a bootstrap sampling method. The bootstrap creates subsets by sampling with replacement from the popula-

tion (these must have the same pitch data). The system creates 500 subsets from each population of pitch data.

A decision tree is then created for each subset. The feature used for branching is not selected from all features, but from several randomly selected candidate features at the node of each

Figure 19. SIFT features in a pitching scene

Figure 20. Detection of the billboard region

Figure 21. List of features

1	2	3	4	5	6	7	8	9	10	11	12	13	14	15	16	17	18	19	20	21	22	23	24	25	26	27	28	29	30	31	32	33
Ball's location																														Ball speed	Catcher's stance	
slope				curvature				motion vector												speed ratio									tracking time			
E	F	C	L	E	F	C	L	E			F			C			L			F-C			C-L			L-F					length	angle
								T	H	V	T	H	V	T	H	V	T	H	V	T	H	V	T	H	V	T	H	V				

branch. Hence, mutually different decision trees are created. The system selects five candidate features at each node. In addition, there is no pruning; therefore, each tree grows to the largest extent possible.

The many decision trees thus generated serve as the classifier. In the recognition process, the pitch type is judged by the various decision trees and the majority decision is output as the pitch type.

6. EXPERIMENT

6.1. Experimental Conditions

To verify the efficacy of the proposed method, we performed pitch type recognition experiments. We chose five pitchers that have relatively large pitch repertoires from professional live baseball video broadcasts by NHK and created a classifier for each of them.

Figure 22. Random Forest training and recognition

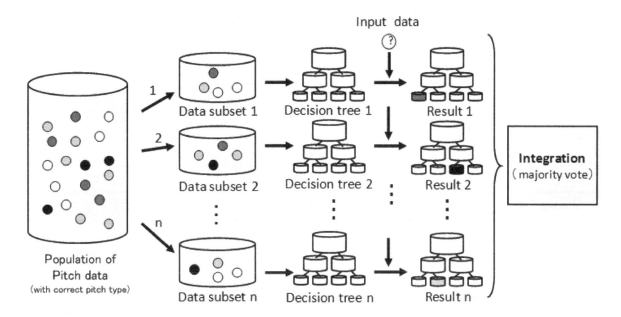

For generality, we included both left-handed and right-handed pitchers in the experiments. The feature data was acquired from at least three games for each pitcher from baseball broadcast video taken in the past three years. However, because the trajectory shape on the screen varies with the camera position of the ballpark, all of the video that we used was from the same ballpark. Figure 23 lists each pitcher's dominant arm and repertoire of pitches and the number of games and pitches in the experiment.

We used two-thirds of the pitching data for training and one-third as test data for cross-validation to evaluate the trained classifiers.

6.2. Results for Individual Pitchers

The results for the five pitchers are presented in Figure 23. The total accuracy for all of the pitchers was 88.96% and an accuracy of over 90% was achieved for four of the pitchers. Figures 24 and 25 show the detailed recognition results for the highest accuracy (pitcher A) and the lowest accuracy (pitcher E). The numerals in the figures

show the number of pitches judged to be each type of pitch. The figures also show the precision and recall for individual pitch types.

Pitcher A pitched straight balls over 40% of the time, and the high recognition rate for straight balls contributed to the overall high rate. The F-measures were very high even for curveballs, sliders, and sinkers. The recall for a screwball, however, was a rather low 28.57%. We believe this low result was caused by insufficient training data, because the screwball is used less than 3% of the time.

As data in support of this supposition, we present the relation between the amount of data and the F-measure for each pitch type for pitcher E (Figure 26). There is quick convergence for pitch types that have particular trajectory shapes or ball speeds, such as curveballs. For other pitch types, however, it takes about 40 pitches to attain convergence. There were only seven instances of data for the screwball of pitcher A, so additional data should improve accuracy.

For pitcher E, the total accuracy is lower than the other pitchers, because he has a large pitching

Figure 23. Accuracy for each pitcher

Pitcher	Dominant arm	Number of type of pitch	Number of games	Number of pitches	Accuracy rate(%)
A	left	5	3	267	93.24
B	right	4	4	277	91.77
C	right	5	3	320	91.62
D	left	5	3	277	90.03
E	right	6	5	401	81.75
Total	right/left	6	14	1544	88.96

Figure 24. Results for pitcher A

	Straight	Screw	Curve	Slider	Sinker	Recall
Straight	120	0	0	0	0	100.00
Screw	4	2	0	0	1	28.57
Curve	0	0	25	0	1	96.15
Slider	1	0	0	55	3	93.22
Sinker	1	0	0	5	49	89.09
Precision	95.24	100.00	100.00	91.67	90.74	93.24

Figure 25. Results for pitcher E

	Straight	Screw	Cutball	Curve	Slider	Fork	Recall
Straight	77	11	5	0	0	1	81.91
Screw	19	28	2	0	0	0	57.14
Cutball	6	0	122	0	6	0	91.04
Curve	0	0	0	35	0	0	100.00
Slider	0	0	18	1	28	1	58.33
Fork	0	1	1	0	1	38	92.68
Precision	75.49	70.00	82.43	97.22	80.00	95.00	81.75

repertoire. However, the F-measures were above 60% for all pitch types, and recognition was possible without bias for particular types of pitches.

6.3. Feature Analysis

For a finer analysis of the features, we calculated the importance of each feature. We used the Gini coefficient as a branching index in constructing decision trees by Random Forests, and the importance of features can be evaluated by the amount of reduction in the Gini coefficient that results from branching. Feature importance is shown in graph form in Figure 27.

The features in order of importance were ball speed, speed ratios, curvature, slope, and the catcher's stance. The features concerning the ball speed ranked high. This result is consistent with the criteria used by the experts to judge pitch type.

The system depends on the ball speed feature and it cannot be used if the ball speed was not obtained. However, the system can still be used for broadcast videos that have no superimposed characters registering ball speed. Figure 28 shows the results of a comparison of a classifier trained without the ball speed feature. High accuracy was maintained for almost all pitchers, and the accuracy for pitcher B was almost the same. It seems that the speed ratio and motion vectors calculated from the ball's location complement the ball's speed. The experiment shows the system can accurately identify pitch types even when the ball speed is not available.

The recognition accuracy of the catcher's stance is relatively low compared with those of ball speed and ball trajectory. The reason is that the timing of switching from another scene to the pitching scene was sometimes late. When the timing was late, the system could not detect the catcher's mitt position because of changes in the catcher's stance. However, it contributes to higher recognition rates for breaking balls. For a right-handed pitcher, for example, the catcher

tends to move to the right to position the mitt for a screwball, and adding the catcher stance feature improves the F-measure by 2.38%.

6.4. Comparison with Other Learning Algorithms

Our system uses the random Forests learning algorithm for creating the pitch type classifier. The algorithm is noise robust, fast at learning and recognition, and can calculate the importance of features. We performed the comparative experiments with SVM, Adaboost (Zhang, 2004), Bagging (Kotsiantis & Pintelas, 2004), Decision tree (Menzies & Hu, 2003), and the K-Nearest Neighbor method (Geng, Liu, Qin, Amold, Li, & Shum, 2008).

Adaboost is a classification algorithm for constructing a "strong" classifier from a "weak" learning algorithm. Adaboost finds a sequence of weak hypotheses, each of which is appropriate for the distribution on training example, and combines the weak hypotheses by a weighted majority vote.

Bagging is an ensemble machine learning algorithm designed to improve the stability and classification accuracy of classification and regression models by aggregating weak hypotheses. It also reduces variance and helps to avoid overfitting. We used decision trees as weak hypotheses for Adaboost and Bagging in these experiments.

Decision tree is a predictive model, mapping from observations about an item to conclusions about its target value. In the tree structure, leaves represent classifications and branches represent conjunctions of features that lead to those classifications.

The k-Nearest Neighbor (k-NN) algorithm is a simple machine learning algorithm. An object is classified by a majority vote of its neighbors, with the object being assigned to the class most common among its k nearest neighbors. The nearest neighbors of an object are defined in terms of the standard Euclidean distance.

Figure 26. Relation of amount of data to F-measure

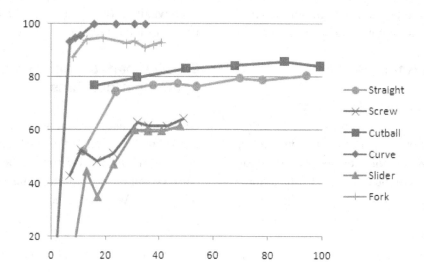

Figure 27. Features importance

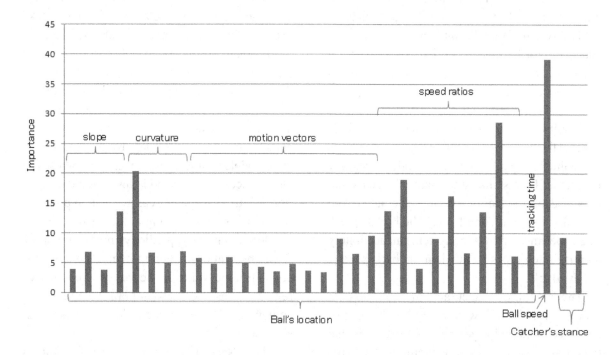

We compared 6 classifiers, each created from different learning algorithms. We used two-thirds of the 400 pitching data of pitcher E for training and one-third as test data for cross-validation. Figure 29 shows the resulting recognition accuracies and processing times in training (267 pitch data) and recognition (133 pitch data).

Adaboost achieved the best recognition rate, and Random Forests, SVM, Bagging followed. Although the accuracy of Adaboost is little bit

Figure 28. Comparison of the classifiers which was trained with all features and trained without ball speed

Pitcher / Classfier	A	B	C	D	E
Trained with all features (%)	93.24	91.77	91.62	90.03	81.75
Trained without ball speed (%)	90.26	91.26	88.19	88.74	73.32

higher than Random Forests, its processing speed is much slower than Random Forests. Processing speed is an important factor in live broadcast programs, so we chose the Random Forests learning algorithm.

Random Forests does not have to normalize the units of features, so it seems that its accuracy may be higher than some learning algorithms that need to normalize them. This is especially suitable for our task that uses various units of features.

Random Forests can also calculate the importance of each feature, and the processing cost can be reduced by referring to the importance. We created an Adaboost classifier trained with ten high rank features calculated by Random Forests. The classifier could recognize the pitch types in 0.94 seconds and had a recognition accuracy of over 80% (Specifically, 80.14%). Thus, by referring to the importance calculated by Random Forests, we can create a classifier that quickly and accurately identifies the pitch type.

This framework for creating a noble classifier can be used for other sports such as softball, bowling, and golf.

6.5. Generalization of the Classifier

We created classifiers for each pitcher because the number of pitch types, ball speed, and trajectory vary depending on the pitcher. A system that is to be used in broadcasts must have high accuracy. Hence, we gave priority to recognition accuracy rather than system generality.

For comparison, we also created a general classifier trained with all pitch data. Figure 30 compares it with the proposed classifier trained for each pitcher. The accuracies of general classifier are lower for all pitchers. In particular, the accuracy for pitcher E is lower by as much as 38.36%. It seems that this result is because the ball speed and the trajectory will vary depending on the pitcher. For example, the speed of a straight ball thrown by a low-speed pitcher might be similar to the ball

Figure 29. Comparison with other learning algorithms (pitcher E)

		Random Forests	SVM	Adaboost	Bagging	Decision tree	kNN
Recognition accuracy(%)		81.75	79.1	82.31	78.96	74.67	74.22
Processing time(sec)	training	0.66	0.76	14.61	13.72	0.08	0.02
	recognition	0.03	0.06	1.41	1.42	0.01	0.01

Figure 30. Comparison of the individual classifiers and general classifiers

Classfier \ Pitcher	A	B	C	D	E
Individual (%)	93.24	91.77	91.62	90.03	81.75
General (%)	68.17	87.37	89.06	60.29	43.39

speed of a breaking ball thrown by a high-speed pitcher. Although the system's generality is low, it is necessary to create a classifier for each pitcher to obtain high accuracy. The individual classifier would be needed even if three-dimensional ball trajectory were measured.

However, it's laborious to create classifiers for every pitcher of professional baseball, so we plan to create the general classifier in the future. The accuracies of pitcher B and pitcher C hardly fell. To create a general classifier, we will have to analyze the differences between the pitchers for whom the system lost accuracy and those for whom it did not lose it.

We also plan to create a general classifier for any ballpark because the camera position changes from ballpark to ballpark and the shape of trajectory on the screen slightly changes. As described above, we gave priority to recognition accuracy for nine kinds of individual pitch types in this study. Hence, we created classifiers for the most popular ballpark in Japan, one that is frequently used for broadcasts by NHK.

Although we experimented with baseball videos broadcast from one broadcasting station, the classifier can be used by other broadcasters because the camera is set up in the same position in the ballpark regardless of the broadcaster, and the same pitch data can be extracted.

CONCLUSION

We developed a system that can automatically recognize nine kinds of individual pitch types in live baseball broadcasts. The system can identify the pitch types only from single-view video sequences of baseball broadcast videos. The features used by the system are the ball's location obtained from pitched ball trajectory, the ball speed obtained by character recognition of numbers superimposed on the video, and the catcher's stance obtained from the locus of the catcher's mitt. These features were learned by the Random Forests ensemble-training algorithm to construct pitch classifiers. Tests on actual broadcast video images resulted in a total accuracy of 88.96%, and accuracies of over 90% for four of the five pitchers.

Our next objective will be to improve the recognition accuracy by increasing the training data. We plan to create a general classifier that can identify the pitch type of any pitcher in any ballpark. We will also apply this framework for other sports.

REFERENCES

Alaways, L. W. (1998). *Aerodynamics of the Curve-Ball: An Investigation of the Effects of Angular Velocity on Baseball Trajectories*. Unpublished doctoral dissertation, University of California, Davis.

Ando, R., Shinoda, K., Furui, S., & Mochizuki, T. (2007). A Robust Scene Recognition System for Baseball

Breiman, L. (2001). Random Forests. *Machine Learning, 45*, 5-23.Chang, P., Han, M., & Gong, Y. (2002). Extract Highlights from Baseball Game Video with Hidden Markov Models. In *Proceedings of the International Conference on Image Processing* (pp. 609-612).

Broadcast using Data-Driven Approach. In *Proceedings of the ACM International Conference on Image and Video* (pp.186-193). New York: ACM Publishing.

Chen, H.-S., Chen, H.-T., Tsai, W.-J., Lee, S.-Y., & Yu, J.-Y. (2007). Pitch-by-Pitch Extraction from Single View Baseball Video Sequences. In *Proceedings of the IEEE International Conference on Multimedia and Expo* (pp. 1423-1426)

Chen, H.-T. (2006). A Trajectory-Based Ball Tracking Framework with Enrichment for Broadcast Baseball Videos. In *Proceedings of the International Computer Symposium* (pp. 1145-1150).

Chen, P. H., Lin, C. J., & Schölkopf, B. (2005). A Tutorial on v-Support Vector Machines. *Applied Stochastic Models in Business and Industry, 21*, 111–136. doi:10.1002/asmb.537

Chu, W.-T., Wang, C.-W., & Wu, J.-L. (2006). Extraction of Baseball Trajectory and Physics-Based Validation for Single-View Baseball Video Sequences. In *Proceedings of the IEEE International Conference on Multimedia & Expo* (pp. 1813-1816).

Geng, X., Liu, T.-Y., Qin, T., Amold, A., Li, H., & Shum, H.-Y. (2008). Query Dependent Ranking using K-Nearest Neighbor. In *Proceedings of the International Conference on Research and Development in Information Retrieval, 2008*, 115–122.

Gray, A. (1997). *Modern Differential Geometry of Curves and Surfaces with Mathematica* (2nd ed.). Boca Raton, FL: CRC Press.

Gueziec, A. (2002). Tracking Pitches for Broadcast Television. *IEEE Computer, 35*(3), 38–43.

Hoshikawa, D. (2006). Utilization of IT in Professional Baseball. *Operations Research as a Management Science Research, 51*(1), 37–39.

Jin, M., & Masakatsu, M. (2007). Authorship Identification using Random Forests. *Institute of Statistical Mathematics, 55*(2), 255–268.

Kon'ya, Y., Kuwano, H., Yamada, T., Kawamori, M., & Kawazoe, K. (2005). Metadata Generation and Distribution for Live Programs on Broadcasting-Telecommunication Linkage Services. In *Proceedings of the Pacific Rim Conference on Multimedia* (pp. 224-233).

Kotsiantis, S. B., & Pintelas, P. E. (2004). Combining Bagging and Boosting. *International Journal of Computational Intelligence, 1*(4), 324–333.

Liddy, E. D., Allen, E., Harwell, S., Corieri, S., Yilmazel, O., Ercan Ozgencil, N., et al. (2002, August). Automatic Metadata Generation & Evaluation. In *Proceedings of the 25th Annual International ACM SIGIR Conference on Research and Development in Information Retrieval*, Tampere, Finland (pp. 401-402). New York: ACM Publishing.

Lien, C.-C., Chiang, C.-L., & Lee, C.-H. (2007, February). Scene-Based Event Detection for Baseball Videos. *Journal of Visual Communication and Image Representation, 18*(1), 1–14. doi:10.1016/j.jvcir.2006.09.002

Lowe, D. G. (2004). Distinctive Image Features from Scale-Invariant Keypoints. *International Journal of Computer Vision, 60*(2), 91–110. doi:10.1023/B:VISI.0000029664.99615.94

Menzies, T., & Hu, Y. (2003). Data Mining for Very Busy People. *Computer*, *36*(11), 22–29. doi:10.1109/MC.2003.1244531

Panasonic. (n.d.). *Color OCR Library*. Retrieved November 10, 2008, from http://panasonic.co.jp/pss/pstc/products/colorocrlib/

Rander, P. (1998). *A Multi-Camera Method for 3D Digitization of Dynamic, Real-World Events* (Tech. Rep.CMU-RI-TR-98-12). Pittsburgh, PA: Robotics Institute, Carnegie Mellon University.

Schölkopf, B., Platt, J. C., Shawe-Taylor, J., Smola, A. J., & Williamson, R. C. (2001). Estimating the Support of a High-Dimensional Distribution. *Neural Computation*, *13*, 1443–1471. doi:10.1162/089976601750264965

Shibata, S. (2007). *Digital Baseball Scoring System Using XML*. Retrieved April 25, 2009, from http://www.ipa.go.jp/SPC/report/01fy-pro/dcaj/techadvn/baseball/baseball.pdf

Shum, H., & Komura, T. (2004). A Spatiotemporal Approach to Extract the 3D Trajectory of the Baseball from a Single View Video Sequence. In Proceedings of the *IEEE International Conference on Multimedia & Expo* (pp. 1583-1586).

Stadium, D. (n.d.). *Data Stadium Inc*. Retrieved April 25, 2009, from http://www.datastadium.co.jp/

Takahashi, M., Misu, T., Tadenuma, M., & Yagi, N. (2005). Real-Time Ball Trajectory Visualization using Object Extraction. In *Proceedings of the Conference on Visual Media Production* (pp. 62-69).

Theobalt, C., Albrecht, I., Haber, J., Magnor, M., & Seidel, H.-P. (2004). Pitching a Baseball: Tracking High-Speed Motion with Multi-Exposure Images. In *Proceedings of ACM SIGGRAPH* (pp. 540-547). New York: ACM Publishing.

Yamauchi, Y., Fujiyoshi, H., Hwang, B.-W., & Kanade, T. (2008). People Detection Based on Co-Occurrence of Appearance and Spatiotemporal Features. In *Proceedings of the International Conference on Pattern Recognition* (pp. 1-4).

Yu, X., Xu, C., Tian, Q., & Leong, H. W. (2003). A Ball Tracking Framework for Broadcast Soccer Video. In *Proceedings of the IEEE International Conference on Multimedia & Expo, II*, 273–276.

Zhang, T. (2004). Convex risk Minimization. *Annals of Statistics*, *32*, 56–85. doi:10.1214/aos/1079120130

This work was previously published in the International Journal of Multimedia Data Engineering and Management, Volume 1, Issue 1, edited by Shu-Ching Chen, pp. 12-36, copyright 2010 by IGI Publishing (an imprint of IGI Global).

Chapter 9
Ontology Instance Matching Based MPEG-7 Resource Integration

Hanif Seddiqui
Toyohashi University of Technology, Japan

Masaki Aono
Toyohashi University of Technology, Japan

ABSTRACT

Heterogeneous multimedia contents are annotated by a sharable formal conceptualization, often called ontology, and these contents, regardless of their media, become sharable resources/instances. Integration of the sharable resources and acquisition of diverse knowledge is getting researchers' attention at a rapid pace. In this regard, MPEG-7 standard convertible to semantic Resource Description Framework (RDF) evolves for containing structured data and knowledge sources. In this paper, the authors propose an efficient approach to integrate the multimedia resources annotated by the standard of MPEG-7 schema using ontology instance matching techniques. MPEG-7 resources are usually specified explicitly by their surrounding MPEG-7 schema entities, e.g., concepts and properties, in conjunction with other linked resources. Therefore, resource integration needed schema matching as well. In this approach, the authors obtained the schema matching using their scalable ontology alignment algorithm and collected the semantically linked resources, referred to as the Semantic Link Cloud (SLC) collectively for each of the resources. Techniques were addressed to solve several data heterogeneity: value transformation, structural transformation and logical transformation. These experiments show the strength and efficiency of the proposed matching approach.

DOI: 10.4018/978-1-4666-1791-9.ch009

INTRODUCTION

The proliferation of heterogeneous digital media contents along with the rapid growth of current World Wide Web endures a formidable task of information integration across media. The digital media is often represented by text, image, audio, video, and graphics and so on. Due to the heterogeneity and availability of large number of digital contents, digital media turns out to become hardly manageable without fine-grained computerized support (Garcia & Celma, 2005). Furthermore, the most of state-of-the-art researches are borne to focus on monotonic digital media, either concentrating on text or image or other media contents independently. Recently a number of structured resource annotation standards are proposed for knowledge acquisition from heterogeneous digital media.

The heterogeneous contents of digital data, regardless of their media, become structured resources containing knowledge source in an interoperable format by means of MPEG-7 (Nack & Lindsay, 1999; Nack, Lindsay, & GMD-IPSI, 1999; Salembier & Smith, 2002), or MPEG-21 (Bormans & Hill, 2002) standards. MPEG-7, formally named *Multimedia Content Description Interface* (Salembier & Smith, 2002), is developed by the Moving Picture Experts Group[1] (MPEG). MPEG-7 is standardized by means of *Descriptors* (Ds), *Description Schemes* (DSs) and the relationships between them. The descriptors correspond either to the low- level data features (e.g., visual texture, camera motion, audio spectrum and so on) or semantic resources (e.g., places, actors, events and objects). The description schemes are used for grouping the descriptors into more abstract description entities. The descriptors, the schemes and their relationships are represented using the *Description Definition Language* (DDL) in W3C XML Schema recommendation[2]. However, XML is a semi-structured context having a little semantic with hardly sharable structure.

The XML schema lacks to express formal semantics. However, an ontology has formal semantic with reusability and is defined as a formal specification of a shared conceptualization (Gruber, 1993). It has capability to alleviate the limitation. An ontology contains sets of concepts, properties, axioms and instances. Furthermore, it contains concept hierarchy and property hierarchy. Several researchers converted MPEG-7 schema into ontologies to enhance the semantic expressiveness using *Web Ontology Language* (OWL) (McGuinness & van Harmelen, 2004).

There are a number of MPEG-7 ontologies. They are *Hunter's ABC ontology*[3] (Lagoze & Hunter, 2001) used for digital libraries (Hunter, 2002; Hunter, 2003) and eResearch field (Bloehdorn, et al., 2005), *DS-MIRF*[4] (Tsinaraki, Polydoros, & Christodoulaki, 2004), (Tsinaraki, Polydors, & Christodoulakis, 2007), *Rhizomik*[5] (Garcia & Celma, 2005) and *COMM*[6] (Arndt, Troncy, Staab, Hardman, & Vacura, 2007). COMM is developed based on their previous work (Troncy, 2003; Isaac & Troncy, 2004). A comprehensive research work compares the ontologies (Troncy, Celma, Little, Garcia, & Tsinaraki, 2007). Moreover, the description of an annotated digital media can be obtained either manually or automatically in XML format. This annotating description can also be converted automatically into RDF description (Garcia & Celma, 2005).

Using MPEG-7 ontologies, multimedia resources are annotated by the concepts, properties and other schema entities of MPEG-7. We can divide the MPEG-7 contents into two parts: schema and resources. The schema entities, often called as terminology, are collectively defined as TBox, assertion for describing a set of concepts and properties in terms of controlled vocabularies of ontologies. On the other hand, the instances of concepts of TBox are collectively called as ABox i.e. assertion of control statements on instances of the concepts. We call the MPEG-7 based instances as multimedia resources. A multimedia resource is specified with the help of schema entities of TBox and other resources of ABox.

Integrating annotated contents or descriptions of the resources of several digital media is often a formidable task, as they are annotated by differently by various users of diverse area of locality with different viewpoints and with different metadata ontologies. The language, culture and the way of description affect the annotation of a media adversely. There are several factors as typographical errors, abbreviating words, individual psychological behavior and so on which affect the contents. Therefore, resource consolidation is required for identifying equivalent resources to achieve the semantic benefits like efficient integration, acquisition of sharable knowledge against gigantic media contents of the World Wide Web.

We have an experience of developing scalable ontology alignment algorithm called Anchor-Flood to match even very large ontology schemas efficiently (Seddiqui & Aono, 2009) (Seddiqui & Aono, 2008). We achieved the best runtime (Caracciolo et al., 2008) in ontology alignment during *Ontology Alignment Evaluation Initiative (OAEI), 2008 Campaign*[7] with our Anchor-Flood algorithm. We also develop instance matching algorithm recently. We use our scalable schema matching and ontology instance matching algorithm to integrate MPEG-7 based heterogeneous resources of multimedia.

Our approach intends to match semantic resources rather than the low-level binary contents of the digital media. In this regard, our ontology alignment algorithm first aligns a pair of TBox. The resulted aligned pairs, i.e. concept to concept or property to property across ontology schemas, are fed into our proposed instance matching algorithm. Our matching algorithm then starts matching resources or instances across ABox. We compare the literals associated to one semantic resource with those of the other resources across heterogeneous digital media. And our system produces a list of aligned pairs to attain interoperability and integration.

The main contribution of our approach is of attaining the aligned resources or instances across heterogeneous digital media by a novel method considering the neighboring semantic links. It helps integrating information and producing a consolidated knowledge base. The integrated information and the consolidated knowledge base have a wide impact on Information Access (IA), Information Retrieval (IR) and many other data and web mining applications over heterogeneous media.

The rest of the paper is organized as follows. The following section focuses on the multimedia metadata and resource annotation. The subsequent section describes the state-of-the-art methods of MPEG-7 integration. Then we focus on the resource integration challenges. We describe our techniques to solve the challenges consequently. Our approach of multimedia resource integration is elaborated on the next. The section of 'Experiments and Evaluation' focuses on our experimental results and their strength and weakness. At last we conclude our paper along with our future direction.

MULTIMEDIA METADATA AND RESOURCE ANNOTATION

Before going into details of our proposed method, description of the structure of MPEG-7 metadata would be helpful to comprehend the content of this paper. This section focuses on the MPEG-7 framework, MPEG-7 ontologies and resource annotation.

MPEG-7 Framework

The MPEG-7 standard contains components for multimedia description. This standard is implemented in XML, composed of 1182 elements, 417 attributes, and 377 complex types. They are divided into four main components: the Description Definition Language (DDL), Audio Descriptors, Visual Descriptors, and Multimedia

Description Scheme (MDS). The DDL is a basic building block of the MPEG-7 metadata and describes the relationship among Descriptors (Ds) and Descriptor Schemas (DSs). Audio descriptors contain the descriptive elements for audio, while the visual descriptors describe elements for video. Moreover, the MDS focuses on the elements for capturing the semantic aspects of multimedia contents (e.g., places, actors, objects, events, etc.). MPEG-7, implemented in XML, lacks formal semantics. It causes serious interoperability issues for multimedia processing and exchange (Nack, Van Ossenbruggen, & Hardman, 2005; Van Ossenbruggen, Nack, & Hardman, 2004; Troncy & Carrive, 2004). The semantics of information encoded in XML are specified within each framework. Hence it is hard to integrate the information across frameworks. To overcome the limitations, a number of researchers are trying to develop semantically rich MPEG-7 ontologies.

MPEG-7 Ontologies

There are at least four ontologies, which formalize the MPEG-7 standard using semantic web languages. They are characterized and compared comprehensively in (Troncy et al., 2007). We are going through a short discussion of Hunter's ontology for the MPEG-7 standard as it is relatively simpler to comprehend. The other ontologies of MPEG-7 are created to satisfy the similar goal of attaining interoperability and understandability. The current version of Hunter's MPEG-7 ontology is an OWL ontology containing classes to define the media types (Audio, Audiovisual, Image, Multimedia, Video) and containing the decompositions from the MPEG-7 MDS part (Manjunath, Salembier, & Sikora, 2002). The descriptors for recording information about the production and creation, usage, structure and the media features are also defined. Moreover, the ontology also contains a large number of object property and datatype property in OWL construct. These properties, their values and the hierarchical

relation of concepts play an important role in our process of integration. The schema of ontology, which includes concepts and properties, is used to annotate multimedia resources.

Resource Annotation

We consider Hunter's ABC ontology to annotate multimedia resources. We consider two famous images of Abraham Lincoln, the president of the United States and his youngest son Thomas Tad Lincoln and their URLs are http://en.wikipedia.org/wiki/File:A%26TLincoln.jpg and http://en.wikipedia.org/wiki/File:Tad_Lincoln_in_uniform.jpg respectively in Wikipedia. These two images are annotated by RDF descriptions. The annotation contains the media identification and locators, which define still regions SR1 and SR2. The short RDF annotations of these two images are displayed in Figure 1 and 2 respectively. The figures depict the illustration of decompositions of images into still regions with some simple semantics.

Observations of the above annotations revive the necessity of SLC, where the neighboring semantically linked information specifies a resource. The resource 'Abraham Lincoln' (#uri_SR1) is specified by the resources #uri_001, #uri_SR2, #uri_p1 and their property values (see Figure 1). Similarly, the resource #SR1 in Figure 2 is specified with #uri_i1, #uri_p001 and their property values.

INTEGRATION STATE-OF-THE-ART

The approach in (Garcia & Celma, 2005) contributes a complete and automatic mapping of the whole MPEG-7 standard to OWL. It is based on a generic XML Schema to OWL mapping. This is a schema level mapping that facilitates data integration in a semantic space enormously. However, the mapping does not reveal on instance or resource integration.

Figure 1. A simplified part of RDF description of image <url= http://en.wikipedia.org/wiki/ File:A%26TLincoln.jpg> compliant with Hunter's ABC ontology

```
<mpeg7:image rdf:about="#uri_001">
    <mpeg7:MediaLocator> http://en.wikipedia.org/wiki/File:A%26TLincoln.jpg
    </mpeg7:MediaLocator>
    <mpeg7:depicts> US President Abraham Lincoln is reading a book with his
    youngest son</mpeg7:depicts>
    <mpeg7:spatial_decomposition rdf:resource="#uri_SR1"/>
    <mpeg7:spatial_decomposition rdf:resource="#uri_SR2"/>
    <mpeg7:creator rdf:resource="#uri_p1"/>
</mpeg7:image>
<mpeg7:StillRegion rdf:about="#uri_SR1">
    <mpeg7:dim> 2 4</mpeg7:dim>
    <mpeg7:Coords>194 30 194 148 290 148 290 30 </mpeg7:Coords>
    <mpeg7:depicts> Abraham Lincoln </mpeg7:depicts>
</mpeg7:StillRegion>
<mpeg7:StillRegion rdf:about="#uri_SR2">
    <mpeg7:dim> 2 4</mpeg7:dim>
    <mpeg7:Coords>348 75 348 170 429 170 429 75 </mpeg7:Coords>
    <mpeg7:depicts> Tad </mpeg7:depicts>
</mpeg7:StillRegion>
<mpeg7:Creator rdf:about="#uri_p1">
    <mpeg7:name> Mathew Brady </mpeg7:name>
    <mpeg7:creation_date> 1864-2-9</mpeg7:creation_date>
    <mpeg7:creation_location> White House, USA</mpeg7:creation_location>
</mpeg7:Creator>
```

Figure 2. A simplified part of RDF description of image <url= http://en.wikipedia.org/wiki/File:Tad_Lincoln_in_uniform.jpg> compliant with Hunter's ABC ontology

```
<mpeg7:image rdf:about="#uri_i1">
    <mpeg7:MediaLocator>
    http://en.wikipedia.org/wiki/File:Tad_Lincoln_in_uniform.jpg</
    mpeg7:MediaLocator>
    <mpeg7:depicts> Portrait of Tad Lincoln, son of Abraham Lincoln, standing,
    wearing a military-style uniform</mpeg7:depicts>
    <mpeg7:spatial_decomposition rdf:resource="#SR1"/>
    <mpeg7:creator rdf:resource="#uri_p001"/>
</mpeg7:image>
<mpeg7:StillRegion>
    <mpeg7:dim>2 4</mpeg7:dim>
    <mpeg7:Coords>259 24 259 100 334 100 334 24 </mpeg7:Coords>
    <mpeg7:depicts> Thomas Tad Lincoln </mpeg7:depicts>
</mpeg7:StillRegion>
<mpeg7:Creator rdf:about="#uri_p001">
    <mpeg7:name> Mathew Brady </mpeg7:name>
    <mpeg7:creation_date> 1860s</mpeg7:creation_date>
    <mpeg7:creation_location> White House, USA</mpeg7:creation_location>
</mpeg-7:Creator>
```

There is another approach to integrate OWL ontology to the MPEG-7 XML content by (Tsinaraki et al., 2004). However, they also focus on the schema level of MPEG-7, rather than concentrating on resource integration.

The research described in (Mitschick, Nagel, & Meissner, 2008) focuses on the instance consolidation detailing on data cleansing. The task of data cleansing comprises the detection and resolution of errors and inconsistencies from a data collection. Typical tasks are normalization and standardization, error correction and duplicate detection. Their proposed methods certainly help the process of resource integration. However, they do not reveal the experimental results of instance merging or instance integration. Furthermore, our approach of instance matching differs from their approach in various aspects. We consider the typographic errors, value transformation, logical and structural transformations which might be appear in a real instance. To the best of our knowledge, our approach considers these transformations for the first time in the field of multimedia resource integration.

RESOURCE INTEGRATION CHALLENGES

The ontology schema, which includes concepts, properties and other relations, is relatively stable part of ontology. However, concepts and properties of an ontology are instantiated by instances very often by different users in different styles. In order to find out proximity between two instances referred to the same real-world resource, a resource integration or instance matching algorithm is needed to solve the problem of different kinds of heterogeneity: value transformation, structural transformation and logical transformation.

Value Transformation

Resources contain lexical information as their property values that may contain errors (like typographical errors) or be represented using different standard formats, such as dates or person name in different countries. This issue has been addressed in the field of record linkage research too. For example, person name *Masaki Aono* is also written as *M. Aono* and date variants *16ᵗʰ December, 1965* or *December 16, 1965* or *16/12/1965* or *1965-12-16* are representing a unique date.

Structural Transformation

Unlike record linkage, schema and instances are more strictly related in instance matching. For a resource/instance of a concept, ontology users use a property, either an object property or a datatype property to specify lexical information. Properties, having domains and ranges, always behave like the notion of relation of discrete mathematics. There is a great variation of using properties in their range values. The range of an object property is another resource while the range of a datatype property is an absolute value. There is always a chance of defining an object property of an ontology as a datatype property in another ontology and vice versa. The cases of defining a property impose a great challenge in resource integration by introducing different levels of depth in property representation. Again, different aggregation criteria of properties, like *full-name* as represented by *first-name* and *last-name* together, induces extra level of difficulties in instance matching. Furthermore, missing values of properties, and multiple values of a single property across knowledge base introduce heterogeneity to represent same real world resources differently.

Logical Transformation

There are a number of factors influencing logical heterogeneity in resource representation. Identical resources can be instantiated into different subclasses of the same class or into more general classes without altering the meaning. *"Hanif"*, being a *Person*, can be defined by a subclass *Man* without altering its meaning. Moreover, implicit value specifications and implicit similar classes defined by restrictions also introduce heterogeneity in defining similar instances. However, instances defined by disjoint classes are having different meaning even if they are containing similar type of descriptions.

OUR TECHNIQUES TO SOLVE THE CHALLENGES

As there are a number of challenges in resource integration, we incorporate several techniques in a combination. This section includes details of our techniques.

To Value Transformation

We resolve typographical variation by the methods of data cleansing. The task of data cleansing comprises the detection and resolution of errors and inconsistencies from a data collection. Typical tasks are syntax check, normalization, and error correction. First of all, our syntax check and normalization process check the data type of an instance and classify on three important information types: time data (using regular expression), location data (using GeoNames Webservice[8]) and personal data. In our current realization, we use a couple of manually defined normalization rules for each information type. We implement the techniques in a modular way, so that the used algorithm and rules of normalization can be extended and substituted.

To Logical Transformation

We focus on the logical transformation when resources are instantiated in neighboring concepts like subclass, siblings or parents, but not by disjoint class. This logical transformation is obtained by defining a relational block of neighboring concepts. From the types of two resources we obtain two relational blocks. Then we find at least a relation or an aligned pair of schema entities across the blocks. Therefore, we need schema matching to resolve the logical transformation. This section focuses on the *relational block* and our *schema matching algorithm*.

- **Relational block:** In resource integration, we look up the type (concept as a type of a resource) match of resources first. To cope with the logical variation, we first look up at least an aligned pair across two *relational blocks* each from a type of two resources of different knowledge base. A *relational block* is defined as follows:

Definition 1 *(Relational block): As concepts are organized in a hierarchical structure called a taxonomy, we consider a relational block of a concept c as a set of concepts and simply referred to 'block' throughout this paper, and defined as:*

block(c)={children(c) U siblings(c) U parents (c) U grand-parents(c)} - disjoint(c)

where children(c) and parents(c) represent the children and the parents of a particular concept c, respectively within a taxonomy, whereas siblings(c) is defined as children(parents(c)-{c} and grand-parents(c) is defined as parents(parents(c)) and disjoint(c) comprises the classes disjoint to c.

- **Ontology Schema Matching Algorithm:** As there are a number of ontologies to represent the schema of the MPEG-7 standard, users are free to use any of them to define their own multimedia contents. Unless aligning entities, e.g., concepts, properties or other relations across ontologies, resource integration is not achievable. Therefore, we use our scalable and efficient ontology alignment algorithm called *Anchor-Flood* to obtain the alignment between ontology pair used to define resources of two different multimedia resources.

Our ontology schema matching algorithm takes the essence of the *locality of reference* by considering the neighboring concepts and relations to align the entities of ontologies. The algorithm starts off a seed point called an *anchor*, where the notion *anchor* is a pair of "look-alike" concepts from each of two ontologies. Starting off an anchor point our scalable algorithm collects two sets of neighboring concepts across ontologies. Then it computes the structural and terminological similarity among the collected concepts and produces a list of aligned pairs. Our algorithm extends the produced aligned pairs to align their properties or relations as well. Then it completes one cycle of operation. The collected concept pairs are again considered as further seed points or anchors. Therefore, the operation cycle is repeated for each of the newly found aligned concept pairs. The cycle is stopped if there is no more new concept pair left to be considered as an anchor.

To Structural Transformation

We focus on four types of structural transformation: different levels of depth in property representation, different aggregation criteria of properties, missing values of properties, and multiple values of a single property. Different levels of depth in property representation are resolved by property consolidation that converts object property into datatype property. *Semantic Link Cloud (SLC)* settles multiple values of a single property and some of the aggregation criteria of properties, whereas we use a co-efficient factor (α) in struc-

tural similarity measure (this is described in the Section of 'Similarity Measure') to reduce the effect of missing values of properties.

- **Property consolidation:** Due to the structural variations of instances with object property and datatype property across ontologies, instance matching becomes a challenging task. Therefore, we consolidate the property types before terminological similarity measure. Instances comprise of descriptions as values of properties. The range of a datatype property is directly an absolute value, whereas the range of an object property is another instance. Furthermore, the instance may again contain object property. Therefore, we collect all the values iteratively against the primary object property of the starting instance and covert it as a datatype property.

- **Semantic link cloud (SLC):** In an ontology, neither a concept nor an instance comprises its full specification in its name or URI (Uniform Resource Identifier) alone. Therefore we consider the other semantically linked information that includes other concepts, properties and their values and other instances as well. They all together make an information cloud to specify the meaning of that particular instance. The degree of certainty is proportional to the number of semantic links associated to a particular instance by means of property values and other instances. We refer the collective information of association as a *Semantic Link cloud (SLC)*, which is defined as below:

Definition 2 *(Semantic Link Cloud): A Semantic Link Cloud (SLC) of an instance is defined as a part of knowledge base (Ehrig, 2007) that includes all linked concepts, properties and their instantiations which are related to specify the instance sufficiently.*

In the Figure 3, a resource depicts *"Tad"* as a still image and is a spatial decomposition of a well known picture of Abraham Lincoln and his youngest son. Although Tad may have different meanings across web, it is specified in the figure with the help of the neighboring resources and depicts: *Tad is the youngest son of US president Abraham Lincoln.* To solve the problem of structural variations to define instances we use the essence of SLC quite efficiently.

OUR APPROACH OF MULTIMEDIA RESOURCE INTEGRATION

Multimedia resources are defined by content annotation with the concepts and properties of the MPEG-7 ontologies in RDF as described in Figure 1 and Figure 2. An RDF data is sharable and reusable by its nature. Therefore, the annotated multimedia contents turn out to become sharable and reusable too. We use our ontology instance matching algorithm to integrate resources.

Our proposed method of multimedia resource integration contains data cleansing and normaliza-

tion, generation of blocks with the neighboring concepts, property consolidation, and formation of *SLCs* along with ontology schema matching algorithm to deal with various transformations. We need similarity measure among SLCs across different digital media contents to calculate structural similarity of resources as a resource affinity.

Similarity Measure

Instances or resources contain their lexical information as values of properties. We apply normalization and data cleansing methods to reduce the effect of value transformation. Then the normalized and standardized lexical information is compared against that of another property value for identity recognition. Eventually identity recognition of properties across pair of SLCs integrates resources by measuring the structural similarity (or affinity).

String based similarity measure is often called as terminological similarity measure. The terminological similarity measures are widely used in ontology alignment and instance matching techniques. We use terminological similarity measures

Figure 3. Specification of an instance with its Semantic Link Cloud (SLC)

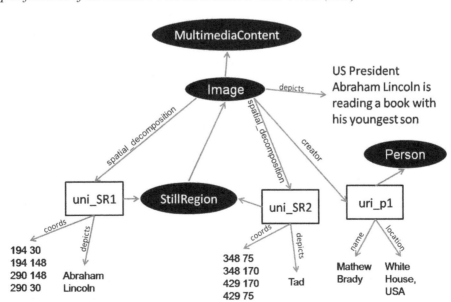

using string metric (Stoilos, Stamou, & Kollias, 2005) in our algorithm. The string metric based similarity is defined as:

Definition 3 *(String Metric): Let s_p be a string and s_q be another string. The string metric based similarity between s_p and s_q is then measured as follows:*

Sim (s_p, s_q) = comm. (s_p, s_q) - diff (s_p, s_q) + winkler (s_p, s_q)

where comm.(s_p, s_q) stands for the commonality between s_p and s_q, diff(s_p, s_q) for the difference and winkler(s_p, s_q) for the improvement of the result using the method introduced by Winkler (1999).

Two property values s_p and s_q are equal if their string similarity is greater or equal to a threshold. Therefore, we define an equality function, E (p, q) as follows:

Definition 4 *(Equality Function): Let p and q be two properties having s_p and s_q as their property values for resources r_i and r_j respectively. The properties p and q are said to have same values if the similarity between their values is greater than a threshold, otherwise they are considered to be different. This Equality Function, E (p,q) is defined mathematically as:*

$$E(p,q) = \begin{cases} 1, & \text{if } Sim(s_p, s_q) \geq \delta_1 \\ 0, & \text{otherwise} \end{cases}$$

where δ_1 is a threshold.

Moreover, an instance contains a list of property values in an SLC. Therefore, an *SLC* based structural matching plays an important role in our resource matching. To calculate the similarity between two SLCs, we use a structural similarity measure, defined in (Mitschick et al., 2008) as:

Sim$_{struct}$ (r_i, r_j) = 2*x/(2*x+α(y+z))

where x is the total number of entities similar, i.e., $|E(p,q)=1|=x$, across two SLCs, y is the number of entities available in an SLC of r_i, however, not available in the cloud of r_j, z is the number of entities in an SLC of r_j, however, not available in the cloud of r_i, and α is the weighting factor ($0 < \alpha < 1$) to reduce the influence of the missing elements. We use 0.3 as the weighting factor.

Overall Matching Model

The operational block of the instance matching combines ontology alignment, generation of SLCs of instances and instance matcher to produce matched instance pairs (See Figure 4).

The algorithm in Figure 5 portrays a simple flow of the matching algorithm. For every SLC of an instance or resource of one media content is matched against the SLCs of the instances of another media content (line 1 through 4 in Figure 5) if and only if there is an aligned point across *Block(ins$_i$.type)* and *Block(ins$_j$.type)* (as there exists a condition at line 5 in Figure 5). *Block(concept)* is a relational block defined earlier at definition 1 and *generateSLC(ins, ab)* generates an SLC against an instance *ins* in an ABox *ab*. An SLC usually contains concepts, properties, and their consolidated values. Every value of an SLC is compared with that of another SLC (as of line 6 of Figure 5). Once similarity value is greater than the threshold, it is collected as an aligned pair (as stated at line 7 in Figure 5). Finally, the algorithm produces a list of matched instance pairs.

Threshold Values

In this paper, we incorporate two thresholds (δ_1 and δ_2) and one weighting factor (α). The threshold value δ_1 is used in Equality Function to observe that two strings associated to two properties of resources are sufficiently similar. The threshold value δ_2 is used to check that the affinity between two resources considering their property values is sufficiently high to be similar. On the other hand,

Figure 4. The basic operational block of the instance matching algorithm

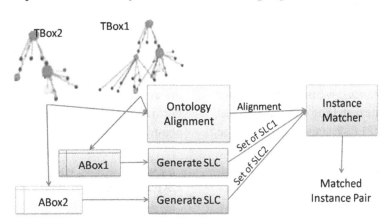

the weighting factor α is used to reduce the effect of missing property values.

Equality Function $E(p,q)$ uses string metric, which we describe earlier. This string metric is quite commonly used in ontology alignment field. In the string metric, the dissimilarity stretches the range of the similarity metric over the interval $[-1, 1]$. This stretching makes it less probable to get same values for a string when it is compared to a large set of other strings, and thus satisfying the property of discrimination. In (Stoilos et al., 2005), the authors claim that the threshold δ_1 can range 0.4 to 0.7 in ontology alignment and

data integration and retrieval. We evaluate our ontology instance matching based multimedia integration model against the ISLab Instance Matching Benchmark (IIMB)[9] datasets and set the threshold value to 0.5.

On the other hand, to reduce the influence of missing elements, weighting factor (α) is added to measure Jaccard-Similarity-Coefficient and we call this metric as a structural similarity. As the MPEG-7 standard has a large number of elements to describe three major types of multimedia data: audio, image and video. The possibility of the influence of missing elements in the MPEG-7

Figure 5. Macro steps of our instance matching algorithm, where a is an aligned pair that contains concepts c_1 and c_2 and belongs to set A

Algorithm *ResourceMatch* (ABox ab_1, ABox ab_2, Alignment A)

1. for each $ins_i \in ab_1$
2. $slc_i = generateSLC(ins_i, ab_1)$
3.   for each $ins_j \in ab_2$
4. $slc_j = generateSLC(ins_j, ab_2)$
5.   if $\exists a(c_1, c_2) \in A \wedge c_1 \in Block(ins_i.type) \wedge c_2 \in Block(ins_j.type)$
6.   if $Sim_{struct}(slc_i, slc_j) \geq \delta_2$
7. $imatch = imatch \bigcup makeAlign(ins_i, ins_j)$

based multimedia contents is high, because of the diversity of the MPEG-7 elements. Therefore, we set the value of α as 0.3 considering that every category is having equal weight.

Finally, as the structural similarity ensures the affinity between instances, we introduce another threshold to decide the matching relation between resources. As the MPEG-7 standard has a large number of elements, the missing elements are often appeared in a resource and reduce the affinity in spite of their relatedness. Therefore, we consider smaller threshold value to decide matching pairs among resources. We set an empirical value for δ_2 as 0.4.

In our multimedia resource integration, our algorithm learns efficient threshold experimenting with IIMB datasets. Furthermore, we have a future plan to incorporate machine learning technique to define threshold automatically.

Computational Complexity

The computational complexity of our instance matching algorithm depends on its constituents: ontology schema matching, generation of SLC and Block and the similarity computation. For ontology schema matching, we use our scalable Anchor-Flood algorithm that achieves the best runtime in Ontology Alignment Evaluation Initiative (OAEI) 2008 and 2009 and the computational complexity is O(N log(N)) (Seddiqui & Aono, 2009) where N is the average size of ontology. Moreover, RDF data is organized into graph structure. Therefore, generation of SLC and Block requires O(N) complexity where N is their size. The time consuming task is the similarity computation. Each cloud of one ABox is compared to every cloud of another ABox. In our system, we generate cloud for each instance before proceeding to loop operation. Moreover, with the condition at line 5 of our *Resource-Match* algorithm, we only compare instances of similar classes. It enhances the performance in a distributed knowledge base, where instances are

equally distributed among classes. The complexity would be O(N log(N)) on an average. However, comparison against a monotonic knowledge base where the instances are of similar classes requires the worst case complexity of O(N^2). Therefore, the average computational complexity of our algorithm is O(N log(N)), whereas the worst case complexity is O(N^2).

EXPERIMENTS AND EVALUATION

We run our implemented system against two types of datasets. One is for the general purpose instance matching benchmarks and another is a synthetic dataset based on 10 different images with 10 artificial variants of each of the image-data. The number of resources in each variant is around 5.

IIMB Benchmarks

A generated benchmark constituted using one dataset and modifying it according to various criteria. The benchmark is generated using the IIMB, used on a dataset from the OKKAM[10] project.

The test-bed provides OWL/RDF data about actors, sport persons, and business firms taken from OKKAM. The main directory contains 37 sub-directories and the original ABox and the associated TBox (abox.owl and tbox.owl). The original ABox contains about 300 different instances.

Each sub-directory contains a modified ABox (abox.owl + tbox.owl) and the corresponding mapping with the instances in the original ABox (refalign.rdf). The introduced modifications are the following:

- Dataset 001: It contains an identical copy of the original ABox.
- Datasets 002 - 010: The datasets contain ABoxes to test value transformations.
- Datasets 011 - 019: These are for testing structural transformations.

- Datasets 020 - 029: The datasets represent ABoxes of logical transformations.
- Datasets 030 - 037: Several combinations of the previous transformations.

Precision-Recall on IIMB

From the precision, recall and f-measure of Table 1 we observe that our algorithm is capable of matching instances perfectly instead of changing the instance id or URI. Our instance matching algorithm produces excellent precision and recall, although the property values are transformed (datasets 2~10).

The hardiest part of the benchmark is structural transformation (datasets 11~19). There are four types of structural transformation: different levels of depth in property representation, different aggregation criteria of properties, missing values of properties, and multiple values of a single property. Although our integration system deals with different levels of depth in property representation efficiently, it still has some inability to handle a part of aggregation criteria of properties. Missing values of properties have negative impact on results in spite of using weighting factor. These lead our system in poor result in the region of the structural transformation.

The algorithm shows its strength in logical transformation group. Although the types of instances are changed and are scattered around neighboring concepts, it produces good precision and recall (datasets 20~29).

The last group of test set combines different transformation including structural transformation. Therefore, our algorithm produces relatively lower precision and recall. The overall performance is satisfactory and convincing. Annex includes the detailed results against the IIMB benchmarks.

The recall-precision graph (see Figure 6) compares different systems including our *AFlood* against IIMB benchmarks, where all of the participants participated in OAEI-2009 campaign (Euzenat et al., 2009). Although our system produces fourth best results, the first three systems are using manually tuned weight factors to each of the properties of the dataset TBox. However, our system has no manual tuning weight factors and therefore, it has a salient feature of ontology and knowledge base independence.

Runtime Efficiency

The IIMB benchmark has monotonic instances classified by only 3 to 6 classes. The smallest unit of information specification of an instance is triple. A triple is defined as a sequence of <subject, predicate, object> organization. The average triples and the average elapsed time displayed in Table 1 depicts runtime efficiency against various groups of IIMB datasets. No other system that was participating in the IIMB benchmark datasets provides their elapsed time. Therefore, it is hard compare the runtime efficiency against that of other systems.

Table 1. Summary results of ontology instance matching

Datasets	Transformation	Prec.	Rec.	F-Measure	Avg. Triples	Avg. Elapsed Time (sec)
001	Random changes in Instance ID	1.00	1.00	1.000	1774	90
002~010	Value transformations	0.99	0.99	0.991	1774	92
011~019	Structural transformations	0.72	0.79	0.751	2601	51
020~029	Logical transformations	1.00	0.96	0.981	1751	83
030~037	Several combinations of the previous transformations	0.75	0.82	0.786	2951	65

Figure 6. Precision/recall graphs for IIMB

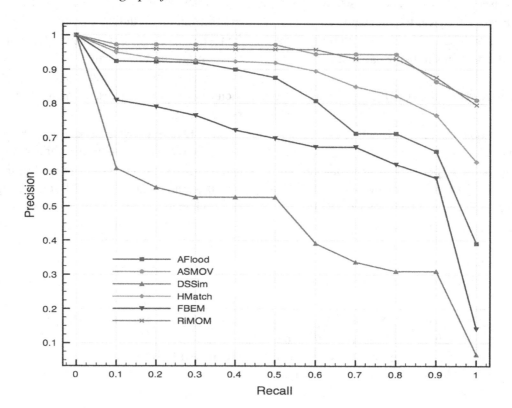

Our Synthetic Datasets

We also created a small list of the MPEG-7 image data by our own for experiments. We annotated and retrieved the annotating data by using third party software. We used the semantic objects or resources which were annotated by the shallow textual contents for 10 different images and with 10 artificial variants by value transformation, logical and structural transformation.

To the best of our knowledge, there is no system for ontology based multimedia resource integration. Moreover, the other instance matching algorithm (participated in IIMB benchmark datasets) manually tunes the property weights for the benchmark datasets. We could not test their system against our synthetic multimedia datasets. Therefore, we create a baseline system by replacing string metric with simple edit distance and removing the formation of Blocks and SLCs from our algorithm. We compare our results with the baseline results in Table 2.

Table 2. Summary result against our synthetic MPEG-7 multimedia data

Systems	Prec.	Rec.	F-Measure	Elapsed Time (sec)
Our Proposed System	0.83	0.76	0.79	7
Baseline (Using Edit-Distance & removing Block and SLC)	0.87	0.43	0.58	5

CONCLUSION AND FUTURE WORK

This paper proposes a novel method of ontology instance matching based algorithm to integrate multimedia contents for facilitating retrieval engines across media. In the process, our algorithm collects SLCs of instances or multimedia resources and measures the similarity among SLCs to produce the matching pairs. SLC helps to improve our result in all groups of transformation, especially in the group of structural transformation. In spite of the difficulties in this group, we find competitive results in some cases. Moreover, the aligned pair of a type of a resource is searched in a block of other resource type, instead of searching one-to-one direct correspondence. This improves our results in a group of logical transformation. Although the precision-recall graph shows that we are among the four best systems, the best three systems are using manual tuned weight to each of the properties in TBox.

The average computational complexity of our system is $O(N \log(N))$, whereas it is $O(N^2)$ in the worst case. Moreover, we compute results using a baseline system and compare with our proposed system.

We test our algorithm against both of the general purpose ontologies and their instances and the multimedia resources as well. The results against both of the general purpose instances and the MPEG-7 multimedia resources are satisfactory and convincing. Our algorithm runs efficiently and has a salient feature of scalability.

Our future work is to extend our experiments with real world multimedia contents of the MPEG-7 standard and to improve the similarity computation and to develop a more efficient process of retrieving the *Semantic Link Clouds (SLCs)*. Moreover, we have a future plan to incorporate machine learning technique to define threshold values automatically.

ACKNOWLEDGMENT

This study was supported by Global COE Program "Frontiers of Intelligent Sensing" from Japan's Ministry of Education, Culture, Sports, Science and Technology (MEXT).

REFERENCES

Arndt, R., Troncy, R., Staab, S., Hardman, L., & Vacura, M. (2007). COMM: Designing a well-founded multimedia ontology for the web. *Lecture Notes in Computer Science, 4825*, 30–43. doi:10.1007/978-3-540-76298-0_3

Bloehdorn, S., Petridis, K., Saathoff, C., Simou, N., Tzouvaras, V., Avrithis, Y., et al. (2005). Semantic Annotation of Images and Videos for Multimedia Analysis. In *Proceedings of the 2nd European Semantic Web Conference (ESWC 2005m)* (pp. 592-607). New York: Springer.

Bormans, J., & Hill, K. (2002). MPEG-21 Overview v.5. *ISO/IEC JTC1/SC29/WG11, 5231.* Retrieve from http://www.chiariglione.org/mpeg/standards/mpeg-21/mpeg-21.htm

Caracciolo, C., Euzenat, J., Hollink, L., Ichise, R., Isaac, A., Malaise, V., et al. (2008). Results of the Ontology Alignment Evaluation Initiative 2008. In *Proceedings of Ontology Matching Workshop of the 7th International Semantic Web Conference*, Karlsruhe, Germany (pp. 73-119).

Ehrig, M. (2007). *Ontology Alignment: Bridging the Semantic Gap.* New York: Springer.

Euzenat, J., Ferrara, A., Hollink, L., Joslyn, C., Malaise, V., Meilicke, C., et al. (2009). Preliminary Results of the Ontology Alignment Evaluation Initiative 2009. In *Proceedings of Ontology Matching Workshop of the 8th International Semantic Web Conference*, Chantilly, VA

Garcia, R., & Celma, O. (2005). Semantic Integration and Retrieval of Multimedia Metadata. In *Proceedings of the 5th International Workshop on Knowledge Markup and Semantic Annotation (SemAnnot'05)*, Galway, Ireland. Citeseer.

Gruber, T. (1993). A Translation Approach to Portable Ontologies. *Knowledge Acquisition*, *5*(2), 199–220. doi:10.1006/knac.1993.1008

Hunter, J. (2002). *Combining the CIDOC CRM and MPEG-7 to Describe Multimedia in Museums*. ERIC Clearinghouse.

Hunter, J. (2003). Enhancing the Semantic Interoperability of Multimedia through a Core Ontology. *IEEE Transactions on Circuits and Systems for Video Technology*, *13*(1), 49–58. doi:10.1109/TCSVT.2002.808088

Isaac, A., & Troncy, R. (2004). Designing and Using an Audio-Visual Description Core Ontology. In *Proceedings of the Workshop on Core Ontologies in Ontology Engineering*.

Lagoze, C., & Hunter, J. (2001). The ABC ontology and model. *Journal of Digital Information*, *2*(2).

Manjunath, B., Salembier, P., & Sikora, T. (2002). *Introduction to MPEG-7: Multimedia Content Description Interface*. New York: Wiley.

McGuinness, D., & van Harmelen, F. (2004). *OWL Web Ontology Language Overview*. Retrieved from http://www.w3.org/TR/owl-features/

Mitschick, A., Nagel, R., & Meissner, K. (2008). Semantic Metadata Instantiation and Consolidation within an Ontology-based Multimedia Document Management System. In *Proceedings of the 5th European Semantic Web Conference ESWC*, Tenerife, Spain.

Nack, F., & Lindsay, A. (1999). Everything you wanted to know about MPEG-7 (Part I). *IEEE MultiMedia*, *6*(3), 65–77. doi:10.1109/93.790612

Nack, F., & Lindsay, A., & GMD-IPSI, D. (1999). Everything you wanted to know about MPEG-7 (Part 2). *IEEE MultiMedia*, *6*(4), 64–73. doi:10.1109/93.809235

Nack, F., Van Ossenbruggen, J., & Hardman, L. (2005). That Obscure Object of Desire: Multimedia Metadata on the Web (part 2). *IEEE MultiMedia*, *12*(1), 54–63. doi:10.1109/MMUL.2005.12

Salembier, P., & Smith, J. (2002). Overview of Multimedia Description Schemes and Schema Tools. In Manjunath, B., Salembier, P., & Sikora, T. (Eds.), *Introduction to MPEG-7: Multimedia Content Description Interface*. New York: John Wiley & Sons.

Seddiqui, M. H., & Aono, M. (2008). Alignment Results of Anchor-Flood Algorithm for OAEI-2008. In *Proceedings of Ontology Matching Workshop of the 7th International Semantic Web Conference*, Karlsruhe, Germany (pp. 120-127).

Seddiqui, M. H., & Aono, M. (2009). An Efficient and Scalable Algorithm for Segmented Alignment of Ontologies of Arbitrary Size. In *Proceedings of the Web Semantics: Science, Services and Agents on the World Wide Web* (2008). doi:10.1016/j.websem.2009.09.001

Seddiqui, M. H., Seki, Y., & Aono, M. (2006). Automatic Alignment of Ontology Eliminating the Probable Misalignments. In *Proceedings of the 1st Asian Semantic Web Conference (ASWC2006)*, Beijing, China (pp. 212-218). New York: Springer.

Stoilos, G., Stamou, G., & Kollias, S. (2005). A String Metric for Ontology Alignment. In *Proceedings of the 4th International Semantic Web Conference (ISWC2005)*, Galway, Ireland (pp. 623-637). New York: Springer.

Troncy, R. (2003). Integrating Structure and Semantics into Audio-Visual Documents. *Lecture Notes in Computer Science*, 566–581.

Troncy, R., & Carrive, J. (2004). A Reduced yet Extensible Audio-Visual Description Language. In *Proceedings of the 2004 ACM Symposium on Document Engineering* (pp. 87-89). New York: ACM.

Troncy, R., Celma, O., Little, S., Garcia, R., & Tsinaraki, C. (2007). Mpeg-7 based Multimedia Ontologies: Interoperability Support or Interoperability Issue. In *Proceedings of the 1st International Workshop on Multimedia Annotation and Retrieval enabled by Shared Ontologies (MAReSO)*, Genova, Italy.

Tsinaraki, C., Polydoros, P., & Christodoulaki, S. (2004). Interoperability Support for Ontology-based Video Retrieval Applications. *Lecture Notes in Computer Science*, 582–591.

Tsinaraki, C., Polydors, P., & Christodoulakis, S. (2007). Interoperability Support between MPEG-7/21 and OWL in DS-MIRF. *IEEE Transactions on Knowledge and Data Engineering*, 19(2), 219–232. doi:10.1109/TKDE.2007.33

Van Ossenbruggen, J., Nack, F., & Hardman, L. (2004). That Obscure Object of Desire: Multimedia Metadata on the Web, Part-1. *IEEE MultiMedia*, 11(4), 38–48. doi:10.1109/MMUL.2004.36

Winkler, W. (1999). *The State of Record Linkage and Current Research Problems (Tech. Rep.)*. Washington, DC: U. S. Census Bureau, Statistical Research Division.

ENDNOTES

1. http://www.mpeg.org/
2. http://www.w3.org/XML/Schema
3. metadata.net/mpeg7/
4. http://www.music.tuc.gr/ontologies/MPEG703.zip
5. http://rhizomik.net/ontologies/mpeg7ontos
6. http://multimedia.semanticweb.org/COMM/
7. http://oaei.ontologymatching.org/2008/
8. http://www.geonames.org/export
9. http://islab.dico.unimi.it/iimb/
10. http://www.okkam.org/

This work was previously published in the International Journal of Multimedia Data Engineering and Management, Volume 1, Issue 2, edited by Shu-Ching Chen, pp. 18-33, copyright 2010 by IGI Publishing (an imprint of IGI Global).

Chapter 10
Synthetic Video Generation for Evaluation of Sprite Generation

Yi Chen
University of Alabama in Huntsville, USA

Ramazan S. Aygün
University of Alabama in Huntsville, USA

ABSTRACT

Sprite generation is the process of aligning, warping, and blending of pixels that belong to an object in a video. The evaluation of the correctness of a sprite is usually accomplished by a combination of objective and subjective evaluations. Availability of ground-truth image would help mere objective evaluation. In this paper, the authors present video generation from an image based on various camera motion parameters to be used as ground-truth for the sprite evaluation. This paper introduces a framework for evaluation of sprite generation algorithms. Experiments under the proposed framework were performed on the synthetic videos of different camera motion patterns to reveal the components of the sprite generation algorithm to be improved.

INTRODUCTION

The term "sprite" refers to the composition of pixels that belong to a video object in a video. Sprite generation (Lu, 2003) is the process of generating sprites for objects in videos. The most common object for sprite generation is the background, and the corresponding sprite is usually referred as the background sprite. It was used for

video compression under MPEG-4 video standard (Sikora, 1997). Sprite coding is only supported by MPEG-4 Main Profile and requires the availability of the sprites. In MPEG-4, a sprite may be generated for each object, and objects are layered on top of each other. Instead of sending the complete background scene for every frame, sprite coding encodes and transmits static background sprite once. The individual frames can be regenerated from the sprite with the support of motion compensation. Thus, sprite coding leads

DOI: 10.4018/978-1-4666-1791-9.ch010

to good subjective quality with very low bitrates (Jinzenji, 2001).

Sprite generation has been also studied as background extraction (Lai, 2008), photo stitching (Baudisch, 2007; Brown, 2007; Baudisch, 2005; Zomet, 2006), and panoramic image generation (Farin, 2008). Sprite generation research has gained significant attraction since late 1990s due to its application in many domains such as object-based coding (Wantanabe, 2001), video compression (Jinzenji, 2001), video indexing (Grammalidis, 1999), virtual environments (Jaillon, 1994), object tracking (Lin, 2002), and security surveillance (Cheng, 2007). Sprite generation is mostly applied to the background in the video. In the rest of the paper, we will use the term sprite for the background sprite unless stated otherwise. Since background scene may not be captured in a single frame of a video, sprite is generated by correctly overlapping between sequential frames. Sprite is usually generated when there is a significant global motion and the background regions eventually become visible. Therefore, sprite generation algorithms process every frame (usually in order) to incorporate occluded backgrounds as they become visible and newly visible backgrounds. Sprite generation is mostly applied in order sequentially for all frames in the video, since the global motion is limited for consecutive frames. The consecutive frames are aligned and the newer one is blended into the sprite.

The three main steps of sprite generation are global motion estimation, warping and blending. Global motion estimation aims at calculating the motion between two (consecutive) frames. For background sprite, it is usually assumed that global motion estimation corresponds to camera motion if the moving objects are not too large. Global motion estimation is the most computation intensive component of sprite generation. Warping maps coordinates of pixels in one frame to coordinates of pixels in the other frame without changing pixel values. In other words, it aligns the frames that are processed. Blending determines what the pixel values should be after aligning the frames (e.g., averaging).

Global motion estimation depends on the motion models used for the estimation. The most common motion models are 2D motion models, such as perspective, affine, or translational models, due to their performance. Since cameras capture 3D environments where object distances to camera vary and some local objects may move in a different direction from the camera motion, the 2D models may not be 100% accurate to model the environment. Hence, 2D global motion estimation algorithms can only approximate the actual global motion. If the estimated global motion is close enough to the actual motion, the sprite can still be generated by using enhanced methods such as long-term global motion estimation (Smolic, 1999). If the global motion is not estimated correctly, neither warping nor blending may produce satisfactory results.

The evaluation of sprite generation is composed of subjective and objective evaluation steps. An expert looks at the sprite and the video and determines whether it is an appropriate sprite or not in the subjective evaluation. In the objective evaluation, the typical measure is peak signal-to-noise ratio (PSNR) (Li, 2003). The PSNR (Smolic, 2003; Sheikh, 2006) is used to calculate the difference between the generated frame and original frame. The visual quality was maintained despite decrease in PSNR (Smolic, 2003). Sheikh et al. (Sheikh, 2006) state that the correlation of mean squared error (Li, 2003) and PSNR is not a tight indication of human judgment quality. The problem for sprite evaluation is that the PSNR value can be ∞ even for an incorrectly generated sprite if the frames are concatenated without any overlapping. In the objective evaluation, the original frames can be regenerated exactly the same although the sprite is not correct at all. However, the generated sprite is not correct. (To check the correctness of the sprite, we regenerated the original frames, and the original frames can be regenerated exactly the same although the sprite is not correct at all).

It can be concluded that PSNR is not sufficient to determine the quality of sprite. Sprite generation has three main steps: global motion estimation, warping, and blending. The algorithms for these steps may be independent of each other. So, the reason for a better sprite may be due to an improvement in any of these steps. A sprite generation algorithm with good global motion estimation but with a poor blending algorithm may perform poorly. Therefore, just comparing the final result is not enough to compare two sprite generation algorithms. In the literature, the outputs of intermediate steps are not shared. Knowing that PSNR is not enough for evaluating sprites, the comparison of PSNR values is also doubtful. Since many researchers experimented on specific videos to prove their sprite generation, it is not strong enough to prove the strength of an algorithm. The major problem for sprite generation evaluation is the absence of the correct sprite. If there had been a ground-truth, we could tell how good our sprite is. It is necessary to adapt the ground-truth to evaluate the sprite generation and to establish a framework to utilize a combination of reasonable criteria.

Previous Work

In the literature, the sprite evaluation has subjective and objective evaluation. Experts look at the generated results and check the correctness subjectively, and then they compare the PSNR values. For this purpose, it is common to see that MPEG test sequences such as 'coastguard' (Xiph. org) and 'stefan' (Xiph.org) are used repeatedly to compare results. Hence, there is no formal framework for sprite generation evaluation. The introduction of a framework is a novelty by our paper. Since we use synthetic video generation in our framework, we have identified research that used synthetic video generation for ground-truth generation. If the sprite (or ground-truth image) is available, a video can be generated for evaluating sprite generation. Numerous works generated and used ground-truth video to evaluate the performance of video processing. The two major areas that used synthetic videos are object tracking and video surveillance.

Ambardekar et al. (2009) proposed a tool (GTVT) that allows users to establish the ground-truth video and ground-truth information file to compare the vision given by video surveillance applications. Similarly, D'Orazio et al. (2009) presented a semi-automatic system to generate initial ground-truth estimation, and users can manually verify and validate later. In object tracking, Black and Ellis (Black, 2003) generated the ground-truth tracks and integrated them into videos to track the video tracking algorithm with dynamic occlusions. In the light of tracking the objects, ground-truth was used to check the performance of specific algorithm. In our case, the ground-truth is used to check the correctness of the global motion estimation in

For object detection, Nascimento et al. (2006) detected 5 errors statistically: splits of foreground regions, merges of foreground regions, false alarms and detection failures by comparing the ground-truth with the output of object detection algorithms. Erdem et al. (2001) applied two metrics including color and motion difference around the boundary of the estimated video object plane and the color histogram difference between the current object plane and its temporal neighbor without ground-truth in the object tracking, and Erdem et al. (2000) presented four objective metrics with ground-truth: misclassification, penalty, shape penalty, motion penalty and combined penalty. It is interesting to note that while object tracking deals with the motion of foreground objects in the video, the background sprite generation deals with the global motion in the video. Ishikawa et al. (2008) generated an image with rotating certain amount of cameras in a scene. In our synthetic video generation, frames are generated sequentially following camera motion patterns.

Our Approach

In this paper, we extend the work we proposed in (Chen, 2009a; Chen, 2009b). In those two papers, we proposed camera motion patterns including Zigzag, Spiral, Earthquake, Zoom, Rotate, Affine, pan-tilt-zoom (PTZ) and combined patterns. We generated the synthetic videos from high resolution images and tested the sprite generation algorithm on those synthetic videos. In addition, we proposed new metrics for evaluation of sprite including picturePSNR and sprite size using the ground-truth images and files. In this paper, we further introduce a framework to evaluate sprite generation algorithms, improve patterns that include zoom operations, and explain the workflow of this framework.

Through our sprite evaluation framework (SEF), we can evaluate sprite generation algorithm in three aspects:

1. Evaluation of the sprite generation algorithm for *a specific motion pattern* by comparing the results on *several high resolution images* with various textures.
2. Evaluation of the sprite generation algorithm for *various specific motion patterns* on *a specific high resolution image*.
3. Evaluation of the sprite generation algorithm and global motion estimation.

We have improved the zoom-in and zoom-out patterns. The zoom operation is smoother in this version. Hence, the PTZ, zoom-in and zoom-out, and combined patterns are new in this paper since they have a smooth zoom. Therefore, our experiments reflect the results according to this new zoom-in and zoom-out patterns.

The contributions of our paper are as follows:

*   We introduce a new framework for sprite generation evaluation
*   We have a new zoom-in, zoom-out, PTZ, and combined patterns for synthetic video generation.

This paper is organized as follows. The following section concisely covers camera motion patterns and synthetic videos. The next section explains the sprite evaluation framework (SEF). Using SEF and providing experimental results is then presented.

MOTION ESTIMATION AND CAMERA MOTION PATTERNS

In this section, we firstly provide information about 2D global motion estimation and then introduce camera motion parameters that are used for synthetic video generation.

Global Motion Estimation

The traditional motion estimation models can be classified as 2-dimensional (2D) and 3-dimensional (3D). 2D motion models (Aygun, 2002) are usually preferred to 3D motion models (Zhu, 2005) due to its simplicity as well as the less computation cost. In addition, 2D motion models in general provide acceptable good results. 2D motion can be determined by the following transformation matrix:

$$T = \begin{bmatrix} a_2 & a_5 & a_0 \\ a_4 & a_3 & a_1 \\ a_6 & a_7 & 1 \end{bmatrix}$$

The computation of coordinates is performed as

$$\begin{bmatrix} x' \\ y' \\ 1 \end{bmatrix} = T \times \begin{bmatrix} x \\ y \\ 1 \end{bmatrix}$$

where (x,y) is the coordinate before the motion and (x',y') denotes the new coordinates after the motion. The motion estimation basically corresponds to estimation of these 8 parameters in transformation matrix T. The complexity of motion helps to determine the values of these parameters. The simplest motion is considered as translational motion. In translational motion, $a_2 = a_3 = 1$ and $a_3 = a_4 = a_6 = a_7 = 0$. The only two parameters to be estimated are a_0 and a_1 for the translational motion. Rotate motion is actually represented with a single angle parameter, θ. If there is only rotation, $a_0 = a_1 = a_6 = a_7 = 0$; and $a_2 = a_3 = \cos\theta$, $a_4 = \sin\theta$, and $a_5 = -\sin\theta$. If there is only zoom (i.e., zoom-in or zoom-out), $a_5 = a_0 = a_4 = a_1 = a_6 = a_7 = 0$. The only parameter that needs to be estimated is a_2 where $a_2 = a_3$. In pan-tilt-zoom motion, translational and zoom parameters need to be estimated. In affine motion, 6 parameters need to be computed. They are a_0, a_1, a_2, a_3, a_4, and a_5. In perspective motion, all 8 parameters need to be estimated We used the same notation in our ground-truth file.

Assume that the motion needs to be computed between consecutive frames in a video. If the motion parameters in general provide good results for all pixels in a video frame, the motion is considered global motion. The global motion does not always represent the camera motion. If moving objects are very large (similar to the frame size), the global motion corresponds to the motion of these objects.

Camera Motion Patterns

One of the major components of sprite generation is the global motion estimation. In our observation, affine motion model provided good results for global motion estimation and sprite generation. Therefore, we try to estimate the 6 parameters of the affine motion model. The camera motion patterns should include all these 6 parameters. The camera motion parameters should also allow us to check the computation of a subset of these parameters.

The synthetic videos were generated using camera motion patterns including *Zigzag, Spiral, Earthquake, Zoom, Rotate, Affine, Pan-Tilt-Zoom (PTZ)* and *Combined Pattern*. These eight patterns cover various camera effects: translational, rotation, zoom, scaling, pan-tilt-zoom, and affine transformations. In our data set, the typical high resolution image size was 450x450. The video size is chosen smaller than this image size.

Translational Patterns

One of our goals while using translational patterns is to cover the complete ground-truth image so that the sprite that is generated will be similar to the ground-truth image. In translational patterns, only two translational parameters (i.e., a_0 and a_1 in transformation matrix in Section 2.1) need to be estimated. Translational patterns include *Zigzag, Spiral* and *Earthquake*. *Zigzag* and *Spiral* patterns use 150 x 150 pixels as video frame size. Selected original images whose sizes are 450 x 450 were divided into 9 sub-images. All patterns are based on using paths along the sub-images. The center of the frame moved along the path in constant or variable speed and produced a series of sequential images. Figure 1 depicts *Zigzag, Spiral* and *Earthquake* under category of translational camera pattern. For the *Zigzag* pattern, the starting point is at sub-image (1, 1). The subsequent destinations of the path will be sub-images (1, 3), (2, 3), (2, 1), (3, 1), and (3, 3). For the *Spiral* pattern, assume that the starting point is the sub-image at (x, y). The subsequent destinations of the path will be (x, y-1), (x-1, y-1), (x-1, y+1), (x+1, y+1), (x+1, x-1). In the presence of 9 sub-images, it will be sub-images (2, 2), (2, 1), (1, 1), (1, 3), (3, 3), and (3, 1).

Earthquake pattern uses a sub-image almost having the original image size to scan the original image with random direction from the center of the original image. This sub-image is moved left-right and up-down. The scanning process will continue till the whole image is scanned. In other words, the scanning process will stop when all four corners of the original image are covered.

Figure 1. Translational Camera Motion Patterns. This figure illustrates the translational camera motion pattern including Zigzag, Spiral and Earthquake.

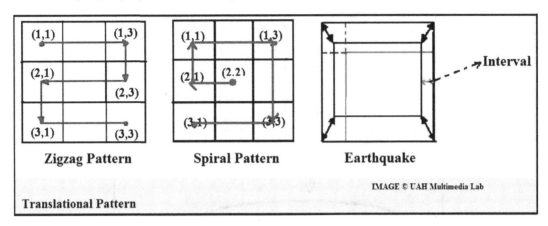

Zoom Patterns

Zoom patterns as shown in Figure 2 are aimed to create the effect of pure zoom-in, pure zoom-out, and combination of both. In zoom pattern, only one parameter (i.e., *a2* in transformation matrix in Section 2.1 and note that $a_2=a_3$) needs to be estimated. In this version of paper, the zoom we adapted is a smooth zoom in which the next zoom depends on the previous zoom. For example, assume that the number of pixels for zoom is 10 pixels (i.e., if image size is 100 x 100, the new region for the frame will be either 110 x 110 or 90 x90). We select the middle point in the big image as the center for zoom patterns. If current region size for the frame is 80 x 80, the next region size will be 90x 90 or 70x70. All regions will be mapped to uniform frames having constant size such as 50x50. The adapted smooth zoom is more natural since it resembles the zoom in traditional camcorders. In our case, the frame expands at a zoom factor of 10 pixels in Zoom-Out pattern and shrinks at a zoom factor of 10 pixels in Zoom-In pattern at each iteration. ZoomInZoomOut pattern is the combination of performing random zoom factor (multiples of 10 pixels) in a number of iterations. The zoom action will start with the same frame as zoom out by applying either zoom in or zoom out effect.

Pan-Tilt-Zoom Pattern

The Pan-Tilt-Zoom (PTZ) pattern as shown in Figure 3 moves the frame in horizontal direction (Pan), vertical direction (Tilt), and performs zoom in and zoom out. It repeats for a number of iterations. PTZ pattern needs to deal with 2 translational parameters and one zoom parameter (i.e., a_0, a_1, and a_2 in transformation matrix in Section 2.1 and note that $a_2=a_3$).

Rotate Pattern

Rotate pattern as shown in Figure 4 spins the frame around the center of the original image to generate a series of consecutive images. Rotate pattern needs to estimate one rotation angle (i.e., a_2, a_3, a_4 and a_5 in transformation matrix in Section 2.1 depend on the rotation angle). The *Rotate* pattern has two modes. Either it rotates the frame constantly for 90 iterations with constant 4 degrees at each iteration or rotates the frame with a random degree under 4 to finish one complete rotation.

Affine Pattern

In Affine pattern as shown in Figure 5, three points A, B, and C of the parallelogram will move to A', B' and C', respectively. The movements of A,

Figure 2. Zoom Camera Motion Patterns. This figure illustrates the Zoom In, Zoom Out, and Zoom-InZoomOut pattern.

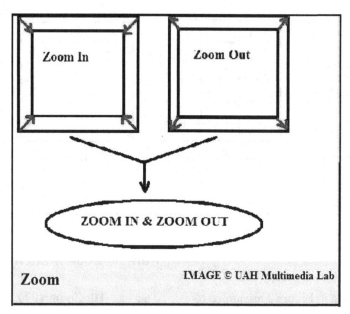

B, and C points are less than 5 pixels. Note that if three points are provided for a parallelogram, the fourth one can be computed from the rest. We calculated the transformation matrix and generated the parallelogram. Then we mapped the points in the parallelogram to the square grid of the video frame. In Affine pattern, 6 parameters (i.e., a_0, a_1, a_2, a_3, a_4, and a_5 in transformation matrix in Section 2.1) need to be estimated.

Combined Patterns

The combined patterns are presented to have all types of aforementioned motion patterns. Two types of combined patterns are proposed: Combined Pattern I (CPI) and Combined Pattern II (CPII). Both combined patterns contain translational, smooth PTZ, Rotate, and Affine patterns. CPI follows Zigzag (5 pix), smooth PTZ, Rotation,

Figure 3. PTZ camera motion pattern

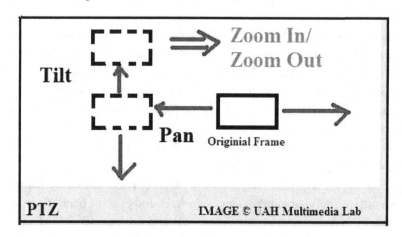

Figure 4. Rotate camera motion pattern

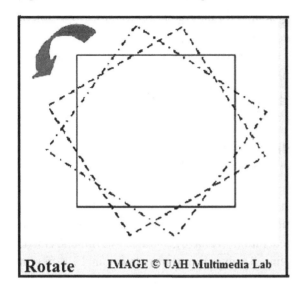

Figure 5. Affine camera motion pattern

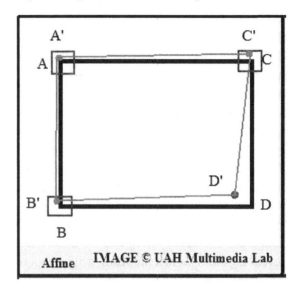

Affine and Zigzag (5 pix) patterns. CPII follows Spiral pattern (5 pix), smooth PTZ, Rotation, and Affine patterns. Since the subsequent frame should have the same frame size as the previous frame and the frame size for Earthquake pattern is larger than the frame sizes of other patterns, Earthquake pattern is not included in the combined patterns.

SPRITE EVALUATION FRAMEWORK (SEF)

In this section, we explain the framework, a sprite generation algorithm, our data set, and evaluation methods.

The Framework

Our sprite evaluation framework has three stages (Figure 6). The first stage of our evaluation framework is to generate synthetic videos. A high resolution image is selected. Eight camera motion patterns are applied to the high resolution image. For each camera pattern, a ground-truth image, a ground-truth file that maintains motion parameters and synthetic video are generated.

The second stage is to apply the sprite generation algorithm on the synthetic video produced in the first stage. The sprite generation algorithm generates the sprite. In addition, it should also generate a global motion file that includes global motion parameters. This file can be used for further analysis and to identify the problem during sprite generation. Moreover, it is beneficial to compute the PSNR for each frame (framePSNR) by reconstructing each frame from the sprite.

The third stage evaluates the sprite. Since the ground-truth image is produced in the first stage and the sprite is generated in the second stage, picturePSNR can be calculated if the sizes of the ground-truth image and sprite are similar. In addition, since the ground-truth file and the global motion file are available, the frames that had incorrect motion estimation can be found out. Accuracy for motion estimation can also be provided.

A Sprite Generation Algorithm

Most sprite generation algorithms have three components. The global motion estimation of sprite generation algorithm we selected is based on hierarchical global motion estimation in (Dufaux, 2000; Bergen, 1992; Anandan & P. A, 1987; Dengler, 1986; Bergen, 1980; Horn, 1986; Waxman, 1985). There are three levels of hierarchical global estimation. The original image is downsampled by 2, and then the downsampled image is again downsampled by 2. At the lowest level, the motion estimation is performed as translational motion estimation for the complete frame. In the intermediate level, the translational parameters are multiplied by 2. The Levenberg-Marquardt iterative nonlinear minimization algorithm is repeatedly applied to optimize the error. The translational parameters are again multiplied by 2, and the Levenberg-Marquardt minimization algorithm is again applied. For the blending phase, the average

of pixel values is taken. Figure 7 shows the sprite generated for the frames between 250 and 298 of *stefan* test sequence.

No special processing is made to remove the moving object in Figure 7. Additional sprites for various videos can be checked at http://sprite. cs.uah.edu.

High Resolution Images in Our Dataset

In this section, we provide information about the high-resolution images used for synthetic video generation. We have generated 91 synthetic videos using 8 camera motion patterns in 13 different ways from 7 high resolution original test files

Figure 6. Workflow of sprite evaluating framework

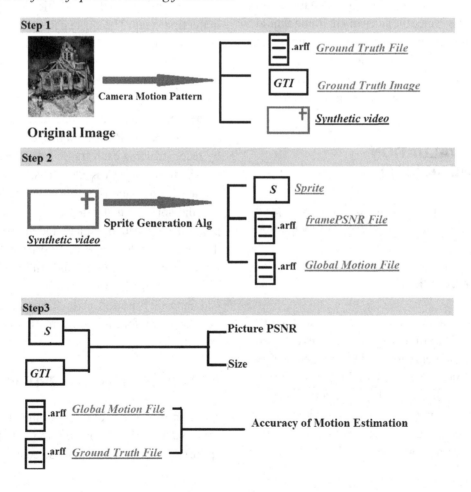

Figure 7. The sprite generated for frames (250-298) of Stefan sequence

(Chen, 2009a; Chen, 2009b) 6 of these images are obtained from NASA and one of them is the Mona Lisa image. The repetition of textures in these images aggravates the sprite generation. That is one of the reasons why we have chosen these images. The sizes of original images are 450 x 450. These images are used to check the performance of sprite generation. In this paper, we introduced another two high resolution images for the framework. Figure 8 shows two sample images used in this paper.

We proposed SpriteDB Tool (Chen, 2009c) as an open access environment to view and download synthetic videos generated on the camera motion patterns. Synthetic videos can be downloaded and tested at by following http://sprite.cs.uah.edu.

Resources for Evaluating Sprite Generation

The traditional sprite evaluation usually consists of two phases: subjective and objective. In the subjective phase, an expert looks at both the sprite and the video and determines whether the sprite is appropriate for the video. In the objective phase, the frames are regenerated from the sprite. The PSNR is computed between the original and the corresponding regenerated frame (this is called framePSNR). PSNR computation is based on mean squared error (MSE). PSNR is computed as

$$PSNR = 10 \log_{10} \left(\frac{MAX_I^2}{MSE} \right) = 20 \log_{10} \left(\frac{MAX_I}{\sqrt{MSE}} \right)$$

where MAX_I denotes the maximum error and MSE represents mean squared error.

Figure 8. High resolution images

Starry Night

Satellite by NASA

We use PSNR in two ways: framePSNR and picturePSNR (Chen, 2009a; Chen, 2009b). The framePSNR corresponds to traditional PSNR computation for each frame. The framePSNR is used to compute the difference between the original frame and the generated frames from the sprite. However, framePSNR only is not a satisfactory measure to evaluate the correctness of sprite. The common example is that framePSNR value becomes infinite when all the frames of a video are concatenated. PicturePSNR corresponds to the PSNR computation between the ground-truth image and the generated sprite. However, if the size of the sprite is different from the size of the ground-truth, picturePSNR cannot be applied directly. If the difference in the sizes is not significant, the sprite is resized and picturePSNR is computed. However, if the difference is significant, computing picturePSNR is not necessary since it will be very low anyway. Size is also an indication of using picturePSNR or not (Chen, 2009a; Chen, 2009b). Lu et al. (2003) present sprites with PSNR values around 23. Sprites with (average) PSNR values higher than 23 usually are of acceptable quality. FramePSNR values between 25 and 30 (Aygun, 2002) can be considered to have very good quality. FramePSNR values above 30 are desirable if they can be achieved. There is no formal mapping between PSNR values and quality. We obtained these values by looking at the results of PSNR values for sprite generation in the literature.

In our approach, our advantage is the availability of the ground-truth image. Since the synthetic video generation uses specific motion patterns, the motion parameters are maintained in a ground-truth file. This helps to identify the correctness of motion estimation for each frame in the sequence. In addition, the size is the most straight-forward metric to evaluate the sprite itself. The relationship between size and picturePSNR can directly judge the quality of the sprite.

Ground-truth Image (GTI) is the exact area covered in the original image by the movement of camera motion pattern. In the translational and zoom patterns, the GTI will be the whole original image. Since the coverage of rotate, affine and PTZ will be part of the original image, the GTI will only be the covered part. In the case of combined patterns, the GTI will cover same as the transla-

Figure 9. Ground-truth Images(GTI) of Satellite from NASA

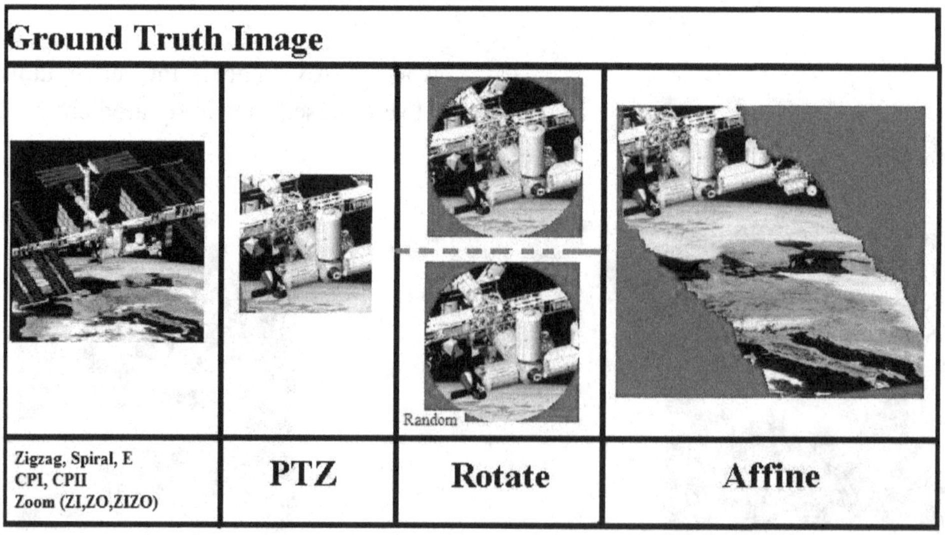

Ground Truth Image			
Zigzag, Spiral, E CPI, CPII Zoom (ZI,ZO,ZIZO)	PTZ	Rotate	Affine

IMAGE © UAH Multimedia Lab

tional patterns (i.e., the whole original image). Figure 9 presents the exact ground-truth image of 8 patterns with satellite image from NASA.

Ground-truth File (GTF) is the arff (Wiki, 2009) file created to track the motion parameters which camera motion patterns applied to the high resolution image. It records the information of the current frame number, the x and the y displacements, rotate angle (degree) for the Rotate pattern, and a_2 and a_3 parameters for zoom. The red-circled line in Figure 10 shows that the third frame in the video has 15-pixel displacement in x coordinate and 0-pixel displacement in y coordinate, rotate degree is 0 and no zoom (the corresponding parameters are both 1). There is no rotation, so a_3 and a_5 are 0, and a_6 and a_7 are 0 since it is not perspective motion. Currently (in the third frame), the current camera motion pattern applied is ZSC (Zigzag pattern at constant speed without overlapping). The frame size we used is 150 x150.

Figure 10. Ground-truth File for Combined pattern 1

```
% 1. Title: Sprite video generation database

% 2. Source:
% (a) Creator:Yi Chen
% (b) Donor: Dr Aygun Ramazan
% (c) Date12/29/2009 7:53:34 PM
% Original Image name: testfile10
% Original Image size |Width:450 Height:450
% Output framesize |Width:150 Height:150
% Initial framesize |Width:150 Height:150
% Initial frame location |X:0 Y:0

@RELATION spritevideogeneration
@ATTRIBUTE frame number NUMERIC
@ATTRIBUTE X NUMERIC(a0)
@ATTRIBUTE Y NUMERIC(a1)
@ATTRIBUTE Rotate NUMERIC
@ATTRIBUTE a2
@ATTRIBUTE a3
@ATTRIBUTE a4
@ATTRIBUTE a5
@ATTRIBUTE a6
@ATTRIBUTE a7
@ATTRIBUTE Pattern String
@ATTRIBUTE frmheight NUMERIC
@ATTRIBUTE frmwidth NUMERIC


@DATA

0     0     0     0     0     0     0     0     0     0     ZSC   150
      150
1     5     0     0     1     0     0     1     0     0     ZSC   150
      150
2     10    0     0     1     0     0     1     0     0     ZSC   150
      150
3     15    0     0     1     0     0     1     0     0     ZSC   150
      150
4     20    0     0     1     0     0     1     0     0     ZSC   150
      150
5     25    0     0     1     0     0     1     0     0     ZSC   150
      150
```

APPLYING THE FRAMEWORK

We applied the framework according to three steps in Figure 6.

Ground Truth Generation

We chose the high resolution images in Figure 8. In the first stage, we applied camera motion patterns on the chosen high resolution images. Figure 11 shows the interface for selecting the regions for frames from Satellite image using Spiral Pattern.

The framework generates corresponding arff files for each pattern and Ground-truth Image files as in Figure 6. Figure 12 and Figure 13 are the synthetic video snapshots for Figure10 included in the framework.

Figure 11. Camera motion tool at UAH Multimedia Lab

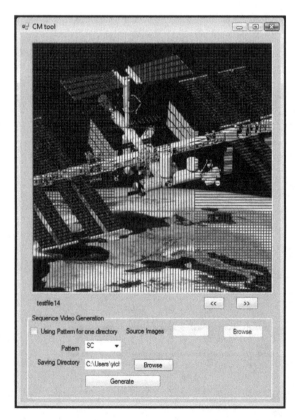

Evaluation with Respect to Camera Patterns

After applying the sprite generation algorithm, we obtain the sprite, framePSNR files and motion estimation files generated by the sprite generation algorithm. Then, we compare the sprite and ground-truth images.

Translational Patterns

There are two parameters that are used for zigzag pattern: speed and overlap. The speed determines whether the motion is at constant speed or not. In the original zigzag pattern, there is no overlap between rows (except while moving down). In the overlap version, the height of the synthetic video frame is increased to have an overlap with the previous row. In the spiral pattern, the speed is the control parameter we applied. Table 1 is the summary of size of the original image and sprite of Starry Night and Satellite images.

According to the Table 1, the size difference is less than 10 pixels, less than 2% compared with 450. So we adapted the picturePSNR. Figure 14 shows the sprites generated from these two high resolution images for both Zigzag and Spiral patterns. It depicts that the Zigzag pattern without overlapping has misalignment in the middle of the sprite in Zigzag pattern without overlapping at variable speed. According to our experience, the misalignment may also happen in Zigzag pattern without overlapping at constant speed (Chen, 2009a). Since image content is very unique in the subsequent frame, the problem did not happen. To resolve the misalignment, the overlapping in both horizontal and vertical direction relieves this problem. (Chen, 2009a)

Comparing Figure 15 with Figure 16 and Figure 17 with Figure 18 demonstrates that the speed of change influences the performance of selected sprite generation. Average framePSNR reduces about 10 for this resolution image in both overlapping and non-overlapping mode.

Figure 12. Translational synthetic video snapshots

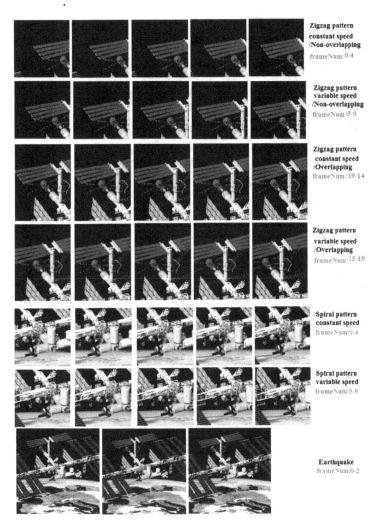

By analyzing figures 15 through 18, we can deduce that using overlapping mode does not necessarily improve the performance. Average framePSNR is higher for Zigzag pattern at constant speed than Zigzag pattern at constant speed with overlapping. Average framePSNR is lower for Zigzag pattern at variable speed than Zigzag pattern at variable speed with overlapping

ZSC is the mode of zigzag pattern at constant speed without overlapping; ZSR is the mode of zigzag pattern at variable speed without overlapping; ZRC is the mode of zigzag pattern at constant speed with overlapping; and ZRR is the mode of zigzag pattern at variable speed with overlapping. In Figure 19, the average framePSNR value is not similar to the picturePSNR value. However, the trends of these two are similar in Figure 19.

In Figure 20, the average framePSNR is nearly 50, and picturePSNR is close to 30, and size information is 454 x 452. In Figure 21, picturePSNR is not calculated since the size is 484 x 451. Hence, picturePSNR is likely to be very low here. Although the high framePSNR is not indication that the sprite has a high quality; low framePSNR is an indication that the sprite is not satisfactory.

Figure 13. Complex Synthetic Video snapshots

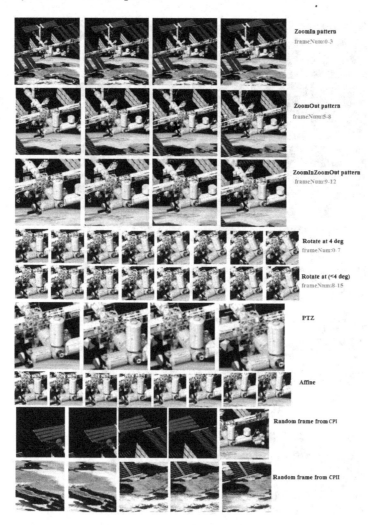

Since the average framePSNR for Earthquake pattern is infinite, we do not present the chart of framePSNR. The picturePSNR indicates that the sprites are satisfactory. The picturePSNR for Satellite is 33 and the picturePSNR for Starry Night is 29. Figure 22 displays sprites look the same as the ground-truths.

Zoom, Affine, and Rotate Patterns

In Figure 23, the sprites that are generated for synthetic video having zoom pattern are not good. In the hierarchical motion estimation, the first step

Table 1. Size difference table of Starry Night and Satellite

	Starry Night	**Satellite**
Zigzag (constant/Non-overlapping)	454 x 452	452 x 452
Zigzag (variable/Non-overlapping)	451 x 453	456 x 452
Zigzag (constant/Overlapping)	452 x 453	452 x 452
Zigzag (variable/Overlapping)	451 x 450	455 x 451

Figure 14. Zigzag pattern and Spiral Pattern sprite

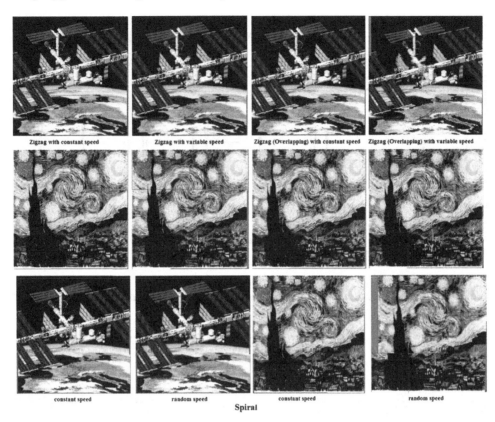

Figure 15. PSNR values of Zigzag pattern at constant speed without overlapping for Satellite

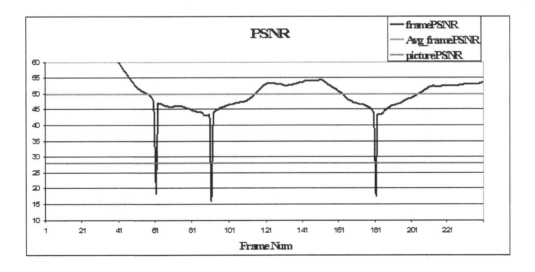

Figure 16. PSNR values of Zigzag pattern at variable speed without overlapping for Satellite

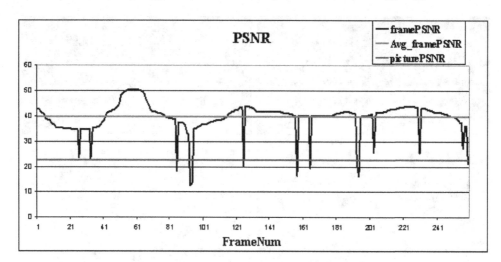

Figure 17. PSNR values of Zigzag pattern at constant speed with overlapping

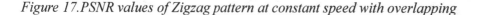
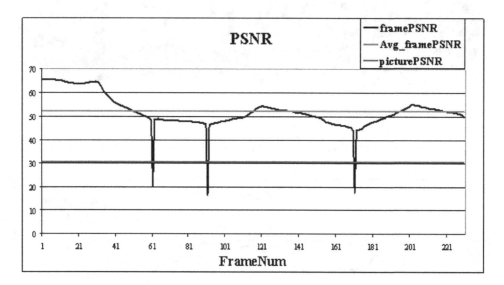

is to calculate translational parameters. The motion parameters are computed using optimization of error at the next two levels. If the first level does not have good estimation, the error may propagate to other levels.

For the Affine pattern, the size of Satellite sprite is 292 x 256, and the size of the corresponding GTI is 269 x 264 (Figure 24). The size of Starry Night sprite is 303 x 270 and the size of the corresponding GTI is 277 x 256 (Figure 24).

Calculating picturePSNR is not applicable due to 10% difference in sizes. The sprites look good. Figure 25 provides framePSNR and average framePSNR for StarryNight for the affine pattern. The average framePSNR is 27.

For the Rotate pattern, the size of Satellite sprite is 292 x 256 and the size of the corresponding GTI is 269 x 264 (Figure 26). The size of Starry Night sprite is 303 x 270 and the size of the corresponding GTI is 277 x 256 (Figure 26).

Figure 18.PSNR values of Zigzag pattern at variable speed with overlapping for Satellite

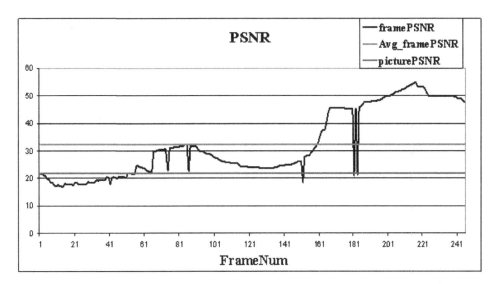

Calculating picturePSNR is not applicable due to 10% difference in sizes. The sprites look good in Figure 26. According to Figures 27 and 28, the trends of rotate pattern and random rotate pattern are very similar.

PTZ and Smooth PTZ Patterns

For the PTZ pattern, sprites for both synthetic videos are not good (Figure 29). We believe this is due to the zoom pattern (Chen, 2009a). The sprites should be equivalent to the whole original image. We may deduce that when the combination

Figure 19.The relationship between framePSNR and picturePSNR for Satellite and Starry Night in Zigzag pattern

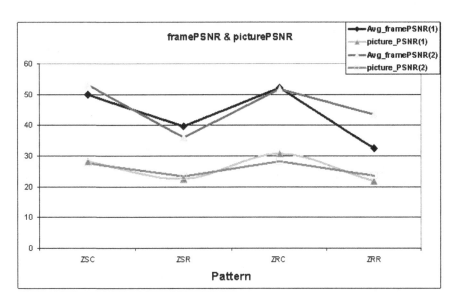

Figure 20. PSNR values of Spiral pattern at constant speed of Satellite

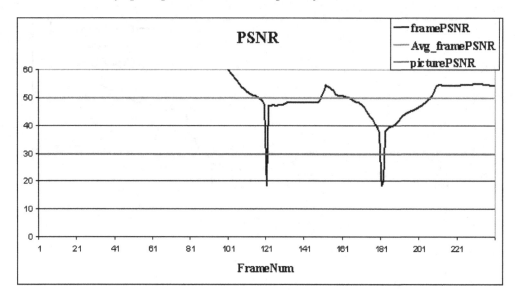

of translational and other patterns are combined, the sprite generation algorithm does not perform well. Smooth PTZ is the improved version, which is more close to the conventional camera motion pattern since it has a smooth zoom. In Figure 30, the size of the GTI for the Satellite image is 116 x 119 and the size of the sprite is 241 x 240. The

size of the GTI for the Starry Night is 119 x 117 and the size of the corresponding sprite is 338 x 386. The sprite of Satellite looks pretty good by itself. However, its size is almost 4 times the size of the GTI. In Figure 31, low average framePSNR indicates the poor quality of the sprite.

Figure 21. PSNR value of Spiral pattern at variable speed of Satellite

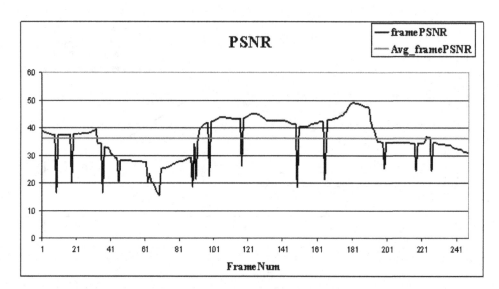

Figure 22. Sprite of Earthquake pattern on Satellite and Starry Night Image

Earthquake

Figure 23. Sprite of Zoom pattern on Satellite and Starry Night Image

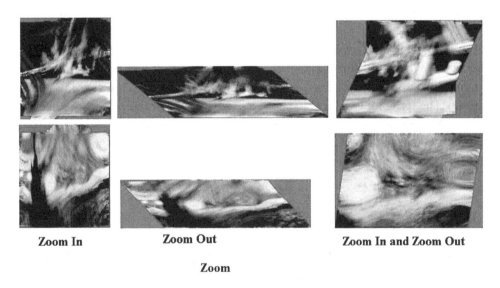

Zoom In   **Zoom Out**   **Zoom In and Zoom Out**

Zoom

Figure 24. Sprite of Affine pattern on Satellite and Starry Night

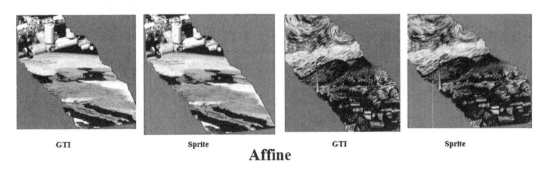

GTI   **Sprite**   **Affine**   **GTI**   **Sprite**

Figure 25. framePSNR on Starry Night

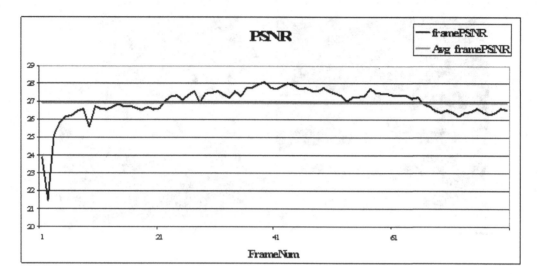

Combined Patterns

In Figure 32, we do not show the sprite for CBI pattern of the Satellite Image because sprite generation algorithm gave errors (possibly due to huge size of the sprite). The sprite for CBII is not at an acceptable level. According to the sprite of CBI on Starry Night, we found that the beginning part and the ending part of sprite are acceptable. The middle part has wrong global motion estimation since the biggest star has repetition. This can also be concluded from Figure 33. In the middle of the chart, during frames from 101 to 201 the framePSNR values are very low. From the GTF, we realize that the problem is due to switching among Zigzag, PTZ, Rotate and Affine patterns. The sprite of CBII on Starry Night is acceptable. However, the size is 494 x 454 where there is

Figure 26.Sprite of Rotate pattern

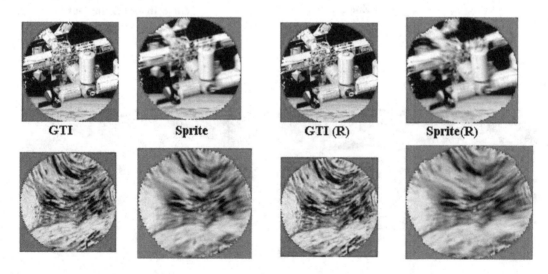

Figure 27. framePSNR of Rotate pattern on Satellite

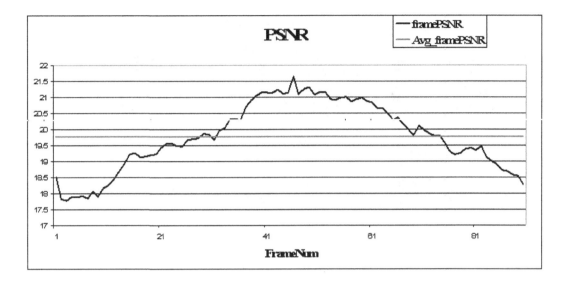

nearly 40-pixel difference when comparing to the size of GTI (equal to high resolution image). In the middle part of the sprite, we have blurring problem since revisiting the same region by PTZ, Rotate and Affine patterns. In Figure 34, it can be seen that there are problems towards the end of the video.

DISCUSSION

Based on these results, we may deduce that the selected sprite generation algorithm react well to translational and rotate patterns. The algorithm is likely to fail if there is zoom involved in the video. For the smooth PTZ pattern, the algorithm may be acceptable from the subjective evaluation.

Figure 28. framePSNR of Random Rotate pattern on Satellite

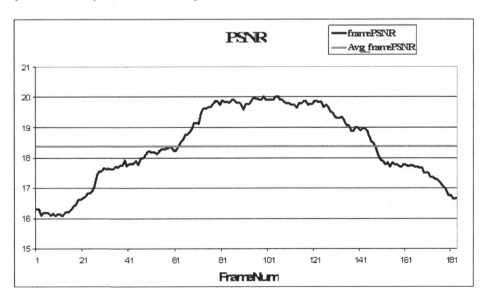

Figure 29. Sprite of PTZ on Satellite and Starry Night

977*367

2379*358

121*121

GTI   Sprite

However, the sizes of sprites are not correct if the ground-truth images are known. The algorithm may perform sometimes well for affine pattern (especially in CBII). However, if an error is made, it is likely that the error will propagate and an incorrect sprite is generated. The error for zoom may come from hierarchical motion estimation. An error at the low levels is propagated to the higher levels. In other words, Levenberg-Marquardt method cannot optimize properly from an incorrect set of parameters. The selected sprite generation algorithm is not sensitive to switching between the camera motion patterns.

In terms of measures to check the correctness of the sprite, high framePSNR values do not necessarily indicate a good quality sprite and low framePSNR indicates a bad quality of sprite. PicturePSNR values indicate the problems in the sprite quality. In our experiments for PTZ pattern, the size became a good indicator of the sprite quality for Satellite image. By looking at the sprite and the corresponding GTI, we may determine the problematic areas in the sprite. By analyzing the framePSNR, we may identify the frame numbers

Figure 30. Sprite of Smooth PTZ on Satellite and Starry Night

GTI

GTI

Sprite

Smooth PTZ

Figure 31. framePSNR of Smooth PTZ on Satellite

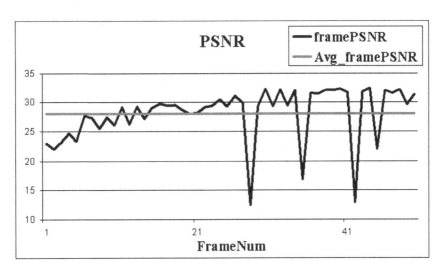

Figure 32. Sprite of combined pattern on Satellite and Starry Night

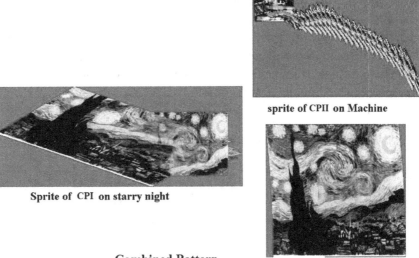

Sprite of CPI on starry night

sprite of CPII on Machine

Combined Pattern

sprite of CPII on starry night

having problems. Then using the GTF, we may determine the reason for error. We only used the correctness of motion parameters for translational patterns since sprites had good quality. The comparison of motion parameters yielded that the algorithm made mistakes in translational motion estimation. Since the frame numbers for incorrect

motion estimation are known, the algorithm can be improved by identifying the reasons for errors.

These measures (framePSNR and pictureP-SNR) complete each other. Firstly, picturePSNR makes sense when the sizes of the ground-truth and the sprite are similar. Secondly, low (average) framePSNR indicates low quality regardless of

Figure 33. framePSNR of combined pattern 1 on Starry Night

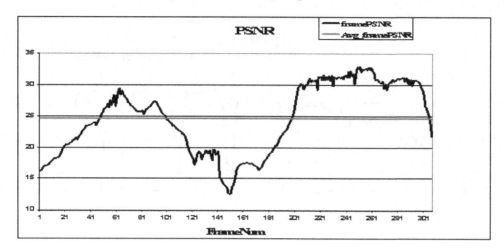

the picturePSNR value. Actually, low framePSNR indicates also low picturePSNR. When (average) framePSNR is high, picturePSNR and size play an important role. If the sizes are very different, this indicates a significant error while generating the sprite. This possibly may have happened few times. If framePSNR is high and sizes are similar, picturePSNR is likely to be high. If framePSNR is high (in this case sizes should be almost the same), this indicates that for every frame the global motion is estimated almost correctly. Therefore, framePSNR is also likely to be high. In other words, when picturePSNR is high, we do not expect low (average) framePSNR.

These results also indicate that our framework is good enough to identify the problems of a sprite generation algorithm.

Figure 34. framePSNR of combined pattern 2 on Starry Night

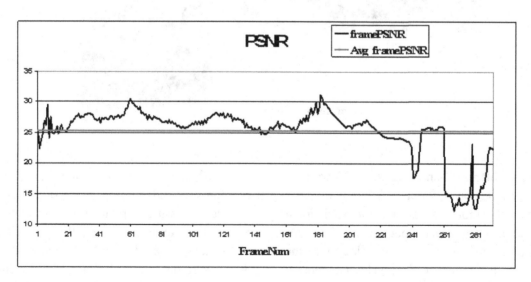

CONCLUSION

In this paper, we introduce and then experiment use our sprite evaluation framework by selecting one of the sprite generation algorithms to evaluate our framework as well as the sprite generation algorithm. It can systemically be used to analyze a sprite generation algorithm by using various synthetic videos that are generated from different high-resolution images with various camera motion patterns. We also provide the results of our sprite generation algorithm in an open environment to be used by other researchers for comparison. Our framework has synthetic video generation, which is the process of a video based on a high-resolution image following camera motion patterns. Our synthetic video generation algorithm supports a variety of camera motion patterns including zigzag, spiral, earthquake, zoom-in, zoom-out, zoom in and zoom out, affine, smooth PTZ and combined patterns. Since the videos are generated from an available image, the ground-truth images are available to check the correctness of the sprite. The comparison of sizes of the sprite and the ground-truth indicates presence of errors in motion estimation. Since the video is generated following camera motion patterns, motion parameters that are used to generate the synthetic videos are available to check the correctness of motion parameters for each frame. Our experimental results indicate that synthetic videos are effective for sprite generation evaluation. We were able to determine the weaknesses of the sprite generation algorithm and more importantly identify when they happen. This helps researcher to isolate the problem and remedy the weaknesses.

ACKNOWLEDGMENT

This material is based upon work supported by the National Science Foundation under Grant No. 0812307.

REFERENCES

Ambardekar, A., Nicolescu, M., & Dascalu, S. (2009). Ground-truth verification tool (GTVT) for video surveillance systems. In *Proceedings of ACHI '09, Second International Conferences on Advances in Computer-Human* (pp. 354-359).

ARFF. (n.d.). Retrieved from http://www.cs.waikato.ac.nz/~ml/weka/arff.html

Aygun, R. S., & Zhang, A. (2002) Reducing blurring-effect in high resolution mosaic generation.

Azzari, P., Stefano, L., & Bevilacqua, A.(2005). An effective real-time mosaicing algorithm apt

Baudisch, P., Tan, D., Steedly, D., Rudolph, E., Uyttendaele, M., Pal, C., & Szeliski, R. (2005, November 21-25). Panoramic viewfinder: providing a real-time preview to help users avoid flaws in panoramic pictures. In *Proceedings of the 17th Australia Conference on Computer-Human interaction: Citizens online: Considerations For Today and the Future*, Canberra, Australia (Vol. 122, pp. 1-10).

Baudisch, P., Tan, D., Steedly, D., Rudolph, E., Uyttendaele, M., Pal, C., & Szeliski, R. (2007). An Exploration of User Interface Designs for Real-Time Panoramic. *Australasian Journal of Information Systems*, *3*, 1327.

Black, J., Ellis, T., & Rosin, P. (2003). A novel method for video tracking performance. In *Proceedings of the IEEE PETS Workshop*.

Brown, M., & Lowe, D. G. (2007). Automatic Panoramic Image Stitching using Invariant Features. *International Journal of Computer Vision*, *74*(1), 59–73. doi:10.1007/s11263-006-0002-3

Chen, L., Lai, Y., & Liao, H. (2006). Video scene extraction using mosaic techinque. In *Proceedings of the 18th International Conference on Pattern Recognition (ICPR'06)* (Vol. 4, pp. 723-726).

Chen, Y., & Aygun, S. R. (2009a). Synthetic video generation with camera motion patterns to evaluate sprite generation. *Advances in Multimedia, 0*, 140–145.

Chen, Y., & Aygun, S. R. (2009b). Synthetic video generation with complex camera motion patterns to evaluate sprite generation. In *Proceedings of the Fifth IEEE International Workshop on Multimedia Information Processing and Retrieval (MIPR 2009)*.

Chen, Y., Deshpande, A. A., & Aygun, S. R. (2009). *SpriteDB* (Version 1.1 software). Retrieved from http://sprite.cs.uah.edu

Chen, Y., Deshpande, A. A., & Aygun, S. R. (2009c). SpriteDB tool – a web-tool for comparing sprite generation results. In *Proceedings of the IEEE International Symposium on Multimedia (ISM2009)*.

Cherng, D., & Chien, S. (2007, May). Video Segmentation with Model-Based Sprite Generation for Panning Surveillance Cameras. In Proceedings of *IEEE International Symposium on Circuits and Systems (ISCAS 2007)* (pp.2902-2905).

Coastguard Video. (n.d.). Retrieved from http://media.xiph.org/video/derf/

Dufaux, F., & Konrad, J. (2000). Efficient robust and fast global motion estimation for video coding. *IEEE Transactions on Image Processing, 9*, 497–500. doi:10.1109/83.826785

Erdem, C., & Sankur, B. (2000). Performance evaluation metrics for object-based video segmentation. In *Proceedings of the X European Signal Processing Conference (EUSIPCO)*.

Erdem, C., Sankur, B., & Tekalp, A. M. (2001). Metrics for video object segmentation and tracking without ground-truth. In *Proceedings of the IEEE International Conference on Image Processing (ICIP '01)*.

Farin, D., Haller, M., Krutz, A., & Sikora, T. (2008, October). Recent developments in panoramic imageGeneration and sprite coding. In *Proceedings of the IEEE 10th Workshop on Multimedia Signal Processing* (Vol. 8, No. 10, pp. 64-69).

Grammalidis, N., Beletsiotis, D., & Strintzis, M. G. (1999). Sprite Generation and Coding of Multiview Image Sequences. In *Proceedings from ICIAP'99: 10th Image Analysis and Processing, International Conference on* (p. 95).

Ishikawa, A., Panahpour Tehrani, M., Naito, S., Sakazawa, S., & Koike, A. (2008). Free viewpoint video generation for walk-through experience using image-based rendering. In *Proceedings from MM '08 ACM: In Proceeding of the 16th ACM international Conference on Multimedia* (pp. 1007-1008).

ISO/IEC 14496-2. (1999). *Information Technology – Coding of audio-visual objects– Part 2: Visual*.

Jinzenji, K., Watanabe, H., Okada, S., & Kobayashi, N. (2001). MPEG-4 Very Low Bit-rate Video Compression Using Sprite Coding. In *Proceedings from ICME'01: IEEE International Conference on Multimedia and Expo*.

Kunter, M., Kim, J., & Sikora, T. (2005, December). Super-resolution Mosaicing using Embedded Hybrid Recursive Flow-based segmentation. In *Proceedings of the Int. Conf. on Information, communications and Signal Processing (ICICS '05)*.

Lai, A.-N., Yoon, H., & Lee, G. (2008). Robust background extraction scheme using histogram-wise for real-time tracking in urban traffic video. In *Proceedings from CIT 2008: 8th IEEE International Conference* (pp. 845-850).

Li, Z.-N., & Drew, M. S. (2003). *Fundamentals of Multimedia*. Englewood Cliffs, NJ: Prentice-Hall.

Lim, S.-C., Na, H.-R., & Lee, Y.-L. (2007). Rate Control Based on Linear Regression for H.264/MPEG-4 AVC. *Signal Processing Image Communication, 22*(1), 39–58. doi:10.1016/j.image.2006.11.001

Lin, G., Wang, C., Chang, Y., & Chen, Y. (2002, December). Realtime object extraction and tracking with an active camera using image mosaics. In Proceedings of the *Multimedia. Signal Processing, 9*(11), 149–152.

Lu, Y., Gao, W., & Wu, F. (2003, May). Efficient background video coding with static sprite generation and arbitrary-shape spatial prediction techniques. In *Proceedings of the Circuits and Systems for Video Technology, IEEE Transactions* (Vol. 13, No. 5, pp. 394-405).

MPEG-4. (n.d.) Retrieved from http://www.chiariglione.org/mpeg/standards/MPEG-4/MPEG-4.htm

Multimedia and Expo. 2002. In *Proceedings of the IEEE International Conference (ICME '02)* (Vol. 2, pp. 537-540).

Nascimento, J.-C., & Marques, J.-S. (2006). Performance evaluation of object detection algorithms for video surveillance. In *Proceedings from ICPR '02: 16th International Conference on Pattern Recognition* (Vol. 3, p. 30965).

Orazio, D.-T., Leo, M., Mosca, N., Spagnolo, P., & Mazzeo, P. L. (2009). A semi-automatic system for ground-truth generation of soccer video sequences. In *Proceedings from AVSS '09: the 2009 Sixth IEEE International Conference on Advanced Video and Signal Based Surveillance* (pp. 559-564).

Sheikh, H. R., & Bovik, A. C. (2006, February). Image information and visual quality. In Proceedings of *Image Processing IEEE Transactions* (Vol. 15, No. 2, pp.430-444).

Sirkora, T. (1997). The mpeg-4 video standard verification model. *IEEE Transactions on Circuits and Systems for Video Technology, 7*, 19–31. doi:10.1109/76.554415

Smolic, A., Sikora, T., & Ohm, J. R. (1999). Long-term global motion estimation and its application for sprite generation, content description and segmentation. *IEEE Transactions on Circuits and Systems for Video Technology, 9*, 1227–1242. doi:10.1109/76.809158

Stefan Video. (n.d.). Retrieved from http://media.xiph.org/video/derf/

Szeliski, R. (2002). Video mosaics for virtual environments. *IEEE Computer Graphics and Applications, 16*(2), 22–30. doi:10.1109/38.486677

To detect motion through background subtraction using a PTZ camera. In *Proceedings of the Advanced Video and Signal Based Surveillance (AVSS 2005)* (pp. 511-516). Washington, DC: IEEE.

Wantanabe, H., & Jinzenji, K. (2001). Sprite coding in object-based video coding standard: MPEG-4. In *Proccedings of World Multiconf, on SCI 2001* (pp. 420-425).

Zhu, Z., & Hanson, A. R. (2005, September 11-14). Mosaic-based 3D scene representation and rendering. In Proceedings of the IEEE International Conference on *Image Processing (ICIP 2005)* (Vol. 1, p. 633).

Zomet, A., Levin, A., Peleg, S., & Weiss, Y. (2006). Seamless image stitching by minimizing false edges. *IEEE Transactions on Image Processing, 15*(4), 969–977. doi:10.1109/TIP.2005.863958

This work was previously published in the International Journal of Multimedia Data Engineering and Management, Volume 1, Issue 2, edited by Shu-Ching Chen, pp. 34-61, copyright 2010 by IGI Publishing (an imprint of IGI Global).

Chapter 11
Archive Film Comparison

Maia Zaharieva
Vienna University of Technology, Austria

Matthias Zeppelzauer
Vienna University of Technology, Austria

Dalibor Mitrović
Vienna University of Technology, Austria

Christian Breiteneder
Vienna University of Technology, Austria

ABSTRACT

In this paper, the authors present an approach for video comparison, in which an instantiated framework allows for the easy comparison of different methods that are required at each step of the comparison process. The authors' approach is evaluated based on a real world scenario of challenging video data of archive documentaries. In this paper, the performed experiments aim at the evaluation of the performance of established shot boundary detection algorithms, the influence of keyframe selection, and feature representation.

INTRODUCTION

Video copy detection is an active research area driven by ever-growing video collections. The detection of video duplicates allows for the efficient search and retrieval of video content. Existing applications for content-based video copy detection comprise video content identification (Yuan, Duan, Tian, & Xu, 2004), copyright protection (Joly, Frélicot, & Buisson, 2003; Ke, Sukthankar, & Huston, 2004), identification of duplicated news stories (Zhang & Chang, 2004), and TV broadcast monitoring and detection of commercials (Shen, Zhou, Huang, Shao, & Zhou, 2007). Presented experiments are often limited to high quality video clips of pre-defined fixed length and synthetically generated transformations such as resizing, frame shifting, contrast and gamma modification, Gaussian noise additions, etc.

In contrast, film and video comparison reaches beyond the boundaries of a single shot and aims at the identification of both reused and unique film

DOI: 10.4018/978-1-4666-1791-9.ch011

material in two video versions. The compared videos can be two versions of the same feature film, e.g., director's cut and original cut, or two different movies that share a particular amount of film material, such as documentary films and compilation films. Archive film material additionally challenges existing approaches for video analysis by the state and the nature of the material. The analysis of archive film material is often impeded by the loss of the original film versions. Remaining copies are usually low-quality backup copies from film archives and museums. Different versions vary significantly not only by the actual content (e.g., loss of frames/shots due to censorship or re-editing) but also due to material-specific artifacts such as mold, film tears, flicker, and low contrast. The movies are often monochromatic and silent which limits the set of available modalities and feasible techniques. Furthermore, existing algorithms often provide only limited robustness to illumination changes, affine transformation, cropping, and partial occlusions, which restricts their applicability for low-quality archive films. Archive film material is well-suited for the evaluation of video comparison techniques since it contains a large number of natural (not synthetically generated) transformations among different film versions and represents a complex real world scenario for film comparison and copy detection.

In general, a video comparison process passes well-defined steps from a shot boundary detection to shot representation and matching. At each step different algorithms can be applied. The combination of and the interaction between the selected methods are crucial for the overall comparison process. In this paper, we shortly describe a methodology for video comparison that accounts for the overall video structure at frame, shot and video level as presented in (Zaharieva, Zeppelzauer, Mitrović, & Breiteneder, 2009). The approach allows for the selection of the appropriate hierarchical level for a given task and, thus, enables different application scenarios

such as the identification of missing shots or the reconstruction of the original film version.

In this paper we extend our previous work in the following aspects: *First*, we account for the temporal ordering of corresponding keyframes from matched shots. *Second*, to further increase the performance, we additionally investigate shots that are labeled as unknown by the system. *Third*, we extend the performed experiments. We evaluate the performance of established shot boundary detection algorithms on a larger set of archive documentaries and investigate the influence of keyframe selection on the video comparison. *Finally*, we extend the video data and account for four different type of artifacts:

1. Artifacts originating from the analog film-strips, e.g., contrast and exposure changes, blurring, frame shift, dirt, film tears;
2. Digitization artifacts, e.g., coding transformations;
3. Technical transformations, e.g., changes in video format, resizing, cropping; and
4. Editorial operations such as frame/shot insertion and frame/shot deletion.

This paper is organized as follows. We first present related work on video copy detection. Following, we describe the underlying methodology for video comparison and the methods for shot boundary detection, keyframe extraction and feature representation. Finally, we present the performed experiments and discuss the results.

RELATED WORK

Existing approaches for video copy detection usually rely on the extraction of local and/or global features that are matched against a video reference set. In general, algorithms based on global features allow for efficient computation, search, and indexing. Typical features include color, edge, and motion information (Bertini, Bimbo, & Nunziati,

2006; Leon, Kalva, & Furht, 2009; Kim, Lee, Liu, & Lee, 2008; Li, Jin, & Zhou, 2005; Yeh & Cheng, 2009). Despite their effectiveness, global features often provide limited robustness to illumination changes, cropping, and partial occlusions. In contrast, approaches based on local features are robust to various video modifications at higher computational cost. Sand & Teller propose an image-registration method for aligning two videos recorded at different times into the spatio-temporal domain (2004). The authors combine Harris interest point-based matching and local motion estimation (Kanade-Lucas-Tomasi Feature Tracker, KLT) for frame alignment. The proposed method has low invariance to affine transformation and high computational costs of several minutes per second of video. Joly, Frélicot, and Buisson (2003) apply an improved version of the Harris corner detector and a differential description of the local region around each interest point. This approach was shown to be superior over further methods used in the literature such as ordinal intensity signatures or space-time interest points (Law-To, Chen, Joly, Laptev, Buisson, Gouet-Brunet, Boujemaa, & Stentiford, 2007). Recently, Douze, Jégou, and Schmid (2010) apply a combination of Hessian-Affine detector and Scale Invariant Feature Transform (SIFT) descriptor and integrate it into a bag-of-features framework. The authors report best results on the TRECVID 2008 copy detection task providing manifold video modifications such as contrast change, blur and noise introduction, occlusions and cropping.

Our work differs from previous research in the area of video copy detection in several aspects. *First*, we aim at the comparison of complete film versions. The additional knowledge about the video structure allows for the easy integration of temporal constrains of matched video frames and shots and increases the overall matching performance. *Second*, we evaluate the combination and influence of different state-of-the-art algorithms for shot boundary detection, keyframe selection and feature representation. *Third*, we perform the evaluation on a real-world video data set of archive film material exposing challenging artifacts such as contrast and exposure changes, dirt, film tears, coding transformations, size changes, frame/shot dropping, etc.

Underlying Methodology

From a technical point of view, a video consists of temporally aligned shots. Each video shot is a continuous sequence of frames recorded from a single camera. We present an approach, which accounts for this logical structure of a video and does not require any additional. Starting form a raw and unsegmented video, the first step is to determine shot boundaries automatically. Following, each shot is represented by a set of robust and distinctive features. Finally, our matching and decision process is applied to the segmented video stream. Figure 1 visualizes the workflow and information propagation within the framework.

Frame-Level

Video frames are the basic building blocks of a video sequence. Since a single frame represents a still image, manifold global and local features can be applied to describe its content. For performance reasons, features are usually not extracted for each frame of the shot but only for selected keyframes. Each keyframe is represented by a set of features and compared to each frame of the second video. The similarity between frame features is used to assign a keyframe to a shot by means of frame voting. Dependent on the selected feature, various distance metrics can be applied to measure the visual similarity. In our work, we use nearest neighbor ratio matching based on Euclidean distances, i.e., two features are considered similar if the distance to the second most similar feature is above a predefined threshold. Furthermore, we introduce a frame confidence measure, c_f, based on the distance spreading of all matches, i.e. if all distances lie closely together, the corresponding

Figure 1. Workflow and information propagation

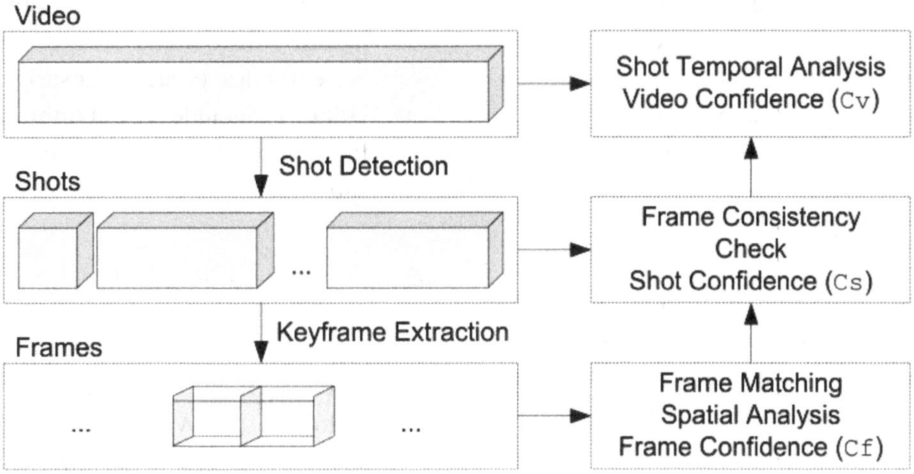

match is considered less reliable. In contrast, an outlier suggests a high matching confidence:

$$c_f = 1 - \frac{d_m}{d},$$

where d_m is the mean matching distance of the matched features, and d – the mean matching distance of all descriptors. Finally, the comparison for each keyframe results in a quadruple holding the frame's position in the current shot, the frame's confidence, the frame voting and the positioning of the frame within the matched shot.

Shot-Level

Since each shot is represented by a set of keyframes, three factors influence the shot matching decision: 1) frames' votes, 2) corresponding frames confidences, and 3) the temporal ordering of the frames. Thus, the shot confidence, c_s, is defined as:

$$c_s = \frac{\sum\limits_{i=1}^{n} s_i \times c_{fi} \times w_{fi}}{\sum\limits_{i=1}^{n} s_i} \quad \begin{cases} s = 1 & \text{for a voting frame} \\ s = 0 & \text{otherwise} \end{cases}$$

where c_{fi} is the frame confidence of the i-th frame, n the number of keyframes in the shot, and w_{fi} the weight factor for the corresponding temporal position. If matched keyframes have corresponding temporal positions within the respective shots, $w_{fi} = 1$, otherwise $w_{fi} = 0.8$. The consideration of the temporal ordering of the frames increased the precision score by up to 10% in experimental tests. Additionally, we apply the majority rule, i.e. the majority of the keyframes have to vote for the same shot otherwise the shot is rejected and classified as unknown.

Video-Level

In the domain of video comparison corresponding shots in different video versions build a well-defined sequence. This additional knowledge is used to eliminate falsely matched shots, which do not fit in the overall ordering sequence. To detect outliers we apply local minima and maxima suppression on the sequence formed by the corresponding shot positions. The average confidence score of matched shots is defined as video confidence c_v.

To further improve the matching performance, we additionally investigate all missed shots. Shots, which are labeled as unknown by the system and are at similar positions in both video streams, are pairwisely compared. For the final assignment of the shots the matching criteria is relaxed by decreasing the threshold. Since the search range for corresponding shots is limited to a well-defined area, the matching performance can easily be improved with low additional computational costs.

Methods Compared

The choice of underlying technology is crucial at each step of the video comparison process. The proposed approach defines the logic of the comparison process. It does not define the specific techniques used at each processing step. The user has the opportunity to select the adequate method at each step of the process. The three most important factors are: 1) the selection of shot detection algorithm; 2) the selection of keyframes as representatives for a given shot; and 3) the feature representation of the keyframes. In this section we give a brief description of different approaches for shot boundary detection, keyframe selection, and feature extraction.

Shot Boundary Detection

Shot boundary detection is a basic preprocessing step for most high-level video analyses tasks such as scene segmentation and video summarization. Many different techniques have been proposed in the last decades. The principle behind different approaches is similar. Usually, differences between consecutive frames are computed. If the differences exceed a certain threshold a shot cut is identified. In shot cut detection the single frames are usually represented by compact features, which are based on color, intensity, edges, motion, and frequency information. We evaluate three standard methods in cut detection, which are based on edges and intensity information. The fourth method (self-similarity matrix) is based on edge and frequency information and was specifically adapted to low-quality archive material.

- **Intensity Histogram (IH).** This method is based on the bin-wise differences of the intensity histograms between two consecutive frames (Gargi, Katsuri, & Strayer, 2000). To include spatial information, each frame is divided into M non-overlapping sub-images:

$$D_{F_1,F_2}^{IH} = \frac{1}{MN} \sum_{j=1}^{M} \sum_{i=1}^{N} \left| h_{1,j}[i] - h_{2,j}[i] \right|,$$

where h_j is the corresponding sub-image histogram and N – the number of bins. A shot cut is detected if the difference exceeds a predefined threshold.

- **Adaptive Threshold (AT).** Instead of using a global threshold on the histogram differences, Truong, Dorai, and Venkatesh (2000) propose the use of a simple adaptive thresholding method to detect peaks in the histogram difference curve. An adaptive threshold usually adapts better to local properties of the difference curve such as motion and flicker. The authors consider a sliding window along the temporal axis. They detect a shot cut if a given histogram difference 1) has the maximum value within the window, and 2) is α-times greater than the mean of remaining histogram differences within the window.

- **Edge Change Fraction (ECF).** The basic idea of this approach is that the positions of edges change considerably at shot boundaries: existing edges disappear and new edges appear where there were no edges before (Zabih, Miller, & Mai, 1995). The first step of the method is to apply an edge detection algorithm to two consecutive frames F_1 and F_2. The next step is the dilation of the edges (thickening) in order to compensate for small object and camera motions. Following, the method determines the fraction of appearing edge pixels ρ_{in} and vanishing edge pixels ρ_{out} in the frame F_2. The edge change fraction (ECF) ρ is defined as:

$$\rho = \max(\rho_{in}, \rho_{out}).$$

The ECF is computed for all pairs of consecutive frames in the video. Eventually, the peaks of the edge change fraction indicate shot boundaries.

- **Self-Similarity Matrix (SSM).** This method is based on the self-similarity between adjacent video frames (Zeppelzauer, Mitrović, & Breiteneder, 2008). First, each frame is split uniformly into blocks and for each block an edge histogram (EH) and the low-frequency DCT coefficients are extracted. The EH captures the orientations of the edges and is robust to frame displacements and flicker. The DCT feature represents the coarse spatial intensity distribution across a frame and is robust against dirt and scratches. The DCT and the EH features are well-suited for combination, since they capture complementary information.

Next, the similarity matrices for both features are computed separately. Sequences of similar frames produce bright squares along the diagonal of the matrix. Shot cuts are detected by moving a Gaussian weighted checkerboard kernel along the diagonal of the similarity matrix. The checkerboard kernel yields high correlation at the shot cuts and low correlation at other positions. Finally, the two similarity matrices result in two kernel correlation functions that are linearly combined. Shot boundaries are located by means of peak detection.

Keyframe Selection

There are different approaches for the selection of keyframes from a given video shot. Simple techniques do not account for the shot content but rather select the keyframes according to a predefined pattern. More sophisticated methods consider the visual dynamics of a shot and perform keyframe selection based on visual characteristics (e.g., color histograms) or motion information. Recently, Law-To, Chen, Joly, Laptev, Buisson, Gouet-Brunet, Boujemaa, and Stentiford (2007) select keyframes corresponding to extrema of the global intensity of motion in a comparative study of video copy detection algorithms. Originally, this approach was proposed by Eickler and Müller (1999).

To explore the influence of keyframe selection on the video comparison, we evaluate the following approaches:

- **KS1:** always select the first frame as a keyframe (Ng, King, & Lyu, 2001),
- **KS2:** the first and the last frames (Rui, Huang, & Mehrotta, 1999),
- **KS3:** the first, middle and last frames (Zaharieva, Zeppelzauer, Mitrović, & Breiteneder, 2009), and
- **KS4:** motion-based selection of keyframes (Eickeler & Müller, 1999).

Eickeler & Müller define *intensity of motion* as:

$$i(t) = \frac{\sum_{x,y} d(x,y,t)}{XY},$$

where $d(x,y,t)$ is the difference image of the gray values of adjacent frames (1999). To overcome the problem of abrupt visual changes caused by e.g., flashes, the authors propose to use the smaller value of the motion intensities for the frames *(t, t+1)* and *(t-1, t+2)*.

Feature Extraction

Different features can be used for the representation of keyframes. We compare three different types of features with a complementary structure. The edge histogram is a global statistical descriptor, the SIFT features are local image descriptors and the differential-based descriptors capture representative information for an entire shot.

- **MPEG-7 Edge Histogram Descriptor (EHD).** The MPEG-7 edge histogram describes the distribution of orientations of edges. Each frame is divided into 4 × 4 non-overlapping sub-images and for each sub-image a local edge histogram with 5 bins (0°, 45°, 90°, 135°, and non-directional edges) is computed. Thus, the edge histogram descriptor for the entire frame contains 4 × 4 × 5 = 80 bins (ISO/IEC, 2002). EHD is an effective feature for image similarity retrieval (Manjunath, Ohm, Vasudevan, & Yamada, 2001) and possesses promising characteristics for the comparison of archive films. The feature captures global information within each block and, thus, is highly robust against frame displacements and invariant to flicker. Since it captures high-frequency information, it is prone to local artifacts (e.g. scratches, dirt) and reflects global artifacts such as tears across the entire frame.

- **Scale Invariant Feature Transform (SIFT) Features.** SIFT features capture the gradient distribution in salient regions (Lowe, 2004). Keypoints are identified by means of a Gaussian function applied in scale space. Keypoint location, scale and orientation (defined by the peak of the gradient histograms) are associated with each SIFT feature. The resulting SIFT descriptor has 128 dimensions (4 × 4 location grid × 8 gradient orientations).

SIFT descriptors are highly discriminative local features. They are invariant to changes in translation, scale, and rotation and partially invariant to changes in illumination and affine distortions. Thus, frame displacement and flicker have no influence on the features. Artifacts, which result in loss of visual information (scratches, dirt, tears), automatically lead to loss of potential keypoints. However, since there is a large number of keypoints per frame, their fraction does not impede the matching process significantly.

- **Differential Descriptors (DD).** Recently, several authors report outstanding performance of differential-based descriptors in the context of video copy detection (Joly, Frélicot, & Buisson, 2007; Law-To, Buisson, Gouet-Brunet, & Boujemaa, 2006; Law-To, Chen, Joly, Laptev, Buisson, Gouet-Brunet, Boujemaa, & Stentiford, 2007). In this evaluation we follow the approach proposed by Law-To, Buisson, Gouet-Brunet, and Boujemaa (2006), which was reported as top-performing in a comparative study on video copy detection algorithms (Law-To, Chen, Joly, Laptev, Buisson, Gouet-Brunet, Boujemaa, & Stentiford, 2007).

The differential descriptors are computed in three steps. First, keypoints are identified using the Harris corner detector (Harris & Stephens, 1988) in each frame of a shot. Following, local features are computed at four spatial positions around the keypoints as Gaussian differential decomposition of the grey-level signal until the second order:

$$f = \left(\frac{\partial I}{\partial x}, \frac{\partial I}{\partial y}, \frac{\partial I}{\partial xy}, \frac{\partial^2 I}{\partial x^2}, \frac{\partial^2 I}{\partial^2 y} \right).$$

The resulting feature vector is a 20-dimensional descriptor. Finally, keypoints along frames are associated to build trajectories that are represented by the average descriptors. Unlike the original approach, we do not distinguish between motion and background trajectories. Bouncy and unsteady video sequences often exhibit high motion characteristics, which may lead to mislabeling and, thus, misclassification.

EVALUATION

In this section we discuss the performed experiments. First, we present the video data and corresponding application scenarios. Following, we present the results on shot boundary detection as a preprocessing step for the comparison of archive documentaries. Finally, we explore the influence of keyframe selection and feature extraction within the presented application domain.

Video Data

Subject of our experiments are historical artistic documentaries by the Soviet avant-garde filmmaker D. Vertov from the 1920s and 1930s. The films have a distinctive structure characterized by a high number of short, repeating shots with high visual similarity (see for examples Figure 2).

The films do not contain any narrative structure, which makes them different from material that is usually analyzed such as news broadcasts, sports videos, and feature film. Additionally, the director used advanced montage techniques to create

complex transitions, multiple exposures, and split screen compositions. The film material is 35mm monochrome and mostly silent film. The filmstrips were digitized frame-by-frame to make them processable.

We explore ten films grouped into three case studies. The first case study (*CS1*) investigates two films in two versions respectively. All films originate from tape-based analog sources and range from 64 to 86 min length. In one case, the copies were derived from the original source with several decades in between. They differ greatly in image quality and censored content. In the other case, the two versions originate from the same analog copy. One copy is the result of an effort to manually reconstruct the original film by manually adding and removing shots. The second case study (*CS2*) investigates again two films in two different versions whereas the second copies originate from unknown sourced DVDs. Additionally to the differences in image quality and content, digitization artifacts further impede the process of video comparison. The films' length ranges from 55 to 82 min. The last case study (*CS3*) compares two different but related analog films: an original documentary by D. Vertov (59 min) and a compilation film by A.V. Blum (23 min) where a number of shots from the former have been reused.

Existing filmstrips of archive films are often multiple-generation copies that were never intended for other purposes but backups. In most

Figure 2. Examples for highly similar repeating shots (each shot is represented by its first frame)

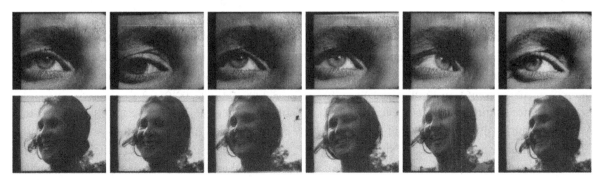

cases the original filmstrips do not exist any more, hence the available backup copies are the only existing source material left. The state of film material degrades significantly during storage, copying and playback over the decades. Important artifacts in archive film material include:

- Scratches, which are usually introduced by dirt in the film projector.
- Dirt (dust, liquids, mold), which propagates and increases from one copy to the next.
- Visible framelines, which result from copying misaligned filmstrips and the shrinking of the film material. Since the filmstrips are made of organic material they contract over time. Contraction occurs horizontally and vertically and results in shaking and misaligned frames.
- Low contrast which is a result of repeated copying.
- Flicker, which results from the fact that film transports in early cameras was performed manually (variable exposure time).
- Frame displacements, which result from shrinking of the filmstrips.

These artifacts accumulate from generation to generation with each copy. The large number of artifacts makes the material challenging for film comparison.

Shot Boundary Detection

The first step of automatic video comparison is shot boundary detection. Shot boundary detection is widely seen as solved for contemporary video material. However, experiments with shot boundary detection demonstrate the task being still challenging in the context of archive film material (see Table 1 for summary of the achieved results). Artifacts, such as dirt, scratches and film tears, generate abrupt visual changes and significantly impede the process of shot boundary detection.

Such unintended alterations of the content interfere with established algorithms that are based on pixel differences (*Intensity Histogram*, IH, and *Adaptive Threshold*, AT) and edge information (*Edge Change Fraction*, ECF). Furthermore, these methods are sensitive to motion (camera shaking, large object and camera motions, etc.) In such cases, preceding motion compensation is required. However, tests showed that prior motion compensation of archive film material introduces new artifacts that adversely affect shot boundary detection using the ECF method. The *Self-Similarity Matrix* (SSM) outperforms significantly the other tested methods in terms of recall and precision and proves robustness for the complex spatio-temporal structure and manifold artifacts of archive film material. The use of robust image features and the larger analysis window (checkerboard window size of up to 8 frames) significantly increases the robustness of the method. Thus, all following experiments are performed based on the shots detected by the SSM approach.

Video Comparison

In this section we present the evaluation results of different keyframe selection methods (KS1-4) in combination with the MPEG-7 edge histogram descriptor (EHD) and the SIFT features. Since the differential descriptors (DD) are based on feature trajectories and, thus, process each frame of a shot, their performance is reported only at the shot- and video-level.

EHD features are matched using simple Euclidean distance. Local feature descriptors (SIFT and DD) additionally identify the first two nearest neighbors in terms of Euclidean distances. A descriptor is accepted if the nearest neighbor distance ratio is below a predefined threshold of 0.8. Since the local descriptors represent the characteristics of a small area around a point of interest, these approaches usually result in a high number of matching descriptors. Given the

Table 1. Recall(R)/Precision(P) performance for shot boundary detection

		R	P
CS1	Intensity Histogram (IH)	0.68	0.68
	Adaptive Threshold (AT)	0.67	0.65
	Edge Change Fraction (ECF)	0.67	0.67
	Self-Similarity Matrix (SSM)	**0.91**	**0.91**
CS2	Intensity Histogram (IH)	0.82	0.77
	Adaptive Threshold (AT)	0.88	0.92
	Edge Change Fraction (ECF)	0.77	0.76
	Self-Similarity Matrix (SSM)	**0.95**	**0.95**
CS3	Intensity Histogram (IH)	0.77	0.77
	Adaptive Threshold (AT)	0.80	0.81
	Edge Change Fraction (ECF)	0.75	0.76
	Self-Similarity Matrix (SSM)	**0.93**	**0.93**

partially high similarity between different shots, the total number of matches is often misleading. To increase the reliability of detected matches we ignore all ambiguous matches, i.e. all descriptors are eliminated that match several features in the other frame. Additionally, the RANdom Sample Consensus (RANSAC) algorithm is applied to remove outliers that do not fit a homography transformation (Fischler & Bolles, 1981). Finally, a video frame votes for the shot of the frame with the most matches. However, if less than 5% of the descriptors are matches or if the frame confidence is below 50-60% (depending on the features extracted), the match is considered unreliable and is ignored, i.e., the frame is classified as unknown. At shot-level, the required shot confidence score is set initially to 60-70%. All shots with lower confidence score are rejected and classified as unknown. At video-level, we account for the temporal alignment of matched shots and discard shots that do not fit in the ordering sequence by applying peak (local minima and maxima) detection. Finally, all unknown shots are re-evaluated by reducing the required confidence score for a positive match by 10%.

- **Case Study 1 (CS1).** The first case study focuses on the comparison of analog-sourced films. The different film versions share around 90% of all shots. In general, the remaining (unique) shots are the result of loss in the process of storage or copying during the years. However, corresponding shots bear also partially large differences due to e.g., film tears, contrast differences and removed frames (see for examples Figure 3).

Table 2 summarizes the experimental results in terms of recall-precision measures. In general, the SIFT features outperform the remaining descriptors independently of the keyframe selection method and on all three levels of the comparison. Surprisingly, the performance difference to MPEG-7 edge histogram (EHD) is very low. EHD proves to be a very competitive descriptor and as performant as the computationally more expensive SIFT algorithm. In terms of recall and precision, EHD scores 90% and 98% respectively whereas SIFT achieves 92% and 99%. Although the differential descriptors (DD) build on information from each frame of a given shot, they show very low performance. An analysis of the extracted features shows very low variance, which results in low distinctiveness of the computed descriptors. Thus, such descriptors are only applicable for highly discriminative data. In a scenario of multiple low quality shots with high visual similarity, this approach fails to correctly assign corresponding shots.

The comparison of the keyframe selection methods shows that – for the given case study – KS1 (first frame is a representative for the shot) outperforms the remaining methods closely followed by KS3 (selection of the first, middle, and last frame for a shot) and KS4 (motion-based selection of keyframes). KS2 (first and last frames are keyframes for a shot) results in lower performance due to the majority decision rule on the frame-level of the framework, i.e. if both key-

Figure 3. Examples for differences in corresponding shots in different film versions (each shot is represented by its first frame). First shot: film tear and illumination differences. Second shot: additional frame displacement (see the black lines on the corresponding frame borders. Third shot: frame mark removed in the second film version. Fourth shot: high contrast difference.

frames vote for different shots, the votes are discarded and the shot is classified as unknown even if one of the frames is assigned correctly. In general, the performances of all keyframe selection methods lie closely together. However, the computational costs differ significantly. KS1 results in a single frame as representative for each shot. In contrast, within the given video set, KS4 results in the selection of 1 to 30 keyframes per

shot, which increases the number of required comparisons significantly.

An analysis of the false positives reveals two facts. *First*, the investigated films contain a large number of static, repeating shots. In general, such shots are assigned correctly outside of the context of a complete film. Within the given context, they are often assigned to an identical shot that appears on a different position in the video sequence. Thus, a generally correct match is classified as a false

Table 2. Recall(R) / Precision(P) results for CS1

		Frame-Level		Shot-Level		Video-Level	
		R	P	R	P	R	P
EHD	KS1	0.89	0.90	0.89	0.90	**0.90**	**0.98**
	KS2	0.85	0.87	0.84	0.95	0.87	0.97
	KS3	0.88	0.87	0.89	0.93	0.90	0.96
	KS4	0.83	0.85	0.89	0.90	0.90	0.96
SIFT	KS1	0.92	0.90	0.92	0.90	**0.92**	**0.99**
	KS2	0.86	0.90	0.82	0.96	0.85	0.98
	KS3	0.86	0.91	0.89	0.96	0.90	0.97
	KS4	0.87	0.83	0.89	0.91	0.90	0.94
DD	-	-	-	0.58	0.62	0.59	0.96

positive. *Second*, the large number of shots with high perceptual similarity also increases the false positives at frame- and shot-level (see Figure 4 for examples). Since the video-level of the framework accounts for the temporal ordering of the shots, such false positives are easily identified and correctly re-assigned.

- **Case Study 2 (CS2).** The second case study compares different film versions of different origin: analog and digital. The film versions share around 70% of all shots. Additionally to the already discussed artifacts in archive film material, artifacts that result from a preprocessing of the material (e.g. noise reduction, stabilization, contrast enhancement) as well as the coding technology lead to large differences in the visual perception of different shots (see Figure 5).

The results of the experiments are presented in Table 3. Again, SIFT features are the top performing approach. In contrast to the first case study,

the selection of three keyframes as representatives for the shot proves to be the best keyframe selection method. The manifold artifacts presented in this case study require for a robust decision rule at shot- and video-level of the framework. In general, all recall-precision scores are slightly lower than those achieved in the first case study because of the intensification of the presented artifacts as well as the introduction of new artifacts due to preprocessing and video coding. MPEG-7 edge histogram bears higher sensitivity to motion artifacts in shots (see for examples the last two shots pictured in Figure 5) and, thus, often fails to classify shots with large motion. The differential-based descriptors completely fail to achieve any reasonable results due to the experimental nature of the video data set. The low performance of the method on the shot-level of the framework does not allow for further evaluation on video-level. The video-level involves peak detection in the ordering sequence of shots and requires a precision of at least 51% for the detection of a reliable sequence.

Figure 4. Examples for false positives. The assigned shots bear high visual similarity. In the first three examples the shots present the same scene settings with slightly different motives (e.g. people walking by or different workers). Despite the different subjects in the last example, both shots have identical composition and action flow.

Table 3. Recall (R) / Precision (P) results for CS2

		Frame-Level		Shot-Level		Video-Level	
		R	**P**	**R**	**P**	**R**	**P**
EHD	KS1	0.65	0.56	0.65	0.56	0.81	0.82
	KS2	0.57	0.57	0.58	0.62	0.81	0.78
	KS3	0.69	0.60	0.69	0.75	**0.85**	**0.82**
	KS4	0.63	0.57	0.68	0.58	0.79	0.79
SIFT	KS1	0.81	0.88	0.81	0.88	0.87	0.85
	KS2	0.76	0.75	0.76	0.77	0.76	0.88
	KS3	0.79	0.74	0.83	0.84	**0.91**	**0.88**
	KS4	0.79	0.80	0.81	0.83	0.86	0.84
DD	-	-	-	0.03	0.02	-	-

- **Case Study 3 (CS3).** The last case study compares an original documentary and a compilation film that uses less than 5% of the shots. This case study clearly outlines the limitations of the MPEG-7 edge histogram and the differential-based descriptors: both approaches fail to find sufficient corresponding shots. However, SIFT features also achieve very low performance. Best recall and precision scores are 40% and 70% respectively using the KS1 keyframe selection method.

CONCLUSION

We presented an approach for video comparison, which accounts for the overall video structure. The approach is embedded in a framework that allows for the easy comparison of different methods required at each step of the comparison process. Within this framework we compared state-of-the-art methods for shot boundary detection as well as feature representation and investigated the influence of keyframe selection on the performance of the video comparison process. We

Figure 5. Examples for differences in corresponding shots as result from a preprocessing step (e.g. noise reduction and contrast enhancement) and coding and compression technology

presented the results of the evaluation based on a real world scenario on challenging archive film material. Where SIFT is starting to be more and more the universal weapon with which to attack such problems, MPEG-7 edge histogram proves to be almost as performant as the computationally much more expensive SIFT. Despite the low video quality and partially large differences between corresponding shots, MPEG-7 edge histogram descriptors achieve outstanding performance in terms of recall and precision that is only marginally lower than those of SIFT features.

ACKNOWLEDGMENT

This work was partly supported by the Vienna Science and Technology Fund (WWTF) under grant no. CI06024: "Digital Formalism: The Vienna Vertov Collection".

REFERENCES

Bertini, M., Bimbo, A. D., & Nunziati, W. (2006). Video clip matching using mpeg-7 descriptors and edit distance. In *Proceedings of the International Conference on Image and Video Retrieval* (LNCS 4071, pp. 133-142).

Douze, M., Jégou, H., & Schmid, C. (2010). An image-based approach to video copy detection with spatio-temporal post-filtering. In *Proceedings of IEEE Transactions on Multimedia*.

Eickeler, S., & Müller, S. (1999). Content-based video indexing of tv broadcast news using hidden markov models. In *Proceedings of the IEEE International Conference on Acoustics, Speech, and Signal Processing* (pp. 2997-3000).

Fischler, M. A., & Stephens, M. (1988). A combined corner and edge detector. In *Proceedings of the Alvey Conference* (pp. 147-152).

Gargi, U., Kasturi, R., & Strayer, S. H. (2000). Performance characterization of video-shot-change detection methods. In *Proceedings of IEEE Transactions on Circuits and Systems for Video Technology, 10*(1), 1–13. doi:10.1109/76.825852

ISO/IEC. (2002). *Information Technology - Multimedia Content Description Interface - part 3: Visual. Number 15938-3*. Geneva, Switzerland: ISO/IEC, Moving Pictures Expert Group.

Joly, A., Frélicot, C., & Buisson, O. (2003). Robust content-based video copy identification in a large reference database. In *Proceedings of the International Conference on Image and Video Retrieval* (pp. 414-424).

Joly, A., Frélicot, C., & Buisson, O. (2007). Content-based copy detection using distortion-based probabilistic similarity search. *IEEE Transactions on Multimedia, 9*(2), 293–306. doi:10.1109/TMM.2006.886278

Ke, Y., Sukthankar, R., & Huston, L. (2004). Efficient near-duplicate and sub-image retrieval. In *Proceedings of the ACM International Conference on Multimedia* (pp. 869-876).

Kim, H.-s., Lee, J., Liu, H., & Lee, D. (2008). Video linkage: group based copied video detection. In *Proceedings of the International Conference on Content-based Image and Video Retrieval* (pp. 397-406).

Law-To, J., Buisson, O., Gouet-Brunet, V., & Boujemaa, N. (2006). Robust voting algorithm based on labels of behavior for video copy detection. In *Proceedings of the ACM International Conference on Multimedia* (pp. 835-844).

Law-To, J., Chen, L., Joly, A., Laptev, I., Buisson, O., Gouet-Brunet, V., et al. (2007). Video copy detection: a comparative study. In *Proceedings of the International Conference on Image and Video Retrieval* (pp. 371-378).

Leon, G., Kalva, H., & Furht, B. (2009). Video identification using video tomography. In *Proceedings of the IEEE International Conference on Multimedia and Expo* (pp. 1030-1033).

Li, Y., Jin, J., & Zhou, X. (2005). Video matching using binary signature. In *Proceedings of the International Symposium on Intelligent Signal Processing and Communication Systems* (pp. 317-320).

Lowe, D. G. (2004). Distinctive image features from scale-invariant keypoints. *International Journal of Computer Vision*, 60(2), 91–110. doi:10.1023/B:VISI.0000029664.99615.94

Manjunath, B., Ohm, J.-R., Vasudevan, V., & Yamada, A. (2001). Color and texture descriptors. *IEEE Transactions on Circuits and Systems for Video Technology*, 11(6), 703–715. doi:10.1109/76.927424

Ng, C. W., King, I., & Lyu, M. R. (2001). Video comparison using tree matching algorithm. In *Proceedings of the International Conference on Imaging Science, Systems and Technology* (pp. 184-190).

Rui, Y., Huang, T. S., & Mehrotra, S. (1999). Constructing table-of-content for videos. *Multimedia Systems*, 7(5), 359–368. doi:10.1007/s005300050138

Sand, P., & Teller, S. (2004). Video matching. *ACM Transactions on Graphics*, 592–599. doi:10.1145/1015706.1015765

Shen, H. T., Zhou, X., Huang, Z., Shao, J., & Zhou, X. (2007). Uqlips: a real-time near-duplicate video clip detection system. In *Proceedings of the International Conference on Very Large Data Bases* (pp. 1374-1377).

Truong, B. T., Dorai, C., & Venkatesh, S. (2000). New enhancements to cut, fade, and dissolve detection processes in video segmentation. In *Proceedings of the ACM International Conference on Multimedia* (pp. 219-227).

Yeh, M.-C., & Cheng, K.-T. (2009). Video copy detection by fast sequence matching. In *Proceedings of the ACM International Conference on Image and Video Retrieval* (pp. 1-7).

Yuan, J., Duan, L.-Y., Tian, Q., & Xu, C. (2004). Fast and robust short search using an index structure. In *Proceedings of the ACM SIGMM International Workshop on Multimedia Information Retrieval* (pp. 61-68).

Zabih, R., Miller, J., & Mai, K. (1995). A feature-based algorithm for detecting and classifying scene breaks. In *Proceedings of the ACM International Conference on Multimedia* (pp. 189-200).

Zaharieva, M., Zeppelzauer, M., Mitrović, D., & Breiteneder, C. (2009). Finding the missing piece: Content-based video comparison. In *Proceedings of the IEEE International Symposium on Multimedia* (pp. 330-335).

Zeppelzauer, M., Mitrović, D., & Breiteneder, C. (2008). Analysis of historical artistic documentaries. In *Proceedings of the International Workshop on Image Analysis for Multimedia Interactive Services* (pp. 201-206).

Zhang, D.-Q., & Chang, S.-F. (2004). Detecting image near-duplicate by stochastic attributed relational graph matching with learning. In *Proceedings of the ACM International Conference on Multimedia* (pp. 877-884).

Zhou, J., & Zhang, X.-P. (2005). Automatic identification of digital video based on shot-level sequence matching. In *Proceedings of the ACM International Conference on Multimedia* (pp. 515-518).

This work was previously published in the International Journal of Multimedia Data Engineering and Management, Volume 1, Issue 3, edited by Shu-Ching Chen, pp. 41-56, copyright 2010 by IGI Publishing (an imprint of IGI Global).

Section 4
Audio Data Processing and Indexing

Chapter 12
Fast Caption Alignment for Automatic Indexing of Audio

Allan Knight
University of California, Santa Barbara USA

Kevin Almeroth
University of California, Santa Barbara, USA

ABSTRACT

For large archives of audio media, just as with text archives, indexing is important for allowing quick and accurate searches. Similar to text archives, audio archives can use text for indexing. Generating this text requires using transcripts of the spoken portions of the audio. From them, an alignment can be made that allows users to search for specific content and immediately view the content at the position where the search terms were spoken. Although previous research has addressed this issue, the solutions align the transcripts only in real-time or greater. In this paper, the authors propose AUTOCAP. It is capable of producing accurate audio indexes in faster than real-time for archived audio and in real-time for live audio. In most cases it takes less than one quarter the original duration for archived audio. This paper discusses the architecture and evaluation of the AUTOCAP project as well as two of its applications.

INTRODUCTION

Over the past 10 years, automatic speech recognition has become faster, more accurate, and speaker independent. One tool that these systems rely on is *forced alignment*, the alignment of text with speech. This application is especially useful in automated captioning systems for video play out.

Traditionally, forced alignment's main application was training for automatic speech recognition. By using the text of recognized speech ahead of time, the Speech Recognition System (SRS) can learn how phonemes map to text. However, there exist other uses for forced alignment.

Caption alignment is another application of forced alignment. It is the process of finding the

DOI: 10.4018/978-1-4666-1791-9.ch012

exact time all words in a video are spoken and matching them with the textual captions in a media file. For example, closed captioning systems use aligned text transcripts of audio/video. The result is that when the audio of the media plays, the text of the spoken words is displayed on the screen at the same time. Finding such alignments manually is very time consuming and requires more than the duration of the media itself, i.e., it cannot be performed in real-time. Automatic alignment of captions is possible using the new generation of SRS, which are fast and accurate.

There are several applications that benefit from these aligned captions. Foremost, and quite obviously, are captions for media. Providing consumers of audio and video with textual representations of the spoken parts of the media has many benefits. Other uses are also possible. For example, indexing the audio portion of the media is a useful option. By aligning media with the spoken components, users can find the exact place where text occurs within the audio content. This functionality makes the media searchable.

The technical challenge is how to align the transcript of the spoken words with the media itself. As stated before, manual alignment is possible, but requires a great deal of time. A better solution would be to find algorithms to automatically align captions with the media. There are, however, several challenges to overcome in order to obtain accurate caption timestamps. The first is aligning unrecognized utterances. No modern SRS is 100% perfect, and therefore, any system for caption alignment must deal with this problem. The second challenge is determining what techniques to apply if the text does not exactly match the spoken words of the media. This problem arises if the media creators edit transcripts to remove grammatical errors or other types of extraneous words spoken during the course of the recorded media (e.g., frequent use of the non-word "uh"). The third challenge is to align the caption efficiently. For indexing large archives of media,

time is important. Therefore, any solution should balance how much time it takes with the greatest possible accuracy.

The work discussed in this paper is part of a project called AUTOCAP. The goal of this project is to automatically align captured speech with their transcripts while directly addressing the questions above. AUTOCAP includes of two previously available components: a language model toolkit and a speech recognitions system. By combining these components with an alignment algorithm and caption estimator, developed as part of this research, we are able to achieve accurate timestamps in a timely manner. Then, using the longest common subsequence algorithm and local speaking rate, AUTOCAP can quickly and accurately align long media files that include audio (and video) with a written transcript that contains many edits, and therefore, does not exactly match the spoken words in the media file.

While other researchers have previously addressed a similar problem (Hazen, 2006; Moreno & Jeorg, 1998; Placeway & Lafferty, 1996; Robert-Ribes & Mukhtar, 1997), they use different techniques and do not accomplish the task as fast as AUTOCAP can. The cited projects either do more work than is needed, such as a recursive approach (Moreno & Joerg, 1998), or add more features than are needed (Hazen, 2006), for example, correcting the transcripts. In either case, both approaches, while very accurate, take real-time or longer to align each piece of media. And as mentioned previously, for processing large archives of media, shorter processing times are critical. Finally, and most importantly, these works do not address the issue of edited transcripts.

Our research shows that AUTOCAP can accurately and efficiently align edited transcripts. AUTOCAP's accuracy, as measured by how closely aligned the spoken words are with when the text appears on the screen, is well within two seconds of the ground truth. This two second value is what other research cites as the minimum level of accuracy (Hazen, 2006; Moreno & Jeorg, 1998; Robert-Ribes & Mukhtar, 1997). Furthermore, in most cases, AUTOCAP is well below this two-second threshold. Also, it is capable of aligning captions in faster than real-time. That is to say, it can align the transcripts in time no greater than the length of the recorded audio itself. In most cases, it produces accurate alignments in approximately 25% of real-time. This result is possible using a system implemented in Java.

The remainder of this paper is organized as follows. Section 2 provides more details about the challenges of caption alignment. Section 3 describes the AUTOCAP architecture and the tools and algorithms it uses. Section 4 examines our claims about the accuracy and efficiency of AU-TOCAP. Section 5 describes in greater detail the previously mentioned related work along with other similar research. Finally, Section 6 provides a brief summary of our findings and final remarks about the AUTOCAP project.

ALIGNING CAPTIONS

Caption alignment is a specialized problem for automatic speech recognition. This section outlines the specific problems that AUTOCAP addresses. It also specifies which problems it does not address. The main functionality of AUTOCAP is forced alignment. As AUTOCAP is not useful for automatic speech recognition training, we start by describing the usual purpose of forced alignment, then differentiate the purpose of AUTOCAP forced alignment, and finally, offer details about the real application of AUTOCAP and how it can be used to enrich media.

The following subsections discuss the major concepts associated with aligning audio media and transcripts. Their purpose is to create a common understanding of the terms used throughout this paper for the sake of clarity.

FORCED ALIGNMENT

Usually forced alignment is associated with SRS training. By feeding a known collection of utterances to an SRS, it can learn to properly map utterances from audio signals to text. The process involves first breaking the known utterances into individual phonemes and then aligning them with recognized phonemes from the audio source. Modern SRSs uses the Viterbi algorithm for performing these alignments.

Other applications of forced alignment also exist, and not necessarily at the same linguistic level. For example, AUTOCAP aligns audio with written transcripts. For this problem, there is no need to match at the phoneme level (though the SRS will still operate at this level), but instead operates at the word, or even text segment level. Here the goal is not to train the SRS, but rather to align an already transcribed text to an audio file for other purposes than SRS training.

MEDIA AND TRANSCRIPTS

While there are many reasons for alignment of media and transcripts, there are three major reasons we deem important. First is accessibility. Closed captioning has existed for many years. However, in today's media rich world, captioning is a vital part of maintaining accessibility for people of differing capabilities. The problem is, however, that finding the time that each utterance or transcript segment is spoken is time consuming. Automatic means of aligning captions and media provide a more scalable solution for this problem. Such techniques are particularly important as more and more media content are produced.

Indexing is also a powerful tool driven by the growing availability of media and the increasingly varied ways in which it is used. Indexing allows media consumers to search for the exact content that interests them. Since most current indexing technologies require some form of text to associate with the media, alignment of text and audio media is a powerful means of indexing audio media. Other characteristics of media may be used in the future, but the textual content of media will always maintain a basic level of importance for quickly searching media.

Finally, internationalization is also a major concern as the global economy continues to expand and evolve. By aligning textual transcripts with media, content providers not only provide caption and indexing capabilities in the native language of the media, but can also provide translations for multiple languages. This added benefit provides access to a larger audience of consumers for media content.

EDITED TRANSCRIPTS

For the set of media and transcripts on which we tested AUTOCAP, we used edited transcripts. These were transcripts professionally edited by experts with domain-specific knowledge in the fields addressed by the media.

Aligning edited transcripts with media has its own unique set of problems. First, unlike the work by Hazen (2006), the transcripts were considered correct and no additional editing was necessary. However, because the transcripts were edited, they often did not match verbatim what was said in the audio media. This fact imposed two problems for the normal forced alignment problem. First, not every word spoken in the audio was reflected in the transcript. Mistakes by the speaker, such as stuttering or using filler non-words such as "um", were removed from the transcript. Second, not every word in the transcript was necessarily spoken in the audio. For example, if the speaker used the wrong word, the edited transcript instead included the correct phrasing. For these two reasons, aligning the two media at a lower linguistic level is not only a much harder problem but also unnecessary.

ALIGNING EDITED TRANSCRIPTS WITH MEDIA

The application for which AUTOCAP is intended is very specific. When content producers wish to take edited transcripts and align them with audio or video content, AUTOCAP can accomplish this task not only accurately, but in faster than real-time. Also, because AUTOCAP allows for edited transcripts, the basic problem is reduced to edit distance, and therefore the longest common subsequence algorithm is used to align audio and text. The following two sections discuss how AUTOCAP accomplishes this task and describes how AUTOCAP is able to perform it accurately.

AUTOCAP

AUTOCAP employs five processing steps that are necessary to align a transcript with its audio. First, the audio file, sometimes as part of a media file that includes video, must be trans-coded into a Sphinx compatible codec. Second, a language model is built using the Carnegie-Mellon University Cambridge Statistical Language Modeling Language toolkit (CMU-CAM). Third, both the audio and language model are then used as input to the Sphinx SRS. The SRS produces a list of utterances. Fourth, AUTOCAP aligns these recognized utterances with the transcript and, where unable to use exact timestamps, estimates the timestamp instead. Finally, a transcript file is produced that contains all the segments used for captioning and the necessary timestamps to synchronize with the audio/video media.

AUTOCAP is not simply a software program, but rather is a software system integrated with a Java program that performs alignment. The purpose of this section is to describe the entire AUTOCAP system as well as the software itself and how they interact to accomplish caption alignment and audio indexing. Upon reading this section the reader should expect to have a good understanding of how AUTOCAP accomplishes this task. Figure 1 illustrates all of the components that make up the AUTOCAP architecture.

ARCHITECTURE

The architecture of AUTOCAP is composed of two levels: the system and the software levels. The system level represents the collection of tools, both previously available and those developed as part of this effort, used to perform the task of caption alignment. Figure 1 outlines this level and illustrates the flow of media through the system. The media starts as a file and a transcript file. Once all processing is complete, it outputs the same transcript used as input, with time codes for each transcript segment. The software level represents the actual programming code written as part of this research project by the authors. Its entire contents are original to the project. Figure 2 outlines this level and illustrates the flow of media through it. Figure 2 is an expanded view

of the AUTOCAP element shown in the middle of Figure 1. The software takes as its input both the original transcript and the audio portion of the original media file. The transcript is normalized to remove capitalization for alignment later in the process, and the SRS to retrieve as many recognizable utterances as is possible from the audio portion of the original media. As in the system level, the output of this level is the time coded transcript file. The rest of this section describes the various processes used by AUTOCAP to align transcripts and audio media.

MEDIA TRANS-CODING

Before alignment can begin, the media must be converted to an appropriate format. Furthermore, if the media includes videos, the Java Speech API (JSAPI) (Sun Microsystems, 2009) requires that the video be stripped from the media. Once the video is removed, the audio must be encapsulated in a header readable by JSAPI at an appropriate

Figure 1. AUTOCAP system architecture

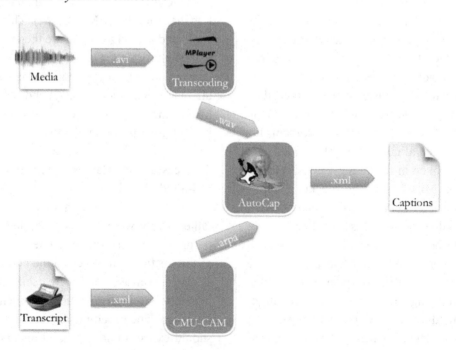

Figure 2. AUTOCAP Software Architecture

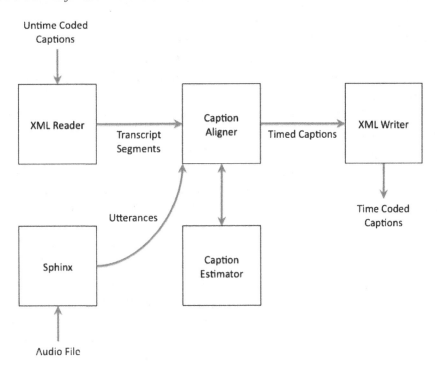

sampling rate and in a suitable codec. To accomplish this task, AutoCap uses MPlayer (The MPlayer Project, 2008). This general-purpose media player can transcode a wide range of audio and video formats as well as change frame rates and sampling rates. Using this freely available open source tool, we found that we were able to convert just about any media file to suit the requirements of the JSAPI.

BUILDING THE LANGUAGE MODEL

In order to decrease the word error rate of automatic speech recognition, it is first necessary to create a language model. Since the edited transcript file contains the exact language model of the media, AUTOCAP uses it instead of a larger, static language model. We have observed a reduction in the Word Error Rate (WER) on the order of 25% to 40% by using the transcript to build the language model. For this purpose, AUTOCAP uses the CMU-CAM

Statistical Language Modeling Toolkit (Clarkson & Rosenfeld, 1997).

First, the text is stripped from the transcript, removing all XML tags. Then the raw text is fed into a pipeline of tools that create a language model for use with automatic speech recognition. The language model is saved in the Advanced Research Project Agency (ARPA) file format.

RECOGNIZING SPEECH

Once the media is extracted, trans-coded, and the language model is built, the SRS takes caption and media files to begin the process of aligning the captions. The SRS provides two pieces of information necessary for alignment. First, it recognizes as many utterances as it can. Second, it provides timestamps for each of the words recognized in each utterance. Each utterance is made up of consecutive recognized words and is retained for alignment during the next stage of processing.

AUTOCAP uses the Sphinx SRS (Huang & Hon, 1992) from Carnegie-Mellon University. This SRS was selected for several important reasons. Most importantly, Sphinx is open source and provides an intuitive API. Second, because it is implemented in Java, it runs on multiple platforms with no modification. Finally, Sphinx is a speaker-independent SRS. Because the corpus of media we acquired for testing pre-existed, training the SRS would have been impossible. Furthermore the speaker independence feature allows for multiple speakers during a media presentation.

The result of this phase is a collection of utterances. This collection represents a set of anchor points for the alignment phase to match with the transcript during the next phase.

ALIGNING SPEECH

The process of aligning utterances with the transcripts is actually a longest common subsequence problem. The application of this algorithm, however, cannot begin until the entire media file has been processed. Using the classic dynamic programming algorithm, AUTOCAP aligns as many words from the transcript as it can while using a minimum burst size. This burst size prevents misalignments, which is especially possible in small utterances of function words, or other common short utterances.

Once the alignment is complete, timings are calculated for each of the segments provided in the transcript. At this point, one of two possibilities occurs. If the first word of the segment was part of a recognized utterance, an exact timestamp for that segment is already available. If, however, the first word is not recognized, an estimation of when the time first word of the segment was spoken must be provided. Providing an estimation of any unrecognized segment start, based on the local speaking rate, is the goal of the next phase of the architecture.

ESTIMATING CAPTIONS

At this point in the process, AUTOCAP has recognized as many words as it can and matched those recognized words with the transcript. Within the words, AUTOCAP has indentified "islands" (Huang & Hon, 1992) of recognized words with anchor points at the edges of recognized and unrecognized bursts of words. If the beginning of transcript segments (captions) is within these islands, no more work is required. The timestamp for the word returned by the SRS is used as the timestamp of the caption. If, however, the beginning of the segment is not within an island, then other techniques are necessary to find that timestamp. While Moreno (1998) used a recursive approach to recognize more and more utterances, AUTOCAP uses an estimation scheme that results in similar accuracy and less processing time. Rather than spending more time attempting to do more recognition, it uses two adjacent anchor points and the speaking rate between the two corresponding islands to estimate the timestamp of the first word of a caption.

The estimation technique used in AUTOCAP is simple and uses local speaking rate to make estimations. To calculate the estimation of a caption, AUTOCAP counts the number of words between two adjacent anchor points and the difference between their corresponding timestamps. From these two values, a local speaking rate is computed in terms of words per second. Next, it finds the distance from the nearest anchor point to the beginning of the caption. This distance is then multiplied by the speaking rate and added to the closest anchor timestamp to estimate the actual time the first word of a caption is spoken. The formula for this calculation is then:

$$D_{Anchor_i} (T_{Anchor_i} - T_{Anchor_{i+1}}) / (Anchor_{i+1} - Anchor_i) + T_{Anchor_{closest}}$$

OUTPUTTING CAPTIONS

Once all alignments are made, the timestamps are saved, along with the segmented transcripts, producing a caption file. For the files used in developing and testing AUTOCAP, the original transcript and that produced by AUTOCAP were the same, except for the timestamps, missing from the original. Other applications of AUTOCAP need not follow this same pattern.

The resulting caption files are then used to produce a more media rich experience. Figure 3 shows an example of this richer experience. Not only is the video and audio displayed, but captions are as well.

Figure 3. Example of using caption files to enhance the richness of a media experience

But we've been able to apply them with a vengeance because Toyota had thought through so well some of the concepts of Lean production. This is a fairly standard representation of the Toyota Production System.

EVALUATION

Using forced alignment for the purpose of aligning captions is not only possible but also efficient. The following analysis shows that AUTOCAP is capable of accurately aligning captions using open source technology. Furthermore, AUTOCAP achieves this alignment using currently available computing hardware in less than real-time. Finally, the transcripts used for the captions need not match word for word with the audio spoken in the media.

Establishing these claims takes several steps. First this document discusses the methodology and equipment used in conducting all of our experiments. Next, it examines the makeup of the experiments themselves and describes collecting all the data used in this analysis. Finally, a discussion of the results and findings of the experiments shows that forced alignment for the purposes of automatic captions is possible using open source tools on commodity PCs.

METHODOLOGY

In analyzing the effectiveness of AUTOCAP, a single computer with the following configuration executed all of our experiments: an Intel Core 2 Quad Q6600 running at 2.40 GHz with 2 GB of RAM and using the Fedora Core 8 Linux distribution with kernel version 2.6.23.1-42.fc8. The operating system ran in a typical configuration with X-windows and daemons for SSH and other system functions.

In addition to the hardware and operating system, AUTOCAP and other aspects of the experiments used the following software applications and libraries: AUTOCAP builds with and runs on the standard Java HotSpot Server Virtual Machine build 1.5.0_15-b04 (Sun Microsystems, 2009) and uses the Sphinx4 beta release 1.0 (Carnegie Mellon University, 2004) for its speech recognition engine. For media processing, two utilities were necessary. For language model creation,

AUTOCAP used the CMU-Cambridge Statistical Language Modeling toolkit version 2 (Clarkson, 1999) from Carnegie Mellon University. We used this toolkit because it produces language models in the ARPA format and are directly usable by Sphinx. To extract audio and transcode it for use with Java compatible codecs, all experiments used MPlayer version dev-SVN-r26936-4.1.2.

These experiments used all videos from a collection of 26 involving a single speaker with good audio quality. In total, these videos represent 172 minutes of audio, 673 captions and 26,049 words. Altogether, our system spent approximately 501 minutes conducting all of the experiments, excluding the time to trans-code and builds languages models.

The source of these videos is a manufacturing consultancy and the content is very domain specific. Experts with the proper domain knowledge edited the produced transcript, which are therefore considered to be completely accurate with respect to their language usage. The experts also created timestamps for the captions manually. We used these manually determined timestamps as the ground truth to compare against our automatically generated timestamps to judge the accuracy of our system. The manually generated timestamps given with the captions, are, however, naturally prone to error. We discuss and quantify this error in the results section.

EXPERIMENTS

Execution of these experiments involved transcoding each video, creating an appropriate language model for each and then using the Sphinx SRS to align the transcripts. The alignment phase took the bulk of processing time. This process occurred nine times for varying values of the Absolute Beam Width (ABW) parameter used by Sphinx. The ABW directly affects both the amount of work done by the SRS and the accuracy of any recognition. As we discuss this parameter we are

using it as a means of gauging the time required to perform the speech recognition phase of the caption alignment and indexing process. We further describe this parameter to give the reader a better idea of how it affects processing time.

As the recognition progresses, the number of possible Viterbi paths increases. Each of these paths represents potential matches for a particular utterance. As the number of paths increases, however, so too does the amount of memory and work required to perform the match. By limiting the number of paths, the SRS can more quickly find possible text matches for the audio. As a consequence of this pruning action, the real match may be pruned, negatively impacting the accuracy of the SRS. The goal, then, is to find a balance between accuracy and the required time for processing. In order to identify the proper balance, the experiments used the following ABW values: 100, 250, 500, 750, 1000, 1250, 2000, and 3000. As the ABW increases, the number of Viterbi paths also increases and, therefore, the amount of processing time also increases, while the WER decreases. The results section discusses the degree to which these parameters are related. For each experiment we saved the caption file, statistics about the resources used, and the accuracy of the experiment.

RESULTS

To discuss the accuracy of the alignments found by AUTOCAP, we require a ground truth. Fortunately, the videos provided to us already included manual caption times. The problem then is how accurate the manual captions are if they are to be used as ground truth.

The media files provided to us contained a video file and a caption file with pre-segmented caption text with timestamps for each. The challenge, then, is to determine the accuracy of each timestamp, specifically, when each segment actually begins. Human determination of these times is precisely the problem, so having another human measure this metric simply adds another source of error. Instead, we used for this study the time-stamps from the first word of a caption segment, if recognized by the SRS. These timestamps are accurate to the tenths of seconds, but rounded to the nearest second because the manual timestamps are only accurate to the nearest second. Therefore, to determine the overall accuracy of the manually determined timestamps within the ground truth, we compared all ground truth timestamps to those of the recognized segment starts. The caption error is the absolute value of the distance of the manual timestamps from the actual timestamps as determined by the SRS. Table 1 shows the findings of this phase of the analysis.

The results from Table 1 show that, overall, the manual caption timestamps are within 0.4s of the correct time. For future discussion, we can

say that our system is at least as accurate as manual timestamps if they are within the same range. As our later results show, not all alignments achieved this accuracy. However, these automatically generated timestamps led to errors with which people were comfortable. In actuality, people are able to tolerate even longer errors. While we have not found any usability studies that directly address this issue, we believe that caption time stamps within 2 seconds of the actual text being spoken is more than accurate enough.

With regard to the actual accuracy of AutoCap, Figure 4 illustrates the results of the experiments performed. The objectives of the evaluation were threefold. First, our goal was to show that Auto-Cap exhibited tolerable error rates for caption alignments. Second, accurate alignments should be obtainable in less than real-time. Third, more

Figure 4. WER vs. ABW

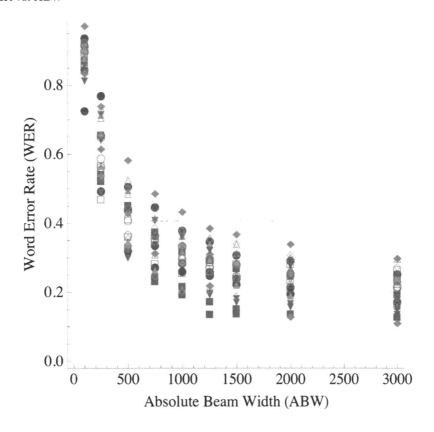

Table 1. Results of measuring the accuracy of ground truth

Total Caption Segments	673
Recognized Caption Segments	408
Percentage of Caption Segments Recognized	60.6%
Total Caption Error in Ground Truth	149 s
Average Caption Error per Caption Segment	0.4 s

processing (i.e., higher ABW values) should reduce error rates, but only to a point, beyond which, increased accuracy is minimal and unnecessary. Further discussion of these objectives and the corresponding results follows.

The graph in Figure 4 explores the relationship between the WER and the ABW. Along the X-axis are the varying ABW values, from 0 to 3000. The Y-axis records the corresponding WER values and can vary from 0.0 to 1.0. Each symbol rep-

resents a different media file. As there are 26 different media files, a complete list is not given. As the ABW increases, the WER decreases. Put another way, as the number of possible utterances tracked increases (and thereby the amount of work for the SRS), the less likely the SRS is to make a mistake. As the SRS makes fewer and fewer mistakes, there should be a corresponding drop in the caption error. Figure 5 verifies this prediction.

Figure 5 is similar to Figure 4. Along the X-axis are the ABW values. Along the Y-axis is the Average Caption Error. We define the average caption error as the absolute value of the timestamp for each caption as found by AUTOCAP minus the timestamp from the ground truth. For clarity, a caption timestamp is for the beginning of a caption segment, not for each individual word. For this graph, the average per media file was calculated

Figure 5. Average caption error vs. ABW

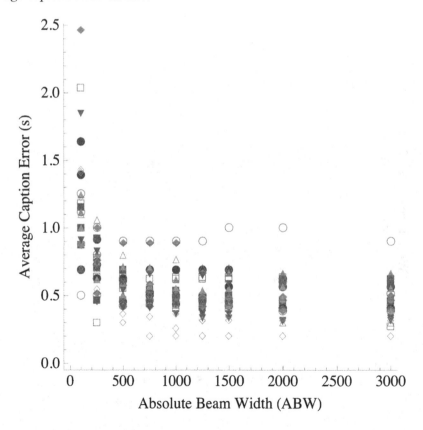

and recorded. The results confirm our predictions. As the ABW is increased, there is a corresponding drop in the average caption error rate.

The question still remains, though; about how much more processing can be done in order to further decrease the caption error. Figures 6 and 7 address this question. Figure 6 shows the relationship between the word error rate and the processing time required to align captions. The X-axis records the ratio of processing time to media length time. We use this measure as a means of normalizing the metric over all the media files. The Y-axis records the WER. The individual points also indicate the ABW values used. The graph is similar to the graph from Figure 6, and similar conclusions can be drawn from it. However, there are other trends observable in the graph.

First, the obvious trend that can be inferred from Figure 6 is that more processing time means lower WER. Second, as the ABW is increased, the variance in the processing ratio also increases. This observation is clear as the clusters of media processed with the same ABW value become more spread out as the ratio tends towards one. Finally, the returns on extra processing time also diminish as more processing time is dedicated to each media file. The main idea behind this graph is that obtaining a WER suitable for caption alignment with AutoCap requires less that real-time. Other systems we have looked at required greater than real-time to align captions.

Lastly, Figure 7 gives more insight into the diminishing return of longer and longer processing times. This graph displays the change in average caption error with changes in the WER. The X-axis records the average caption error and the Y-axis records the WER. While the WER varies from 0.0 to 1.0, the average caption error varies from less than 1.0s to 2.5s. What is observable in this graph is that, as the WER decreases, so too does the average caption error, however, by smaller and smaller amounts. At the bottom of the graph around the point (0.5, 0.2), the results start to bunch up and there is no discernable difference

in effectiveness, even with more processing time. This behavior is especially true for ABW values above 1000. A reasonable conclusion is that while more processing time would result in slightly better caption timings, it is not enough to justify further increases in processing time.

Next, we address the question of how much accuracy is needed. As previously stated, for a good experience from a usability standpoint, the captions need only be within two seconds of the ground truth. Therefore, the question is: how much processing is required to achieve the necessary accuracy? The graphs in Figures 8-11 address this question. All four figures represent the histograms of caption errors across all tested media. We varied the ABW to determine an optimal ABW value, and therefore better estimate the amount of time needed to process each media file.

Figure 8 shows the histogram for an ABW value of 100. While the amount of processing required for this setting is about 10% of the length of the original media, the overall distribution of caption errors is not ideal. Caption error for this test ranged from 5 seconds too early to 10 seconds too late. Overall, the number of captions with errors less than or equal to two seconds (the agreed upon threshold) is 83% of the total captions. To achieve more accurate captions, the SRS needs to do more work to increase its overall accuracy, and therefore, generate more captions within the acceptable range.

Here we see that the distribution is closer to the target. First, the number of caption errors within two seconds represents 99.7% of all the captions aligned. Only two captions of the 673 had a caption error greater than two seconds, and no caption errors were greater than four seconds. Also, the number of caption errors less than or equal to one second represents 94% of all captions.

The question still remains, however, of whether more processing leads to even better accuracy. Figures 10 and 11 directly address this question. For these two histograms, the ABW values were 2000 and 3000, respectively. These ABW values

Figure 6. WER vs. media length ratio

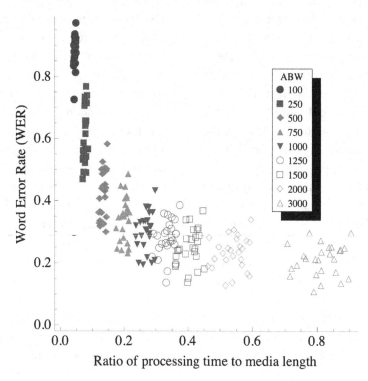

Figure 7. WER vs. average caption error

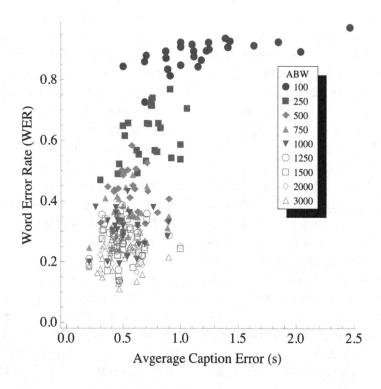

Figure 8. ABW=100

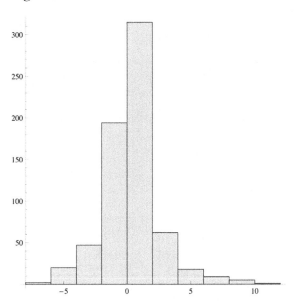

Figure 9. ABW=1000

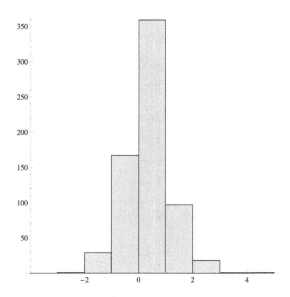

represent approximately 2 to 3 times more processing than an ABW value of 1000. Yet, what we see is that they do not yield any more accuracy than with an ABW value of 1000. For each, the number of captions aligned to within the two-second threshold is also 99.7%. Therefore, nothing is really gained, in terms of accuracy, by increasing the processing times by 2 to 3 times. The ABW value of 1000 seems ideal since it requires less than real-time (approximately 25% of the actual media length) to process and still maintains a high accuracy level.

Table 2 lists all the accuracy results from each of the test runs. The interesting finding is that for this set of media, the ABW value of 1000 is slightly more accurate than for higher ABW values. This anomaly is due either to the inaccuracy of the ground truth (because of human error), or the fact that there may exist more incorrect Viterbi paths with higher scores than for the actual spoken words. Either way, the difference is negligible and unlikely to occur in other collections of media.

RELATED WORK

We have found six projects similar in nature and spirit to AutoCap. First, Moreno suggests a similar technique for transcript alignment (Moreno & Joerg, 1998). However, this work uses recursion to re-process portions unrecognized by automatic speech recognition, and using a more constrained speech domain, recognizes at least part of the unrecognized portions. The recursion process ends once no more words are recognized for all of the unrecognized portions. While this work represents a similar goal to our efforts, it does more work than is necessary for our goals. Aligning pre-segmented transcripts does not require that all words be recognized, just those at the beginning of a segment. Furthermore, our technique gives similar accuracy scores, with in 1 or 2 seconds of the actual the actual time, but with less work overall as ours runs in at most real-time, and usually less.

Second, Hazen (2006) suggest techniques similar to AutoCap, but adds correction to the technique. Under this system, it corrects the given

Figure 10. ABW=2000

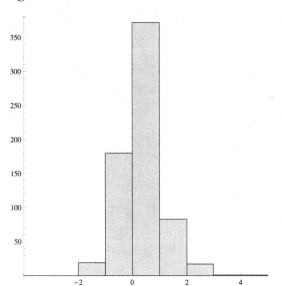

Figure 11. ABW=3000

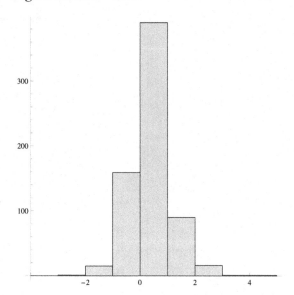

transcripts based on processing done by the SRS. Our work specifically deals with edited transcripts from domain experts, and the transcript, therefore, represents the correct textual representation of the spoken words. Therefore, there exists no need for transcript editing. Adding this feature to AUTOCAP would unnecessarily increase processing time and would not lead to more accurate captioning information.

Third, Placeway and Lafferty (1996) use imperfect transcripts, generated in real-time for the purpose of closed captioning, to improve word error rates. The goal of this research, however, is to improve speech recognition, and not to align

transcripts and audio for the purposes of captioning. Also, recent advances improve recognition without the necessity of the suggested techniques.

Fourth, Robert-Ribes and Mukhtar (1997) also discusses work that has a similar overall objective to ours. The goal of their project is to hyperlink text to audio recordings. The key here is to find the exact times that the first word of a transcript segment is spoken. Our work similarly finds the beginning of segments, but in a very different way. The major difference between this work and ours is that we use the transcripts themselves to improve recognition. Our system also has the goal of completing a video in real-time or less.

Table 2. Processing time and resultant error rates

ABW	% Time	Error > 1 s	Error >2 s	% Error ≤1 s	% Error ≤ 2 s
100	~5	215	121	68	82
500	~13	50	3	93	99.6
1000	~25	38	2	95	99.7
1250	~33	34	1	95	99.9
1500	~40	35	2	95	99.7
2000	~50	33	3	95	99.6
3000	~80	34	3	95	99.6

Robert-Ribes and Mukhtar ignore the need for real-time processing, which makes processing any large corpus of material overly time consuming.

Finally, two projects use a technique similar to ours for aligning the captions with the audio. Both of the works by Martone et al. (2004) and Huang (2003) use automatic speech recognition and the longest common subsequence to address the alignment problem. Huang uses a slightly different technique: using closed caption (CC) timings to eliminate certain path in their dynamic programming approach. While this technique also works without CC, it loses some accuracy. Martone's work is very similar to ours. This work, however, does not provided much in the way of analysis of the accuracy of the technique. Both projects also do not address the problem of edited transcripts and how they impact accuracy. Nor do they use the transcripts they do have to build language models to increase the accuracy of speech recognition.

CONCLUSION

In this paper we have described and evaluated AUTOCAP. We have shown that AUTOCAP is capable of accurately and efficiently aligning captions with all sorts of media. Furthermore, with a proper ABW setting that takes into account both speed and accuracy, AUTOCAP can do so in less than real-time and within a tolerable amount of error. And while other projects have similar goals, they do so with more processing than is necessary. While the other works used disparate corpora, making direct comparison impossible, none had the stated goal or conclusion of doing caption alignment in real-time. Also, the related work does not address the issue of edited transcripts. Instead, these other projects expect exact transcriptions of the exact words spoken. Using a tool such as AUTOCAP can lead to more and easier integration of media as well

as better and faster indexing of more media types. Using similar techniques as described in this work, researchers and owners of large corpora of media can efficiently and accurately incorporate media into their productions and make them searchable.

REFERENCES

Carnegie Mellon University. (2004). *Sphinx-4*. Retrieved from http://cmusphinx.sourceforge.net/sphinx4/

Clarkson, P. (1999). *Statistical Language Modeling Toolkit*. Retrieved from http://www.speech.cs.cmu.edu/SLM/CMU-Cam_Toolkit_v2.tar.gz

Clarkson, P., & Rosenfeld, R. (1997). Statistical language modeling using the CMU-Cambridge Toolkit. In *Proceedings of the European Conference on Speech Communication and Technology – Eurospeech* (pp. 2707-2710).

Hazen, T. J. (2006). Automatic alignment and error correction of human generated transcripts for long speech recordings. In *Proceedings of the International Conference of the International Speech Communication Association – INTERSPEECH*.

Huang, C. (2003). *Automatic closed caption alignment based on speech recognition transcripts* (Tech. Rep. No. 005). New York, New York: Columbia University.

Huang, X., Alleva, F., Hon, H. W., Hwang, M. Y., Lee, K. F., & Rosenfeld, R. (1992). The SPHINX-II speech recognition system: an overview. *Computer Speech & Language*, *7*(2), 137–148. doi:10.1006/csla.1993.1007

Martone, A. F., Taskiran, C. M., & Delp, E. J. (2004). Automated closed-captioning using text alignment. *Proceedings of the Society for Photo-Instrumentation Engineers*, *5307*, 108–116.

Moreno, P. J., Joerg, C., Thong, J. M., & Van Glickman, O. (1998). A recursive algorithm for the forced alignment of very long audio segments. In *Proceedings of the International Conference on Spoken Language Processing*.

Placeway, P., & Lafferty, J. (1996). Cheating with imperfect transcripts. In *Proceedings of the International Conference on Spoken Language Processing* (pp. 2115-2118).

Robert-Ribes, J., & Mukhtar, R. G. (1997). Automatic generation of hyperlinks between audio and transcript. In *Proceedings of the Conference on Speech Communication and Technology – Eurospeech* (pp. 903-906).

Sun Microsystems. (2009). *Java Speech API*. Retrieved from http://java.sun.com/products/java-media/speech/

Sun Microsystems. (2009). *Java SE Downloads*. Retrieved from http://java.sun.com/javase/downloads/index.jsp

The MPlayer Project. (2008). *MPlayer*. Retrieved from http://www.mplayerhq.hu/design7/news.html

This work was previously published in the International Journal of Multimedia Data Engineering and Management, Volume 1, Issue 2, edited by Shu-Ching Chen, pp. 1-17, copyright 2010 by IGI Publishing (an imprint of IGI Global).

Chapter 13
Building Tag–Aware Groups for Music High–Order Ranking and Topic Discovery

Dimitrios Rafailidis
Aristotle University, Greece

Alexandros Nanopoulos
University of Hildesheim, Germany

Yannis Manolopoulos
Aristotle University, Greece

ABSTRACT

In popular music information retrieval systems, users have the opportunity to tag musical objects to express their personal preferences, thus providing valuable insights about the formulation of user groups/communities. In this article, the authors focus on the analysis of social tagging data to reveal coherent groups characterized by their users, tags and music objects (e.g., songs and artists), which allows for the expression of discovered groups in a multi-aspect way. For each group, this study reveals the most prominent users, tags, and music objects using a generalization of the popular web-ranking concept in the social data domain. Experimenting with real data, the authors' results show that each Tag-Aware group corresponds to a specific music topic, and additionally, a three way ranking analysis is performed inside each group. Building Tag-Aware groups is crucial to offer ways to add structure in the unstructured nature of tags.

INTRODUCTION

Social tagging is the process of adding metadata by users in the form of keywords to annotate information items. In the case of music, the annotated items can be songs, artists, albums and playlists. Social tags are widely used, as high volume sources of descriptive metadata for music. Tags give the opportunity to a user to express his opinion, aiming to capture his personal view of resources he is interested in, including information about genre, mood, instrumentation and quality. A question is arising, why using tags is beneficial

DOI: 10.4018/978-1-4666-1791-9.ch013

for music information. The paramount motivations are, firstly building playlists by tagging songs and secondly, summarizing and categorizing a user profile using recommendation systems based on tags. This way, social tags have become important for Music Information Retrieval. In particular, tags can provide an insight to user behavior and language usage, e.g., how different is "rap" from "hip-hop". Additional benefits are grouping music items based on tags, finding social groups with shared interests, e.g. people that tag the same items or use the same tags, and generating user profiles from tagging behavior e.g. tag clouds based on tags applied by the user or representing his taste. Therefore, many music discovery and recommendation systems support the social tagging of music. According to Lamere (2008), social tags are used to help searching for items, exploring for new items, finding similar items, and finding other listeners with similar interests.

To assist in exploring and suggesting tags, some systems cluster similar tags together. These tag clusters can assist users in either applying tags or in identifying alternatives that may be useful in their search. Tag clustering has become an important issue for Music Information Retrieval systems. "Tag Radio" and "Tag Cloud" comprise two of the most popular applications of tag clustering. A music search engine can support a user-end tagging or labeling of artists, albums, and songs to create a site-wide folksonomy of music. Users can browse via tags, but the important benefit is the tag radio, permitting users to play music that has been tagged a certain way. The tagging process can be performed by genre "garage rock", mood "chill", artist characteristic "baritone", or any other form of user-defined classification "seen live". Listeners can search for artists or songs that have been tagged with a particular tag, or they can tune into "Tag Radio" where they listen to music that has been tagged with a particular tag.

On the other hand, it has been proved that sometimes tag clustering is not strong enough by itself to satisfy the listeners' requirements. Often users

need to obtain results in a ranked list, where the position of each result should be taken into account. A question arising is why ranking is important in Music Information Retrieval. In the more general field of Information Retrieval, ranking of query/search answers has become mandatory for internet searches. When the answers of a query or search are varying in quality and are large in numbers, it is necessary to rank/order these answers based on some criteria. From a users' viewpoint, ranking is extremely useful especially when associated with the retrieval of a few (top-k) answers. This way, ranking has also become an important issue in music search engines, a basic application of Music Information Retrieval on the internet.

A premature form of ranking in music search engines can be found. For example, people often run upon tag clouds, while visiting music search engines, e.g., Last.fm. A particular song, artist or user can be described by a tag cloud. For example, if a tag cloud describes a certain artist, by clicking on a particular tag in the tag cloud, all artists that have been frequently tagged with that tag will be displayed. In particular, we note that larger fonts in such displays indicate most popular tags, like in Figure 1, where the font size is scaled by the tag's weight (popularity or rank).

Tag clouds consist of collective information from users and provide a visual illustration for these tags. They effectively provide a good overview about a certain music topic like "The Beatles" in Figure 1, and describe it in instant. However, although tag clouds virtually hide the notions of users and music objects (such as songs, artists, albums etc), these two dimensions, e.g., users and music objects are visually missing from a (regular) tag cloud and simultaneously the respective ranking is also omitted. Therefore, from a social music tagging system there is a demand for a more powerful grouping and representation of information based on these three entities (i.e., tags, users, music objects), in which also a ranked list should be provided. Instead of just using tags, here we propose an enriched representation of the three

Figure 1. A tag cloud from Last.fm, describing the artist "The Beatles"

entities by embedding them into a group called *Tag-Aware* group, in which the results are provided in ranked lists and each group refers to a certain music topic.

Next, an example of a Tag-Aware group referring to Beatles and similar artists is provided, whereas further discussion about this group follows in the results' subsection. Figure 2 presents four clouds, i.e., user, tag, song and artist clouds, quite opposite of Figure 1, where only one tag cloud appears. Evidently, a Tag-Aware group provides extra information about users and specifies correlated music objects. As social music tag systems are built upon humans, the extra information obtained from a Tag-Aware group becomes important. Having in mind a cloud as that of Figure 2, in Last.fm these users are called *neighbors*. While each user needs to discover users with similar preferences, the system should provide a convincing explanation to explain why they are correlated and which their respective links are. For example, if user "Vincent" prefers songs "You Never Give Me Your Money" and "Sun King", he would discover that the users "The Quarrymen" and "Xenob" have similar taste, since they tagged these songs as "Classic Pop" and "Rock and Roll" (note that user nicknames are not drawn from our dataset but have been randomly selected for the sake of the example). This way "Vincent"

would understand why users in this group are relevant to his preferences. At the same time, a Tag-Aware group provides additional information about similar artists, while representing songs as links between them, since the linkage between the artist and the song cloud is based on the fact that all of them correspond to a specific music topic. Parallel, a user can observe which of these items are more relevant to his preferences, since each cloud contains results in a ranked form.

The Tag-Aware group production is based on the three dimensions: users, tags and music objects. To model these dimensions the proposed method uses multidimensional arrays, called *tensors*. An M-way or M-order tensor is an element of the tensor product of M vectors, each one with its own coordinate system. A first-order tensor is a vector, a second-order tensor is a matrix, whereas tensors of order three or higher are called higher-order tensors. This way, all dimensions are taken into account in the Tag-Aware group's generation process. A multilinear Algebra method called *Parallel Factors Decomposition* (PARAFAC) is applied to this tensor. An overview for tensor decompositions and applications appears at Kolda and Bader (2008).

In mathematics, multilinear algebra extends the methods of linear algebra. More specifically, just as linear algebra is built on the concept of

Figure 2. A Tag-Aware group based on artist "The Beatles" and similar artists

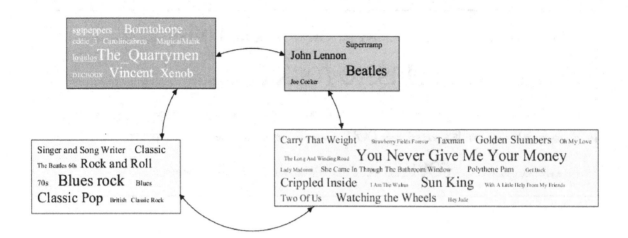

vectors and develops the theory of vector spaces, multilinear algebra builds on the concept of tensors and develops the theory of *tensor spaces*. A vector space is a mathematical structure formed by a collection of vectors, which may be scaled and added. In particular, a tensor space assigns a tensor to each point of a Euclidean space. While applying PARAFAC to a tensor, a ranking based on the three considered dimensions is achieved. The proposed approach produces ranked lists, similar to the HITS algorithm developed by Kleinberg (1999), a link analysis algorithm for Web pages. It determines two values for a page: its authority that estimates the value of the page content, and its hub value that estimates the value of its links to other pages.

In this paper we propose an algorithm for building Tag-Aware groups, which aims at: (a) high order ranking, and (b) topic discovery. Our method develops the tensor model with data triplets of users, songs and tags gathered from Last. fm. On this real dataset we apply PARAFAC to factorize the tensor model and to generate *factors*, a kernel step of our algorithm, where each factor represents a Tag-Aware group (i.e., a meaningful division of the data). By summarizing these factors, the initial tensor can be constructed. In particular,

the resulting Tag-Aware groups refer to a certain music topic, such as an artist, a mood or a genre description, while performing ranking to the three resulted lists (tags, users and music objects lists). Using this real dataset, experimentally we show the effectiveness of the proposed approach, since the two goals are achieved. More precisely, our contribution provides ways to:

- Demonstrate the rich representation provided by Tag-Aware groups in an effective way,
- Produce Tag-Aware groups, each of them corresponding to a specific music topic, such as an artist, a mood or a genre description, while the tag clouds are those which describe the respective topic,
- Link tags, songs, artists and users inside each group and offer a transparent explanation for their relevance degree to explore similar preferences, since all clouds are correlated to the respective music topic, and
- Face the vocabulary problem, a main challenge for social tags in Music Information Retrieval, by grouping synonymous tags together in music concepts.

The rest of this paper is organized as follows. The next section describes related work for implemented algorithms based on tags and how building Tag-Aware groups differs. In the following sections Tag-Aware groups are defined, and the problem description is provided. Next, a section introduces a methodology for producing Tag-Aware groups, whereas its next section reports the experimental results. The last section concludes this paper and proposes future work.

RELATED WORK

Symeonidis et al. (2008) introduce a method to generate personalized recommendations of musical items. They construct a three order tensor, to model altogether users, tags and musical items. Consequently, they proceed to unfold the tensor, where three new matrices are built. They apply SVD (Singular Value Decomposition) in each matrix and then the resulting tensor is built. In this resulting tensor, the latent components that govern the associations among the triplets user-tag-items can be discovered. Thus, the musical items can be recommended according to the captured associations. That is, given a user and a tag, the purpose is to predict whether and how much the user is likely to label with this tag a specific music item. In particular, considering a specific triplet in form (user, tag, music item), the likelihood that user1 will tag with tag1 the music item1 equals to the value in the reconstructed tensor at the respective coordinates (user1,tag1,music item1). In our approach we built a three order tensor to model users, tags and items, in an analogous manner to the initial step of the previous described method. Next, instead of reconstructing the tensor and discovering the respective associations, as the previous method do, we decompose the tensor into a number of factors, where each factor corresponds to a meaningful division of the data and describes a certain music topic. This way, for each factor we afford ranked lists of each entity (user,tag,item),

where the tags are used to describe the topic of the respective factor. We should mention that the goal of our implementation is not to recommend musical items, as Symeonidis et al. (2008) do, but to provide a tag-aware group corresponding to a certain musical topic, consisting of three ranked lists, as HITS algorithm does, developed by Kleinberg (1999), where a search term in web can result to a ranked list of web sites as answers.

Karydis et al. (2009) focus on similarity-based clustering of tagged items. They try to provide an establishment of user profiles and to discover topics. They model the items, the tags on them and the users who assigned the tags in a multigraph structure. To discover clusters of similar items, they extend spectral clustering, an approach successfully used for the clustering of complex data, into a method that captures multiple values of similarity between any two items. Their scope is to provide a new method being superior to conventional spectral clustering that ignores the existence of multiple values of similarity among the items. Their method can be applicable to a dataset consisting of tags, temperature, pressure values or location names. In contrast to our method, their scope is to focus on spectral clustering. Instead, given a set of triplets {user,tag,music item}, our scope is to discover music topics and to provide ranking lists for each set of users, tags, songs and artists.

Wu et al (2006) also propose to mine latent topics based on the co-occurrence of triplets in the form {user, web page, tag}. Their algorithm input is the triplets and the output is a set of ranked lists. Each derived list refers to a certain topic of a web page. In contrast to our proposed algorithm, which is based on the PARAFAC algorithm, their method is based upon a statistical model for co-occurrence data, proposed by Hofmann and Puzicha (1998). Their method could not be applied in our music dataset, consisting of triplets {user, song, tag}, because our dataset produces a sparse model. Therefore, a sparse tensor model is required as input of our algorithm. To apply a method having as input the sparse tensor model, the proper choice is PARAFAC instead of the method described in Hofmann and Puzicha (1998). Further details about the sparse tensor can be found in subsection Sparse Tensor Model.

Pampalk (2001) demonstrates Islands of music, a visual representation for clustering listeners by tags. In particular, to derive such a Representation: (a) Last.fm listeners are randomly sampled, each one represented by a tag cloud, (b) 2000-dimensions tags are reduced to 120 dimensions using SVD, (c) k-means clustering is used to extract 400 prototypical listeners, and (d) self organizing maps are embedded to create the Islands. The position of each Island depends on the relations between tags, whereas a path is provided to travel from an Island to another. In our approach, Tag-Aware grouping contains information about similar tags and artists as Islands do; moreover, it adds links inside the group with certain songs, tags and users based on their correlation to the music topic. This enhancement is achieved due to the fact that Tag-Aware grouping pays attention on the three dimensions: users, tags and music objects, while performing ranking in each dimension.

Levy and Sandler (2007) notice that tags yield better results than metadata or genres, because they are highly effective in capturing music similarity. In particular, they succeed in creating a browse-by-mood interface for a psychologically-motivated two dimension subspace representing musical emotion. In an analogous manner, we accomplish to produce a Tag-Aware group that refers to a mood description. Additionally, except for topic discovery, such as a mood description, we also perform a three way ranking.

Levy and Sandler (2008) describe a method with latent semantic models to reduce the disadvantages of the vocabulary problem (to be described in the next section). The main algorithm is to project a tag-query into a latent semantic space and discover the closest tags based on semantics. LSA (Latent Semantic Analysis) by Deerwester et al. (1990) assumes that there is some "latent"

structure that relates the items and defines a semantic space. Items that are close together in this space have tags with similar meanings, even if they do not share any actual tags. Previously, some strategies to address many of these shortcomings were described by Guy and Tonkin (2006). Building Tag-Aware groups acts in a very similar way, since each group corresponds to a specific music topic or latent space. Moreover, each time other features are consider than tags, more precisely, users, songs and artists.

On the other hand, to accomplish Tag-Aware grouping we apply Parallel Factors decomposition (PARAFAC), which is a powerful tool for real-world applications. We note that Kolda et al. (2005) have studied PARAFAC related work for web analysis. They succeed to use multi way data representations and tensor decompositions for web search and related tasks. They model a sparse tensor (sparse because the vast majority of elements are 0s in the tensor) with three dimensions: the first two dimensions represent the web pages, whereas the third one adds the anchor text. Subsequently, a three way Parallel Factors (PARAFAC) decomposition of the web graph is applied to produce groups, with URLs associated with prominent topics. In our proposed method, after constructing the tensor by modeling the triplets {user, song, tag}, we apply PARAFAC decomposition of the tensor to group tags, music items and users in music topics.

PROBLEM DESCRIPTION

In this section we define the Tag-Aware grouping and provide the problem description. A Tag-Aware group is defined to a group of three ranked lists: user, tag and song list. Each group corresponds to a specific discovered topic, and its description is provided by the respective tag cloud. More precisely, the two goals are: (a) to perform ranking to three dimensions in each group, and in parallel

(b) to discover a music topic, which corresponds to each group's topic.

A Tag-aware group is a visual representation using three dimensions: users, tags and music objects. In particular, in our method we consider songs and artists as music objects. This way, a Tag-Aware group consists of four clouds for users, tags, songs and artists. They have the ability to correspond to many categories of music topics. In general, collaborative or personal playlists (tag radio), tag groups, and muti-tag searching based on certain preferences comprise motivations for users to tag, whereas often tagging frequencies are arranged by category. Tags can be organized into 9 basic categories: genre, locale, mood, opinion, instrumentation, style, misc (e.g. "name of composers"), personal (e.g., "seen live") and organization (e.g., "check out"). Obtained from Lamere (2008), Table 1 shows that the dominant category for Last.fm is genre. Analogously, as shown later, Tag-Aware groups may refer to these categories of music topics. Apparently, the created groups may belong to more than one category. For instance, we show that the generated group based on "The Beatles" belongs to category misc as a composer based group and to category genre as Classic pop based group. Despite the embedding of more than one category into a group, the proposed method of Tag-Aware grouping proved to be very effective.

Next, aiming at ranking and topic discovery, we would like to introduce some examples to demonstrate the necessary logical steps, starting at one dimension and ending at three dimensions. In case of one dimension, eigenclusters can be produced, since SVD can be applied to e.g. a document matrix, each of them usually corresponding to a topic. In analogous manner, in case of two dimensions, the scores in each eigenvector perform the respective ranking and a topic can be discovered, while applying LSA to a two-dimensional matrix. In our method we face the case of three dimensions. In particular, we perform decomposition to N factors of the three-dimension-al tensor and the produced eigenvectors provide ranking in each dimension (in our case the 3 dimensions are: user, tag and song). Each eigenvector-factor should refer to a topic.

Implemented algorithms based on tags find social groups with shared interests by generating user profiles from tagging behavior. For example, Last.fm groups locate people with common interests not necessarily related to music, such as "ear-chopped-off painter" fans, "car enthusiasts", and people that clearly like meticulous descriptions of their behavior. It is possible to listen to a "group or tag radio", but unfortunately sometimes this is a disappointing experience. This is due to the fact that the playlist was generated by averaging the tastes of the group members. For instance, by considering the average listener's behavior, it is observed that members of the "saxophonists" group listen to far more "Sonny Rollins" than others. Although, they quite often listen to "The Beatles", this is less important as everyone does so often. The average tastes are considered because the number of co-occurrences between two tags (uses of the tags in the same item) is calculated, such as only a high co-occurrence value can suggest a strong similarity between tags. Our method of Tag-Aware grouping ignores the average tastes, but instead implements a method that resembles to the weighting scheme of term frequency - inverse document frequency tf·idf (to be mentioned later).

Table 1. Tagging frequencies by category

Tag Type	Frequency	Examples
Genre	68%	heavy metal, punk
Locale	12%	French, Seattle, NYC
Mood	5%	chill, party
Opinion	4%	love, favorite
Instrumentation	4%	piano, female vocal
Style	3%	political, humor
Misc	3%	Coldplay, composers
Personal	1	seen live, I own it
Organizational	1	check out

In particular, we avoid using the often applied tags in the groups' generation process. Furthermore, we calculate each item's weight in each cloud, scaled to the analogous font size to represent its strength inside the group.

A main challenge for social tags in music information retrieval is the vocabulary problem, which actually has many aspects, provided below:

- Synonyms of tags are often met, e.g., "female vocalists", "female voices" or "female singers".
- Ambiguity and polysemy are problems for tags as well, e.g., "love", could mean music a user loves or music about love.
- The vocabulary problem augments with spelling errors, multi-lingual tags or by using wrong words e.g. "r&b", "r and b".
- Meanwhile some tags may be too subtle for current systems to distinguish, e.g. "power metal" versus "speed metal".

A general definition of the vocabulary problem has been described by Furnas et al. (1987), whereas detailed information can be found in Lamere's survey (2008). The final outcome in the literature is to implement tag grouping to confront all these issues. In this direction, we show experimentally that tags with the same meaning are included to the same tag cloud and we identify their linkage through Tag-Aware grouping. Furthermore, negative tags like abuse tags or tags with no music perceptual description, e.g., "like that song" or "Lazy Eye", may reduce the effectiveness of social tags methods. Since, in general, these tags occur less frequently, in a preprocessing step we remove the negative tags before the process of Tag-Aware grouping starts.

PROPOSED APPROACH

In this section we describe the main algorithm for Tag-Aware grouping, which consists of 3 steps.

The first step is to create the sparse tensor model, the second is to apply PARAFAC onto the sparse tensor to produce Tag-Aware-groups (factors), and, finally, the third one is to generate user, tag, song and artist clouds for each group.

Sparse Tensor Model

As mentioned, our initial step is to create the sparse tensor model based on triplets of the form {user, song, tag}. A tensor is a multidimensional array. More formally, an M-way or M-order tensor is an element of the tensor product of M vectors, each one with its own coordinate system. A first-order tensor is a vector, a second-order tensor is a matrix, whereas tensors of order three or higher are called higher-order tensors. In our approach, a three dimensional sparse tensor model is created, where the three dimensions represent users, songs and tags, respectively. The 1s in a tensor stand for the existence of a triplet and 0s for the absence. Our tensor is sparse since the vast majority of elements are 0s. Figure 3 (spaces denote 0s) shows an example modeling the following 7 triplets:

- {user1, song1, alternative rock}, {user2, song1, alternative rock}
- {user1, song1, 90s}, {user1, song3, 90s}
- {user4, song2, seen live}
- {user1, song2, rock and roll}, {user3, song2, rock and roll}

This example set consists of 5 distinct users, 4 distinct songs and 5 distinct tags. In Figure 3, 5 arrays are illustrated because of the 5 distinct tags, and in each array there are 5 elements in the x-axis because of the 5 distinct users (u1, u2, u3, u4, u5) and 4 elements in the y-axis because of the 4 distinct songs (s1, s2, s3, s4). For example u1 and s1 note user 1 and song 1 respectively, and the upper left 1 inside the bottom array in Figure 3, labeled as alternative rock, notes the triplet {user1, song1, alternative rock}.

Figure 3. A sparse tensor of 7 triplets {user, song, tags}

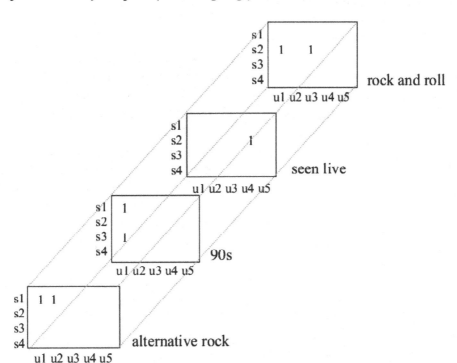

Matrices or tensors are denoted by boldface capital letters, e.g., **A**, whereas vectors are denoted by boldface lowercase letters, e.g., **a**. The element (i,j,k) of a third-order tensor **A** is denoted by $\mathbf{A}_{ijk}$. The *n*-th element in a sequence is denoted by a superscript in parentheses, e.g., $\mathbf{a}^n$ denotes the *n*-th matrix in a sequence, which is equal to the vector with the coordinates of the *n*-th dimension of tensor **A**. Assuming these notations, let **X** denote the adjacency tensor of all triplets, defined as:

$$\mathbf{X}_{ijk} = \begin{cases} 1 \text{ if user } i \text{ tagged song } j \text{ with tag } k \\ 0 \text{ otherwise} \end{cases} \quad (1)$$

Before proceeding to the PARAFAC step, it is important to introduce two terms: "outer product" and "tensor rank". Given a vector $\mathbf{k}=(\mathbf{k}_1,\mathbf{k}_2,\ldots,\mathbf{k}_m)$ with *m* elements and a vector $\mathbf{b}=(\mathbf{b}_1,\mathbf{b}_2,\ldots,\mathbf{b}_m)$ with *n* elements, their outer product $\mathbf{k} \circ \mathbf{b}$, denoted by symbol $\circ$, is defined as the $m \times n$ matrix **A** obtained by multiplying each element of **k** by each element of **b**:

$$\mathbf{k} \circ \mathbf{b} = \mathbf{A} = \begin{pmatrix} \mathbf{k}_1\mathbf{b}_1 & \cdots & \mathbf{k}_1\mathbf{b}_n \\ \vdots & \ddots & \vdots \\ \mathbf{k}_m\mathbf{b}_1 & \cdots & \mathbf{k}_m\mathbf{b}_n \end{pmatrix} \quad (2)$$

In general, the outer product for any two tensors **Q** and **W**, a result tensor **R**, each of whose indices corresponds to an index of **Q** or an index of **W** and each of whose components, is the product of the component of **Q** and the component of **W** with identical values of the corresponding indices.

The term "rank" of a tensor **X** is defined as the smallest number of rank-one tensors that generate **X** as their sum. An *M*-way tensor is rank-one if it can be written as the outer product of *M* vectors based on Equation (2), i.e.,

$$\mathbf{X} = \mathbf{a}^{(1)} \circ \mathbf{a}^{(2)} \circ \ldots \circ \mathbf{a}^{(M)} \quad (3)$$

This means that each tensor element is the product of the corresponding vector elements. For example, if our tensor is a third-order rank-one tensor then it would equal to:

$$\mathbf{X} = \mathbf{u} \circ \mathbf{s} \circ \mathbf{t} \qquad (4)$$

while the following relations must hold:

$$\mathbf{u} = \sum_{i=1}^{N} \mathbf{u}^{(i)} \qquad (5)$$

$$\mathbf{s} = \sum_{i=1}^{N} \mathbf{s}^{(i)} \qquad (6)$$

$$\mathbf{t} = \sum_{i=1}^{N} \mathbf{t}^{(i)} \qquad (7)$$

where vectors $\mathbf{u}$, $\mathbf{s}$, $\mathbf{t}$ represent the set of users, songs and tags, respectively. The size of vector $\mathbf{u}$ equals the number of distinct users, the size of vector $\mathbf{s}$ equals the number of distinct songs, whereas $\mathbf{t}$ the number of distinct tags. As expected, our modeled third-order tensor is a tensor of more than one rank. To express our tensor $\mathbf{X}$ as a sum of small number of rank-one tensors, we have to apply PARAFAC.

Parallel Factors Decomposition - PARAFAC

The second step of our method, i.e. the Parallel Factors decomposition, comprises the kernel of the proposed approach. PARAFAC is applied to the created sparse tensor to produce N factors corresponding to the number of distinct Tag-Aware groups. PARAFAC can be considered as a higher order generalization of the matrix singular value decomposition (SVD) and principal component analysis (PCA). Its goal is to factorize a tensor into a sum of component rank-one tensors. Given our third-order modeled tensor $\mathbf{X}$, PARAFAC scope is to express it in the following form:

$$\mathbf{X} \approx \sum_{i=1}^{N} \mathbf{w}^{(i)} \mathbf{u}^{(i)} \circ \mathbf{s}^{(i)} \circ \mathbf{t}^{(i)} \qquad (8)$$

where each vector is normalized to length one using the weights of vector $\mathbf{w}$.

PARAFAC implementations may vary. In our case, we embed the Alternative Least Squares (ALS) method. ALS method computes an estimate of the best rank-N PARAFAC model of a tensor $\mathbf{X}$ using an alternating least-squares algorithm (where N is the number of factors). The approximation $\approx$ in Equation (8) refers to the fact that there is a residual error between the estimated tensor and the real tensor. The main scope of the ALS algorithm is to minimize this error by repeating the procedure until some convergence criterion is satisfied. For more details readers should refer to Harshman (1970), Faber et al. (2003) or Tomasi and Bro (2005). The ALS procedure for an M-way tensor assumes that the number of factors N must be specified a priori. There is no straightforward algorithm to determine an optimal N value; in fact the problem is NP-hard according to Haastad (1990). The number of factors is estimated empirically based on the level of distinctiveness between the groups and the quality of each group. Also, the degree as to how effectively the tags describe the songs in each group is considered.

PARAFAC offers a three way decomposition that yields users, songs and tags. Figure 4 presents a N-component PARAFAC model, where the created sparse tensor $\mathbf{X}$ is expressed as the sum of N factors (groups), where $\mathbf{u}^i$, $\mathbf{s}^i$ and $\mathbf{t}^i$ are the i-th components in each factor. PARAFAC delivers a score for all items (users, tags and songs) in each dimension for every factor. Thus, for each factor a ranked list for each dimension is provided, having the respective items in descending order according to their scores. This way, we obtain a three way ranking. We should also mention that using ranking in a three dimensional way, becomes a very important issue, since we filter out inappropriate items (users, tags, songs and parallel artists), while keeping only the best of them based on their score (note that artists' score is calculated according to their respective songs). Thus, the remaining items which are faced as possible noise do not belong to the corresponding factors (Tag-Aware groups) and the proposed method becomes more effective.

Generating Clouds

After modeling the triplets to the sparse tensor and applying PARAFAC, we retrieve the ranked lists based on the calculated scores. As mentioned, the effectiveness of the proposed approach will decrease if all the items of each ranked list for every factor are taken into account. Thus, we consider the best 20 items from the lists, where items could be users, tags or songs. We produce user, tag, song and artist clouds for each of N factors e.g., an artist cloud inside a group is a cloud with the respective artists, where the strength of a certain artist into the group is being represented with the analogous font size. In particular, the ranking position of an item depends upon the font size in the cloud. To generate a proper visualization of each cloud, we need to take into account two crucial factors: (a) the respective position of each item (user, tag, song) based on the calculated score acquired by PARAFAC in each ranked list, and (b) the problem of the dominant tags and songs. To consider these two factors, it is necessary to map weights to each item, which represents the third step of the algorithm. Therefore, before proceeding to the third step, it is first necessary to introduce the problem with the dominant tags and songs.

According to Lamere (2008) users apply some tags more often than others and, thus, a few tags and songs may dominate. This becomes a problem for Tag-Aware grouping, since we aim at descriptive factors with representative tags and songs. There is no music perceptual meaning to take into account tags and songs that are often applied from users. To overcome this problem, first, we compute the number of tag and song occurrences in the resulting factors. Then, we calculate the weights of tags and songs by inverting their number of occurrences in each factor. Thus, each item in a cloud is scaled to the analogous font size. The motivation for the proposed weighting scheme, as a high order ranking method, comes from the fact that it effectively acts similarly to *tf·idf* in the popular web ranking method HITS algorithm (Kleinberg, 1999), trying to evaluate how important a link is to a ranked list in a search query on the internet.

Finally, we must mention that a tag, a user or a song cloud is generated by applying our algorithm to the gathered triplets. We consider a threshold for the number of occurrences of a certain user, tag or song into the resulting factors. If a user's, tag's or song's occurrences exceed this threshold, we remove it from the cloud. This way, as depicted in Figure 2 (or later in the following figures), it is possible to retrieve different number of tags or songs for each cloud into the corresponding factors. As there is a lack of artists in the gathered triplets, the artist cloud is provided in a different way. Based on the fact that a song is performed by a certain artist, we add the artist to the artist

Figure 4. Illustration of the PARAFAC model

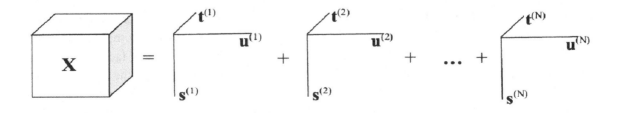

cloud, with the font size equal to font size of the respective song. As observed, sometimes in a group there exists more than one song performed from a certain artist. In this case, we keep the song having the best rank, the larger font size in song cloud and we estimate the artist's font size in the cloud according to this song.

EXPERIMENTS

In the first subsection we describe the method to retrieve the data (triplets), and a toolbox to work with sparse tensors and PARAFAC. Then, we identify the problem of the dominant tags and songs in our dataset. In the second subsection we present the experimental results.

Data Description

To evaluate our method we have chosen a real data set mined from the social music website Last.fm, using the Audioscrobbler web services during July 2008. The extracted data are triplets of the form *{user, song, tag}*. The extraction process starts with the randomly selected user "Metalidol" (note that user nicknames are replaced with distinct ids to respect privacy). The procedure continues by propagating the crawling to his neighbors in a recursive way until 733 distinct users are found. Finally, we collect 70301 *{user, song, tag}* triplets with 985 songs and 3360 unique tags. As our initial choice for the user is a "metal" listener, the vast majority of the gathered songs belong to genre "pop", "rock" or "metal". We also mention that *negative* tags (previous defined) are removed to avoid potential problems.

Next, we run the MA Tensor Toolbox, a toolbox for sparse tensors and PARAFAC, implemented by Brett Bader and Tamara Kolda. The toolbox provides a way to store the values of each triplet to the sparse tensor and to apply the PARAFAC modified method ALS, by calling the parafac_als() function from the toolbox. As expected, few tags and songs dominate into the extracted triplets. This observation becomes apparent in Figure 5, where the frequencies of distinct songs and tags are presented. The most frequent applied tag in our triplets is "rock", having 1486 occurrences in the 70301 triplets (Table 2).

Based on Liekens analysis, it seems that there is a spectrum of musical genres in the population of Last.fm users. The spectrum ranges from "indie" over "alternative" to "rock" and "metal", and then to "hip-hop" and "electronic" music with a sparse gap back to "indie". Tags like "rock", "alternative", "pop", "indie" are often selected by users. In our dataset, the most frequent tagged song is "Hysteria" from the album "Hysteria" by "Def Leppard" from genre "rock" with 1901 occurrences, while the second most frequent tagged song is "Bliss" from the album "Rainbow" by Maria Carey from genre "pop". To overcome the dominant tags and songs problem, after producing the factors by PARAFAC, it is necessary to apply our implemented *tf·idf* method as described in the previous section.

Results

As mentioned in a previous section, to start PARAFAC the number of factors has to be a priori specified. According to the experimental framework of Kolda et al. (2005), the optimal number of factors achieves the best division of the dataset. Since our gathered dataset consists of music items, users and tags, the best division should be considered when each factor refers to a certain music topic. The respective tag cloud provides the description of each music topic. In particular, to ensure that each factor is consistent, irrelevant tags should not be grouped together by the proposed method. Therefore, the exploration concerns the tag clouds as the proper guide, while tuning to different number of factors R in range [1...40]. It was concluded that the optimal number of factors equals to 20. Each factor is a Tag-Aware group with the following components: user, tag,

Figure 5. Frequency of distinct tags (a) and songs (b) into the crawled triplets

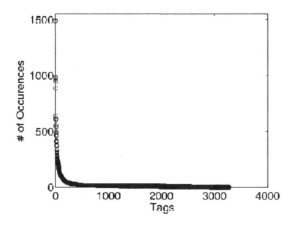
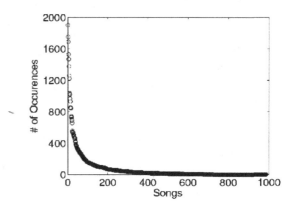

song and artist clouds. Each weight is computed as described in a previous section, and then the font size is scaled linearly by each component's weight in the Tag-Aware group.

To ensure the stability of the discovered Tag-Aware groups, in our experiments we remove or add triplets to the initial dataset. In particular, from Figure 6 it is obvious that even if the dataset size is reduced from 100% to 50%, the tag cloud of factor 9 still describes the respective music topic ("Beatles" in our case). We must mention that the tag clouds are used as a means to prove stability, because they do describe the discovered topic of each factor. To conclude, the proposed method is stable, since the eigenvectors-factors are not modified, when the dataset size is either reduced or increased. Moreover, the high-ranked tags are kept, whereas the new added tags describe appropriately the respective topic equally well. In addition to this experiment, we performed the "stability" experiments for the remaining 19 factors, where we remarked a similar performance.

Since Tag-Aware groups analysis performs a high order ranking and a topic discovery, our evaluation can only be performed by examining: (a) if the respective ranked tag list (tag cloud) properly describes the certain music topic, and (b) if the coherence of each group is maintained, an evaluation method similar to the evaluation

method of the TOPHITS algorithm (Kolda et al., 2005).

In the sequel, we present three factors Tag-Aware groups generated by the proposed method. These factors represent three different types of Tag-Aware groups. Figure 2 shows factor 9, a Tag-Aware group which refers to the music topic of "The Beatles". It also contains their similar artists, the relevant songs, along with the users of similar preferences. We note that in this group "John Lennon" is the second dominant artist, not only as a member of "The Beatles", but as a solo artist as well. Also, "Supertramp" is correlated

Table 2. Top-10 tags and their frequencies in the collection of 70301 extracted triplets

Tag	Freq
Rock	1486
Alternative	981
Alternative rock	966
Classic rock	949
Metal	833
Indie	637
Hard Rock	613
Progressive Rock	609
Punk	602
Electronic	558

Figure 6. Tag cloud transformation of factor 9 (Beatles), while reducing the dataset size to: (a) 100% (b) 90% (c) 80% (d) 70% (e) 60% (f) 50%

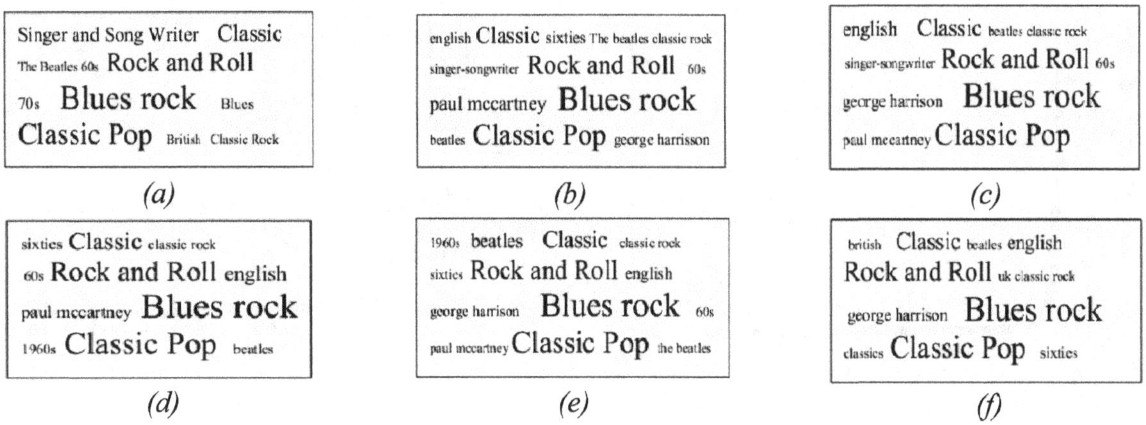

to "The Beatles" as an English progressive rock and pop band. "Joe Cocker" is also connected to "The Beatles", as he is an English rock/blues singer who became popular in the 1960s, and is most known for his gritty voice and his cover versions of popular songs, particularly those of "The Beatles". Their correlation is noted by tags like "classic pop", "blues rock", "british" etc. On one hand, we achieved to discover a Tag-Aware group and provide a rich representation at a glance. On the other hand, the production of such a group is a common task to solve for a system based on artist similarity and can be accomplished using other methods. More information can be found in MIREX (Music Information Retrieval Evaluation eXchange), in *Audio Artist Identification* task or in Downie (2008); however, the relevant links, users, songs and tags will be missing and moreover the respective three way ranking will also be omitted.

Figure 7 depicts a Tag-Aware group which corresponds to a different type of music topic, such as a mood description, "relaxed" music in particular. In general, the songs of "Placebo" are relaxed music. However, a few songs of "Nirvana", like "The Man Who Sold the World", could also belong to this Tag-Aware group. This is a very difficult task to be automatically identified by a

system based on genre or artist similarity, although the particular song can be evaluated as a correct result according to users' preferences for social tags, as users tend to tag the songs of "Placebo" and the corresponding song of "Nirvana" as "chill-out" music. For example, if the proposed method was embedded into a recommendation system to perform ranking and topic searching, then a user could pose a "chill out" music request (see Chen and Chen (2005) for more information on recommendation systems). Then the list retrieved from the system would consist of songs, the vast majority of which, would be songs by "Placebo" and "Coldplay", i.e., the dominant or the higher ranked artists inside the Tag-Aware group, whereas a few songs by "Nirvana" and "Moby" lower ranked artists would be added, in particular "The Man Who Sold the World" and "Natural Blues" respectively. This outcome could be also reached by a select mood system, as Levy and Sandler (2007) claim. We note the absence of a system providing simultaneously artist similarity, like the previous factor 9 and mood – selection like the current factor 3. Additionally, it would be very difficult for a mood selection system to create a recommendation list comprising of "Placebo" and "Nirvana". Also, while associating the two artists with the help of the song "The Man Who Sold the

World", we can provide a transparent explanation to the recommendation system, since their connection is based on the certain music topic, "chillout" music. The appropriate tags establish the connections between components inside this Tag-Aware group. At the same time, a user could discover other users having similar preferences in "relaxed" music, and tune in their "radio" or explore their preferences as well. Moreover they could be based their search or explore on the most prominent, since the resulting items are in a ranked form.

Figure 8 presents factor 19, a Tag-Aware group consisting of "rock" and "metal". Correlated artists and certain songs from these two genres are included. A difficult issue comes up; an association for "rock" and "metal" artists is discovered based on user tags. It is apparent that there is a thin line between these two genres, and, thus, while observing this group we cross from one side to the opposite. In particular, genre overlapping in music is based on the genre folksonomy, described in more details by Lamere (2008). Therefore, this group illustrates a way to locate and explain the overlapping between these two genres.

The three Tag-Aware groups or factors discussed in Figures 2, 7 and 8 are very representative results of the proposed approach applied on our dataset. Another example of group is the "latin" one, which contains users, tags, songs and artists referring to genres "flamenco", "bolero", "bugalu", "cha cha" and "cumbia". Finally, another example is the "melodic rock" group produced by "piano rock" and "symphonic rock" songs and artists, including the relevant users. This group lies at a lower level in hierarchy of genres, under the genre "rock". More information about the hierarchy of genres can be found in Lamere's survey (2008).

We observed that our implementation is capable of dividing the initial unorganized triplets to music topics, by producing 20 concrete Tag-Aware groups. To ensure that effective results are derived, we show that each group provides a good overview and description about a certain music topic. Because the topics of each group belong to music concepts, to prove how each music item of the group is correlated to the respective music topic, we provide explanations for each resulting group based each time on a musical point of view.

CONCLUSION

We have presented an algorithm to implement Tag-Aware grouping by using multilinear algebra. The proposed approach aims at achieving ranking for the three basic elements from a social music tagging system: users, tags and music objects, and additionally each Tag-Aware group correspond to a music topic. We showed experimentally through real data that our method can be very effective, since we achieve a proper division of the data according to the discovered topics. At the same time, the included tags in each group can be very descriptive for the respective songs and artists, based on user preferences.

Three different representative examples for our method have been described. First, a Tag-Aware group which refers to a certain artist has been built; second, a Tag-Aware group relied on mood description, and, third, a Tag-Aware group with correlated-overlapping genres has been constructed. This way, Tag-Aware grouping can be used to build music similarity models. Also, the proposed method creates a multi-way and rich visualization to explore the complex music space and find new, interesting and relevant music. Finally, Tag-Aware grouping can generate transparent and explainable recommendations for their relevance, since the explanation relies on the fact that all clouds are referred to a specific music topic and help users to discover the most prominent users with similar preferences, since ranked lists are provided. This becomes important since social music tagging systems refer to humans.

Figure 7. Factor 3, a Tag-Aware group based on artists and songs with "relaxed" music

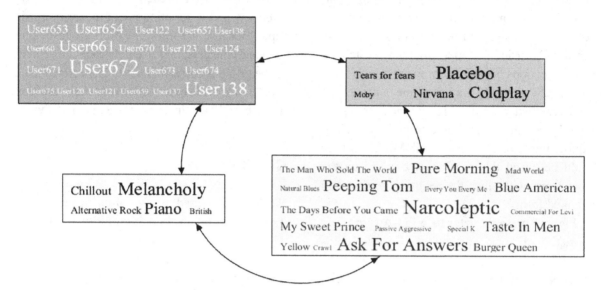

Figure 8. Factor 19, a Tag-Aware group based on a mixture of "rock" and "metal"

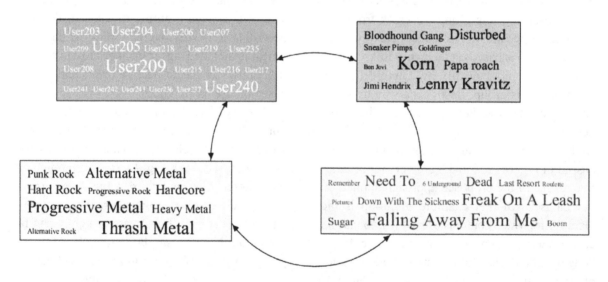

An important topic for future work is the lack of transparency on the relationships between the Tag-Aware groups. These relationships could be calculated based on several criteria, e.g., artist, song or/and tag similarity between two different Tag-Aware groups. This can lead to a visual representation of the considered groups via a graph, where the connecting edges consist of three dimensions: weighted tags, artists and songs.

Apparently, there is always the challenge that the generated groups have different music conceptual meaning and overwhelm the construction of such a graph. Finally, it would be possible to gather triplets from datasets having a priori specified the number of groups. This would offer a direction to our method, such as to measure the precision of our algorithm in a more formal way.

Last, PARAFAC algorithm in sparse tensors causes memory overflows during the tensor factorization process, while using a large dataset. An attempt to solve this 'blowup problem' can be found in Kolda and Sun (2008). Although, they succeeded to reduce the memory consumption, PARAFAC efficiency is questionable with respect to scalable datasets. If a more dramatic reduction is achieved, it would be feasible to apply the proposed algorithm to larger dataset.

REFERENCES

Audioscrobbler. (n.d.). *Web Services for Last.fm*. Retrieved from http://ws.audioscrobbler.com

Bader, B., & Kolda, T. (n.d.). *Tensor MA toolbox*. Retrieved from http://csmr.ca.sandia.gov/~tgkolda/ TensorToolbox/

Chen, H. C., & Chen, A. L. P. (2005). A Music Recommendation System Based on Music and User Grouping. *Journal of Intelligent Information Systems: Intelligent Multimedia Applications, 24*(2), 113–132.

Deerwester, S. C., Dumais, S. T., Landauer, T. K., Furnas, G. W., & Harshman, R. A. (1990). Indexing by Latent Semantic Analysis. *Journal of the American Society for Information Science American Society for Information Science, 41*(6), 391–407. doi:10.1002/(SICI)1097-4571(199009)41:6<391::AID-ASI1>3.0.CO;2-9

Downie, J. S. (2008). The Music Information Retrieval Evaluation Exchange (2005-2007): a Window into Music Retrieval Research. *Acoustical Science and Technology, 29*(4), 247–255. doi:10.1250/ast.29.247

Faber, N. K. M., Bro, R., & Hopke, P. K. (2003). Recent Developments in CANDECOMP/PARAFAC Algorithms: a Critical Review. *Chemometrics and Intelligent Laboratory Systems, 65*(1), 191–137. doi:10.1016/S0169-7439(02)00089-8

Furnas, G. W., Landauer, T. K., Gomez, L. M., & Dumais, S. T. (1987). The Vocabulary Problem in Human-system Communication. *Communications of the ACM, 30*(11), 964–971. doi:10.1145/32206.32212

Guy, M., & Tonkin, E. (2006). Tidying up Tags. *D-Lib Magazine*. Retrieved from www.dlib.org/dlib/january06/guy/01guy.html

Haastad, J. (1990). Tensor Rank is NP-complete. *Journal of Algorithms, 11*, 644–654. doi:10.1016/0196-6774(90)90014-6

Harshman, R. A. (1970). Foundations of the PARAFAC Procedure: Models and Conditions for an 'Explanatory' Multi-modal Factor Analysis. *UCLA working papers in phonetics, 16*, 1-84.

Hofmann, T. &. Puzicha, J. (1998). *Statistical models for co-occurrence data* (Tech. Rep. 1635). Cambridge, MA: MIT.

Karydis, I., Nanopoulos, A., Gabriel, H., & Spiliopoulou, M. (2009). Tag-aware spectral clustering of Music Items. In *Proceedings of the International Society for Music Information Retrieval Conference*, Kobe, Japan (Vol. 10, pp. 159-164).

Kleinberg, J. (1999). Authoritative Sources in a Hyperlinked Environment. *Journal of the ACM, 46*(5), 604–632. doi:10.1145/324133.324140

Kolda, T. G., & Bader, B. W. (2009). Tensor Decompositions and Applications. *SIAM Review, 51*(3), 455–500. doi:10.1137/07070111X

Kolda, T. G., Bader, B. W., & Kenny, J. P. (2005). Higher-Order Web Link Analysis Using Multilinear Algebra. In *Proceedings of the IEEE International Conference on Data Mining*, Houston, TX (Vol. 5, pp. 242-249).

Kolda, T. G., & Sun, J. (2008). Scalable Tensor Decompositions for Multi-aspect Data Mining. In *Proceedings of the IEEE International Conference on Data Mining*, Pisa, Italy (Vol. 8, pp. 363-372).

Lamere, P. (2008). Social Tagging and Music Information Retrieval. *Journal of New Music Research, 37*(2), 101–114. doi:10.1080/09298210802479284

Last.fm. (n.d.). *A social music platform*. Retrieved from http://www.last.fm

Levy, M., & Sandler, M. (2007). A Semantic Space for Music Derived from Social Tags. In *Proceedings of the International Conference on Music Information Retrieval*, Vienna, Austria (Vol. 8, pp. 411-416).

Levy, M., & Sandler, M. (2008). Learning Latent Semantic Models for Music from Social Tags. *Journal of New Music Research, 37*(2), 137–150. doi:10.1080/09298210802479292

Liekens, A. (2007, March 28-April 2). *Data mining music profiles*. Retrieved from http://anthony. liekens.net/index.php/ Computers/DataMining

Pampalk, E. (2001). *Islands of Music: Analysis, Organization and Visualizations of Music Archives*. Unpublished master thesis, Vienna University of Technology, Vienna, Austria.

Symeonidis, P., Ruxanda, M., Nanopoulos, A., & Manolopoulos, Y. (2008). Ternary Semantic Analysis of Social Tags for Personalized Music Recommendation. In *Proceedings of the International Conference on Music Information Retrieval*, Philadelphia (Vol. 8, pp. 219-224).

Tomasi, G., & Bro, R. (2005). PARAFAC and Missing Values. *Chemometrics and Intelligent Laboratory Systems, 75*(2), 163–180. doi:10.1016/j.chemolab.2004.07.003

Wu, X., Zhang, L., & Yu, Y. (2006). Exploring social annotations for the semantic web. In *Proceedings of the international Conference on World Wide Web*, New York (Vol. 15, pp. 417-426).

This work was previously published in the International Journal of Multimedia Data Engineering and Management, Volume 1, Issue 3, edited by Shu-Ching Chen, pp. 1-18, copyright 2010 by IGI Publishing (an imprint of IGI Global).

Section 5
Multimedia Applications:
Integration of Multimedia Management
and E-Learning Technology

Chapter 14
Content Adaptation in Mobile Learning Environments

Sergio Castillo
Universidad de las Américas Puebla, México

Gerardo Ayala
Universidad de las Américas Puebla, México

ABSTRACT

In this paper, the authors present their proposal for adaptation of educational contents of learning objects to a particular mobile device and a specific learner. Content adaptation in mobile learning objects implies user adaptation and device adaptation, and requires additional metadata categories in comparison with SCORM 2004. This learning object content model, ALMA (A Learning content Model Adaptation), inherits from the SCORM standard a subset of metadata categories, and extends it with three top level metadata categories for content adaptation, i.e., Knowledge, Use, and Mobile Device Requirements (Castillo & Ayala, 2008). For user adaptation, the authors developed NORIKO (NOn-monotonic Reasoning for Intelligent Knowledge awareness and recommendations On the move), a belief system based on DLV, a programming system based on Answer Set Programming paradigm. For device adaptation the authors designed CARIME (Content Adapter of Resources In Mobile learning Environments), which uses trans-coding and transrating to adapt media content to suit the device characteristics.

INTRODUCTION

Content adaptation is the process of automatically modify the characteristics of the learning object educational contents, in order to enhance the user experience, considering her/his interests and specific mobile device. User adaptation implies a learner model and a personalization process in order to select and present to the learner contents appropriates to her current interests. In the other hand, the number and variety of mobile devices characteristics, makes very common to vary the details of format of images, image sizes, or bit-rate of media when delivering content to mobile

DOI: 10.4018/978-1-4666-1791-9.ch014

devices. We consider a mobile learning object (MLO) as an information entity, digital, interactive, adaptable and reusable in different contexts, designed to support an educational objective through a mobile device in situated or collaborative learning activities (Castillo & Ayala, 2007). ARMOLEO (ARchitecture for MObile LEarning Objects) is the architecture for the design, development and use of learning objects in mobile learning environments. In this paper we discuss our proposal for content adaptation, both user and device adaptation, as we designed in ARMOLEO (Castillo & Ayala, 2008).

ARMOLEO (ARCHITECTURE FOR MOBILE LEARNING OBJECTS)

ARMOLEO is our proposal for the design, development and use of learning objects aimed to be used in mobile learning environments. With ARMOLEO we have proposed three models for the design and use of LOs in mobile learning environments, based on their respective learning strategies and the required awareness support (Ayala & Castillo, 2008):

1. Personalization model, based on Personalization Learning and supporting Knowledge Awareness.
2. Interaction model, based on Situated Learning and supporting Context Awareness, and
3. Collaboration model, based on Collaborative Learning and supporting Social and Knowledge Awareness.

The architecture (see Figure 1) is composed by the following components:

- The deductive database of Learner models,
- Database for Device's Profiles,

- MLOs repository, composed by ALMA Packages and Metadata database,
- Database for Collaboration scripts,
- Learner and Device identifier,
- NORIKO, the learner's models manager,
- MLOs selector,
- CARIME, the MLOs device adapter,
- Collaboration Script selector, and
- ALMA Packager.

In ARMOLEO, the personalization model implies a deductive database of learner models and is maintained by a beliefs revision system named NORIKO (NOn-monotonic Reasoning for Intelligent Knowledge awareness and recommendations On the move). This Java based system interacts with DLV, a programming system based on Answer Set Programming paradigm, and allows us to insert, remove and consult beliefs, and performs a beliefs revision process any time a new belief is included or removed to/from the inductive database. Beliefs are relevant because a computational model of beliefs is suitable to include both, cognitive and psychological aspects of learners, which permits to obtain a more comprehensive and whole-person model of the learner. In the other hand, ASP paradigm has been recognized as a contribution and a significant evolution in the areas of Logic Programming and Artificial Intelligence. ASP is more expressive than normal (disjunction free) logic programming and allow us to deal with uncertainty. It uses two types of negation: weak negation (not X), that means "there is no evidence of X", and strong negation (~X) which means "there is evidence that X is false". These features made this programming paradigm a powerful tool for knowledge representation, commonsense reasoning and modeling of incomplete knowledge (Leone et al., 2002). NORIKO keeps the learner model updated by monitoring his/her interaction with mobile learning objects in order to keep a registration and deduction of the interests and capabilities of the learner based on his/her selection and use of mobile learning

Figure 1. ARMOLEO components

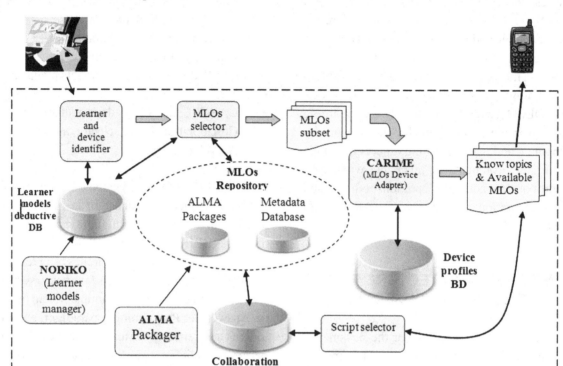

Figure 2. Personalization model in ARMOLEO

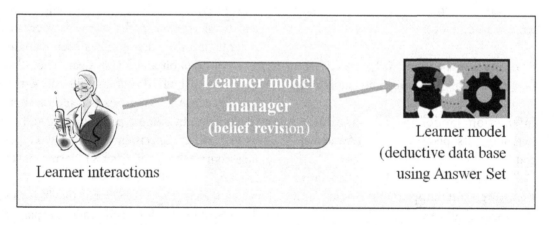

objects (Ayala, 2005; Castillo & Ayala, 2008 b). Figure 2 illustrates the personalization model that we propose for ARMOLEO. It consists of a Learner model manager, based on NORIKO, and a deductive database generated using ASP programming.

PERSONALIZATION MODEL

Personalization of learning contents must be based on a learner model, which is a type of user model. There have been several approaches for modeling the users of learning environments. Berri et al. (2006) propose a personalization framework based on ontologies for context awareness in mobile learning in order to facilitate the design, transfer and presentation of personalized learning resources to mobile learners. Shi et al. (2002) proposed a connectionist approach to personalized learning. They proposed a system in which an intelligent agent exploits a connectionist model of the learner behavior based on the self organizing maps (SOM) training algorithm. Albayrak et al. (2005) proposed personalization based on multiagent systems. They developed an agent-based information system named Personal Information Agents (PIA). PIA combines push (system initiative) and pull (user initiative) techniques allowing users to be informed automatically about relevant information and to search explicitly for specific information, classified in pre-work, work and recreation categories based on end-user daily routine. PIA maintains the learner model updated based on the interaction of the user with the learning environment, however, the personalization process is based on the learner daily routine more than on topics of interests or capabilities.

For us, personalization is the adaptation of the content of learning objects to interests and capabilities of specific learner; therefore we base the personalization process and the learner model in the interests and capabilities of learner, which we consider are more representatives of her/his learning aims and possibilities.

NORIKO, the learner model manager of AR-MOLEO, allows adding of basic beliefs about capabilities of learner when s/he explicitly indicates that s/he is able to apply knowledge represented in a learning object. This is accomplished by the following rule:

addBelief(hasAccomplishedTask, LearnerId, TaskId).

NORIKO also generates derived beliefs, by inferring that learner is able to apply the knowledge represented in the learning object, based on the results of a learning task:

capability(LearnerId, LearningObjectId):-
hasAccomplishedTask(LearnerId, TaskId),
knowledgeUsedInTask(LearningObjectId,TaskId).

or by inferring that learner is not able to apply the knowledge represented in the learning object, based on the results of a learning task:

-capability(LearnerId, LearningObjectId):-
-hasAccomplishedTask(LearnerId, TaskId),
knowledgeUsedInTask(LearningObjectId,TaskId).

The recommendation of a specific learning object to a particular learner, according to her/his interests and/or capabilities, is generated by the rule:

learningObjectRecommendation(LearnerId,KnowledgeElementId,LearningObjectId):-
hasInterestInTopic(LearnerId, TopicId),
topicOfKnowledge(TopicId, LearningObjectId),
knowledgeRepresentedInObject(KnowledgeElementId,LearningObjectId),
not capability(LearnerId, KnowledgeElementId).

In order to have a personalized interaction with the specific learner, according to her/his interests and/or capabilities, content recommendation for the learning object, is generated by the rule:

learningObjectContentRecommendation(LearnerId,LearningObjectId,ContentId):-
hasInterestInTopic(LearnerId, TopicId),
topicOfKnowledge(TopicId, KnowledgeElementId),
knowledgeRepresentedInObject(KnowledgeElementId,LearningObjectId),
learningObjectContent(LearningObjectId, ContentId),
knowledgeRepresentedInContent(KnowledgeElementId,ContentId),
not capability(LearnerId, KnowledgeElementId).

COLLABORATION MODEL

In a collaborative learning environment, persons are able to participate in a community of practice, working with other members of the community, and simultaneously creating their own mental models of domain. Collaborative learning allows construction of knowledge and developing of problem solving skills in the group members in such a way that would not be possible without group participation (Ayala, 1996).

The collaboration model in ARMOLEO allows social interactivity and connectivity. To accomplish these, collaboration model supports the awareness of those who are or have been interacting with a given mobile learning object (knowledge awareness), and awareness of the interests and capabilities of other learners (social awareness). Assistance recommendation is accomplished through the application of rules such as the following ones:

maybeCannotUseSuccessfully(LearnerId, KnowledgeElementId):-
knowledgeUsedInTask(KnowledgeElementId ,TaskId),
-hasAccomplishedTask(LearnerId,TaskId).
assistanceRecommendation(KnowledgeElementId, LearnerId,excellent):-
capability(LearnerId, KnowledgeElementId),
not maybeCannotUseSuccessfully(LearnerId, KnowledgeElementId),
learnerAvailable(LearnerId).
assistanceRecommendation(KnowledgeElementId, LearnerId,familiar):-
canUseSuccessfully(LearnerId, KnowledgeElementId),
maybeCannotUseSuccessfully(LearnerId, KnowledgeElementId),
learnerAvailable(LearnerId).

INTERACTION MODEL

In ARMOLEO, the interaction model has two functions: to keep the learner aware of other learners and mobile learning objects (knowledge awareness), and to provide adaptation of the content of mobile learning objects to the specific mobile device of the current learner.

Knowledge awareness is accomplished through a set of rules, such as the next ones:

haveToMakeAwareOfOtherLearner(LearnerId, LearningObjectId, OtherLearnerId):-
learnerAvailable(LearnerId),
learnerAvailable(OtherLearnerId),
OtherLearnerId <> LearnerId,
isInteractingWithALearningObject(LearnerId ,LearningObjectId),
hasInteractedWithALearningObject(OtherLearnerId, LearningObjectId),
capability(OtherLearnerId, KnowledgeElementId),
knowledgeRepresentedInObject(KnowledgeElementId,LearningObjectId).
haveToMakeAwareOfLearningObject(LearnerId,KnowledgeElement, LearningObject):-
hasInterestInTopic(LearnerId, TopicId),
topicOfKnowledge(TopicId, KnowledgeElement),
knowledgeRepresentedInObject(KnowledgeElement, LearningObject),
not capability(LearnerId, KnowledgeElement).

In order to accomplish adaptation of the content of mobile learning objects to the specific mobile device of the current learner, we designed CARIME (Content Adapter of Resources In Mobile learning Environments), one of the software components of ARMOLEO. CARIME needs information about the characteristics of the target mobile device and the minimal requirements of the content to be adapted. In order to obtain this information, CARIME makes access to a database, which provides profile information about diverse mobile devices. CARIME also needs information about some features of the contents of a mobile learning object. We include the "Mobile Device Requirements" as a new top level category to ALMA metadata set. This category includes two tags which refer to:

1. The minimum acceptable screen size for the presentation of the contents.
2. The format of the content, in case of graphics, audio and video.

With both of these sets of data of a given MLO, together with the mobile device characteristics of the user, CARIME will be able to determine the feasibility of the adaptation and, in such a case, to adapt the contents of the MLO to be properly presented to the current learner in her/his device.

ALMA (A LEARNING CONTENT MODEL ADAPTATION)

There have been several proposals to adapt standards to specific learning environments. Katz and Worsham (2005) tried to integrate mobile technologies into SCORM 2004. The UK Learning Object Metadata Core attempted to optimize the LOM (Learning Object Metadata) standard for use it within the context of the UK public education system (Campbell, 2007). The CanCore Learning Object Metadata Profile (Friesen et al., 2002) is an initiative to adapt the SCORM standard to the specifics needs of the Canadian public education system.

In the context of mobile learning, Chan et al. (2004) have proposed to modify the SCORM standard in order to extend it to mobile learning adding three top level metadata categories: Learning object, to describe learning resources, Learner, to describe learner profile and learner model, and Setting, to describe context state of the learning environment. In this last category they include

the Equipment tag to describe characteristics of the mobile device of the learner.

For modeling the contents of mobile learning objects we propose ALMA (**A L**earning **M**odel content **A**daptation), which is a subset of SCORM 2004 standard metadata categories. ALMA extended SCORM 2004 with three top level categories: Knowledge Metadata, Use Metadata and Mobile Device Requirements Metadata.

Knowledge Metadata

The Knowledge Metadata category is included to register the domain of the knowledge contained in the learning object in order to enable the use of the mobile learning object in informal learning scenarios, or learning activities independent of an educational program or course. It includes three tags:

- **KnowledgeId:** Identifier of the knowledge item.
- **Domain:** The domain the knowledge item is about of.
- **Description:** A brief description of this knowledge item.

Use Metadata

The Use Metadata category is included to register the history of use of the mobile learning object. This is necessary in order to provide knowledge awareness (who are or have been interacting with a given mobile learning object) as well as social awareness (interests and capabilities of other learners). It includes two tags:

- **UserId:** Learner id of a learner that has used the learning object in a learning situation.
- **Situation:** Brief description of the learning situation of use of this mobile learning object.

Mobile Device Requirements Metadata

In order to determine the requirements for adaptation of specific mobile learning objects, we include a new metadata top category named Mobile Device Requirements with the following tags:

1. minRequiredScreenSize
2. mimeMediaTypes, to specify image, video or audio format.

The minRequiredScreenSize tag specifies the minimum screen size acceptable to display images. With the mimeMediaTypes tag we specify the image, audio and video formats of the contents included as resources in the mobile learning object. These MIME media types can be obtained automatically from content files included in the ALMA package.

ALMA Packager

We have also developed ALMA Packager with the aim to facilitate the assembly and labeling of mobile learning objects. This Java based software element allows us to pack files and create the manifest file, assembling mobile learning objects that fulfill the ALMA metadata set.

In the ALMA Packager, the MIME type is obtained from the filename extension. When a new file is added as a resource to the current mobile learning object, the ALMA Packager obtains its filename extension and it determines and registers its MIME type. In case of graphics contents, to determine the minimum acceptable screen size, any time an image file is added to the mobile learning object, the ALMA Packager analyzes it in order to obtain its size. In case of multiple image files, the image with the greatest size will determine the minimum acceptable size. This way, the minimum required screen size tag will contain a single element, while MIME media types tag could contain a list of images, video and/

or audio formats. Our ALMA Packager allows us to create new learning objects and to edit already created learning objects.

Creation of ALMA Learning Objects packages

Figure 3 shows the Create Learning Object interface of ALMA Packager. For the creation of learning objects, the developer must enter some of the tags we describe in this section. The general metadata category includes the following tags:

- Identifier
- Serial Id
- Language
- Title
- Keywords
- Description.

Identifier is entered by the MLO developer and Serial Id is automatically created in order to define a unique General Identifier combining Identifier and Serial Id tags. In the Language tag, the MLO developer must select the primary human language used to communicate with the intended learner. In the Title tag, the MLO developer enters the name of the MLO. In the Keywords and Description tags should be entered keywords and phrases descriptive of the learning object by the MLO developer.

The LifeCycle metadata category allows the developer to define a version number and a development Status for the learning object, which can be Draft, Final, Revised or Unavailable.

The Metametadata category allows describing the metadata record itself. The MLO developer can specify a Metametadata identifier and language, but the value of the Schema tag must be LOMv1.0, as SCORM indicates. Identifier implies Catalog and Entry tags. For the Catalog tag, some types of cataloging systems may be Universal Resource Identifier (URI), Universal Resource Name (URN), Digital Object Identifier

Figure 3. Create Learning Object Interface of ALMA Packager

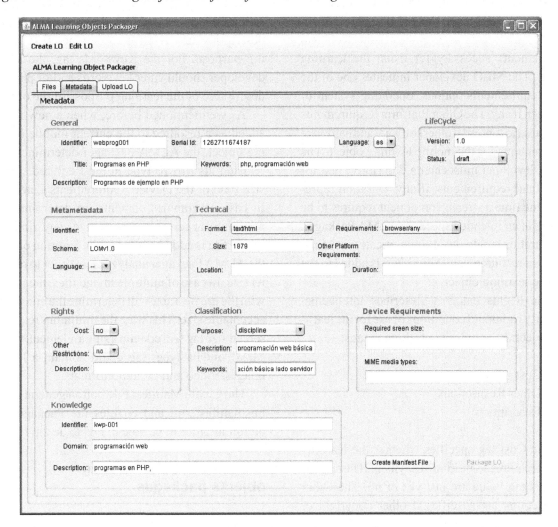

(DOI), International Standard Book Numbers (ISBN), or International Standard Serial Numbers (ISSN). The values for the Entry tag depend on the cataloging system. Organizations are free to choose any cataloging and entry schemes that satisfy their needs, but is recommended that a common scheme be chosen. The value for the Language tag represents the default language for all Language tags.

The Technical metadata category is aimed to describe technical characteristics and requirements of the mobile learning object. The tags of this category are:

- Format
- Size
- Location
- Requirements
- Other Platform Requirements
- Duration

The Format tag refers to technical data type of all the resources used in the learning object, expressed as MIME types. Size refers to total size of digital contents in bytes. In ALMA Packager, Size is automatically updated each time a new resource is added to the mobile learning object. Location describes one or more alternative locations where a resource of the mobile learning object can also be found, in addition to the learning object itself. The Requirements tag represents the technical requirements necessary for using the learning object. The MLO developer indicates one of the two Requirements options: operating system or browser, if any. The Other Platform Requirements tag is used to represent other software and hardware requirements for the mobile learning object. The MLO developer must enter a descriptive text for additional requirements, if any. Duration represents the time a stream component requires to be played at an intended speed. In ALMA Packager, this duration is calculated automatically each time a stream resource (audio or video) is added to the mobile learning object.

The Rights category describes intellectual property rights and conditions of use for the learning object. It includes the following tags:

- Cost
- Other Restrictions
- Description

The Cost tag specifies whether the learning object requires some kind of payment. The options for this tag value are just yes or no. The Other Restrictions tag specifies if other copyright or restrictions apply to the use of the mobile learning object. In case the developer chooses the yes option for this tag, the Description tag is enabled to allow her/him to enter a description text.

Classification category describes where current learning object falls within a specific classification system. The tags for this category are:

- Purpose
- Description
- Keywords

The purpose tag defines the learning purpose of the mobile learning object. The options for this tag are discipline, idea, prerequisite, educational objective, accessibility restrictions, educational level, skill level, security level, and competency. In the Description tag, developer should enter a description text relative to the specified learning purpose. For the Keywords tag, the MLO developer should enter keywords and/or phrases descriptive of the learning purpose of the object.

As we mentioned before, when a new file is added as a resource to the current mobile learning object, the ALMA Packager determines and registers its MIME type in the Required screen size field of the Device Requirements Category. In case of graphics contents, to determine the minimum acceptable screen size, any time an image file is added to the mobile learning object, the ALMA Packager analyzes it in order to obtain its size. In case of multiple image files, the image with the greatest size will determine the minimum acceptable size. This way, the minimum required screen size tag will contain a single element, while MIME media types tag could contain a list of images, video and/or audio formats.

The Create Manifest File button generates the imsmanifest.xml and enables the Package LO button in order to be able to create de zip file.

Edition of ALMA learning objects packages

In Figure 4 we show the Metadata interface of ALMA Packager that corresponds to the edition of a learning object. In this interface we have two sections, Use category and Relations category, in addition to those that appear in the creation interface.

The Use metadata tags are automatically filled based on the up to date application of the learning object, recording who has used this mobile learning object, and the corresponding situations of its use.

The Relation category registers the relationship between this and others learning objects, if any. The tags for this category are Kind and Resource. The Kind tag values may be ispartof, haspart, isversionof, hasversion, isformatof, hasformat,

Figure 4. Edit Learning Object Interface of ALMA Packager

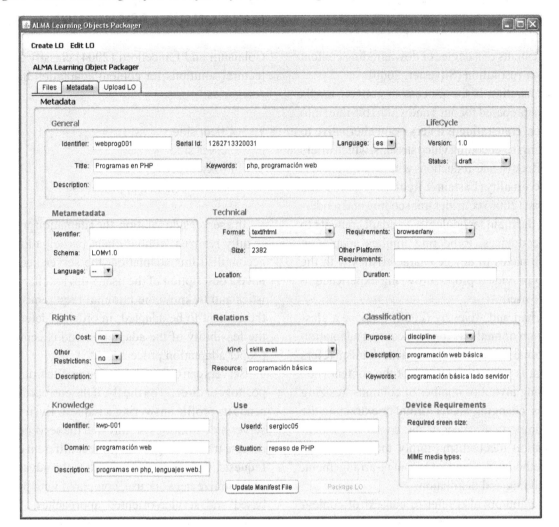

references, isreferedby, isbasedon, isbasisfor, requires, and isrequiredby. The Resource tag will contain the General Identifier of other mobile learning object related with the mobile learning object under description. The Relation category is used to infer the learner interests about the mobile learning objects of the repository.

The Update Manifest File button updates the "imsmanifest.xml" file, and, as in the case of creation of a learning object, enables the "Package LO" button in order to be able to create the corresponding zip file.

TECHNOLOGIES FOR CONTENT ADAPTATION

Concerning adaptation of videos to mobile devices, Tang (2008) indicates that the underlying technologies behind broadband to mobile content rendering are transcoding and transrating. Transcoding is the ability to change the format and resolution of graphics contents, both static images and videos. Transcoding is the coding and recoding of digital content from one compressed format to another, in order to enable transmission over different media and playback over various devices. Transcoding can be accomplished in several ways, for example, conversion from MPEG-2 to H.264 format, changing the bit rate to meet requirements of a device or downgrading content to lesser resolution (Silvester, 2006).

Transrating is the process to convert media content prepared for one bandwidth (bit-rate) into another. Transrating is a very good alternative to decoding/re-encoding video streams, which offers cost effective rate-reductions with a minimum loss of video quality (Lastein & Reul, 2003). Frost and Sullivan (2006) consider transcoding and rendering as the main technologies to adapt contents to mobile devices. Rendering implies adaptation of web pages to device characteristics with the aim to provide a proper browsing experience to mobile users.

Farhan and Abawajy (2008) propose a classification of methods for Web content adaptation for mobile devices. For them, a mechanism refers to what is going to do to adapt the content (i.e., changing layout or number of columns, resizing images, changing media format or extracting the most important aspect of the content). Content adaptation mechanisms imply the corresponding methods, like content layout re-arrangement, transcoding and distillation.

The authors also refer to context of content adaptation. Context refers to who the content is going to be adapted: to a particular device or to a particular user. In device adaptation, the adaptation process is based on the characteristics of the target device, while in user adaptation, user's preferences are considered to guide the adaptation process.

In ARMOLEO, the personalization model provides user adaptation, while the interaction model provides device adaptation. For device adaptation we use transcoding as method to adapt the images format and/or resizing them to fit the characteristics of the particular mobile device screen. Other method for device adaptation that we apply is transrating, used to change the bit-rate of media content to suit the device characteristics.

ARCHITECTURAL SOLUTIONS FOR CONTENT ADAPTATION

Colajanni and Lancellotti (2004) classify architectural solutions for content adaptation in four categories:

1. Client side
2. Server side
3. Proxy-based
4. Service-oriented approaches

In a server side solution, the adaptation process is fully realized without client participation. To accomplish this adaptation, the server needs to have a description of the user's device characteristics and to know the minimal requirements of the content to be adapted, in order to determine the feasibility of the adaptation and execute the proper adaptation process.

Servers can obtain the device profile from a repository or directly on the fly, if the current device sends its profile answering a request. Even when server-side solutions require that the servers have diverse transcoding skills to meet different client requests, this kind of solution has the advantage of minimize network use, compared with proxy-based and service-oriented approaches. These two advantages make server-side solutions very attractive for mobile clients, because they usually have devices with limited processing power and low bandwidth data communications.

In ARMOLEO, CARIME is designed to implement adaptation as a server-side solution. In this way, the diverse mobile devices of the learners, as clients, do not require any additional processing or resources for the adaptation process.

DESCRIBING MOBILE DEVICES CHARACTERISTICS

Mobile devices are in constant innovation, and the number and variety of these devices grows constantly. In order to be able to adapt contents to mobile devices it is necessary to describe essential device characteristics.

The Device Independence Working Group of the W3C organization (2003), consider the following features to describe mobile devices:

- Screen Size and Resolution
- Color capability
- Video capability
- Audio capability
- Input capabilities

Georgieva and Georgiev (2007) propose the following characteristics to model mobile devices for content adaptation processes:

- Screen resolution.
- Screen mode (portrait or landscape).
- Supported markup and script languages.
- Supported multimedia file formats.

They also propose the following ways for the recognition of mobile devices characteristics:

- Analyze the HTTP User-agent information.
- Composite capabilities/Preferences Profiles (CC/PP), which is a description of device capabilities and user preferences aimed to be used to guide the adaptation of content presented to specific devices.
- Wap User Agent Profile (UAPROF).
- Wireless Universal Resource File (WURFL).

In ARMOLEO, we designed CARIME to use HTTP User-agent and CC/PP for device characteristics recognition. In this way, mobile learning objects selected to be delivered to the learner, could be properly adapted to her mobile device characteristics, if mobile device features allow it.

MOBILE LEARNING OBJECTS FOR SECOND LANGUAGE LEARNING

The objective of second language learning is to develop communicative competences that imply to enhance listening, reading, writing and speaking abilities in the students. In our current research, we are developing mobile learning objects to support the second language learning of Japanese (Ayala et al., 2010)

A language pattern is the appropriate combination of different types of words: nouns, verbs, etc., for construction of correct sentences following grammar rules. An expression is a combination of words with a specific meaning and communicative intention which does not follow grammar rules. We consider words, language patterns and expressions as the fundamental knowledge elements for communicative situations. Speech acts are uttering expressions performed in accordance with certain constitutive rules. Searle (1969) states that "speaking a language is performing speech acts, such as making statements, giving commands, asking questions, making promises, and so on".

For second language learning activities, we consider words, grammar patterns and expressions as the fundamental units of learning contents, and we use speech acts to describe communicative situations.

Mobile learning objects for language learning are aimed to provide:

- Learning activities for vocabulary acquisition.
- Learning activities for grammar rules acquisition.
- Learning activities for expressions acquisition.
- Collaborative construction of dialogues.
- Collaborative development of multimedia learning objects.

For language learning, we consider the use of mobile learning objects from two perspectives of use:

1. Just in time knowledge, providing vocabulary, grammar rules and expression support in communicative situations.
2. Simulated Learning activities, which correspond to authentic activities wherever and whenever the learner wants to perform them.

We consider vocabulary learning objects as elemental learning objects. In GRACILE, Ayala (1996) organized vocabulary in dictionaries, and classified words in the following categories: place, thing, abstract, animal, and grammar particle. We propose the following categories for vocabulary learning objects classification:

*   Animals

*   Family and social relations
*   Names
*   Not living things
*   Numbers
*   Places
*   Plants

The Center for Advanced Research on Language Acquisition (CARLA) of the University of Minnesota, classifies speech acts in the following categories:

*   Apologies, for example, I am sorry.
*   Complaints, for example, I was harassed by a police officer.
*   Compliments/Responses, for example, you look great!
*   Refusals, for example, no thanks!
*   Requests, for example, Can I just take …?
*   Thanks.

Figure 5. Prototype of a vocabulary midlet. a) Asking the meaning of the word cat, category Animals, b) Showing the meaning with options to play the pronunciation and to view the writing.

(a)
Asking meaning midlet

(b)
Showing meaning midlet

We propose the following categories for communicative situations:

1. Request, for example:
   ◦ Positive request (Please go)
   ◦ Negative request (Please don't go).
2. Inform, for example:
   ◦ Refusal (I will not go)
   ◦ Acceptance (I will go)
   ◦ Positive inform if (If I go…)
3. Others, for example:
   ◦ Proposal (let's go)
   ◦ Explanation (I go because…)

Figure 5 a shows the prototype of a midlet to ask for vocabulary support, and Figure 5b shows the response, where we can see the options to play the pronunciation and to view the writing of the meaning.

CONCLUSION

Content adaptation in mobile learning objects implies both user adaptation and device adaptation. It requires additional metadata categories in comparison with SCORM 2004. For user adaptation, the Knowledge Metadata category allows the personalization of contents according to the learner interests, and the Use metadata category is included in order to register the history of use of the mobile learning object (knowledge awareness) in diverse situations. In order to determine the requirements for device adaptation, the Mobile Device Requirements metadata is also necessary.

In ARMOLEO, CARIME is the software component responsible for device adaptation. CARIME is designed to use transcoding as the method to adapt the images format and/or resizing them to fit the characteristics of the particular mobile device screen. Other method for device adaptation that CARIME applies is transrating, used to change the bit-rate of media content to suit the device characteristics.

The implementation of adaptation is as a server-side solution. In this way, the diverse mobile devices of the learners, as clients, do not require any additional processing or resources for the adaptation process. We propose to use HTTP User-agent and CC/PP for device characteristics recognition. In this way, mobile learning objects selected to be delivered to the learner can be properly adapted to the characteristics of the specific mobile device.

We have developed ALMA Packager with the aim to facilitate the assembly and metadata specification for mobile learning objects.

Currently we are developing MLOs to support second language learning. We consider words, grammar patterns and expressions as the fundamental units of learning contents, and we use speech acts to describe communicative situations.

REFERENCES

W3C. (2003). W3C Device Independence Working Group. *Authoring Challenges for Device Independence. W3C Working Group. Note 1 September 2003*. Retrieved November 5, 2009, from http://www.w3.org/TR/acdi/

Albayrak, S., Wollny, S., Varone, N., Lommatzsch, A., & Milosevic, D. (2005). Agent technology for personalized information filtering: the PIA system. In *Proceedings of SAC'05,* Santa Fe, NM.

Ayala, G. (1996). *Intelligent Agents for Supporting the Effective Collaboration in a CSCL Environment.* Unpublished doctoral dissertation, Department of Information Science and Intelligent Systems, The University of Tokushima, Japan.

Ayala, G. (2005). An Analytic Model based on ASP for Maintaining ZPDs in CSCL Environments. In Looi, C.-K., Jonassen, D., & Ikeda, M. (Eds.), *Towards Sustainable and Scalable Educational Innovations Informed by the Learning Sciences, Frontiers in Artificial Intelligence and Applications* (pp. 3–10). Amsterdam, The Netherlands: IOS Press.

Ayala, G., & Castillo, S. (2008). Towards Computational Models for Mobile Learning Objects. In *Proceedings of the Fifth IEEE International Conference on Wireless, Mobile, and Ubiquitous Technology in Education* (pp. 153-157). ISBN:978-0-7695-3108-3

Ayala, G., Paredes, R. G., & Castillo, S. (2010). Computational models for mobile and ubiquitous second language learning. *International Journal of Mobile Learning and Organisation, 4*(2), 192–213. doi:10.1504/IJMLO.2010.032636

Berri, J., Benlamri, R., & Atif, Y. (2006). Ontology-based framework for context-aware mobile learning. In *IWCMC '06*, Vancouver, BC, Canada.

Campbell, L. (2007). Learning Object Metadata (LOM). In S. Ross & M. Day (Eds.), *DCC Digital Curation Manual*. Retrieved November 5, 2009, from http://www.dcc.ac.uk/resource/curation-manual/chapters/learning-object-metadata

CARLA. Center for Advanced Research on Language Acquisition, University of Minnesota. (2008, December 15). *Descriptions of Speech Acts*. Retrieved from http://www.carla.umn.edu/speechacts/descriptions.html

Castillo, S., & Ayala, G. (2007). Towards Mobile Learning Objects: Learning Approaches, Awareness and Computational Models. In *Proceedings of the 15th International Conference on Computers in Education*, Hiroshima, Japan.

Castillo, S., & Ayala, G. (2008). ARMOLEO: An Architecture for Mobile Learning Objects. In *Proceedings of the 18th International Conference on Electronics, Communications and Computers (conielecomp 2008)*, Cholula, Puebla, México. ISBN: 978-0-7695-3120-5

Castillo, S., & Ayala, G. (2008b). A personalization Model for Learning Objects in Mobile Learning Environments. In *Proceedings of the 16th International Conference on Computers in Education (ICCE 2008)*, Taiwan. Retrieved October 11, 2009, from http://www.apsce.net/ICCE2008/papers/ICCE2008-paper137.pdf

Chan, T., Sharples, M., Vavoula, G., & Londsdale, P. (2004). Educational Metadata for Mobile Learning. In *Proceedings of the 2nd IEEE International Workshop on Wireless and Mobile Technologies in Education (WMTE '04)* (p. 197).

Colajanni, M., & Lancellotti, R. (2004). *System architectures for Web content adaptation services, Web Systems Invited Article, IEEE Distributed Systems Online*. Retrieved October 11, 2009, from http://dsonline.computer.org/portal/site/dsonline/menuitem.9ed3d9924aeb0dcd82ccc6716bbe36ec/index.jsp?&pName=dso_level1&path=dsonline/topics/was&file=adaptation.xml&xsl=article.xsl&

Farhan, M., & Abawajy, J. (2008). *A classification for Content Adaptation System*. In *Proceedings of iiWAS 2008*, Linz, Austria.

Friesen, N., Roberts, A., & Fisher, S. (2002). CanCore: Learning Object Metadata. *Canadian Journal of Learning and Technology, 28*(3).

Frost & Sullivan. (2006). *Research overview of Strategic Insight into Mobile Content Adaptation Markets - Porting with Transcoding and Rendering.* Retrieved October 11, 2009, from http://www.marketresearch.com/product/display.asp?productid=1327087

Georgevia, E., & Gerogiev, T. (2007). *Methodology for mobile devices characteristics recognition.* Paper presented at the International Conference on Computer Systems and Technologies.

Katz, H. A., & Worsham, S. (2005). Streaming mLearning Objects via data resolution and web services to mobile devices: design guidelines and system architecture model. In *Proceedings of the MLEARN 2005*, Cape Town, South Africa. Retrieved November 5, 2009, from http://www.mlearn.org.za/CD/papers/Katz%20&%20Worsham.pdf

Lastein, L., & Reul, B. (2003). *Transrating Efficiency -- Bit-rate reduction methods to enable more services over existing bandwidth.* Retrieved November 5, 2009, from http://www.broadcastpapers.com/whitepapers/IBCBarconetTransratingEfficiency.pdf?CFID=37604273&CFTOKEN=42a178598bba5024-FC0BFE9E-0F72-5D57-AEB8738937907188

Leone, N., Pfeifer, G., Faber, W., Eiter, T., Gottlob, G., Perri, S., & Scarcello, F. (2002). *The DLV System for Knowledge Representation and Reasoning* (Tech. Rep. No. cs.AI/0211004). arXiv.org. Retrieved April 14, 2008, from http://www.dbai.tuwien.ac.at/proj/dlv/#publications

Searle, J. R. (1969). *Speech Acts, an Essay in the Philosophy of Language.* New York: Cambridge University Press.

Shi, H., Revithis, S., & Chen, S. S. (2002). An agent enabling personalized learning in e-Learning Environments. In *Proceedings of the AAMAS'02*, Bologna, Italy.

Silvester, I. (2006). *Transcoding: The future of the Video Market Depends on It* (IDC Executive Brief). Retrieved October 15, 2009, from http://www.edchina.com/ARTICLES/2006NOV/2/2006NOV10_HA_AVC_HN_12.PDF

Tang, R. (2008). *Mobile Content Adaptation. Product Marketing Dilithium Networks.* Retrieved October 11, 2009, from http://www.dilithiumnetworks.com/pdfs/white_papers/MKT_ART_MobileContentAdaptation.pdf

This work was previously published in the International Journal of Multimedia Data Engineering and Management, Volume 1, Issue 4, edited by Shu-Ching Chen, pp. 1-15, copyright 2010 by IGI Publishing (an imprint of IGI Global).

Chapter 15
Board Game Supporting Learning Prim's Algorithm and Dijkstra's Algorithm

Wen-Chih Chang
Chung Hua University, Taiwan

Te-Hua Wang
Chihlee Institute of Technology, Taiwan

Yan-Da Chiu
Chung Hua University, Taiwan

ABSTRACT

The concept of minimum spanning tree algorithms in data structure is difficult for students to learn and to imagine without practice. Usually, learners need to diagram the spanning trees with pen to realize how the minimum spanning tree algorithm works. In this paper, the authors introduce a competitive board game to motivate students to learn the concept of minimum spanning tree algorithms. They discuss the reasons why it is beneficial to combine graph theories and board game for the Dijkstra and Prim minimum spanning tree theories. In the experimental results, this paper demonstrates the board game and examines the learning feedback for the mentioned two graph theories. Advantages summarizing the benefits of combining the graph theories with board game are discussed.

INTRODUCTION

Game based learning (GBL) is a kind of serious games serving for special educational purposes, such as management, politics, city planning, defense and skill training. GBL is mainly comprised of learning content, strategies and even

the learning outcome. Generally GBL aims to cultivate learners' ability for specific educational purposes to apply the methods, strategies and attitude to the real world. Games often include interesting, interactive and fantasy elements to engage players in a learning activity through the predefined storylines.

Computer games have become an integral part of the popular culture in modern societies.

DOI: 10.4018/978-1-4666-1791-9.ch015

Moreover, "game-based learning" is the latest buzz word in the computer science educational curriculum. Research (Feldgen & Clua, 2004) shows that students today have a totally different way of learning – react more to interactive learning. If they are not entertained while they learn, the instructor has lost them. However, much of content that needs to be learned by students today lacks of motivation to them. The word "boring", "dry" and "too technical" often crosses their lips (Prensky, 2003). Finally, it leads to frustration. A good game helps students to enhance their learning techniques, such as learning by doing, learning from mistakes, goal-oriented learning, discovery learning, task-based learning, question-led learning, and etc (Din, 2006). Although game-based learning has been made a good progress in academic research (Squire et al., 2002), using computer games for educational purposes has been rather uncommon. Although learning by playing has been reported to education (Roussou, 2004), nevertheless, it is still less popular in post-elementary education.

Some educational researches discuss game based learning in various application domains, such as discovery learning, learning pyramid and learning by doing. Discovery Learning belongs to the inquiry-based instruction which is considered as a constructivist based approach to education. Learners can draw their own experience and prior knowledge by discovering and solving problems. Students interact with their environment by exploring and manipulating objects, brain storming with questions and arguments with peers, or performing experiments. Although Ausubel and Robinson (1969) have found that discovery learning not the best learning method, especially when there is no deliberate design in learning activities. Dole (1954) proposed teaching methods in audio-visual media. Another similar theory which is called learning pyramid also mentioned how people memorize knowledge. More concrete learning activities leave more memory for people. People learned 75% from what they learned in practical action. People learned 50% from what they learned

in group discussion. People learned 30% from what they learned when they see a demonstration. People learned 20% from what they learned from audio-visual. People learned 10% from what they learned from reading. People learned 5% from what they learned from lecture. Learning-by-doing is a concept of economic theory. It refers to the capability of workers to improve their productivity by regularly repeating the same type of action. The increased productivity is achieved through practice, self-perfection and minor innovations.

GBL assists teachers with changing their teaching functions. It provides an attractive and practical learning environment. In GBL, students have to deal with challenging tasks or missions themselves. After completing the assigned task, learners can get encouragement or reward according to the game rules. This is also the most important motivation for students. However even though there exist quite a lot of benefits brought by GBL, but we still can find the weakness of GBL. For example, instructors have to arrange the learning materials precisely to each leaner according to individual ability, and this is hard for instructors to make the general game rules.

The organization of this paper is as follows. First, related techniques are introduced followed by a description of the three minimum spanning tree algorithms. Next, the board game "Ticket to Ride" is demonstrated showing the ways of combining graph theories with the board game "Ticket to Ride". Then the difference between our work and other researchers are compared. Finally, we discuss the experimental result and the analysis of learning performance followed by a conclusion.

RELATED WORK

GBL makes learning more interesting and attractive, but not all of the games make learning effectively. Van Eck (2006) mentioned card game, *Jeopardy*-style game, Arcade-style game and

Adventure game are suitable for learners in some learning situations. Card game makes students compare and match the concepts and recognize the abstract concept. Arcade-style games are likely to promote the response speed and visual processing. Adventure games makes people learning hypothesis the situation and problem solving in some specific events. Some games need blended strategies to compete with others.

Games motivate players and let players experience and challenge various situations. Players can play different roles in games (Gee, 2003), such as the producers or the consumers in games. Players grow up at initial level and learn complex skill, knowledge and conquer obstacles to raise their levels.

Prensky (2003) pointed out digital game based learning makes kids learn without pressure, provide more opportunities to gather information from games and complete missions or make decisions. Some games support simulation environment for players to understand complex concept, to simulate real life, and to create ideas and strategies to overcome difficulties. diSessa (2000) mentioned motivation is the key factor to drive learning. Motivation leads learning and playing. Students keep learning and playing when motivation increases.

Problem-based game cultivates learners' problem solving skill. Learners can experience from the problem solving in the game. Natvig and Line (2004) applied an on-line game that consists of computer history knowledge. Learners have to answer different types of computer history and evolution questions. The result shows learners were willing to spend more time on this game and 95% learners increase the motivation better than traditional teaching. Makansi (2001) designed a board game for learners to realize the nuclear power plant construction, which includes planning, employee recruit, equipment purchase and employee training. Peitz, Björk, and Jäppinen (2006) designed a Wizard's Apprentice board game, and they found computer supported board game is more attractive than traditional board game. Bekir, Cable, Hashimoto, and Katz (2001) propose the board game integrating Engineering Ethics. The research shows this kind of teaching environment could be applied to wider age than traditional teaching. Learners will not feel bored to lower the learning motivation. Game promotes learning motivation and assists learners to establish the Engineering Ethics.

Lots of card games applied in education could be found in many GBL researches. And some equipment was utilized to strengthen the authenticity of the card game. Diaz, Moisies, Lourdes, and Isaac (2006) designed a networked virtual card game for multiple users. It used some devices to bring learners in visual environment augmented with the reality. Learners can use this device anywhere when the internet connection is available. At the same year, Lam, Chow, Yau, and Lyu (2006) proposed a technique to enhance existing trading card game. It used visual device to support prototyping to increase the practicability of card game. According to players' input, the system identifies and then responses. The game can retain the original playing rules and style. In 2005, Katayose and Imanishi developed a trading card game based on augmented reality technology (ART). Learners can gain experience with the device on their arms.

For educational card game, Baker, Navarro, and Hoek (2003) and Baker, Navarro, and Hoek (2005) designed a card game which helps learners to gain the experience about software process in class. Learners who studied this course lacked effective experience in the past. In addition, Carrington (2005) devised a physical card game "Problems and Programmers (PnP)" which is a competitive card game in 2002. The game's rules and methods are based on Waterfall model. This game allows learners to find out the procedure of Waterfall through the game. The trouble and tool in game can make learners study in progressive methods. Learners gain practical experience from the competitive and interesting game.

In addition to software engineering domain, Chandra et al. (2006) designed a financial trading market simulating card game. Learners can use it to simulate trading environment. One player who serves as the marketing and sales director role uses different market tactics, marketing and stock option to obtain the largest profit as the goal. Another player who acts as the businessman in the market buys products and sells it according to the market manager's market tactics. This game simulates marketing and sales director and businessmen's tactics that aim at market environment and strategy. Another subject is about object-oriented thinking learning, Kim et al. (2006) designed Smalltalk Card Game (SCG). Students can experience and understand Object Oriented concepts by expending basic rules of game.

Traditional teaching approach cannot always keep students' engagement, not even an hour – certainly no shouting with glee at their successes and no desire to overcome their failures (Prensky, 2003). It is because there is no fun in the formal teaching. Draper (1999) suggests that fun is associated with playing for pleasure with the sake of freedom of choice. Carroll (2004) summaries "fun" as "Things are fun when they attract, capture, and hold our attention by provoking new or unusual emotions in contexts that typically arouse none, or arousing emotion not typically aroused in a given context."

To provide an engaging learning environment, keeping students' attention by providing fun should be a considerable way. Edutainment may be a solution for teaching computer programming courses. Baker et al. (2003) and Baker et al. (2005) developed an educational card game to help students who gained little practical experience in software process. Alex, who made software engineering course more practical by using card game, tried to overcome the limitation by providing a simulation of the software process.

There is also physical card game, named "Problems and Programmers (PnP)", which is invented by Carrington et al. (2005). PnP is a competitive

physical card game to help students to understand software engineering. This game simulates the process from requirements specification to product delivering. Kaur and Haar (2005) used the fuzzy logic to simulate the card game called "Euchre". Chang and Chen (2007) designed an operation system process card game to assist learners to gain practical experience. Learners will challenge the task to fulfill the requirements and modify their play tactics. Another subject is regarding object-oriented thinking learning. Kim et al. (2006) designed Smalltalk Card Game (SCG). Participants can experience and understand Object Oriented concepts by extending basic rules of game.

Virtual reality technology is utilized as a modern tool for fun learning of Physics Biology and Molecular Biology (Amon, 2006; Lu, Liu, & Yao, 2003). Currently, researchers begin to consider the edutainment approach to teach programming course. Rajaravivarma (2005) proposed a game-based approach for teaching the introductory programming course. He used two broad categories of game, word games and number games, in his course materials. The course started from some simple games containing basic programming skill and additional programming skills were required through the course progress. However, these two games are text-based without interaction and even the background music. Goschnick and Balbo (2005) aimed to motivate students by giving assignments of 2D board game such as *Snakes and Ladders*, *Ludo* and *Checker* for the Information System students. However, those students had to firstly learn the SG_Board library (Goschnick, 1992) and then they could deliver the assignment. SG_Board Library is a generic board game class developed in Java language. Their approach looks like a game programming course, but not an introductory programming course. The board games supported by the library are mainly for the primary school students to play. Therefore, students who take the course may not really enjoy the game that they have developed. Nevison and Wells (2004) presented a case study based on a maze as an example that provided a complex framework to teach an introduction course in Computer Science. They found that using different structures for maze could be a rich source for illustrating design patterns. They claimed that one of the authors had used this concept in an introductory Java programming class with great success. Lam et al. (2003) proposed a prototype of the Augmented Reality Table for card games to enhance existing trading card games. With the support of visual input devices, the game remained the original playing style and rules. The system identified players' input commands. Katayose and Imanishi (2005) developed an enhanced and virtual trading card game involved with Augmented Reality technologies. Players can experience battles with the equipment on their arms.

With respect to computer sciences, graph theories are important. There are many computer science's concepts relate with graph theory, and many researchers try to combine these science concepts to games. For example, we can connect the concept of network and Prim's minimum spanning tree (Grimald, 1994), or link the graph and the concept of searching (Lim, 2007). Knowledge related to the graph theories in computer science is quite useful. It helps to describe some virtual concepts, like network connection. Among various graph theories, the concept of minimum spanning tree is mostly utilized. And, in this work, we choose the minimum spanning tree theories as our targeted concepts.

Accordingly, how to make student to learn graph theories more efficiently and arise the learning interest are the key essentials to computer science. In order to increase the learning interest, using board game to help learning is a good method. Accordingly, we combine the board game "Ticket to Ride" with well-known graph theories, including Dijkstra's and Prim's minimum spanning tree. In addition to some existed rules, we add and create some considerable rules in the game. As

a result, students are able to use this board game to understand the graph theories more efficiently with higher learning interest.

In the early age, games were just played for fun, especially the board game. Over the years, computer knowledge and technologies are rapidly developed, and accordingly, computer science becomes an important science nowadays. Many researches tried to find the ways to combine computer science learning activity with board game. For example, Henney and Agbinya (2005) used board game to explain the idea about mobile connection. And Steve Goschnick and Sandrine Balbo (2005) linked programming to board games.

From the viewpoints of these researchers, they found the most efficient way to combine computer sciences and board game is to demonstrate the network or graph theory on board game. For example, Komisarczuk and Welch (2006) used board game to teach the internet engineering. Darren Lim (2007) shows the graph theory on the board game. Using games can help teaching computer sciences much more efficiently, especially in teaching graph theory or network concepts on board games. It can use the materiality of board games to describe the virtual of graph theories and network well. In this paper, we target at three graph theories, including the Dijkstra's, Prim's, and Kruskal's minimum spanning tree, with the board game "Ticket to Ride".

THE MINIMUM SPANNING TREE ALGORITHMS

A spanning tree is in an undirected graph containing all of the nodes are connected with no loop or cycle. If we give the weight of each edge from one node to another, the minimum spanning tree algorithm is applied to find the least summation of all the paths' weight (Grimald, 1994).

Dijkstra's Minimum Spanning Tree

Dijkstra's minimum spanning tree describes the concept of minimum spanning tree. The theory can be used in teaching network, like the paths of router and router (James & Keith, 2004). It goes from a start node and then begins to run follow steps: 1. Finding the connected node. 2. Calculating the sum of start node to next node. 3. Choosing the least sum of node as start point next round and avoiding account for loop. It will repeat the three steps until finishing the spanning tree (Grimald, 1994).

Prim's Minimum Spanning Tree

Similar to Dijkstra's minimum spanning tree, the Prim's minimum spanning tree has a start node too. It can be also used in the same knowledge domain in network. After choosing a start node, it finishes the minimum spanning tree by repeating the follow steps: 1. Finding the connected nodes. 2. Choosing the least weight of paths to next node, and avoiding account for loop (Grimald, 1994). After repeating the two steps, a Prim's minimum spanning tree is created.

Kruskal's Minimum Spanning Tree

Unlike the two mentioned theories of minimum spanning tree, the Kruskal's minimum spanning tree needn't a start node. The point is selected according to the least weight of paths and avoiding account for the loop. It finishes the minimum spanning tree by repeating two steps: 1. Choosing the least weight path. 2. Connecting the nodes and avoiding the loop (Grimald, 1994). The concept can be used in network, too.

"TICKET TO RIDE"-ORIGINAL GAME

"Ticket to Ride" is a board game, containing the city name and tracks from one city to another. The maps in "Ticket to Ride" are various, including Europe, South America, and Portugal etc. An example of the board is shown in Figure 1.

The main ideas of this game are: 1.Players can choose the mission about connects one city to another, and try to finish the mission to get points. 2. Players have to use their source in hand much more efficiently. 3. There are game plans in the game, such as setting the plans to interrupt others to finish the assigned missions. During playing the game, players get points by finishing missions or building the longest tracks. Player who gets the highest points is the winner, and frankly speaking, this is a game of deceit.

THE DESIGN OF COMBINING MINIMUM SPANNING TREE THEORIES AND TICKET TO RIDE

In the section we updated some rules from the original, and made a new edition of board game "Ticket to Ride". The new edition of Ticket to ride is combined with the concept of board game Ticket to Ride and three minimum spanning tree theories: the Dijkstra, Prim, and Kruskal's minimum spanning tree.

Necessary Properties of the Game

In this game, a set of components is needed to set up the game environment, including:

1. Railway map (We use Portugal railway map as an example in Figure 1)
2. Starting Point Card (It presents the start point of each player)
3. Ticket Card (It indicates the link from Start point station to Destination station, and the score after the player completed the route)
4. Knowledge Card (It identifies which algorithm is applied on the railway stations and the completed score. The related algorithms include the Dijkstra's algorithm for the short-

Figure 1. A sketch of competition players' interface

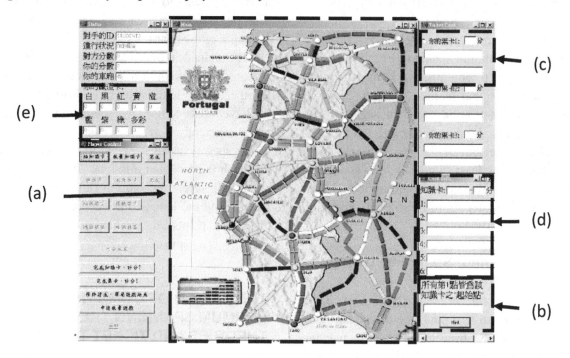

est path algorithm, and Prim's algorithm for the minimum spanning tree.

5. Railway Card (Each section railway of the map has a specific color which is composed of white, black, red, yellow, orange, blue, purple, green and full-color.) Each player has 45 railway carriages with its special color. The Number of each color card (white, black, red, yellow, orange, blue, purple, green) are thirty five, and the number of full-color is fifteen.

The Limitation of this Game

The limitations of this game includes the follows,

1. Players range: 2-3 players
2. End conditions of single round game:
    a. When one of the players ran out of the 45 railway carriages
    b. When one of the players cannot put his/her railway carriages

c. When one of the players reached scores over 150

3. Completed conditions of the entire game: (A game consists of two single round games.)
    a. When one of the players reached scores over 300
    b. When one of the players completed all the three knowledge card missions which involved Dijkstra and Prim algorithms. The winner has to complete each knowledge card.

4. All the players have to learn the related knowledge about the shortest path algorithm and minimum spanning tree.

Game Progress

In our proposed "Ticket to Ride" board game, we fixed some rules based on original rules because of our ideal – combining the board game and three minimum spanning tree theories. The progress is similar to the original game. The main difference between new and old edition games is that we gave the new game an additional element. The element is the concept of start location and minimum spanning tree theories cards. First, players should cast a start point and knowledge card. After casting start point and knowledge cards, players begin to a single turn.

In the single turn, players can do four steps:

1. Draw two of the railway cards or choose one which is opened directly.
2. Draw three of the 3 ticket cards, and reserve the selected ticket.
3. Re-cast new start point card and knowledge cards.
4. Put the railway carriages on the map to establish the route. Players also can skip the step if there is no available condition.

In principle, the game will repeat these four steps until a player reach the end conditions of a single round game. The game progress is demonstrated in Figure 2.

Game Regulations

The game regulations are set as the follows.

1. The station recorded in the start point card has to match the stations in the knowledge card; otherwise the player cannot play the game (as shown in Table 1).
2. Regulations of drawing the railway card:
   a. Railway card color: white, black, red, yellow, orange, blue, purple, green, full-color.

Figure 2. Single round for each player

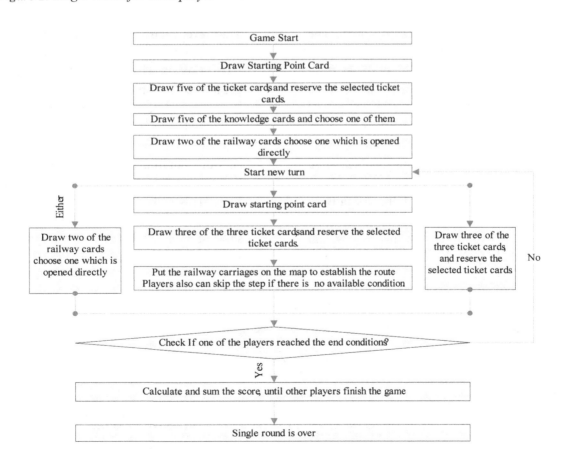

b. In the beginning of each round, the railway cards are divided into two piles. One is composed of five opened cards and the other is covered pile of cards.

c. When drawing the cards, each player can either select two cards from the covered pile of cards or select the card from five opened cards. In other words, player can get the preferable card which is opened.

3. Players can give up the knowledge card in hands, and player's score will be detected according to the card. Then the player proceeds game from the starting point.

4. After the player completed one knowledge card, player can decide if he/she will continue draw the next knowledge card.

5. Establish the player's railway routes:

a. The color of the railway card and spaces of the map routes are matched, and then the railway cards can occupy the routes of the railway map. The full-color card can occupy any color routes on the map. For example, there are three white spaces on the route [BRAGANCA-BENAVENTE], and the player can occupy the route with the combination of the three railway cards. The first one contains three white railway cards, the second one contains two white and one full-color railway cards, the third one contains one white and two full-color railway cards, and the last contains three full-color railway

cards. The other card combinations are useless in such cases.

b. Grey route is available for all colors. For example, there are three grey spaces on the route [BRAGANCA-SALAMANCA], and any kind of the colors of railway cards are acceptable, such as two orange and one red railway cards.

c. The quantity of the railway cards and spaces of the map routes are matched, and then the railway cards can occupy the routes of the railway map.

d. If the route of the map is occupied, this route cannot be used anymore.

Score Rules

The score rules of this game are listed as follows:

1. The player gains 10 points if the player used the most railway carriages.

2. If the ticket card is completed, the player will get the score on the card. On the contrary, the score will be deducted if the player did not complete the ticket card.

3. The score of ticket card is calculated by the shortest path from starting point to destination. For instance, the route, [VALENCA-VERIN] is with the shortest path "3" and the route [VALENCA-BRAGA] is with the shortest path "2". Other routes follow the same rules for calculating the shortest path.

Table 1. Example of choosing start point card and knowledge card

The starting point card player owned	The recorded linked stations on the knowledge card	Result
VERIN	VALENCA, BRAGA, CHAVES, VILA REAL, BRAGANCA	Useless knowledge card
VERIN	VALENCA,BRAGA, CHAVES, VERIN, BRAGANCA	Usable knowledge card

Table 2. Example of accomplish Knowledge cards and ticket cards

Connected Railway Stations	Knowledge	Partial Score	Completed Score
VALENCA,VERIN,BENAVENTE,BRAGANCA,CHAVES,BRAGA, PORTO	Dijkstra's algorithm	spaces number of the route*3	14
VALENCA,VERIN,BENAVENTE,BRAGANCA,CHAVES,BRAGA, PORTO	Prim's algorithm	spaces number of the route *2	14
VALENCA,VERIN,BENAVENTE,BRAGANCA,CHAVES,BRAGA	Prim's algorithm	spaces number of the route *2	12

4. The knowledge card score consists of two parts; the first one gains partial score when the player completed part of the answer route, and the other gains full score when the player completed all the answer routes. Example can be found in Table 2.

In order to encourage the player, high scores were given to the players who follow the correct algorithm. We give an example of Dijkstra's algorithm in Table 2. When the player completed one edge of the answer route and the order of establishing the railway carriages is exactly the same as the Dijkstra's algorithm, the player will get the score with three times of the spaces number of the edge. The edge from VALENCA to VERIN has 3 spaces of railway carriage and scores 9 points (i.e., 3*3).

The full score is based on the railway stations in the knowledge card. After players completed the card in correct order of the algorithm and then players get the full score.

COMPARISON

In this section, we compare our work with traditional education and Darren Lim's theory (2007), respectively from various viewpoints as shown in Table 3. After the comparison, we can clearly find the advantages in teaching minimum spanning tree theories with combining the board game. These advantages are:

1. **Efficiency in learning:** Students can practically manipulate the board game with various types of cards to realize the minimum spanning tree theories.

2. **Interest in learning:** Due to the essence of game element, students can learn knowledge

Table 3. Comparison with traditional Education and Teaching combining board game

	Traditional Education	Teaching minimum spanning tree theories combining board game	Darren Lim 's theory
Efficiency in learning	Teachers' ability effect the level of efficiency in learning.	Students can clarify their learning problem with game.	Students can clarify their learning problem with game.
Interest in learning	Hard to let student interested in learning.	Easier to make students interested in learning.	Easier to make students interested in learning.
Students' feeling in learning spanning three theories.	Abstract	Easier to catch the theories	Easier to catch the theories
Prepare before learning	None	Students have to contact this kind of knowledge before.	Students have to contact this kind of knowledge before.
Usable computer science	All computer sciences	Graph theory	Programming, Data Structure, Graph Theory

Table 4. Comparison with Darren Lim's theory

	Teaching minimum spanning tree theories combining board game	**Darren Lim's theory**
If the ideal is computerized?	On cybernation	Not mentioned
How to teach these concepts?	With clear and definite rules to express concepts	Abstract ideal and no detailed description
Usable range in computer science	Only in graph theory	Not only in graph theory, but also in data structure and programming

in an interesting manner. In most cases, playing game is always more attractive than just reading the textbooks in the classroom.

On the other hand, there is a point to note while teaching minimum spanning tree theories with combining the board game. Students have to hold the prerequisite knowledge regarding the main concepts so that they can use the game to help learning. This is also a considerable problem to the Darren Lim's theory.

By comparing our work with Darren Lim's theory, we found Darren Lim's theory is more popular and is utilized widely in computer science. But if we dig further, some concrete ideas were found from the comparison.

In Table 4, we compare our ideal with Darren Lim's theory from the viewpoints of "how to implement", "usable range", and "if the ideal is computerized". We found that the main characteristic of Darren Lim's theory is the extensibility. The Darren Lim's theory can be applied to various domains easily. On the other hand, our ideal will be better while having a clear and definite way to implement it.

EXPERIMENT

Two experiments were designed to evaluate the effectiveness of the proposed system. Experiment 1 applied a pretest-posttest design to evaluate the learning effectiveness for learning Dijkstra and Prim algorithm in the proposed system. Experi-

ment 2 was designed to evaluate the users' subjective attitudes toward the proposed system. The first experiment comprised four computing questions, two Dijkstra algorithm questions and two Prim algorithm questions. Students have sufficient time to solve the questions. We recorded the solving time of the two algorithms. In experiment 1, the hypotheses were listed for the pretest and posttest.

Hypothesis 0: There is no significant difference between the pretest and posttest in Learning Dijkstra algorithm.

Hypothesis 1: There is no significant difference between the pretest and posttest in Learning Prim algorithm.

The experimental results of the pretest and posttest are listed in Table 5. Thirty students attended the pretest and posttest. After the pretest, students use the proposed system to compete with other students and play this system for thirty minutes. Then students attend the posttest consisted of two Hypothesis questions. We applied SPSS (Statistical Package for Social Science) to analyze the difference of the pretest and posttest.

Table 5. Descriptive statistics of pretest and posttest in Learning Dijkstra and Prim algorithm

		No. of subjects	**Mean (Average time for solving problems)**	**S.D.**
Learning Dijkstra	Pretest	30	859.7	447.7
	Posttest	30	331.2	219.2
Learning Prim	Pretest	30	360.5	271.8
	Posttest	30	214.3	121.0

Table 6. Pretest-Posttest of solving problem with Dijkstra algorithm

	N	Lower CL Mean	Mean	Upper CL Mean	Lower CL Std Dev
Difference	30	397.92	528.8	659.68	279.13
	Std Dev	Upper CL Std Dev	Std Err	DF	t Value
	350.49	471.17	63.991	29	8.26
	Pr > |t|(p value)	P<0.05 Reject H0			
	<.0001				

Table 7. Pretest-Posttest of solving problem with Prim algorithm

	N	Lower CL Mean	Mean	Upper CL Mean	Lower CL Std Dev
Difference	30	59.789	146.17	232.54	184.23
	Std Dev	Upper CL Std Dev	Std Err	DF	t Value
	231.32	310.97	42.234	29	3.46
	Pr > |t|(pvalue)	P<0.05 Reject H1			
	0.0017				

Based on the analysis result listed in Table 6 and Table 7, both Hypothesis 0 and Hypothesis 2 are rejected. The result shows the learning performance in the posttest is better than the pretest. The proposed system is helpful to learners when learning Dijkstra algorithm and Prim algorithm.

Experiment 2 was designed to evaluate the learner's attitudes toward our system. Participants in Experiment 2 were asked to browse learning content using our system and competed with other players. The participants in Experiment 2 consisted of 30 Information Management major college students who are 63.33% male and 36.67% female in the same university. There are 20% students spent 2 to 5 hours per week, 33.33% 5 to 8 hours and 46.67% students spend up to 8 hours per week. Only 6.67% students have the experience of playing similar game like the proposed system. After they played the system and completed the game with other classmates, they were asked to fill in an attitude and usefulness questionnaire. The development of the questionnaire was designed based on Likert's five-point scale with "five" being strongly agree and "one"

being strongly disagree. The purpose of the questionnaire was to evaluate the learner's attitudes toward the proposed system.

The attitude questionnaire involves twenty items which were divided into four constructs: perceived ease of use (four items), perceived usefulness (six items), intention and attitude to use (five items) and feel interested to use this tool (five items). The attitude questionnaire is constructed by referring the research of Lu et al. (2003). Perceived ease of use referred to users feel easy to use this system. Perceived usefulness referred to users feels the system is useful when learning Dijkstra algorithm and Prim algorithm. Attitude to use referred to users satisfied the con-

Table 8. The Cronbach α of the system's questionnaire

Constructs	Cronbach α	No. of items
Perceived ease of use	0.671	4
Perceived usefulness	0.710	6
Attitude to use	0.838	5
Feel interested to use	0.737	5

tent and the system. Intention to use referred to users who want to use this system to learn Dijkstra algorithm and Prim algorithm. Feel interested to use this tool referred to users who feel interested in using this system. This system motivates the learner to learn the related concepts.

The questionnaire reliability was checked with Cronbach's α method. The detailed result of the questionnaire showed in Table 8 with high reliabilities (Cronbach's a values: 0.671 for perceived ease of use, 0.710 for perceived usefulness, 0.838 for intention to use, and 0.737 for feel interested to use this tool).

CONCLUSION

Competition motivates learner to study, and computer board game provides solid and clear procedure for the algorithms. Learners can practice the complex algorithms again and again. Learners can see other players' score in real-time graph movement in the system. Interactive feedback and multimedia board game motivates learners. According to the experiment results of pretest and posttest, this system can improve the learner's learning performance. We believe that the proposed system is helpful for students to learn and realize the minimum spanning tree theories. Learners can learn these minimum spanning tree concepts in an efficient way with no more pressure. If the idea – combining the board game "Ticket to Ride" with minimum spanning tree theories can be cybernated, the process of learning activity would be much easier and the learning efficiency would be getting much higher.

ACKNOWLEDGMENT

We would like to thank National Science Council and Chung Hua University. This research was supported in part by a grant from NSC 98-2511-S-216-002 and CHU 98-2511-S-216-002, Taiwan, Republic of China. This paper owes much to the thoughtful and helpful comments of the reviewers.

REFERENCES

Ausubel, D. P., & Robinson, F. G. (1969). *School learning: An introduction to educational psychology*. New York: Holt, Rinehart & Winston.

Baker, A., Navarro, E. O., & Hoek, V. H. A. (2003). Problems and Programmers: an educational software engineering card game. In *Proceedings of the 25th International Conference on Software Engineering* (pp. 614-619).

Baker, A., Navarro, E. O., & Hoek, V. H. A. (2003). An experimental card game for teaching software engineering. In *Proceedings of the 16th Conference on Software Engineering Education and Training* (pp. 216-223).

Baker, A., Navarro, E. O., & Hoek, V. H. A. (2005). An experimental card game for teaching software engineering processes. *Journal of Systems and Software*, 75(1-2), 3–16. doi:10.1016/j.jss.2004.02.033

Bekir, N., Cable, V., Hashimoto, I., & Katz, S. (2001). Teaching engineering ethics: a new approach. In *Proceedings of the 31st Annual Education Conference* (Vol. 1, pp. T2G 1-3).

Carrington, D., Baker, A., & Hoek, V. H. A. (2005). It's All in the Game: Teaching Software Process Concepts. In *Proceedings of the 35th Annual Conference Frontiers in Education* (pp. F4G-13 - F4G-18).

Chandra, N., Herman, B., Kim, Y., Lau, A., Murad, R., Pascarella, W., et al. (2006). A Financial Services Gaming Simulation. In *Proceedings of the IEEE Systems and Information Engineering Design Symposium* (pp. 152-155).

Diaz, M., Moisies, A. M., Lourdes, M. G., & Isaac, R. (2006). Multi-User Networked Interactive Augmented Reality Card Game. In *Proceedings of the International Conference on Cyberworlds* (pp. 172-182).

Din, H. W. H. (2006). Play to Learn: Exploring Online Education Games in Museums. In *Proceedings of the International Conference on Computer Graphics and Interactive Techniques* (No. 13).

diSessa, A. A. (2000). *Changing Minds*. Cambridge, MA: MIT Press.

Dole, E. (1954). *Audio-Visual Methods in Teaching*. New York: The Dryden Press.

Feldgen, M., & Clua, O. (2004). Games as a Motivation for Freshman to Learn Programming. In *Proceedings of the 34th ASEE/IEEE Frontiers in Education Conference* (Vol. 3).

Gee, J. P. (2003). What Video Games Have to Teach Us about Learning and Literacy. *Computers in Entertainment (CIE), 1*(1).

Goschnick, S., & Balbo, S. (2005). Game-first Programming for Information Systems Students. In *Proceedings of the Second Australasian Conference on Interactive Entertainment* (pp. 71-74). Sydney, Australia: Creativity & Cognition Studios Press.

Grimald, R. P. (1994). *Discrete And Combinatorial MatheMatics: An Introduction* (5th ed.). Reading, MA: Addison Wesley.

Henderson, L. (2005). A Significant Cognitive Artifact of Contemporary Youth Culture. In *DiGRA*. Video Games.

Henney, A. J., & Aqbiny, J. I. (2005). Board Games of African Origin on Mobile Phones. In *Proceedings of the Second International Conference on Mobile Technology, Applications and Systems*, Guangzhou, China (pp. 1-8).

James, F. K., & Keith, W. R. (2004). *Computer Networking A Top-Down Approach Featuring the Internet* (3rd ed.). Reading, MA: Addison Wesley.

Katayose, H., & Imanishi, K. (2005). A Trading Card Game using AR Technology. In *ACE* (pp. 354–355). ARMS.

Kim, S. B., Choi, S. K., Jang, H. S., Kwon, D. Y., Yeum, Y. C., & Lee, W. G. (2006). *Smalltalk Card Game for Learning Object-Oriented Thinking in an Evolutionary Way* (pp. 683–684). Portland, OR: OOPSLA.

Komisarczuk, P., & Welch, I. (2006). A Board Game for Teaching Internet Engineering. In *Proceedings of the 8th Austalian conference on Computing education,* Hobart, IN (Vol. 52, pp. 117-123). New York: ACM.

Lam, A. H. T., Chow, K. C. H., Yau, E. H. H., & Lyu, M. R. (2006). ART: Augmented Reality Table for Interactive Trading Card Game. In *Proceedings of the International Conference on Virtual Reality Continuum and Its Applications*, Hong Kong, China (pp. 357-360).

Lim, D. (2007). Taking Students Out for a Ride: Using a Board Game to Teach Graph Theory. In *Proceedings of the 38th SIGCSE technical symposium on Computer science education*, KY (pp. 367-371). New York: ACM.

Lu, J., Yu, C. S., Liu, C., & Yao, J. E. (2003). Technology acceptance model for wireless internet. *Internet Research: Electronic Networking Applications and Policy, 13*(3), 206–222. doi:10.1108/10662240310478222

Makansi, J., & Reactorland. (2001). A board game. *IEEE, 38*(11), 42-43.

Natvig, L., & Line, S. (2004). Age of Computers: An Innovative Combination of History and Computer Game Elements for Teaching Computer Fundamentals. In *Proceedings of FIE 2004, Lasse Natvig, Steinar Line and Djupdal.*

Peitz, J., Björk, S., & Jäppinen, A. (2006). Wizard's apprentice gameplay-oriented design of a computer-augmented board game. In *Proceedings of the ACM SIGCHI international conference on Advances in computer entertainment technology.*

Prensky, M. (2003). Digital game-based learning. *ACM Computers in Entertainment, 1*(1), 1–4.

Rajaravivarma, R. (2005). A Games-Based Approach for Teaching the Introductory Programming Course. *ACM SIGCSE 2005 Bulletin archive, 37*(4).

Roussou, M. (2004). Learning by Doing and Learning Through Play: An Exploration of Interactivity in Virtual Environments for Children. *ACM Computers in Entertainment, 2*(1).

Squire, K., Jenkins, H., & Hinrichs, R. (2002). Games-to-Teach Project: Envisioning the Next Generation of Educational Games. In *Proceedings of the Educational Game Conference*, Edinburgh, Scotland.

Van, E. R. (2006). Digital Game-Based Learning: It's Not Just the Digital Natives Who Are Restless. *EDUCAUSE Review, 41*(2), 16–30.

This work was previously published in the International Journal of Multimedia Data Engineering and Management, Volume 1, Issue 4, edited by Shu-Ching Chen, pp. 16-30, copyright 2010 by IGI Publishing (an imprint of IGI Global).

Chapter 16
Iterative Usability Evaluation for an Online Educational Web Portal

Xin Wang
University of Missouri, USA

DeeAnna Adkins
University of Missouri, USA

Borchuluun Yadamsuren
University of Missouri, USA

George C. Laur
University of Missouri, USA

Anindita Paul
University of Missouri, USA

Andrew Tawfik
University of Missouri, USA

Sanda Erdelez
University of Missouri, USA

ABSTRACT

Online education is a popular paradigm for promoting continuing education for adult learners. However, only a handful of studies have addressed usability issues in the online education environment. Particularly, few studies have integrated the multifaceted usability evaluation into the lifecycle of developing such an environment. This paper will show the integration of usability evaluation into the development process of an online education center. Multifaceted usability evaluation methods were applied at four different stages of the MU Extension web portal's development. These methods were heuristic evaluation, focus group interview and survey, think-aloud interviewing, and multiple-user simultaneous testing. The results of usability studies at each stage enhanced the development team's understanding of users' difficulties, needs, and wants, which served to guide web developers' subsequent decisions.

INTRODUCTION

Online education is the most popular delivery mode of today's distance education. Online education employs multimedia products to improve the effects of teaching and learning and allows learners to participate in various class activities without the boundary of geographic location and time (Richardson & Swan, 2003). This particular form of pedagogy fits well with the increasingly busy lives of learners, especially adult learners who have great motivation to learn but are highly

DOI: 10.4018/978-1-4666-1791-9.ch016

constrained by space and temporal conditions. As such, the landscape of online education is ideal for the promotion of continuing education for adult learners.

Extension units at land-grant universities, a critical arena for expanding higher education, provide a range of scholarly and professional services to state citizens, communities and industries (McLean, 2007). Nowadays, an increasing number of university extension units have adopted various web-based technologies to deliver educational program content, training workshops, credit or non-credit courses, and online degrees to adult learners in order to fulfill students' lifelong learning objectives. University of Missouri Extension (MU Extension), a branch of the land-grant University of Missouri System, is one of these successful examples providing Missourians with a wide range of educational opportunities, informational programs, and materials that are based on university research. In addition, this organization has also employed the distributed learning strategies that use the internet to disseminate educational materials, news stories, video releases, online courses, and reviewed publications in multiple program areas such as agriculture, community development, human environmental sciences, business development, youth development and continuing education.

A great deal of research has been conducted to examine the effect of online education within formal educational settings (e.g., Bannan-Ritland, 2002; Jeong & Joung, 2007; Oh & Jonassen, 2007), while insufficient research has been carried out within professional development or informal learning environments where educational information and programs pertaining to the occupations of adult learners are offered. To date, much attention has been given to the design of online learning environments (e.g., Remidez, Stam, & Laffey, 2007; Scardamalia & Bereiter, 1994) and the potential of online learning to promote collaboration (e.g., Johnson & Johnson, 2008). However, only

a handful of studies have addressed usability of the online education environment (e.g., Ardito et al., 2006; Parlangeli, Marchigiani, & Bagnara, 1999; Saade & Bahli, 2005). Particularly, few studies have integrated the multifaceted usability evaluation into the lifecycle of developing such an environment.

Usability evaluation is vital to a web development team because developers must consider how major users, such as learners and educators, navigate through a web system to accomplish the tasks that lead to teaching and learning. If developers fail to consider the real users' needs and interaction behaviors, learning will be impeded because users' working memory is taxed with unnecessary cognitive load (Chandler & Sweller, 1991).

This paper describes the design challenges and the usability evaluation that was incorporated into the development process of an online continuing education center -- the MU Extension website. The MU Extension website had grown exponentially and chaotically since the first web pages were posted in the mid-1990s. Existing MU Extension websites did not meet the requirements for an ideal educational environment for learners and extension educators due to the lack of understanding of real users' needs. For instance, links and pages were added based on the internal organization of MU Extension rather than logical, content-based organization categories. To better serve the users of the site, the MU Extension web team intended to establish a new web portal that provided a centralized access point to a series of educational materials. The Information Experience Laboratory (IE Lab) of the University of Missouri worked closely with the web team and employed multifaceted usability evaluation methods at four different stages of developing this web portal: heuristic evaluation (Phase I: prototype), focus group interview and survey (Phase II: initial design), think-aloud interviewing (Phase III: detailed website design), and usability testing (Phase IV: website build).

The overall objectives of a series of usability studies for the MU Extension web portal are to investigate the following issues:

1. What are the information needs of the portal's users?
2. Can internal users (faculty, staff, and administrators) and external users (learners and faculty of other programs across the State) of the web portal find information efficiently?
3. What difficulties do users encounter with navigation and information organization on this portal?
4. Does the MU extension portal meet users' expectations and needs?

An important feature of this study was to provide a complete picture of how usability evaluation can be incorporated into the lifecycle of web development. It took nearly two years to finish all the phases of usability evaluation, which seldom occurs in other usability studies. The experiences and lessons learned from this project fill a gap in the literature where few usability studies have been conducted to improve the *informal* online learning environment, particularly for online adult education. In addition, this study revealed the positives and negatives of each evaluation method identified from a series of actual implementation and demonstrated the results of applying these methods. These practices contributed to the improvement of methodology in usability evaluation. At last, this study summarized the resources (See Table 2) needed for execution of each method. These are provided as referral information for other scholars and practitioners who intend to use these methods.

This paper comprises five sections. First, some of the relevant research in online education and usability studies is discussed. Second, the methodology, explaining in detail how to select and carry out these methods is described. Third, the results obtained from each method, such as users' difficulties and recommendations are presented.

Fourth, the positives and negatives of each method are summarized through the real experiences from this study. Fifth, the impact of iterative usability evaluation on online education is reiterated.

LITERATURE REVIEW

University Extension and Online Education

In the United States, university extension units play an important role of democratizing higher education by expanding access to university research to citizens who are not traditional students (McLean, 2007). American university extension divisions provide scholarly and professional services to citizens, communities, and industries through outreach actions or various forms of mass media (Bassett & Reardon, 2007; McLean, 2007). By 1914, more than 30 universities had established extension divisions in the United States (Shannon & Shoenfeld, 1965). A shared goal of these divisions is to enable citizens who are not full-time students to benefit from the resources of the universities.

With the rapid spread of the Internet, university extension units have also shifted much of their knowledge distribution to the web in order to promote higher education and enable citizens' to enjoy lifelong learning at times and places convenient to them. As such, many university extension divisions have established centralized web portals to provide unified access to multiple services such as news, publications, and online courses.

Online Education and the Usability Issue

Online education is an interdisciplinary field that attracts scholars' attention from the fields of distance education, human-computer interaction, instructional technology, and cognitive science

(Larreamendy-Joerns & Leinhardt, 2006). Researchers have noted the need for consideration of usability of online education systems (Ardito et al., 2006). Parlangeli, Marchigiani, and Bagnara (1999) applied Nielson's heuristic checklist (1994) in conjunction with a user interaction questionnaire to examine the relationship between the level of usability of a multimedia course system and learning performance. Ardito et al. (2006) used the systematic usability evaluation (SUE) as the framework for an empirical study of 10 graduate students and found usability elements in the efficacy of both platforms and didactic modules.

In addition to these usability studies of online courseware systems, scholars have also shed light on the usability of online education web portals. For instance, Quintana et al. (2008) conducted usability observation studies with international health professionals to ensure the quality of a continuing education website on the treatment of pediatric catastrophic diseases. Cook and Dupras (2004) pointed out that online learning has a large impact on medical education, but many educational websites fail to facilitate effective learning, and usability testing with target learners should be conducted at various stages of the design process. Because a web portal incorporates a series of communication tools, multi-media, databases, course management systems, and animations, it is critical to establish a successful portal to provide coordinated access to each major function (Pullen & McAndrews, 2004) and enhance the usefulness of educational materials.

User-Centered Design (UCD) and Iterative Usability Evaluation

Barnum (2002) defined User-Centered Design (UCD) as "the product development process based on learning about the users and analyzing what you learn to create products that match users' needs" (p. 121). Because the traditional data-centered approach has suffered from lack of usability (Allen, 1996), Barnum (2002) advocated "early focus

on users and tasks that involve understanding the users, the tasks that users perform, and the environment in which users perform these tasks (p.7)." To date, different UCD design models have been established (Barnum, 2002; Schneiderman, 2005).

Usability evaluation is an iterative process that works best when incorporated into various phases of design (Barnum, 2002). Usability evaluation methods can be categorized into two types: formative evaluation and summative evaluation. Formative evaluation takes place during the development process whereas summative evaluation is usually conducted at or near the completion of the development cycle (Barnum, 2002). Formative evaluation ensures usability at an early design stage. The data gathered then informs the next stage of evaluation. Moreover, from the field of Human-Computer Interaction (HCI), a similar viewpoint indicates that a single method is not adequate for usability testing (Hoppmann, 2009), and that the decision of selecting usability methods should be carefully planned and based on the development life cycle of a project.

Description of the MU Extension Web Portal

The MU Extension web portal has a significant number of visitors who come to the site mainly for educational information such as publications and web pages that deliver research-based information. In Fiscal Year 2009, there were 2,777,629 unique visitors to the MU Extension main site and 2,449,185 unique visitors to the MU Extension publications site (the two sites were integrated during the redesign).

The redesign of the MU Extension web portal started in early 2006. Before beginning usability testing, the MU Extension web team started reorganizing the site with a close look at the site's architecture. Based on electronic card sorts with both internal and external users and discussions with program leaders, the team established a wireframe (See Figure 1) with nine top-level, user-friendly content categories (e.g., Agriculture, Natural Resources, Lawn and Garden, Home and Consumer Life, Nutrition and Health, Families and Relationships, Community and Leadership, Business and Careers, and Emergency Management) and the main navigation elements that would be consistently used in headers and footers across the site. Later, the web team introduced colors and design to the wireframe and formed three prototypes (See Figures 2, Figure 3, and Figure 4). MU Extension began working with the IE Lab on the four stages of usability studies.

METHODS

The design of this usability study was iterative and evolutionary. The selection of each method was informed by the findings from the previous phase. As such, a decision about which method to be employed in each phase was not determined from the outset but was chosen over time as the project evolved. The following usability methods were adopted for each phase: 1) during phase I (Prototype), heuristic evaluation was applied to choose the best prototype from three candidate mockups; 2) during phase II (Initial design), a focus group interview and survey obtained early feedback on the design and structure of the portal from internal users; 3) during phase III (Detailed design), think-aloud interviews were executed to elicit both internal and external users' feedback and understand their performance on this web portal; and 4) during phase IV (Website build), the MUST (Multiple-User Simultaneous Testing) and focus group interview were conducted to test whether the web portal was ready to launch.

Phase I (Prototype): Heuristic Evaluation

For the first usability testing phase in August 2007, the web team developed three design prototypes in PDF format, and the IE Lab team conducted a

heuristic evaluation of these prototypes. Heuristic evaluation, also known as "expert review", is a widely adopted usability inspection method due to its high efficiency of identifying the problems of a website (Barnum, 2002). It is beneficial to carry out a heuristic evaluation on early prototypes before bringing in actual users for usability testing (Ahmed, 2006; Schneiderman & Plaisant, 2005). Heuristic evaluation is usually carried out by three to five evaluators examining a user interface or system and judging its compliance with a set of usability principles, or heuristics. The first step of heuristic evaluation in this study was to establish the heuristic evaluation checklist. Nielsen's (1994) 10 usability heuristic criteria served as a basis for the development of the checklist, but because some criteria were not applicable or were difficult to apply to this web portal, the IE Lab team changed and added some additional criteria (e.g., Skills, and Pleasurable and Respectful Interaction) based on usability literature and Nielsen's usability page at www.useit.com. Eventually, the reviewer team decided to apply 10 heuristic categories with 44 subcategory items to these prototypes.

Three IE Lab graduate students with rich usability evaluation experience individually evaluated the prototypes using the heuristic checklist. The evaluation team had an initial meeting to discuss each item on the checklist to ensure reviewers shared the same understanding about these criteria. The IE Lab team met with the MU Extension web team to understand the scope of evaluation. For instance, due to the lack of functionality offered by the PDF files, issues such as accessibility were not evaluated. The experts had to assume certain functionalities, such as that highlighted links represented on the PDFs would be links in the working version of the website. Each reviewer evaluated all three design prototypes (See Figure 2, Figure 3, and Figure 4; only the home page of each prototype is provided here). All heuristic evaluation sessions were recorded with Morae Recorder software. Eventually, these reviewers

Figure 1. The Wireframe of the Redesign of MU Extension Web Portal. (©2010, University of Missouri Extension. Used with permission)

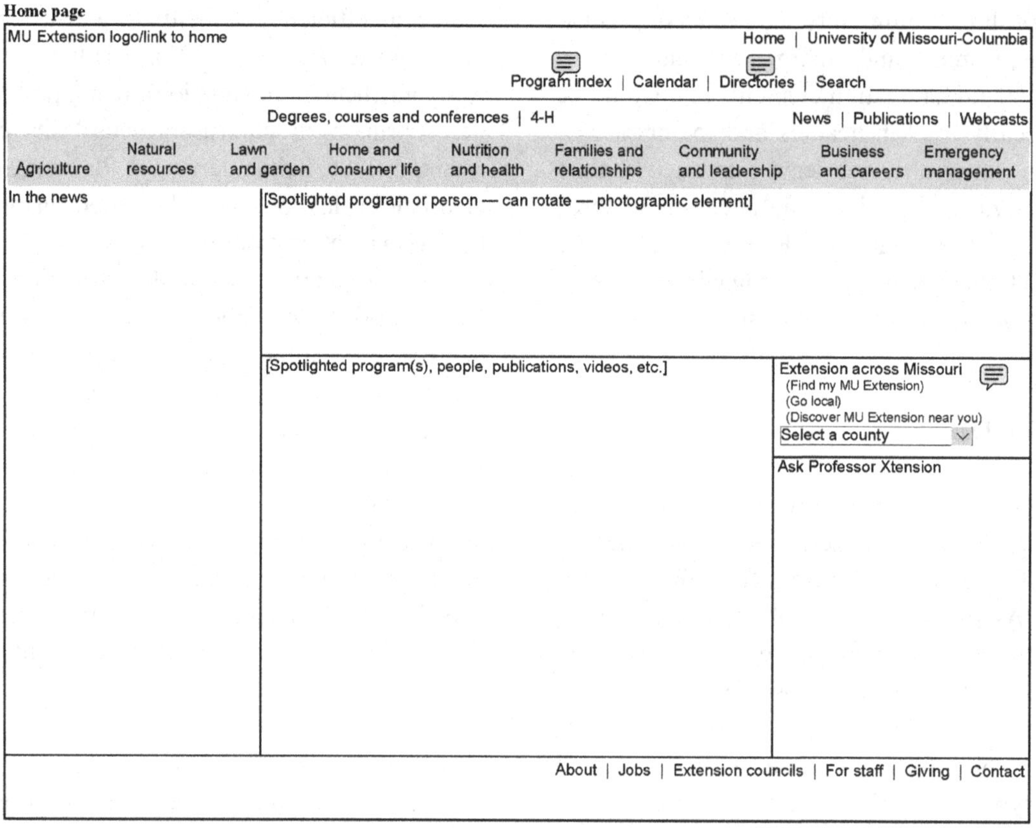

negotiated their rating scores to complete the heuristic evaluation process.

Phase II (Initial Design): Survey and Focus Group Interview

The web team followed recommendations of the heuristic evaluation and created an initial design of the web portal (See Figure 5) based on the prototype Design 3 (See Figure 4) with suggested changes. These changes include selection of a more neutral color scheme, removal of a second news section from the home page, incorporation of two ways for users to easily find local information from the home page and so on. The main goal of the second phase, carried out in November 2007, was

to get early feedback on the design and structure of the portal from *internal* users. A focus group and survey were chosen as the appropriate methods at this stage because the purpose of evaluation was to get rapid feedback on information organization and information architecture of the site rather than on its functionalities. Nine *internal* users, consisting of MU Extension faculty and staff, participated in the focus group and completed a survey.

Phase III (Detailed Design): Think-aloud Usability Testing

For phase III, the MU Extension web team used the feedback obtained from previous studies to further develop the web portal (See Figure 6) with

Figure 2. The Homepage of Prototype Design 1. (©2010, University of Missouri Extension. Used with permission)

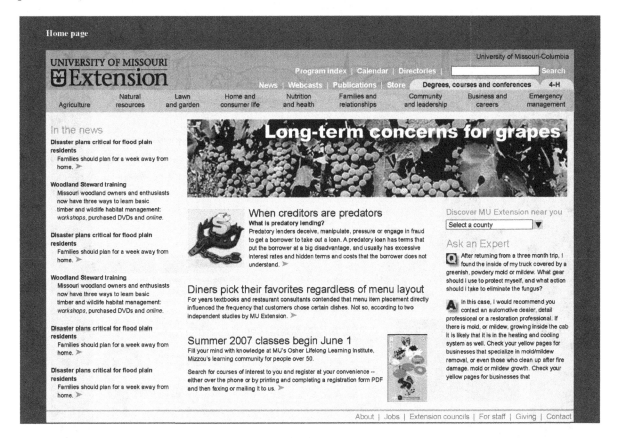

live functionality and with external-user-friendly content categories. This was a major undertaking because the newly designed portal included publications, news stories and videos, webcasts and links to internal websites. To ensure the reorganized portal was usable to major audiences, the think-aloud interview sessions were conducted at the IE Lab.

Think-aloud interviewing is one of the commonly adopted usability evaluation techniques in the HCI community (Nielsen, 2002). The key point of using think-aloud interviews is to undertake interviews as close to the action as possible. It is critical to engage the participants in activities and then have the interviewer ask the participants to discuss talk about what they are doing as they

perform the tasks (Patton, 2002). Users are asked to articulate their reasoning, interpretations, and opinions as they proceed, thus providing additional direct insight. The salient advantage of this method is that researchers can obtain users' concurrent thoughts rather than just retrospective ones (Patton, 2001).

Facilitated by the MU Extension team, 12 users (seven internal and five external) were recruited and invited to the IE Lab. The internal user group consisted of MU Extension educators and staff who all had the experience of developing content for the MU Extension site. The external user group consisted of local citizens with heterogeneous characteristics in terms of gender, age, web skills, and familiarity with the studied site. This was done

Figure 3. The Homepage of Prototype Design 2. (©2010, University of Missouri Extension. Used with permission)

to obtain a representative sample of the diverse audience of the MU Extension web portal.

Through semi-structured interviews, the researchers asked these users to perform a series of tasks and recorded them with the Morae software. While participants were engaged in the assigned tasks, they were asked to comment about what they viewed, clicks, and what kind of difficulties encountered. To keep the situation as natural as possible, the participants were allowed to "give up" on a task if they were unable to find the answer.

Phase IV (Website Build): MUST & Focus Group Interview

The usability test for validation is usually conducted late in the development cycle with the intent to certify product usability (Rubin, 1994).

Figure 4. The Homepage of Prototype Design 3. (©2010, University of Missouri Extension. Used with permission)

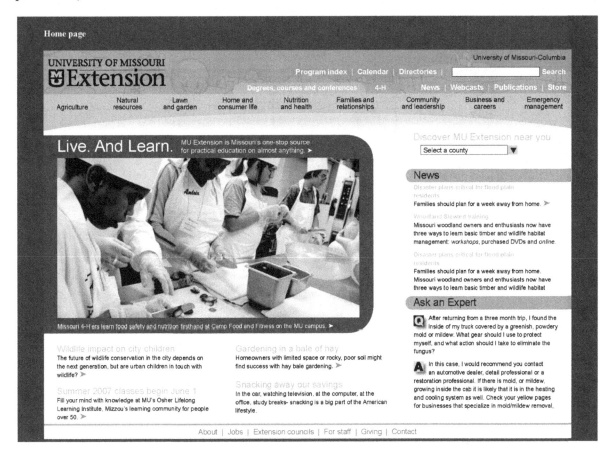

The validation test took place when the MU Extension web portal was considered close to the release stage (See Figure 7) in December 2008. One of the methods used for validation is called Multiple-User Simultaneous Testing (MUST). This method is best applied in the final stages of a study or when there is a time constraint because it allows usability specialists to simultaneously collect data from multiple users. MUST is also useful when performance data is desired. The current study used a self-paced MUST as a data collection method.

Seventeen internal users of the MU Extension portal performed a series of tasks simultaneously, which was followed by a focus group interview with eight of these participants. The eight focus group participants were selected based on the different positions they held and appeared to have difficulty performing the tasks or were quick in performing the tasks during the task analysis session.

Individual task analysis sessions were recorded in a group setting with Morae software in a laboratory. The auto-pilot option in Morae was used to prompt the participants through the sessions and enabled recording of the participants' responses about how difficult they perceived each task to be. Each participant worked on 15 tasks (See Appendix A) individually in a group setting. The tasks were randomly ordered for each participant. After each task, the participants marked on a sheet how easy or difficult it was to complete the given task. A 5-point Likert scale was used to measure difficulty of each task (1-very easy,

Figure 5. The Homepage of Phase II (Initial Design). (©2010, University of Missouri Extension. Used with permission)

2-easy, 3-moderate, 4- difficult, 5-very difficult). The participants also indicated on a 4-point Likert scale how easy it was to find the requested information. At the end of each task, they were asked to provide verbal feedback about individual task performance.

During the focus group interview, participants discussed their overall impressions of the newly designed portal and their task performance in the previous session. All participants completed a survey questionnaire that recorded demographics information and perceived experience with the MU Extension portal.

FINDINGS

This study applied multiple usability evaluation methods with the ongoing development of the MU Extension web portal. This section focuses on reporting the results achieved through these methods.

Phase I (Prototype): Heuristic Evaluation

The goal in this phase was to identify the best prototype. Table 1 displays the percentage of reviewers' agreement with the heuristics for three prototypes. The results reveal that Design 3 (See Figure 4) won the highest heuristic score (92%), followed by Design 1 (72%) and Design 2 (68%). A score of 92% in Design 3 meant that the three experts agreed that the prototype met 92% of all 44 heuristic criteria applied to the evaluation. Thus, Design 3 was chosen as the best prototype for further development.

Figure 6. The Homepage of Phase III (Detailed Design). (©2010, University of Missouri Extension. Used with permission)

Phase II (Initial Design): Survey and Focus Group Interview

At the initial design stage, the web team attempted to acquire quick and early feedback from the users. Because functionalities for external users were not ready, internal users were the major participants at this stage. In the survey, participants were asked about their goals when visiting the website. All participants mentioned that they used the site for work purposes; only 22% of them use the website for leisure reading. Finding forms, reading and downloading publications, and using the staff directory were the participants' top uses of the site.

Following the survey, the focus-group interview revealed a similar pattern of internal visitors' usage of the site. Many participants use the publications on this site. More important, the focus

group participants provided valuable comments and suggestions to improve the newly designed portal. These suggestions touch upon topics about organization of contents, terminology, the use of visual metaphors, presenting major links and tabs.

Phase III (Detailed Design): Think-aloud Usability Testing

As the development of this portal entered the detailed design phase, additional content and functionalities were include accommodating external users. Both external and internal users were recruited for soliciting feedback and examining the usability of the portal. The findings from the external user group were quite informative, especially those points that related to future improvement. Below are some examples:

Figure 7. The Homepage of Phase IV (Website Build). (©2010, University of Missouri Extension. Used with permission)

- Home Link was not available in current portal so subjects had to use the return button in the browser to return to the home page.
- Font size seemed too small to some participants with poor vision. These participants had difficulty reading and performing required tasks on the screen.
- Categories of primary navigation had overlapping meaning.
- Links did not clearly communicate where visitors would be taken. Subjects could not predict link destination due to ambiguous terminology.

To address these identified problems, recommendations provided by the IE Lab team included:

- Add a Home tab to improve users' navigation.
- Improve site readability through making the text size adjustable and accommodate needs of different user groups (such as users with poor vision or older users).
- Compose categories of site contents (navigation tabs) to be more exclusive and avoid ambiguous naming terminologies.
- Hyperlinks should directly communicate where they will lead users.

The think-aloud usability testing phase with external users was an eye-opener for the MU Extension web team. The developers were surprised both by what users could find and by what they couldn't find or see on the web page. For example, the web team thought users would be familiar with the web convention that the organization's

Table 1. Heuristic evaluation scores for each prototype design

Heuristics	Number of Sub-Category Item	Design 1	Design 2	Design 3
1. Visibility of System status	4	67	50	86
2. Match between system and the real world	4	75	0	92
3. Consistency and standards	3	100	67	100
4. Error prevention	2	100	0	100
5. Recognition rather than recall	14	64	71	90
6.Flexibility and minimalist design	1	100	100	100
7. Aesthetic and Minimalist Design	2	100	100	100
8. Help and Documentation	6	60	50	69
9. Skills	3	100	0	75
10. Pleasurable and Respectful Interaction with the User	5	50	100	92
TOTAL	44	72	68	92

logo in the upper left-hand corner was a link to the home page. Because most of the users did not discover this link, the designers added a link entitled Home. Font sizes were also increased based on user feedback.

The above changes were made to the site prior to the think-aloud sessions with internal users. The completion rate for each task reached 100%, which means all subjects were capable of completing all tasks. In addition, a series of usability problems was identified. Some examples are:

- Selected tabs in the primary navigation bar were not highlighted and thus caused users' confusion about where pages were located.
- The space between the two navigation bars created "trapped white space" and thus caused distraction in layout design.
- All subjects at times expressed their need to search for publications because the list of publications seemed too long. Some subjects showed impatience in reading paper titles one by one.
- Terminology of links and navigation tabs caused participants' confusion.

- The "Resources" tab of "MU Extension near you" under "Community and leadership" is not very recognizable.

After the internal think-aloud sessions, the web team made several changes based on the IE Lab recommendations. For instance, the developers were planning to add additional subcategories to further divide the publication lists as time permits.

Phase IV (Website Build): MUST & Focus Group Interview

When the MU Extension web portal was closer to the formal launch, a validation test for was considered beneficial by the researchers. Two measures, "Average Time on Task" and "Participants' Perceptions on Task Completion," were used to examine the efficiency and effectiveness of the site. Average Time on Task ranged from 68.68 seconds to 188.50 seconds across 15 tasks of MUST. Task 13 (*Finding what MU Extension events are happening in Boone County*) seemed to be the easiest task because the Average Time on Task for this task was 68.68 seconds. The participants' perception of the easiest task was also

Table 2. Resources, including time and personnel, implemented for each method

Lifecycle of Design	Methods	Approximate Time of Implementation	Personnel (No. of People)	No. of Participants
Prototype	Heuristic Evaluation	Individual evaluation by each expert (120 minutes) Consolidation meeting (180 minutes)	Evaluation leader (1) Reviewer (3)	N/A
Initial Design	Survey and Focus Group Interview	Survey (5 minutes) Focus group (60 minutes)	Survey (1) Focus group setup (2) Focus group facilitator (1) Note taker (1)	9
Detailed Design	Think-aloud Usability Testing	40 minutes think-aloud interview	Interviewer(1) Facilitator (1) Research supervisor(1) Project manager (1)	12
Website Build	MUST & Focus Group Interview	MUST (All tasks were required to complete within 60 minutes. The least time taken 52 minutes). Focus group (60 minutes)	MUST facilitators (2) MUST machine setup (4) Follow-up Focus Group Facilitation (1) Focus Group setup (2) Focus Group Observer (1)	17 (MUST) 8 (Focus Group)

highest for task 13. Task 12 (*Find the Boone's Lick Chapter of Master Naturalists*) seemed to be the most difficult task because it took the longest time for participants (Average Time on Task was 188.50 seconds) to complete this task. However, the participants' perception of the most difficult task was Task 9.

In addition to performance outcome data, a follow-up focus group interview provided a detailed account of the participants' perception of the portal.

Some of participants' general impressions about the new site included:

- Participants liked the new design of the portal in general. "The website is a great improvement. It is much more intuitive," one user said. They understood that it is impossible to plan for every user difference. A participant commented that "They have done a great job, considering the amount of information there."
- The most useful feature was the search box.

- It took too many clicks to navigate across the site. One user commented that if she can't find the desired information after three clicks, she will start looking for information somewhere else.
- Calendar, People and Locations links on the navigation bar worked well.
- Respondents liked the new functionality for finding people.

Some difficulties users encountered included:

- Certain tabs were confusing for participants. Somebody who never visits this website might not know particular tabs are clickable.
- There were a lot of publications about one topic. Some subcategories were needed to break up the list.
- Participants did not notice that they can click on each county on the map to get specific location information. They suggested that it would be good to have a list of letters for regions on the map (e.g., NW).

The MUST session was very useful as validation for the web team. After changes such as adjusting the look of the tab structure and adjusting the layout to fluid design, the web team launched the site in April 2009.

DISCUSSION

This study presented a comprehensive and iterative course of user-centered evaluation of an online educational web portal. To ensure the appropriate research method was adopted in each phase of the design life cycle, researchers carefully selected the methods based on the literature and the needs from the web team. Researchers were satisfied with the effectiveness of employing these usability methods at each phase, but many important lessons were also learned in terms of implementation of these methods. The following section is a summary of the pros and cons identified during practice for each method.

- Heuristic evaluation provided quick feedback to help the designers choose between the three prototypes. It was beneficial to get feedback on the interface design on early prototypes before real users were brought in for usability testing. The limitations of heuristic evaluation were that usability problems found were restricted to aspects of the interface that are reasonably easy to demonstrate: use of colors, layout and information structuring, and consistency of the terminology.
- A focus group was used to get feedback from several users at the same time in a relatively short period of time. This method encouraged dynamic discussions about the design issues and how to organize information among the focus group participants. The focus group allowed the web developers to get feedback on the important issues at the early stages of the development.

- The main purpose of the survey was to gather background and demographic information from participants efficiently and fast. The survey also supplemented other major research methods. According to Case (2007), the survey method allows researchers to collect responses from a large number of individuals. However, it lacks the ability to capture the complexity of information-seeking behavior and information needs of users. This disadvantage of survey use was offset with other qualitative methods.
- Applying the think-aloud interview enabled the developers to identify many important design issues that caused user difficulties such as poor navigation design, ambiguous terminology, and unfriendly visual presentation. Rich data collected through this qualitative method helped the developers better understand "what" was broken and "why" certain design elements were not usable. However, some inherent limitations of the think-aloud method had also been found. For instance, some users were not able to verbalize their entire thoughts, which was most likely because the verbalization could not keep pace with their cognitive process (Van, Barnard, & Sandberg, 1994). This problem made it difficult for researchers to understand what the users really meant. In addition, the researchers found some participants were not familiar with "thinking aloud" at the beginning. The researchers (or facilitators) had to remind these users to verbalize their thoughts. Last, because only a small sample size of users was involved in the study, researchers could not generalize the findings to make inferential predictions and explanations.
- The MUST session was intended to record the users' efficiency of task performance on a newly completed website and to help

generate feedback about users' perceptions on the site in the follow-up focus group session. Getting the participants to perform a list of tasks on their own without any facilitator prompting ensured the natural flow of the participant task performance. The session was controlled for a task order. Website design was new, and even though the participants were experienced with MU Extension, they had never used the interface before. Therefore, performance of the different tasks on their own allowed the users to explore the website more. The exercise enabled the focus group participants to obtain preliminary ideas about the new website and enhanced discussion in the focus group session. A disadvantage of the self-paced MUST session was that the method affected the structure of the task performance session. The start point of the tasks was not always same across all users. The users were instructed to start each task from the home page, but they did not always adhere to the instructions. Some users used shortcuts, such as searching, to get to the information they needed in spite of being instructed to not use the search function (which the web team forgot to disable). The participants were asked to find all information within the new site, but at times they managed to navigate their way through to the old website, found the information, and thought they were done.

CONCLUSION

Many online education web portals grow chaotically and thus cannot facilitate learning effectively and efficiently (Cook & Dupras, 2004). To better serve learners and educators, web teams of educational organizations often confront the issue of reorganization and redesign of these websites. During the redesign process, how can developers obtain on-time information on whether the new web portal will perform well and enhance users' learning experiences? Usability evaluation is a noteworthy way to address these issues. In this paper, the researchers shared the experiences and lessons learned from studying real and potential users' needs and online behaviors through a series of usability study methods. The goal is to provide first-hand user information to the web development team. The researchers found that understanding users' difficulties, needs, and wants has great impact on web designers' decision making. For example, the MU Extension web team incorporated ideas and recommendations from every phase of this study. They were often surprised to learn what worked and what did not work for users. The team plans to incorporate usability testing of some form into all future design work.

Additionally, iterative development of online education portals can provide a step-by-step approach to dealing with the varied issues that a web portal design might involve: assessing the existing website, prototype evaluation and comparison, obtaining user feedback and matching it up with the possibilities of the development team, and, finally, assessing the efficiency of the final website. Iterative evaluation is a continuous process. With the rapidly changing technology and users' adaptations to new technologies, an iterative development process ensures constant upgrading of an online educational environment to keep it usable and useful.

REFERENCES

Ahmed, S. M., McKnight, C., & Oppenheim, C. (2006). A User-Centered Design and Evaluation of IR Interfaces. *Journal of Librarianship and Information Science, 38*(3), 157–172. doi:10.1177/0961000606063882

Allen, B. L. (1996). *Information Tasks: Toward a User-Centered Approach to Information Systems*. San Diego: Academic Press.

Ardito, C., Costabile, M. F., Marsico, M. D., Lanzilotti, R., Levialdi, S., & Roselli, T. (2006). An approach to usability evaluation of e-learning applications. *Information Sciences, 4*, 270–283.

Bannan-Ritland, B. (2002). Computer-mediated communication, eLearning, and interactivity: A review of the research. *Quarterly Review of Distance Education, 3*(2), 161–179.

Barnum, C. M. (2002). *Usability Testing and Research*. New York: Longman.

Bassett, E. M., & Reardon, M. (2007). Land Use and Health: What Role for Extension? *Journal of Extension, 45*(5).

Case, D. (2002). *Looking for Information: A Survey of Research on Information Seeking, Needs, and Behavior*. New York: Academic Press.

Chandler, P., & Sweller, J. (1991). Cognitive load theory and the format of instruction. *Cognition and Instruction, 8*(4), 293–332. doi:10.1207/s1532690xci0804_2

Cook, D. A., & Dupras, D. M. (2004). A pratical guide to developing effective web-based learning. *Journal of General Internal Medicine, 19*(6). doi:10.1111/j.1525-1497.2004.30029.x

Hoppmann, T. K. (2009). Examining the 'point of frustration': the think-aloud method applied to online search tasks. *Quality & Quantity, 43*(2), 211–224. doi:10.1007/s11135-007-9116-0

Jeong, A., & Joung, S. (2007). Scaffolding collaborative argumentation in asynchronous discussions with message constraints and message labels. *Computers & Education, 48*(3), 427–445. doi:10.1016/j.compedu.2005.02.002

Johnson, D., & Johnson, R. (2008). Cooperation and the use of technology. In Spector, J. M. (Ed.), *M.*

McLean, S. (2007). University Extension and Social Change: Positioning a University of the People in Saskatchewan. *Adult Education Quarterly, 58*(3), 3–21. doi:10.1177/0741713607305945

Merrill, J. Merrienboer, & M. Driscoll (Eds.), *Handbook of Research on Educational Communications and Technology* (pp. 659-670). New York: Routledge.

Nielsen, J. (1994). Heuristic evaluation. In Nielsen, J., & Mack, R. (Eds.), *Usability Inspection Methods*. New York: John Wiley & Sons.

Nielsen, J., Clemmensen, T., & Yssing, C. (2002). Getting access to what goes on in people's heads? In *Proceedings of the Reflections on the think-aloud technique (NordiCHI)*.

Parlangeli, O., Marchigiani, E., & Bagnara, S. (1999). Multimedia systems in distance education: effects of usability on learning. *Interacting with Computers, 12*(1), 37–49. doi:10.1016/S0953-5438(98)00054-X

Patton, M. Q. (2002). *Qualitative Research and Evaluation Methods*. Thousand Oaks, CA: Sage.

Pullen, J., & McAndrews, P. (2004). A web portal for open-source synchronous distance education. In *Proceedings of the Seventh IASTED International Conference on Computers and Advanced Technology in Education* (pp. 428-037).

Quintana Y. O'Brien R. Patel A. Becksfort J. Shuler A. Nambayan A. (2008).

Remidez, H., Stam, A., & Laffey, J. (2007). Web-based template-driven communication support systems: Using Shadow netWorkspace to support trust development in virtual teams. *International Journal of e-Collaboration, 3*(1), 65–83.

Richardson, J. C., & Swan, K. (2003). Examine social presence in online course in relation to students' perceived learning and satisfaction. *Journal of Asynchronous Learning Networks*, 68–88.

Rubin, J. (1994). *Handbook of Usability Testing: How to plan, design, and conduct effective tests*. New York: John Wiley & Sons.

Saadé, R., & Bahli, B. (2005). The impact of cognitive absorption on perceived usefulness and perceived ease of use in on-line learning: An extension of the technology acceptance model. *Information & Management*, *42*(2), 317–327. doi:10.1016/j.im.2003.12.013

Scardamalia, M., & Bereiter, C. (1994). Computer Support for Knowledge-Building Communities. *Journal of the Learning Sciences*, *3*(3), 265–283. doi:10.1207/s15327809jls0303_3

Schneiderman, B. (2005). *Designing the User Interface*. Reading, MA: Addison Wesley.

Shannon, T., & Shoenfeld, C. (1965). *University Extension*. New York: Center for Applied Research.

Van, S., Barnard, Y. F., & Sandberg, J. (1994). *The Think Aloud Method: A Practical Guide to Modelling*. London: Academic Press.

This work was previously published in the International Journal of Multimedia Data Engineering and Management, Volume 1, Issue 4, edited by Shu-Ching Chen, pp. 50-59, copyright 2010 by IGI Publishing (an imprint of IGI Global).

APPENDIX A

Table 3. Task Descriptions

Task	Task description
Task 1	A customer e-mails you. She is preparing her field for planting this spring and wants to find the Soil and Plant Testing Laboratory Web site. Can you find a page on this site with a link to the lab pages?
Task 2	You and a client are looking for information about an online degree in architectural studies. Can you get there from this site?
Task 3	Local cattle were bothered by horn flies last summer. On this site, can you help your clients find a way to get rid of horn flies?
Task 4	There was flooding in your area this year. Several people need information on cleaning up their homes after the flood. Can you find that information on this site?
Task 5	An article ran in the Missouri Conservationist about the Missouri Woodland Steward program, and now people are calling to ask more about it. Can you find out more about this program on this site?
Task 6	One of your customers has two children and is contemplating divorce. Can you find any information on this site to help him prepare the children for divorce?
Task 7	MU Extension's activity pyramid poster shows how much exercise children should get. Can you tell your clients how to order a copy of the poster on this site?
Task 8	Mileage rates have changed, and you need a new copy of the travel expense form. Can you find it on this site?
Task 9	You need to find Extension Technology and Computer Services to drop off your computer, but you don't know where the office is. Can you find the office address?
Task 10	Can you find a list of statewide events for Home and consumer life topics?
Task 11	You remember there's a new community development specialist, maybe based in Mercer County, but you can't remember his or her name. Can you find the name of that person?
Task 12	Go to the Natural resources page. On this page, there's a way to get to the Boone's Lick Chapter of Master Naturalists without going to the Boone County home page. Can you find it?
Task 13	You work in Boone County. Using this site, can you tell your customers how to check what MU Extension events are happening in Boone County this week? How?
Task 14	Can you help potential Boone County 4-H members find contact information on this site? How?
Task 15	You are holding an event at the Boone County Extension Center. Where on this site would participants find directions?

Chapter 17

The Factors that Influence E-Instructors' Performance in Taiwan:
A Perspective of New Human Performance Model

Chun-Yi Shen
Tamkang University, Taiwan

Chiung-Sui Chang
Tamkang University, Taiwan

ABSTRACT

Online teaching is the fastest growing form of delivery in higher education and faculty is expected to integrate technology into their teaching. The purpose of this study is to examine the performance of e-instructors in Taiwan based on the new human performance model. To achieve the purposes, this paper adopted a questionnaire survey and One hundred and six online instructors from 25 universities in Taiwan participated in this study. Correlation and multiple regression are performed to analysis the data. After statistical analysis, the results show that the four factors, advanced skill, basic skill, effort, and self-efficacy, contributed significantly to the model variance of e-instructors' performance in online teaching. The results also provide the evidences of the importance of self-efficacy in online teaching.

INTRODUCTION

The usage of technology among university faculty is a critical issue in higher education. They are expected to integrate technology into their teaching either in classroom or online (Saleh, 2008).

DOI: 10.4018/978-1-4666-1791-9.ch017

Moreover, they are required to be familiar with technology and know how to manage and use it in order to facilitate learning (Coppola, Hiltz, & Rotter, 2002). There is a great volume of references intend to examine faculties' attitude, experiences, and the integration of educational technology in higher education (Chen & Chen, 2006). A study by Haas and Senjo (2004) showed most faculties hold positive views toward educational technology, but far fewer of them are actually integrating technology into their courses. A survey of e-instructor in higher education by Vodanovich and Piotrowski (2005) revealed that about 70% of faculty hold a positive view of using the Internet for instructional purposes and believe the Internet is an effective teaching tool, but there were less than half (47%) of faculty use online instructional approaches to teach in their courses. Saleh (2008) point out that faculty might be afraid to use e-mail, have little confidence in using advanced technology, and resist changing. Furthermore, attitudes toward technology may not be enough to predict the performance of e-instructor in higher education (Vodanovich & Piotrowski, 2005).

Chen and Chen (2006) indicate that e-instructors' self-efficacy is an important factor in efforts to integrate technology into teaching. Self-efficacy originates from Bandura's Social Learning Theory and is "the belief in one's capabilities to organize and to execute the courses of action required to produce given attainments" (Bandura, 1997, p. 2). According to Peterson and Arnn (2005), the new human performance model demonstrates ability, motivation, situational factors, and self-efficacy are the four critical components that impact human performance. The purpose of this study is to examine the performance of e-instructors in Taiwan based on the new human performance model.

THEORETICAL BACKGROUND

According to Goodyear, Salmon, Spector, Steeples, and Tickner (2001), e-instructors have eight competencies for online teaching, which are (a) process facilitator, (b) adviser/counselor, (c) assessor, (d) researcher, (e) content facilitator, (f) technologist, (g) designer, and (h) manager/administrator. The process facilitator is concerned with facilitating the range of online activities that are supportive of student learning. The adviser/counselor works with learners on an individual or private basis, offering advice or counseling to help them get the most out of their engagement in a course. The assessor is concerned with providing grades, feedback, and validation of learners' work. The researcher is concerned with engagement in production of new knowledge of relevance to the content areas being taught. The Content Facilitator is concerned directly with facilitating the learners' growing understanding of course content. The Technologist is concerned with making or helping make technological choices that improve the environment available to learners. The designer is concerned with designing worthwhile online learning tasks. The manager-administrator is concerned with issues of learner registration, security, recordkeeping, and so on (Goodyear et al., 2001). In this study, adviser/counselor and process facilitator were combined as facilitating learning, and other competencies were modified as facilitating learning, research development, content expertise, technology, instructional design, and administration.

As defined by Bandura (1997), self-efficacy is one's judgments of his/her capabilities to organize and execute courses of action required to attain designated types of performances. Hasan (2003) pointed out that self-efficacy has a positive correlation with the usage of information technology and also provides insights into learning performance and the ability to acquire new computer skills. According to the Faseyitan, Libii, and Hirschbuhl (1996), the confidence levels of faculty in using computers are significant factors in the usage of educational technology. In addition, they concluded that computer self-efficacy is a significant factor that can predict faculty's adoption of educational technology. In the study conducted by Kagima and Hausafus (2000), they investigated the relationships between the computer self-efficacy of faculty and integration of electronic communication in teaching. The results showed a statistically significant relationship between technology integration and computer self-efficacy, with high integrators having higher average levels of computer self-efficacy.

According to the study conducted by Georgina and Olson (2008), the technology skill of faculty has a strong positive correlation with pedagogy both in design and delivery. The results revealed that the faculty with high technology ability applies more technology into their instruction.

The first human performance model was developed by Campbell and Pritchard in 1976. The model suggested that ability and motivation are functions of human performance. Based on the research by Peters and O'Connor (1980), the situational factor was added into the revised human performance model. According to the research of Peterson and Arnn (2005), the new human performance model suggested that human performance can be predicted by four factors, which are self-efficacy, ability, motivation, and situational factors. In this study, we focus on the internal factors that affect human performance. The research model is based on the new human performance model and motivation theory. Furthermore, O'Neil (1999) pointed out that motivation can be predicted by two factors, self-efficacy and effort. Self-efficacy and Effort have been found in many self-regulation studies as an element of motivation (Hong & O'Neil, 2001; Zimmerman, 2000; Bandura, 2001). Therefore, the research model of this study is that the hu-

man performance can be predicted by (a) Basic computer skill, (b) Advanced computer skill, (c) effort, and (d) self-efficacy (see Figure 1).

METHODOLOGY

Participants

The study was conducted in universities with a sample of 277 instructors who has experience in online instruction course from 50 universities in Taiwan. All subjects are asked to answer a questionnaire. The questionnaire with a cover letter was distributed to subjects from the researchers. All respondents were asked to complete the survey and their feedback was guaranteed confidentiality. 106 instructors answered the questionnaire (38.3% response rate). Seven missing responses were eliminated and 99 responses were collected. Table 1 describes the sample that consisted of 64 male and 35 female e-instructors.

Instruments

E-Instructors' Performance Questionnaire

The e-instructors' performance questionnaire was based on the studies of Thatch and Murphy

Figure 1. The New Human Performance Model. (Adapted from Peterson & Arnn, 2005)

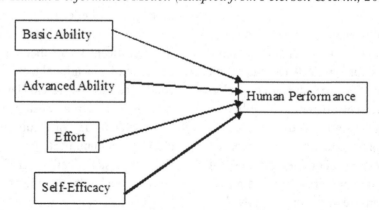

Table 1. Demographic data

Demographic data characteristics	N	Frequency	%
Gender	99		
1. Male		64	64.6
2. Female		35	45.4
Seniority	99		
1. Professor		23	23.2
2. Associate		36	36.4
3. Assistant		18	18.2
4. Lecturer		20	20.2
5. Others		2	2.0
Year of online instruction	99		
1. less than one semester		5	5.1
2. less than one year		14	14.1
3. less than two years		15	15.2
4. less than three years		17	17.2
5. less than four years		20	20.2
6. More than four years		28	28.3
The type of e-Learning Platform	99		
1. WebCT		7	7.1
2. Blackboard		79	79.8
3. Others		13	13.1
The level of training support	98		
1. enough		25	25.3
2. some		53	53.5
3. little		20	20.2
The level of teaching load	99		
1. low		10	10.1
2. average		23	23.2
3. heavy		66	66.7

(1995), Cyrs (1997), Schoenfeld-Tacher and Persichitte (2000), and Goodyear et al. (2001). The first version of the questionnaire consisted of 45 items assigned to seven underlying scales: (a) instructional design, (b) facilitating learning, (c) assessment, (d) technology, (e) administration, (f) content expertise, and (g) research development. Each item employs a four-point Likert response format (almost never = 1, seldom =2, often =3, almost always = 4). Faculty responded to actual and preferred forms of the questionnaire. In the actual form, faculty recorded, for each item, their perceptions of the actual (or real) e-instructors' competencies. Scale scores for each respondent are formed by aggregating the scores for items assigned to the particular scale. After validated by three experienced scholars to investigate the content validity, the questionnaire was conducted

in a pilot study with 32 participants. The research conducted the confirmatory factor analysis (CFA) to examine the construct validity.

In the CFA, the component matrix showed positive, high correlations among the separate items included with each of these seven factors (see Table 4). The KMO statistic and Bartlett's test result ($p < .001$) showed that items constituting each of the factors fit together appropriately for the results of CFA to be meaningful (see Table 2). Also, the value of the Cronbach standardized item alpha for each factor was high. These results verified that a summated rating scale for each other can be formed meaningfully from each of these sets of variables. Items with loadings equal to or greater than 0.50 were retained on each factor. The first factor, which included four items with reliability of 0.72, was named "instructional design". The second factor, named "facilitating learning", consisted of eight items with reliability 0.89. The third factor, named "assessment", consisted of six items with reliability of 0.81. The fourth factor, named "technology", consisted of seven items with reliability of 0.85. The fifth factor, named "administration management", consisted of six items with reliability of 0.84. The sixth factor, named "content expertise", consisted of four items with reliability of 0.82. The seventh factor, named "research development", was composed of four items with reliability of 0.82.

Computer Skill Questionnaire

The questionnaire of computer skill of e-instructors was adapted from the Technology Literacy Survey developed by Georgina and Hosford (2009) and Georgina and Olson (2008). The Cronbach's alpha of Technology Literacy Survey is .951.

Online Teaching Motivation Questionnaire

The questionnaire of e-instructors' motivation of online teaching was adapted from the trait self-

Table 2. Results of reliability analyses

Variables	Item number	KMO and Bartlett	α
Instructional design	7	0.77***	0.72
Facilitating learning	8	0.88***	0.89
Assessment	8	0.80***	0.81
Technology	8	0.78***	0.85
Administration management	6	0.84***	0.84
Content expertise	4	0.73***	0.82
Research development	4	0.78***	0.82

*** $p<.001$

Table 3. Descriptive statistics of variables

Variable	Mean	SD
Instructional design	3.01	0.49
Facilitating Learning	2.63	0.63
Assessment	2.84	0.59
Technology	2.92	0.61
Administration management	3.06	0.63
Content expertise	3.22	0.56
Research development	2.81	0.66
Advanced computer skill	2.95	0.68
Basic computer skill	3.53	0.52
Effort	3.03	0.55
Self-efficacy	3.08	0.53

Note: strongly disagree=1, disagree=2, agree=3, strongly agree=4 for advanced and basic computer skill; almost never=1, seldom=2, often=3, almost always=4 for performance, effort, and self-efficacy.

regulation questionnaire developed by O'Neil and Herl (1998). There was an acceptable reliability of the questionnaire, Cronbach's alpha ranged from .89-.94. The questionnaire consists of 7 items in effort and 14 items in self-efficacy for online teaching.

Results

Table 3 shows the descriptive statistics of each variable. The e-instructors' performance of online teach from high to low are: content expertise (M=3.22, SD=.56), administration management (M=3.06, SD=.63), instructional design (M=3.01, SD=.49), technology (M=2.92, SD=.61), assessment (M=2.84, SD=.59), research development (M=2.81, SD=.66), and facilitating learning (M=2.63, SD=.63). For the computer skill, the e-instructors' basic computer skills (M=3.53, SD=.52) are higher than the advanced computer skill (M=2.95, SD=.68). The mean of effort and self-efficacy of e-instructors are 3.03 (SD=.55) and 3.08 (SD=.53).

Correlation and multiple regression are performed to analysis the data. The correlations among the variables used in the regression models are provided in Table 4. All variables have significantly positive correlations (r=0.22~0.89, p<.05) except facilitating learning-Advanced

computer skill and content expertise-Advanced computer skill.

As shown in Table 5, the four factors (Advanced computer skill, basic computer skill, effort, and self-efficacy) contributed significantly to the model variance of e-instructors' performance in online teaching (ΔR^2=0.52, p < .001). Those four independent variables also contributed significantly to the model variance of all of the seven aspects (ΔR^2=0.24~0.45, p < .001).

In Table 6, effort (β=0.301, p<.05) and self-efficacy (β=0.465, p<.05) are the stronger influent factors for e-instructors' performance in online teaching. In addition, the independent variables contributed significantly to the model variance of instructional design (ΔR^2=0.38, p < .001). Effort (β=0.304, p<.05) and self-efficacy (β=0.436, p<.05) have significantly stronger effect on Instructional design for e-instructors. For facilitating learning, the independent variables contributed significantly to the model variance (ΔR^2=0.24, p < .001). The result shows that advanced computer skill (β=-0.238, p<.05) has a negative correlation for facilitating learning. For assessment, the independent variables also contributed

Table 4. Correlations among the variables used in the regression analysis

Variable	1	2	3	4	5	6	7	8	9	10	11
1. Instructional design	-										
2. Facilitating Learning	0.77*	-									
3. Assessment	0.70*	0.79*	-								
4. Technology	0.47*	0.45*	0.61*	-							
5. Administration management	0.61*	0.63*	0.79*	0.64*	-						
6. Content expertise	0.45*	0.43*	0.52*	0.52*	0.61*	-					
7. Research development	0.56*	0.55*	0.70*	0.67*	0.73*	0.67*	-				
8. Advanced computer skill	0.23*	0.11	0.27*	0.58*	0.22*	0.17	0.33*	-			
9. Basic computer skill	0.25*	0.27*	0.25*	0.46*	0.33*	0.37*	0.34*	0.50*	-		
10. Effort	0.59*	0.46*	0.56*	0.51*	0.58*	0.54*	0.62*	0.43*	0.39*	-	
11. Self-efficacy	0.60*	0.46*	0.57*	0.61*	0.57*	0.57*	0.65*	0.55*	0.49*	0.81*	-

* $p<.05$

significantly to the model variance (ΔR^2 =0.33, $p < .001$) and self-efficacy (β=0.386, $p<.05$) is a strong influential factor. The independent variables contributed significantly to the model variance of technology (ΔR^2 =0.45, $p < .001$). Advanced computer skill (β=0.321, $p<.05$) and self-efficacy (β=0.316, $p<.05$) have significant positive correlations with technology. For administration management, the four factors contributed significantly to the model variance (ΔR^2 =0.36, $p < .001$). As the Instructional design, Effort (β=0.331, $p<.05$) and self-efficacy (β=0.344, $p<.05$) are the strong influential factors. The independent variables contributed significantly to the model variance (ΔR^2 =0.38, $p < .001$) for content expertise. For online teaching, advanced computer skill (β=-0.267, $p<.05$) has a negative effect on content expertise while basic computer skill (β=0.202, $p<.05$) and self-efficacy (β=0.441, $p<.05$) have positive effects on it. The independent variables contributed significantly to the model variance of research development (ΔR^2 =0.43, $p < .001$). As instructional design and Administration management, effort (β=0.271, $p<.05$) and self-efficacy (β=0.436, $p<.05$) have significantly stronger effect on research development for e-instructors.

DISCUSSION AND CONCLUSION

This study tended to investigate the factors that influence the performance of online faculty in Taiwan. The factors were taken into ability and motivation. In addition, ability was divided into basic and advanced computer skill, and motivation is divided into effort and self-efficacy. The findings of the study showed that self-efficacy has significant positive effects on all dimensions of performance except facilitating learning. The results are consistent with previous studies (Hasan, 2003; Faseyitan et al., 1996; Kagima & Hausafus, 2000; Chen & Chen, 2006). The results provide the evidences of the importance of self-efficacy in online teaching. This finding suggests that university should provide the training incorporated attention to self-efficacy (Saleh, 2008).

Effort has a positive effect on performance in three of the dimensions, which are instructional design, administration management, and research development. The results indicate that e-instructors put more effort and time when they design instructional materials, manage courses, and conduct researches. In another word, providing instructional designers, online teaching assistants, and research assistants should be considered by

Table 5. Summary statistics of regression analysis

Dependent Variables	R^2	ΔR^2	F	sig
Instructional design	0.41	0.38	15.86	<.001
facilitating learning	0.28	0.24	8.76	<.001
Assessment	0.36	0.33	12.78	<.001
Technology	0.47	0.45	20.36	<.001
Administration management	0.39	0.36	14.70	<.001
Content expertise	0.40	0.38	15.53	<.001
Research development	0.45	0.43	18.92	<.001

administrators of the university in order to reduce the loading of faculty and encourage them to integrate technology into their instruction.

On the other hand, basic computer skill has a significant positive effect only on content expertise. Advanced computer skill has a significant positive effect on technology and negative effects on facilitating learning and content expertise. Several researchers (e.g., Salomon & Perkins, 1996) pointed out that many applications of educational technology foster only lower-level processing of knowledge and new pedagogical models of using educational technology became more important. Those findings suggest that e-instructors do not need to have the advanced computer skills to facilitate students' learning and have domain knowledge, but they need the basic computer skills to deal with the content. The results suggest that university should provide the training of basic computer skill. However, the results were not consistent with the previous study (Georgina & Olson, 2008) and the New Human Performance Model (Peterson & Arnn, 2005). The possible reason may be that the computer skills are not the conception of the ability for online teaching.

The study involved constructing self-report questionnaires that was designed to assess e-instructors' computer skills and performance of online teaching and their effort and self-efficacy. The scores of performance were not their actual pedagogical practices. The bias from e-instructors' thought about socially desirable answers was the limitation of this study. Another limitation was the insufficient sample size of ninety-nine participants. In addition, it is important to note that this study examine only the internal factors that influence performance, not the external factors in the New Human Performance Model.

The future studies could construct the questionnaire to assess the abilities for online teaching. E-instructors' performance questionnaire Also, the future studies could investigate the relationships among e-instructors' performance, the internal factors (ability, motivation, and self-efficacy), and the external factor (situational factor) based on the New Human Performance Model. In addition, a large amount of sample size is suggested.

Table 6. Summary of standard regression coefficients (β)

	Advanced computer skill	Basic computer skill	Effort	Self-efficacy
Instructional design	-0.134	-0.017	0.304*	0.436*
Facilitating learning	-0.238*	0.131	0.250	0.326
Assessment	-0.053	-0.020	0.278	0.386*
Technology	0.321*	0.111	0.076	0.316*
Administration Management	-0.170	0.112	0.331*	0.344*
Content expertise	-0.267*	0.202*	0.221	0.441*
Research development	-0.051	0.047	0.271*	0.436*

* $p<.05$

RESEARCH LIMITATIONS

According to previous studies (e.g., Wedman, 2009), there are other factors that would influence instructors' performance, such as expectations, feedback, tools, environment, processes, rewards, recognition, incentives, personal innovation, computer anxiety, teaching strategy, desire to perform, and usability of educational technology. However, the research model of this study is based on the New Human Performance Model (Peterson & Arnn, 2005), thus this study only addressed the selected factors, which are basic ability, advanced ability, effort, and self-efficacy.

Another limitation is that the data collected in this study are based the self-report questionnaire. The data are the perceptions of the instructors, but not the actual performance data (e.g., measures of students' performance, motivation, or satisfaction).

REFERENCES

Bandura, A. (1997). *Self-efficacy: The exercise of control.* New York: W. H. Freeman & Company.

Bandura, A. (2001). Impact of Guided Exploration and Enactive Exploration on Self-Regulatory mechanisms and Information Acquisition through Electronic Search. *The Journal of Applied Psychology, 86*(6), 1129–1141. doi:10.1037/0021-9010.86.6.1129

Campbell, J. P., & Pritchard, R. D. (1976). Motivation theory in industrial and organizational psychology. In Dunnette, M. D. (Ed.), *Handbook of industrial and organizational psychology.* Chicago: Rand McNally.

Chen, T.-L., & Chen, T.-J. (2006). Examination of attitudes towards teaching online courses based on theory of reasoned action of university faculty in Taiwan. *British Journal of Educational Technology, 37*(5), 683–693. doi:10.1111/j.1467-8535.2006.00590.x

Coppola, N. W., Hiltz, S. R., & Rotter, N. G. (2002). Becoming a virtual professor: Pedagogical roles and asynchronous learning networks. *Journal of Management Inquiry, 18*(4), 169–189.

Cyrs, T. (1997). Competence in teaching at a distance. *New Directions for Teaching and Learning, 71,* 15–18. doi:10.1002/tl.7102

Faseyitan, S., Libii, J. N., & Hirschbuhl, J. (1996). An inservice model for enhancing faculty computer self-efficacy. *British Journal of Educational Technology, 27,* 214–226. doi:10.1111/j.1467-8535.1996.tb00688.x

Georgina, D. A., & Hosford, C. C. (2009). Higher education faculty perceptions on technology integration and training. *Teaching and Teacher Education, 25,* 690–696. doi:10.1016/j.tate.2008.11.004

Georgina, D. A., & Olson, M. R. (2008). Integration of technology in higher education: A review of faculty self-perceptions. *The Internet and Higher Education, 11,* 1–8. doi:10.1016/j.iheduc.2007.11.002

Goodyear, P., Salmon, G., Spector, J. M., Steeples, C., & Tickner, S. (2001). Competences for online teaching: A special report. *Educational Technology Research and Development, 49*(1), 65–72. doi:10.1007/BF02504508

Haas, S. M., & Senjo, S. R. (2004). Perceptions of effectiveness and the actual use of technology-based methods of instruction: a study of California criminal justice and crime-related faculty. *Journal of Criminal Justice Education, 15*(2), 263–285. doi:10.1080/10511250400085981

Hasan, B. (2003). The influence of specific computer experiences on computer self-efficacy beliefs. *Computers in Human Behavior, 19,* 443–450. doi:10.1016/S0747-5632(02)00079-1

Hong, E., & O'Neil, H. F. Jr. (2001). Construct validation of a trait self-regulation model. *International Journal of Psychology, 36*(3), 186–194. doi:10.1080/00207590042000146

Kagima, L. K., & Hausafus, C. O. (2000). Integration of electronic communication in higher education: Contributions of faculty computer self-efficacy. *The Internet and Higher Education, 2*(4), 221–235. doi:10.1016/S1096-7516(00)00027-0

O'Neil, H. F. Jr. (1999). Perspectives on computer-based performance assessment of problem-solving. *Computers in Human Behavior, 15,* 225–268.

O'Neil, H. F. Jr, & Herl, H. E. (1998). *Reliability and validity of a trait measure of self-regulation. Center for Research on Evaluation, Standards, and Student Testing.* CRESST.

Peters, L. H., & O'Connor, E. J. (1980). Situational constraints and work outcomes: The influences of a frequently overlooked construct. *Academy of Management Review, 5*(3), 391–397. doi:10.2307/257114

Peterson, T., & Arnn, R. (2005). Self-efficacy: The foundation of Human Performance. *Performance Improvement Quarterly, 18*(2), 5–18. doi:10.1111/j.1937-8327.2005.tb00330.x

Saleh, H. (2008). Computer self-efficacy of university faculty in Lebanon. *Educational Technology Research and Development, 56*(2), 229–240. doi:10.1007/s11423-007-9084-z

Salomon, G., & Perkins, D. (1996). Learning in wonderland: What do computers really offer education? In Kerr, S. (Ed.), *Technology and the future of schooling in America: The ninety-fifth yearbook of the national society for the study of education.* Chicago: The University Press of Chicago.

Schoenfeld-Tacher, R., & Persichitte, K. (2000). Differential skills and competencies required of faculty teaching distance education courses. *International Journal of Educational Technology, 2*(1).

Thatch, E., & Murphy, K. (1995). Competencies for distance education professionals. *Educational Technology Research and Development, 43*(1), 57–79. doi:10.1007/BF02300482

Urdan, T., & Midgley, C. (2001). Academic self-handicapping: What we know, what more there is to learn. *Educational Psychology Review, 13,* 115–138. doi:10.1023/A:1009061303214

Vodanovich, S., & Piotrowski, C. (2005). Faculty Attitudes toward Web-Based Instruction May Not Be Enough: Limited Use and Obstacles to Implementation. *Journal of Educational Technology Systems, 33*(3), 309–318. doi:10.2190/V2N7-DMC4-2JWB-5Q88

Wedman, J. (2009). The Performance Pyramid. In R. Watkins & D. Leigh (Eds.), *Handbook of Improving Performance in the Workplace. Volume 2: Selecting and Implementing Performance Interventions.* New York: John Wiley & Sons.

Ziegler, A., & Heller, K. A. (2000). Approach and avoidance motivation as predictors of achievement behavior in physics instructions among mildly and highly gifted eight-grade students. *Journal for the Education of the Gifted, 23*(4), 343–359.

Zimmerman, B. J. (2000). Self-efficacy. An essential motive to learn. *Contemporary Educational Psychology, 25*(1), 82–91. doi:10.1006/ceps.1999.1016

This work was previously published in the International Journal of Multimedia Data Engineering and Management, Volume 1, Issue 4, edited by Shu-Ching Chen, pp. 50-59, copyright 2010 by IGI Publishing (an imprint of IGI Global).

Compilation of References

Agrawal, R., & Srikant, R. (1994). Fast algorithms for mining association rules in large databases, In *Proceedings of the International Conference on Very Large Data Bases (VLDB94)*, (pp. 487-499).

Ahmed, S. M., McKnight, C., & Oppenheim, C. (2006). A User-Centered Design and Evaluation of IR Interfaces. *Journal of Librarianship and Information Science, 38*(3), 157–172. doi:10.1177/0961000606063882

Aksoy, S., Marchisio, G., Tusk, C., & Koperski, K. (2002). Interactive classification and content-based retrieval of Tissue Images. In *Proceedings of the SPIE Annual Meeting, Applications of Digital Image Processing Session* (Vol. 4790, pp. 71-81).

Alaways, L. W. (1998). *Aerodynamics of the Curve-Ball: An Investigation of the Effects of Angular Velocity on Baseball Trajectories.* Unpublished doctoral dissertation, University of California, Davis.

Albayrak, S., Wollny, S., Varone, N., Lommatzsch, A., & Milosevic, D. (2005). Agent technology for personalized information filtering: the PIA system. In *Proceedings of SAC'05,* Santa Fe, NM.

Allen, B. L. (1996). *Information Tasks: Toward a User-Centered Approach to Information Systems.* San Diego: Academic Press.

Ambardekar, A., Nicolescu, M., & Dascalu, S. (2009). Ground-truth verification tool (GTVT) for video surveillance systems. In *Proceedings of ACHI '09, Second International Conferences on Advances in Computer-Human* (pp. 354-359).

Amir, A., Basu, S., Iyengar, G., Lin, C.-Y., Naphade, M., & Smith, J. R. (2004). A multi-modal system for the retrieval of semantic video events. *Computer Vision and Image Understanding, 96*, 216–236. doi:10.1016/j.cviu.2004.02.006

Ando, R., Shinoda, K., Furui, S., & Mochizuki, T. (2007). A Robust Scene Recognition System for Baseball

Anwar, F., & Naftel, A. (2008). Video event modeling and association rule mining in multimedia surveillance systems. In *Proceedings of the International Conference on Visual Information Engineering (VIE08)* (pp. 426-431).

Arbeiter, M., & Patzschke, N. (1996). Random Self-Similar. Multi-fractals. *Mathematische Nachrichten, 181*, 5–42.

Ardito, C., Costabile, M. F., Marsico, M. D., Lanzilotti, R., Levialdi, S., & Roselli, T. (2006). An approach to usability evaluation of e-learning applications. *Information Sciences, 4*, 270–283.

ARFF. (n.d.). Retrieved from http://www.cs.waikato.ac.nz/~ml/weka/arff.html

Arndt, R., Troncy, R., Staab, S., Hardman, L., & Vacura, M. (2007). COMM: Designing a well-founded multimedia ontology for the web. *Lecture Notes in Computer Science, 4825*, 30–43. doi:10.1007/978-3-540-76298-0_3

Audioscrobbler. (n.d.). *Web Services for Last.fm.* Retrieved from http://ws.audioscrobbler.com

Ausubel, D. P., & Robinson, F. G. (1969). *School learning: An introduction to educational psychology.* New York: Holt, Rinehart & Winston.

Ayala, G. (1996). *Intelligent Agents for Supporting the Effective Collaboration in a CSCL Environment.* Unpublished doctoral dissertation, Department of Information Science and Intelligent Systems, The University of Tokushima, Japan.

Ayala, G., & Castillo, S. (2008). Towards Computational Models for Mobile Learning Objects. In *Proceedings of the Fifth IEEE International Conference on Wireless, Mobile, and Ubiquitous Technology in Education* (pp. 153-157). ISBN:978-0-7695-3108-3

Ayala, G. (2005). An Analytic Model based on ASP for Maintaining ZPDs in CSCL Environments. In Looi, C.-K., Jonassen, D., & Ikeda, M. (Eds.), *Towards Sustainable and Scalable Educational Innovations Informed by the Learning Sciences, Frontiers in Artificial Intelligence and Applications* (pp. 3–10). Amsterdam, The Netherlands: IOS Press.

Ayala, G., Paredes, R. G., & Castillo, S. (2010). Computational models for mobile and ubiquitous second language learning. *International Journal of Mobile Learning and Organisation, 4*(2), 192–213. doi:10.1504/IJMLO.2010.032636

Aygun, R. S., & Zhang, A. (2002) Reducing blurring-effect in high resolution mosaic generation.

Aytar, Y., Shah, M., & Jiebo, L. (2008). Utilizing semantic word similarity measures for video retrieval. In *Proceedings of the IEEE International Conference on Computer Vision and Pattern Recognition (CVPR08)* (pp. 1-8).

Azzari, P., Stefano, L., & Bevilacqua, A.(2005). An effective real-time mosaicing algorithm apt

Babu, K. S., & Nagesh, V. (2008, March 9). Optimal solution for image retrieval using integrated region matching. In *Proceedings of the 2ⁿᵈ National Conference on Challenges & Opportunities in Information Technology (COIT-2008),* Mandi Gobindgarh, India (pp. 223-226).

Bader, B., & Kolda, T. (n.d.). *Tensor MA toolbox.* Retrieved from http://csmr.ca.sandia.gov/~tgkolda/TensorToolbox/

Baker, A., Navarro, E. O., & Hoek, V. H. A. (2003). An experimental card game for teaching software engineering. In *Proceedings of the 16th Conference on Software Engineering Education and Training* (pp. 216-223).

Baker, A., Navarro, E. O., & Hoek, V. H. A. (2003). Problems and Programmers: an educational software engineering card game. In *Proceedings of the 25th International Conference on Software Engineering* (pp. 614-619).

Baker, A., Navarro, E. O., & Hoek, V. H. A. (2005). An experimental card game for teaching software engineering processes. *Journal of Systems and Software, 75*(1-2), 3–16. doi:10.1016/j.jss.2004.02.033

Balasubramanian, C., & Duraiswamy, K. (2009). An application of Bayesian classification to interval encoded temporal mining with prioritized items. *International Journal of Computer Science and Information Security, 3*(1), 9250–9259.

Ballard, D. H. (1981). Generalizing the hough transform to detect arbitrary shapes. *Pattern Recognition, 13*(2), 111–122. doi:10.1016/0031-3203(81)90009-1

Bandura, A. (1997). *Self-efficacy: The exercise of control.* New York: W. H. Freeman & Company.

Bandura, A. (2001). Impact of Guided Exploration and Enactive Exploration on Self-Regulatory mechanisms and Information Acquisition through Electronic Search. *The Journal of Applied Psychology, 86*(6), 1129–1141. doi:10.1037/0021-9010.86.6.1129

Bannan-Ritland, B. (2002). Computer-mediated communication, eLearning, and interactivity: A review of the research. *Quarterly Review of Distance Education, 3*(2), 161–179.

Barnum, C. M. (2002). *Usability Testing and Research.* New York: Longman.

Barutcuoglu, Z., Schapire, R. E., & Troyanskaya, O. G. (2006). Hierarchical multi-label prediction of gene function. *Bioinformatics (Oxford, England), 22*(7), 830–836. doi:10.1093/bioinformatics/btk048

Bassett, E. M., & Reardon, M. (2007). Land Use and Health: What Role for Extension? *Journal of Extension, 45*(5).

Baudisch, P., Tan, D., Steedly, D., Rudolph, E., Uyttendaele, M., Pal, C., & Szeliski, R. (2005, November 21-25). Panoramic viewfinder: providing a real-time preview to help users avoid flaws in panoramic pictures. In *Proceedings of the 17th Australia Conference on Computer-Human interaction: Citizens online: Considerations For Today and the Future*, Canberra, Australia (Vol. 122, pp. 1-10).

Baudisch, P., Tan, D., Steedly, D., Rudolph, E., Uyttendaele, M., Pal, C., & Szeliski, R. (2007). An Exploration of User Interface Designs for Real-Time Panoramic. *Australasian Journal of Information Systems*, *3*, 1327.

Bay, H., Tuytelaars, T., & Gool, L. V. (2006, May). Surf: Speeded up robust features. In *Proceedings of the 9th European Conference on Computer Vision*.

Bekir, N., Cable, V., Hashimoto, I., & Katz, S. (2001). Teaching engineering ethics: a new approach. In *Proceedings of the 31st Annual Education Conference* (Vol. 1, pp. T2G 1-3).

Berri, J., Benlamri, R., & Atif, Y. (2006). Ontology-based framework for context-aware mobile learning. In *IWCMC '06*, Vancouver, BC, Canada.

Bertini, M., Bimbo, A. D., & Nunziati, W. (2006). Video clip matching using mpeg-7 descriptors and edit distance. In *Proceedings of the International Conference on Image and Video Retrieval* (LNCS 4071, pp. 133-142).

Black, J., Ellis, T., & Rosin, P. (2003). A novel method for video tracking performance. In *Proceedings of the IEEE PETS Workshop*.

Blockeel, H., Schietgat, L., Struyf, J., Džeroski, S., & Clare, A. (2006). Decision trees for hierarchical multilabel classification: A case study in functional genomics. In *Principle and Practice of Knowledge Discovery in Databases*.

Bloehdorn, S., Petridis, K., Saathoff, C., Simou, N., Tzouvaras, V., Avrithis, Y., et al. (2005). Semantic Annotation of Images and Videos for Multimedia Analysis. In *Proceedings of the 2nd European Semantic Web Conference (ESWC 2005m)* (pp. 592-607). New York: Springer.

Blunt, M. (1989). Geometry of Multi-fractal Systems. *Physical Review A.*, *39*(5), 2780–2782. doi:10.1103/PhysRevA.39.2780

Bormans, J., & Hill, K. (2002). MPEG-21 Overview v.5. *ISO/IEC JTC1/SC29/WG11, 5231*. Retrieve from http://www.chiariglione.org/mpeg/standards/mpeg-21/mpeg-21.htm

Boutell, M. R., Luo, J., Shen, X., & Brown, C. M. (2004). Learning multi-label scene classification. *Pattern Recognition*, *37*(9), 1757–1771. doi:10.1016/j.patcog.2004.03.009

Boutell, M., Shen, X., Luo, J., & Brown, C. (2003). *Multi-label semantic scene classification (Tech. Rep.)*. Rochester, NY: University of Rochester, Department of Computer Science.

Bouzouitz, I., & Elloumi, S. (2007). Integrated generic association rule based classifier. In *Proceedings of the IEEE International Conference on Database and Expert Systems Applications (DEXA07)* (pp. 514-518).

Bradshaw, B. (2000, October 30-November 3). Semantic based image retrieval: A probabilistic approach. In *Proceedings of ACM Multimedia 2000*, Marina del Rey, CA (pp. 167-176).

Breiman, L. (2001). Random Forests. *Machine Learning, 45*, 5-23.Chang, P., Han, M., & Gong, Y. (2002). Extract Highlights from Baseball Game Video with Hidden Markov Models. In *Proceedings of the International Conference on Image Processing* (pp. 609-612).

Broadcast using Data-Driven Approach. In *Proceedings of the ACM International Conference on Image and Video* (pp.186-193). New York: ACM Publishing.

Brown, M., & Lowe, D. G. (2007). Automatic Panoramic Image Stitching using Invariant Features. *International Journal of Computer Vision*, *74*(1), 59–73. doi:10.1007/s11263-006-0002-3

Cai, C. H., Fu, A. W. C., Cheng, C. H., & Kwong, W. W. (1998). Mining association rules with weighted items. *In Proceedings of the IEEE International Conference on Database Engineering and Applications Symposium (IDEAS98)* (pp. 68-77).

Campbell, L. (2007). Learning Object Metadata (LOM). In S. Ross & M. Day (Eds.), *DCC Digital Curation Manual*. Retrieved November 5, 2009, from http://www.dcc.ac.uk/resource/curation-manual/chapters/learning-object-metadata

Campbell, J. P., & Pritchard, R. D. (1976). Motivation theory in industrial and organizational psychology. In Dunnette, M. D. (Ed.), *Handbook of industrial and organizational psychology*. Chicago: Rand McNally.

Cao, J., Jing, H., Ngo, C.-W., & Zhang, Y. (2009). Distribution-based concept selection for concept-based video retrieval. In *Proceedings of the ACM International Conference on Multimedia (MM09)* (pp. 645-648).

Caracciolo, C., Euzenat, J., Hollink, L., Ichise, R., Isaac, A., Malaise, V., et al. (2008). Results of the Ontology Alignment Evaluation Initiative 2008. In *Proceedings of Ontology Matching Workshop of the 7th International Semantic Web Conference*, Karlsruhe, Germany (pp. 73-119).

CARLA. Center for Advanced Research on Language Acquisition, University of Minnesota. (2008, December 15). *Descriptions of Speech Acts*. Retrieved from http://www.carla.umn.edu/speechacts/descriptions.html

Carnegie Mellon University. (2004). *Sphinx-4*. Retrieved from http://cmusphinx.sourceforge.net/sphinx4/

Carrington, D., Baker, A., & Hoek, V. H. A. (2005). It's All in the Game: Teaching Software Process Concepts. In *Proceedings of the 35th Annual Conference Frontiers in Education* (pp. F4G-13 - F4G-18).

Carson, C., Thomas, M., & Belongie, E. A. S. (1999). Blobworld: A system for region based image indexing and retrieval. In *Proceedings of the 3rd International Conference on Visual Information System*, Amsterdam, The Netherlands (pp. 509-516).

Carson, C., Belongie, S., Greenspan, H., & Malik, J. (2002). Blobworld: image segmentation using expectation-maximization and its application to image querying. *IEEE Transactions on Pattern Analysis and Machine Intelligence*, 24(8), 1026–1038. doi:10.1109/TPAMI.2002.1023800

Case, D. (2002). *Looking for Information: A Survey of Research on Information Seeking, Needs, and Behavior*. New York: Academic Press.

Castillo, S., & Ayala, G. (2007). Towards Mobile Learning Objects: Learning Approaches, Awareness and Computational Models. In *Proceedings of the 15th International Conference on Computers in Education*, Hiroshima, Japan.

Castillo, S., & Ayala, G. (2008). ARMOLEO: An Architecture for Mobile Learning Objects. In *Proceedings of the 18th International Conference on Electronics, Communications and Computers (conielecomp 2008)*, Cholula, Puebla, México. ISBN: 978-0-7695-3120-5

Castillo, S., & Ayala, G. (2008b). A personalization Model for Learning Objects in Mobile Learning Environments. In *Proceedings of the 16th International Conference on Computers in Education (ICCE 2008)*, Taiwan. Retrieved October 11, 2009, from http://www.apsce.net/ICCE2008/papers/ICCE2008-paper137.pdf

Ceglar, A., & Roddick, J. F. (2006). Association mining. [CSUR]. *ACM Computing Surveys*, 38(5), 5. doi:10.1145/1132956.1132958

Cesa-Bianchi, N., Gentile, C., & Zaniboni, L. (2006). Incremental algorithms for hierarchical classification. *Journal of Machine Learning Research*, 7, 31–54.

Chan, T., Sharples, M., Vavoula, G., & Londsdale, P. (2004). Educational Metadata for Mobile Learning. In *Proceedings of the 2nd IEEE International Workshop on Wireless and Mobile Technologies in Education (WMTE'04)* (p. 197).

Chandler, P., & Sweller, J. (1991). Cognitive load theory and the format of instruction. *Cognition and Instruction*, 8(4), 293–332. doi:10.1207/s1532690xci0804_2

Chandra, N., Herman, B., Kim, Y., Lau, A., Murad, R., Pascarella, W., et al. (2006). A Financial Services Gaming Simulation. In *Proceedings of the IEEE Systems and Information Engineering Design Symposium* (pp. 152-155).

Chen, H.-S., Chen, H.-T., Tsai, W.-J., Lee, S.-Y., & Yu, J.-Y. (2007). Pitch-by-Pitch Extraction from Single View Baseball Video Sequences. In *Proceedings of the IEEE International Conference on Multimedia and Expo* (pp. 1423-1426)

Chen, H.-T. (2006). A Trajectory-Based Ball Tracking Framework with Enrichment for Broadcast Baseball Videos. In *Proceedings of the International Computer Symposium* (pp. 1145-1150).

Chen, L., Lai, Y., & Liao, H. (2006). Video scene extraction using mosaic techinque. In *Proceedings of the 18th International Conference on Pattern Recognition (ICPR'06)* (Vol. 4, pp. 723-726).

Chen, S.-C., Kashyap, R. L., & Ghafoor, A. (2000). *Semantic models for multimedia database searching and browsing*. New York: Springer.

Chen, S.-C., Shyu, M.-L., & Zhao, N. (2003). Mediamanager: A distributed multimedia management system for content based retrieval, authoring and presentation. In *Proceedings of the International Conference on Distributed Multimedia Systems* (pp. 17-22).

Chen, S.-C., Sista, S., Shyu, M.-L., & Kashyap, R. L. (2000, January). An indexing and searching structure for multimedia database systems. In *Proceedings of the IS&T/SPIE Conference on Storage and Retrieval for Media Databases*, Santa Clara, CA (pp. 262-270).

Chen, Y., & Aygun, S. R. (2009b). Synthetic video generation with complex camera motion patterns to evaluate sprite generation. In *Proceedings of the Fifth IEEE International Workshop on Multimedia Information Processing and Retrieval (MIPR 2009)*.

Chen, Y., Deshpande, A. A., & Aygun, S. R. (2009). *SpriteDB* (Version 1.1 software). Retrieved from http://sprite.cs.uah.edu

Chen, Y., Deshpande, A. A., & Aygun, S. R. (2009c). SpriteDB tool – a web-tool for comparing sprite generation results. In *Proceedings of the IEEE International Symposium on Multimedia (ISM2009)*.

Chen, H. C., & Chen, A. L. P. (2005). A Music Recommendation System Based on Music and User Grouping. *Journal of Intelligent Information Systems: Intelligent Multimedia Applications, 24*(2), 113–132.

Chen, P. H., Lin, C. J., & Schölkopf, B. (2005). A Tutorial on v-Support Vector Machines. *Applied Stochastic Models in Business and Industry, 21*, 111–136. doi:10.1002/asmb.537

Chen, S.-C. (2010). Multimedia databases and data management: a survey. [IJMDEM]. *International Journal of Multimedia Data Engineering and Management, 1*(1), 1–11.

Chen, S.-C., Zhao, N., & Shyu, M.-L. (2007). Modeling semantic concepts and user preferences in content-based video retrieval. *International Journal of Semantic Computing, 1*(3), 377–402. doi:10.1142/S1793351X07000159

Chen, T.-L., & Chen, T.-J. (2006). Examination of attitudes towards teaching online courses based on theory of reasoned action of university faculty in Taiwan. *British Journal of Educational Technology, 37*(5), 683–693. doi:10.1111/j.1467-8535.2006.00590.x

Chen, Y., & Aygun, S. R. (2009a). Synthetic video generation with camera motion patterns to evaluate sprite generation. *Advances in Multimedia, 0*, 140–145.

Cherng, D., & Chien, S. (2007, May). Video Segmentation with Model-Based Sprite Generation for Panning Surveillance Cameras. In Proceedings of *IEEE International Symposium on Circuits and Systems (ISCAS 2007)* (pp.2902-2905).

Chhabra, A., & Jensen, R. (1989). Direct determination of the f(α) singularity spectrum. *Physical Review Letters, 62*(12), 1327–1330. doi:10.1103/PhysRevLett.62.1327

Chu, W.-T., Wang, C.-W., & Wu, J.-L. (2006). Extraction of Baseball Trajectory and Physics-Based Validation for Single-View Baseball Video Sequences. In *Proceedings of the IEEE International Conference on Multimedia & Expo* (pp. 1813-1816).

Chua, T. S., Zhao, Y., & Kankanhalli, M. S. (2002). Detection of human faces in a compressed domain for video stratification. *The Visual Computer, 18*, 121–133. doi:10.1007/s003710100137

Cieplinski, L. (2001). MPEG-7 color descriptors and their applications. In *Computer analysis of images and patterns* (pp. 11-20). Heidelberg, Germany: Springer Berlin.

Clare, A., & King, R. D. (2002). Machine learning of functional class from phenotype data. *Bioinformatics (Oxford, England), 18*(1), 160–166. doi:10.1093/bioinformatics/18.1.160

Clarkson, P. (1999). *Statistical Language Modeling Toolkit*. Retrieved from http://www.speech.cs.cmu.edu/SLM/CMU-Cam_Toolkit_v2.tar.gz

Clarkson, P., & Rosenfeld, R. (1997). Statistical language modeling using the CMU-Cambridge Toolkit. In *Proceedings of the European Conference on Speech Communication and Technology – Eurospeech* (pp. 2707-2710).

Coastguard Video. (n.d.). Retrieved from http://media.xiph.org/video/derf/

Colajanni, M., & Lancellotti, R. (2004). *System architectures for Web content adaptation services, Web Systems Invited Article, IEEE Distributed Systems Online*. Retrieved October 11, 2009, from http://dsonline. computer.org/portal/site/dsonline/menuitem.9ed3d992 4aeb0dcd82ccc6716bbe36ec/index.jsp?&pName=dso_ level1&path=dsonline/topics/was&file=adaptation. xml&xsl=article.xsl&

Cook, D. A., & Dupras, D. M. (2004). A pratical guide to developing effective web-based learning. *Journal of General Internal Medicine, 19*(6). doi:10.1111/j.1525-1497.2004.30029.x

Cooper, M., Foote, J., Girgensohn, A., & Andwilcox, L. (2005). Temporal event clustering for digital photo collections. *ACM Transactions on Multimedia Computing, Communications, and Applications, 1*, 269–288. doi:10.1145/1083314.1083317

Coppola, N. W., Hiltz, S. R., & Rotter, N. G. (2002). Becoming a virtual professor: Pedagogical roles and asynchronous learning networks. *Journal of Management Inquiry, 18*(4), 169–189.

Cyrs, T. (1997). Competence in teaching at a distance. *New Directions for Teaching and Learning, 71*, 15–18. doi:10.1002/tl.7102

Datta, R., Joshi, D., Li, J., & Wang, J. Z. (2008). Image retrieval: Ideas, influences, and trends of the new age. [CSUR]. *ACM Computing Surveys, 40*(2), 1–60. doi:10.1145/1348246.1348248

Deerwester, S. C., Dumais, S. T., Landauer, T. K., Furnas, G. W., & Harshman, R. A. (1990). Indexing by Latent Semantic Analysis. *Journal of the American Society for Information Science American Society for Information Science, 41*(6), 391–407. doi:10.1002/(SICI)1097-4571(199009)41:6<391::AID-ASI1>3.0.CO;2-9

Diaz, M., Moisies, A. M., Lourdes, M. G., & Isaac, R. (2006). Multi-User Networked Interactive Augmented Reality Card Game. In *Proceedings of the International Conference on Cyberworlds* (pp. 172-182).

Dimitrova, N. (2004). Context and memory in multimedia content analysis. *IEEE Multimedia, 11*(3), 7-*11.

Din, H. W. H. (2006). Play to Learn: Exploring Online Education Games in Museums. In *Proceedings of the International Conference on Computer Graphics and Interactive Techniques* (No. 13).

Ding, Q., & Gasvoda, J. (2005). A genetic algorithm for clustering on image data. *International Journal of Computational Intelligence, 1*(1), 75–80.

diSessa, A. A. (2000). *Changing Minds*. Cambridge, MA: MIT Press.

Divakaran, A. (Ed.). (2009). *Multimedia content analysis, theory and applications*. Berlin: Springer Verlag.

Dole, E. (1954). *Audio-Visual Methods in Teaching*. New York: The Dryden Press.

Douze, M., Jégou, H., & Schmid, C. (2010). An image-based approach to video copy detection with spatio-temporal post-filtering. In *Proceedings of IEEE Transactions on Multimedia*.

Downie, J. S. (2008). The Music Information Retrieval Evaluation Exchange (2005-2007): a Window into Music Retrieval Research. *Acoustical Science and Technology, 29*(4), 247–255. doi:10.1250/ast.29.247

Dufaux, F., & Konrad, J. (2000). Efficient robust and fast global motion estimation for video coding. *IEEE Transactions on Image Processing, 9*, 497–500. doi:10.1109/83.826785

Dunckley, L. (2003). *Multimedia databases: An object-relational approach*. Reading, MA: Addison-Wesley.

Ehrig, M. (2007). *Ontology Alignment: Bridging the Semantic Gap*. New York: Springer.

Eickeler, S., & Müller, S. (1999). Content-based video indexing of tv broadcast news using hidden markov models. In *Proceedings of the IEEE International Conference on Acoustics, Speech, and Signal Processing* (pp. 2997-3000).

Erdem, C., & Sankur, B. (2000). Performance evaluation metrics for object-based video segmentation. In *Proceedings of the X European Signal Processing Conference (EUSIPCO)*.

Erdem, C., Sankur, B., & Tekalp, A. M. (2001). Metrics for video object segmentation and tracking without ground-truth. In *Proceedings of the IEEE International Conference on Image Processing (ICIP '01)*.

Esgiar, A. N., & Chakravorty, P. K. (2007). Fractal based classification of colon cancer tissue images. In *Proceedings of the International Symposium on Signal Processing and its Applications* (pp. 1-4).

Euzenat, J., Ferrara, A., Hollink, L., Joslyn, C., Malaise, V., Meilicke, C., et al. (2009). Preliminary Results of the Ontology Alignment Evaluation Initiative 2009. In *Proceedings of Ontology Matching Workshop of the 8th International Semantic Web Conference*, Chantilly, VA

Faber, N. K. M., Bro, R., & Hopke, P. K. (2003). Recent Developments in CANDECOMP/PARAFAC Algorithms: a Critical Review. *Chemometrics and Intelligent Laboratory Systems, 65*(1), 191–137. doi:10.1016/S0169-7439(02)00089-8

Falconer, K. (2003). *Fractal Geometry - Mathematical Foundations and Applications* (2nd ed.). London: Wiley.

Fan, J., Gao, Y., & Luo, H. (2004), Multi-level annotation of natural scenes using dominant image components and semantic concepts. In *Proceedings of the ACM International Conference on Multimedia* (pp. 540-547).

Farhan, M., & Abawajy, J. (2008). *A classification for Content Adaptation System*. In *Proceedings of iiWAS 2008*, Linz, Austria.

Farin, D., Haller, M., Krutz, A., & Sikora, T. (2008, October). Recent developments in panoramic imageGeneration and sprite coding. In *Proceedings of the IEEE 10th Workshop on Multimedia Signal Processing* (Vol. 8, No. 10, pp. 64-69).

Faseyitan, S., Libii, J. N., & Hirschbuhl, J. (1996). An inservice model for enhancing faculty computer self-efficacy. *British Journal of Educational Technology, 27*, 214–226. doi:10.1111/j.1467-8535.1996.tb00688.x

Fawcett, T. (2006). An introduction to ROC analysis. *Pattern Recognition Letters*, 861–874. doi:10.1016/j.patrec.2005.10.010

Fayyad, U. M., & Irani, K. B. (1992). On the handling of continuous-value attributes in decision tree generation. *Machine Learning, 8*(1), 87–102.

Fei-Fei, L., & Perona, P. (2005). A Bayesian hierarchical model for learning natural scene categories. In *Proceedings of Computer Vision and Pattern Recognition, 2*, 524–531.

Fejes Tóth, L. (1972). *Lagerungen in der Ebene auf der Kugel und im Raum* (2nd ed.). Berlin: Springer Verlang.

Feldgen, M., & Clua, O. (2004). Games as a Motivation for Freshman to Learn Programming. In *Proceedings of the 34th ASEE/IEEE Frontiers in Education Conference* (Vol. 3).

Felzenszwalb, P., Mcallester, D., & Ramanan, D. (2008, June). A discriminatively trained, multiscale, deformable part model. In *Proceedings of the IEEE International Conference on Computer Vision and Pattern Recognition*.

Filippas, J., Arochena, H., Amin, S. A., Naguib, R. N. G., & Bennett, M. K. (2003). Comparison of two AI methods for colonic tissue image classification. In *Proceedings of the IEEE Conference of Engineering in Medicine and Biology, 2*, 1323–1326.

Fischler, M. A., & Stephens, M. (1988). A combined corner and edge detector. In *Proceedings of the Alvey Conference* (pp. 147-152).

Friesen, N., Roberts, A., & Fisher, S. (2002). CanCore: Learning Object Metadata. *Canadian Journal of Learning and Technology, 28*(3).

Frost & Sullivan. (2006). *Research overview of Strategic Insight into Mobile Content Adaptation Markets - Porting with Transcoding and Rendering*. Retrieved October 11, 2009, from http://www.marketresearch.com/product/display.asp?productid=1327087

Furnas, G. W., Landauer, T. K., Gomez, L. M., & Dumais, S. T. (1987). The Vocabulary Problem in Human-system Communication. *Communications of the ACM, 30*(11), 964–971. doi:10.1145/32206.32212

Gao, S., Wu, W., Lee, C.-H., & Chua, T.-S. (2004). A MFoM learning approach to robust multiclass multi-label text categorization. In *Proceedings of the International Conference on Machine Learning* (p. 42). New York: ACM Press.

Garcia, R., & Celma, O. (2005). Semantic Integration and Retrieval of Multimedia Metadata. In *Proceedings of the 5th International Workshop on Knowledge Markup and Semantic Annotation (SemAnnot'05)*, Galway, Ireland. Citeseer.

Gargi, U., Kasturi, R., & Strayer, S. H. (2000). Performance characterization of video-shot-change detection methods. In *Proceedings of IEEE Transactions on Circuits and Systems for Video Technology, 10*(1), 1–13. doi:10.1109/76.825852

Ge, J., Qiu, Y., Chen, Z., & Yin, S. (2008). Technology of information push based on weighted association rules mining. In *Proceedings of the IEEE International Conference on Fuzzy Systems and Knowledge Discovery (FSKD08)* (pp. 615-619).

Gee, J. P. (2003). What Video Games Have to Teach Us about Learning and Literacy. *Computers in Entertainment (CIE), 1*(1).

Geng, X., Liu, T.-Y., Qin, T., Amold, A., Li, H., & Shum, H.-Y. (2008). Query Dependent Ranking using K-Nearest Neighbor. In [SIGIR]. *Proceedings of the International Conference on Research and Development in Information Retrieval, 2008*, 115–122.

Georgevia, E., & Gerogiev, T. (2007). *Methodology for mobile devices characteristics recognition.* Paper presented at the International Conference on Computer Systems and Technologies.

Georgina, D. A., & Hosford, C. C. (2009). Higher education faculty perceptions on technology integration and training. *Teaching and Teacher Education, 25*, 690–696. doi:10.1016/j.tate.2008.11.004

Georgina, D. A., & Olson, M. R. (2008). Integration of technology in higher education: A review of faculty self-perceptions. *The Internet and Higher Education, 11*, 1–8. doi:10.1016/j.iheduc.2007.11.002

Ghamrawi, N., & McCallum, A. (2005). Collective multi-label classification. In *Proceedings of the ACM International Conference on Information and Knowledge Management* (pp. 195-200). New York: ACM Press.

Gholap, A., Naik, G., Joshi, A., & Rao, C. V. K. (2005). Content based tissue image mining. In *Proceedings of the IEEE Computational Systems Bioinformatics Conference* (pp. 359-363).

Goodyear, P., Salmon, G., Spector, J. M., Steeples, C., & Tickner, S. (2001). Competences for online teaching: A special report. *Educational Technology Research and Development, 49*(1), 65–72. doi:10.1007/BF02504508

Gool, L. V., Breitenstein, M. D., Gammeter, S., Grabner, H., & Quack, T. (2009). Mining from Large Image Sets. In *Proceedings of the ACM Int. Conference on Image and Video Retrieval.*

Goschnick, S., & Balbo, S. (2005). Game-first Programming for Information Systems Students. In *Proceedings of the Second Australasian Conference on Interactive Entertainment* (pp. 71-74). Sydney, Australia: Creativity & Cognition Studios Press.

Grammalidis, N., Beletsiotis, D., & Strintzis, M. G. (1999). Sprite Generation and Coding of Multiview Image Sequences. In *Proceedings from ICIAP'99: 10th Image Analysis and Processing, International Conference on* (p. 95).

Gray, A. (1997). *Modern Differential Geometry of Curves and Surfaces with Mathematica* (2nd ed.). Boca Raton, FL: CRC Press.

Grimald, R. P. (1994). *Discrete And Combinatorial MatheMatics: An Introduction* (5th ed.). Reading, MA: Addison Wesley.

Grodzicki, R., Mańdziuk, J., & Wang, L. (2008). Improved multilabel classification with neural networks. In *Parallel Problem Solving from Nature* (LNCS 5199, pp. 409-416).

Gruber, T. (1993). A Translation Approach to Portable Ontologies. *Knowledge Acquisition, 5*(2), 199–220. doi:10.1006/knac.1993.1008

Gueziec, A. (2002). Tracking Pitches for Broadcast Television. *IEEE Computer, 35*(3), 38–43.

Guy, M., & Tonkin, E. (2006). Tidying up Tags. *D-Lib Magazine.* Retrieved from www.dlib.org/dlib/january06/guy/01guy.html

Haas, S. M., & Senjo, S. R. (2004). Perceptions of effectiveness and the actual use of technology-based methods of instruction: a study of California criminal justice and crime-related faculty. *Journal of Criminal Justice Education, 15*(2), 263–285. doi:10.1080/10511250400085981

Haastad, J. (1990). Tensor Rank is NP-complete. *Journal of Algorithms, 11*, 644–654. doi:10.1016/0196-6774(90)90014-6

Hamada, M., Martz, H. F., Reese, C. S., & Wilson, A. G. (2001). Statistical practice: finding near-optimal bayesian experimental designs via genetic algorithms. *The American Statistician, 55*(3), 175–181. doi:10.1198/000313001317098121

Hansen, N. (2008). *The CMA evolution strategy: A tutorial.* Retrieved April 2008, from http://lautaro.fb10.tu-berlin.de/user/niko/cmatutorial.pdf

Hardin, R. H., Sloane, N. J., & Smith, W. D. (1997, May 30). *Spherical Coverings.* Retrieved from http://www.sphopt.com/math/question/covering.html

Hardoon, D., Saunders, C., Szedmak, S., & Shawe-Taylor, J. (2006). A correlation approach for automatic image annotation. In *International Conference ADMA* (LNCS 4093).

Harshman, R. A. (1970). Foundations of the PARAFAC Procedure: Models and Conditions for an 'Explanatory' Multi-modal Factor Analysis. *UCLA working papers in phonetics, 16*, 1-84.

Hasan, B. (2003). The influence of specific computer experiences on computer self-efficacy beliefs. *Computers in Human Behavior, 19*, 443–450. doi:10.1016/S0747-5632(02)00079-1

Haupt, R. L., & Haupt, S. E. (2004). *Practical genetic algorithms.* New York: John Wiley & Sons.

Hazen, T. J. (2006). Automatic alignment and error correction of human generated transcripts for long speech recordings. In *Proceedings of the International Conference of the International Speech Communication Association – INTERSPEECH.*

Hemsley, A., & Mukundan, R. (2009). Multi-fractal measures for tissue image classification and retrieval, In *Proceedings of the IEEE International Symposium on Multimedia* (pp. 618-623).

Henderson, L. (2005). A Significant Cognitive Artifact of Contemporary Youth Culture. In *DiGRA.* Video Games.

Henney, A. J., & Aqbiny, J. I. (2005). Board Games of African Origin on Mobile Phones. In *Proceedings of the Second International Conference on Mobile Technology, Applications and Systems,* Guangzhou, China (pp. 1-8).

He, X., King, O., Ma, W.-Y., Li, M., & Zhang, H. J. (2003). Learning a semantic space from user's relevance feedback for image retrieval. *IEEE Transactions on Circuits and Systems for Video Technology, 13*, 39–49. doi:10.1109/TCSVT.2002.808087

Hofmann, T. &. Puzicha, J. (1998). *Statistical models for co-occurrence data* (Tech. Rep. 1635). Cambridge, MA: MIT.

Hong, E., & O'Neil, H. F. Jr. (2001). Construct validation of a trait self-regulation model. *International Journal of Psychology, 36*(3), 186–194. doi:10.1080/00207590042000146

Hoppmann, T. K. (2009). Examining the 'point of frustration': the think-aloud method applied to online search tasks. *Quality & Quantity, 43*(2), 211–224. doi:10.1007/s11135-007-9116-0

Hoshikawa, D. (2006). Utilization of IT in Professional Baseball. *Operations Research as a Management Science Research, 51*(1), 37–39.

Huang, C. (2003). *Automatic closed caption alignment based on speech recognition transcripts* (Tech. Rep. No. 005). New York, New York: Columbia University.

Huang, X., Alleva, F., Hon, H. W., Hwang, M. Y., Lee, K. F., & Rosenfeld, R. (1992). The SPHINX-II speech recognition system: an overview. *Computer Speech & Language, 7*(2), 137–148. doi:10.1006/csla.1993.1007

Hunter, J. (2002). *Combining the CIDOC CRM and MPEG-7 to Describe Multimedia in Museums.* ERIC Clearinghouse.

Hunter, J. (2003). Enhancing the Semantic Interoperability of Multimedia through a Core Ontology. *IEEE Transactions on Circuits and Systems for Video Technology, 13*(1), 49–58. doi:10.1109/TCSVT.2002.808088

Hwang, H., Choi, H., Kang, B., Yoon, H., Kim, H., Kim, S., & Choi, H. (2005). Classification of breast tissue images based on wavelet transform using discriminant analysis, neural network and SVM. In *Proceedings of the International Workshop on Enterprise Networking and Computing in Healthcare Industry* (pp. 345-349).

Isaac, A., & Troncy, R. (2004). Designing and Using an Audio-Visual Description Core Ontology. In *Proceedings of the Workshop on Core Ontologies in Ontology Engineering*.

Ishikawa, A., Panahpour Tehrani, M., Naito, S., Sakazawa, S., & Koike, A. (2008). Free viewpoint video generation for walk-through experience using image-based rendering. In *Proceedings from MM '08 ACM: In Proceeding of the 16th ACM international Conference on Multimedia* (pp. 1007-1008).

ISO/IEC 14496-2. (1999). *Information Technology – Coding of audio-visual objects– Part 2: Visual*.

ISO/IEC. (2002). *Information Technology - Multimedia Content Description Interface - part 3: Visual. Number 15938-3*. Geneva, Switzerland: ISO/IEC, Moving Pictures Expert Group.

Jafari-Khouzani, K., & Soltanian-Zadeh, H. (2005). Radon transform orientation estimation for rotation invariant texture analysis. *IEEE Transactions on Pattern Analysis and Machine Intelligence, 27*, 1004–1008. doi:10.1109/TPAMI.2005.126

James, F. K., & Keith, W. R. (2004). *Computer Networking A Top-Down Approach Featuring the Internet* (3rd ed.). Reading, MA: Addison Wesley.

Jeong, A., & Joung, S. (2007). Scaffolding collaborative argumentation in asynchronous discussions with message constraints and message labels. *Computers & Education, 48*(3), 427–445. doi:10.1016/j.compedu.2005.02.002

Jiang, H., Zhao, Y., & Dong, X. (2008). Mining positive and negative weighted association rules from frequent itemsets based on interest. In *Proceedings of the IEEE International Symposium on Computational Intelligence and Design (ISCID08)* (pp. 242-245).

Jiang, W., Zavesky, E., Chang, S.-F., & Loui, A. (2008). Cross-domain learning methods for high-level visual concept classification. In *Proceedings of the IEEE International Conference on Image Processing (ICIP08)* (pp. 161-164).

Jiang, Y.-G., Ngo, C.-W., & Chang, S.-F. (2009). Semantic context transfer across heterogeneous sources for domain adaptive video search. In *Proceedings of the ACM International Conference on Multimedia (MM09)* (pp. 155-164).

Jiang, Y.-G., Yang, J., Ngo, C.-W., & Hauptmann, A. G. (2010). Representations of keypoint-based semantic concept detection: a comprehensive study. *IEEE Transactions on Multimedia, 12*(1), 42–53. doi:10.1109/TMM.2009.2036235

Jin, M., & Masakatsu, M. (2007). Authorship Identification using Random Forests. *Institute of Statistical Mathematics, 55*(2), 255–268.

Jinzenji, K., Watanabe, H., Okada, S., & Kobayashi, N. (2001). MPEG-4 Very Low Bit-rate Video Compression Using Sprite Coding. In *Proceedings from ICME'01: IEEE International Conference on Multimedia and Expo*.

Ji, R. R., Yao, H. X., & Liang, D. W. (2008). DRM: dynamic region matching for image retrieval using probabilistic fuzzy matching and boosting feature selection. *Signal. Image and Video Processing, 2*(1), 59–71. doi:10.1007/s11760-007-0037-0

Joachims, T. (1998). Text categorization with support vector machines: learning with many relevant features. In C. N'edellec & C. Rouveirol (Eds.), *European Conference on Machine Learning* (pp. 137-142). New York: Springer.

Joachims, T. (1999). *Kernel Methods - Support Vector Learning*. Cambridge, MA: MIT-Press.

Johnson, D., & Johnson, R. (2008). Cooperation and the use of technology. In Spector, J. M. (Ed.), *M*.

Joly, A., Frélicot, C., & Buisson, O. (2003). Robust content-based video copy identification in a large reference database. In *Proceedings of the International Conference on Image and Video Retrieval* (pp. 414-424).

Joly, A., Frélicot, C., & Buisson, O. (2007). Content-based copy detection using distortion-based probabilistic similarity search. *IEEE Transactions on Multimedia, 9*(2), 293–306. doi:10.1109/TMM.2006.886278

Kagima, L. K., & Hausafus, C. O. (2000). Integration of electronic communication in higher education: Contributions of faculty computer self-efficacy. *The Internet and Higher Education*, 2(4), 221–235. doi:10.1016/S1096-7516(00)00027-0

Karydis, I., Nanopoulos, A., Gabriel, H., & Spiliopoulou, M. (2009). Tag-aware spectral clustering of Music Items. In *Proceedings of the International Society for Music Information Retrieval Conference*, Kobe, Japan (Vol. 10, pp. 159-164).

Katayose, H., & Imanishi, K. (2005). A Trading Card Game using AR Technology. In *ACE* (pp. 354–355). ARMS.

Katz, H. A., & Worsham, S. (2005). Streaming mLearning Objects via data resolution and web services to mobile devices: design guidelines and system architecture model. In *Proceedings of the MLEARN 2005*, Cape Town, South Africa. Retrieved November 5, 2009, from http://www.mlearn.org.za/CD/papers/Katz%20&%20Worsham.pdf

Ke, Y., Sukthankar, R., & Huston, L. (2004). Efficient near-duplicate and sub-image retrieval. In *Proceedings of the ACM International Conference on Multimedia* (pp. 869-876).

Kim, H.-s., Lee, J., Liu, H., & Lee, D. (2008). Video linkage: group based copied video detection. In *Proceedings of the International Conference on Content-based Image and Video Retrieval* (pp. 397-406).

Kim, S. B., Choi, S. K., Jang, H. S., Kwon, D. Y., Yeum, Y. C., & Lee, W. G. (2006). *Smalltalk Card Game for Learning Object-Oriented Thinking in an Evolutionary Way* (pp. 683–684). Portland, OR: OOPSLA.

Kim, S.-J., & Lee, K. B. (2003). Constructing decision trees with multiple response variables. *International Journal of Management and Decision Making*, 4(4), 337–353. doi:10.1504/IJMDM.2003.003998

Kim, W.-C., Song, J.-Y., Kim, S.-W., & Park, S. (2008). Image retrieval model based on weighted visual features determined by relevance feedback. *Information Sciences*, 178(22), 4301–4313. doi:10.1016/j.ins.2008.06.025

Kinsner, W., & Zhang, H. (2009). Multi-fractal analysis and feature extraction of DNA sequences. In *Proeedings of the IEEE Intlernational Conference on Cognitive Informatics* (pp. 29-36).

Kleinberg, J. (1999). Authoritative Sources in a Hyperlinked Environment. *Journal of the ACM*, 46(5), 604–632. doi:10.1145/324133.324140

Kocev, D., Vens, C., & Struyf, J. (2007). Ensembles of multi-objective decision trees. In *Proceedings of the European Conference on Machine Learning* (LNCS 4701, pp. 624-631). New York: Springer.

Kolda, T. G., & Sun, J. (2008). Scalable Tensor Decompositions for Multi-aspect Data Mining. In *Proceedings of the IEEE International Conference on Data Mining*, Pisa, Italy (Vol. 8, pp. 363-372).

Kolda, T. G., Bader, B. W., & Kenny, J. P. (2005). Higher-Order Web Link Analysis Using Multi-linear Algebra. In *Proceedings of the IEEE International Conference on Data Mining*, Houston, TX (Vol. 5, pp. 242-249).

Kolda, T. G., & Bader, B. W. (2009). Tensor Decompositions and Applications. *SIAM Review*, 51(3), 455–500. doi:10.1137/07070111X

Komisarczuk, P., & Welch, I. (2006). A Board Game for Teaching Internet Engineering. In *Proceedings of the 8th Australian conference on Computing education*, Hobart, IN (Vol. 52, pp. 117-123). New York: ACM.

Kon'ya, Y., Kuwano, H., Yamada, T., Kawamori, M., & Kawazoe, K. (2005). Metadata Generation and Distribution for Live Programs on Broadcasting-Telecommunication Linkage Services. In *Proceedings of the Pacific Rim Conference on Multimedia* (pp. 224-233).

Kosch, H. (2003). *Distributed multimedia database technologies supported by MPEG-7 and MPEG-21*. Boca Raton, FL: CRC Press.

Kotsiantis, S. B., & Pintelas, P. E. (2004). Combining Bagging and Boosting. *International Journal of Computational Intelligence*, 1(4), 324–333.

Kumar, P., Ranganath, S., Huang, W., & Sengupta, K. (2005). Framework for real time behavior interpretation from traffic video. *IEEE Transactions on Intelligent Transportation Systems*, 6, 43–53. doi:10.1109/TITS.2004.838219

Kunter, M., Kim, J., & Sikora, T. (2005, December). Super-resolution Mosaicing using Embedded Hybrid Recursive Flow-based segmentation. In *Proceedings of the Int. Conf. on Information, communications and Signal Processing (ICICS '05)*.

Lagoze, C., & Hunter, J. (2001). The ABC ontology and model. *Journal of Digital Information, 2*(2).

Lai, A.-N., Yoon, H., & Lee, G. (2008). Robust background extraction scheme using histogram-wise for real-time tracking in urban traffic video. In *Proceedings from CIT 2008: 8th IEEE International Conference* (pp. 845-850).

Lam, A. H. T., Chow, K. C. H., Yau, E. H. H., & Lyu, M. R. (2006). ART: Augmented Reality Table for Interactive Trading Card Game. In *Proceedings of the International Conference on Virtual Reality Continuum and Its Applications*, Hong Kong, China (pp. 357-360).

Lamere, P. (2008). Social Tagging and Music Information Retrieval. *Journal of New Music Research, 37*(2), 101–114. doi:10.1080/09298210802479284

Last.fm. (n.d.). *A social music platform*. Retrieved from http://www.last.fm

Lastein, L., & Reul, B. (2003). *Transrating Efficiency -- Bit-rate reduction methods to enable more services over existing bandwidth*. Retrieved November 5, 2009, from http://www.broadcastpapers.com/whitepapers/IBCBarconetTransratingEfficiency.pdf?CFID=37604273&CFTOKEN=42a178598bba5024-FC0BFE9E-0F72-5D57-AEB8738937907188

Law-To, J., Buisson, O., Gouet-Brunet, V., & Boujemaa, N. (2006). Robust voting algorithm based on labels of behavior for video copy detection. In *Proceedings of the ACM International Conference on Multimedia* (pp. 835-844).

Law-To, J., Chen, L., Joly, A., Laptev, I., Buisson, O., Gouet-Brunet, V., et al. (2007). Video copy detection: a comparative study. In *Proceedings of the International Conference on Image and Video Retrieval* (pp. 371-378).

Leibe, B., Leonardis, A., & Schiele, B. (2008). Robust object detection with interleaved categorization and segmentation. *International Journal of Computer Vision, 77*, 259–289. doi:10.1007/s11263-007-0095-3

Leon, G., Kalva, H., & Furht, B. (2009). Video identification using video tomography. In *Proceedings of the IEEE International Conference on Multimedia and Expo* (pp. 1030-1033).

Leonardi, R., Migliorati, P., & Prandini, M. (2004). Semantic indexing of soccer audio-visual sequences: A multimodal approach based on controlled Markov Chains. *IEEE Transactions on Circuits and Systems for Video Technology, 14*, 634–643. doi:10.1109/TCSVT.2004.826751

Leone, N., Pfeifer, G., Faber, W., Eiter, T., Gottlob, G., Perri, S., & Scarcello, F. (2002). *The DLV System for Knowledge Representation and Reasoning* (Tech. Rep. No. cs.AI/0211004). arXiv.org. Retrieved April 14, 2008, from http://www.dbai.tuwien.ac.at/proj/dlv/#publications

Levy, M., & Sandler, M. (2007). A Semantic Space for Music Derived from Social Tags. In *Proceedings of the International Conference on Music Information Retrieval*, Vienna, Austria (Vol. 8, pp. 411-416).

Levy, M., & Sandler, M. (2008). Learning Latent Semantic Models for Music from Social Tags. *Journal of New Music Research, 37*(2), 137–150. doi:10.1080/09298210802479292

Levy-Vehel, J., Mignot, P., & Berroir, J. (1992). *Texture and Multi-fractals: New Tools for Image Analysis* (Tech. Rep. No. 1706). France: INRIA.

Lew, M. S., Sebe, N., Djeraba, C., & Jain, R. (2006). Content-based multimedia information retrieval: State of art and challenges. *ACM Transactions on Multimedia Computing, Communications and Applications, 2*(1), 1–19.

Li, T. (2005). A general model for clustering binary data. In *Proceedings of the ACM SIGKDD International Conference on Knowledge Discovery in Data Mining* (pp. 188-197).

Li, Y., Jin, J., & Zhou, X. (2005). Video matching using binary signature. In *Proceedings of the International Symposium on Intelligent Signal Processing and Communication Systems* (pp. 317-320).

Liddy, E. D., Allen, E., Harwell, S., Corieri, S., Yilmazel, O., Ercan Ozgencil, N., et al. (2002, August). Automatic Metadata Generation & Evaluation. In *Proceedings of the 25th Annual International ACM SIGIR Conference on Research and Development in Information Retrieval,* Tampere, Finland (pp. 401-402). New York: ACM Publishing.

Liekens, A. (2007, March 28-April 2). *Data mining music profiles.* Retrieved from http://anthony.liekens.net/index.php/ Computers/DataMining

Lien, C.-C., Chiang, C.-L., & Lee, C.-H. (2007, February). Scene-Based Event Detection for Baseball Videos. *Journal of Visual Communication and Image Representation, 18*(1), 1–14. doi:10.1016/j.jvcir.2006.09.002

Lim, D. (2007). Taking Students Out for a Ride: Using a Board Game to Teach Graph Theory. In *Proceedings of the 38th SIGCSE technical symposium on Computer science education,* KY (pp. 367-371). New York: ACM.

Lim, S.-C., Na, H.-R., & Lee, Y.-L. (2007). Rate Control Based on Linear Regression for H.264/MPEG-4 AVC. *Signal Processing Image Communication, 22*(1), 39–58. doi:10.1016/j.image.2006.11.001

Lin, L., & Ravitz, G. Shyu, M.-L., & Chen, S.-C. (2008). Effective feature space reduction with imbalanced data for semantic concept detection. In *Proceedings of the IEEE International Conference on Sensor Networks, Ubiquitous, and Trustworthy Computing (SUTC08)* (pp. 262-269).

Lin, L., & Shyu, M.-L. (2009). Mining high-level features from video using associations and correlations. In *Proceedings of the Third IEEE International Conference on Semantic Computing (IEEE ICSC2009)* (pp. 137-144).

Lin, L., Ravitz, G., Shyu, M.-L., & Chen, S.-C. (2007). Video semantic concept discovery using multimodel-based association classification. In *Proceedings of the IEEE International Conference on Multimedia and Expo (ICME07)* (pp. 859-862).

Lin, L., Ravitz, G., Shyu, M.-L., & Chen, S.-C. (2008). Correlation-based video semantic concept detection using multiple correspondence analysis. In *Proceedings of the IEEE International Symposium on Multimedia (ISM08)* (pp. 316-321).

Lin, L., Shyu, M.-L., & Chen, S.-C. (2009). Enhancing concept detection by pruning data with MCA-based transaction weights. In *Proceedings of the IEEE International Symposium on Multimedia (ISM09)* (pp. 304-311).

Lin, L., Shyu, M.-L., Ravitz, G., & Chen, S.-C. (2009). Video semantic concept detection via associative classification. In *Proceedings of the IEEE International Conference on Multimedia and Expo (ICME09)* (pp. 418-421).

Lin, G., Wang, C., Chang, Y., & Chen, Y. (2002, December). Realtime object extraction and tracking with an active camera using image mosaics. In Proceedings of the *Multimedia Signal Processing, 9*(11), 149–152.

Lin, L., & Shyu, M.-L. (2010). Weighted association rule mining for video semantic detection. [IJMDEM]. *International Journal of Multimedia Data Engineering and Management, 1*(1), 37–54.

Liu, H., & Motada, H. (1998). *Feature selection for knowledge discovery and data mining.* Dordrecht, The Netherlands: Kluwer Academic Publishers.

Liu, Y., & Li, Y. (1997). New Approaches of multi-fractal analysis. In *Proceedings of the IEEE International Conference on Information, Communication and Signal Processing* (Vol. 2, pp. 970-974).

Liu, Y., Mei, T., Wu, X., & Hua, X.-S. (2009). Multigraph-based query-independent learning for video search. *IEEE Transactions on Circuits and Systems for Video Technology, 19*(12), 1841–1850. doi:10.1109/TCSVT.2009.2026951

Li, Z.-N., & Drew, M. S. (2003). *Fundamentals of Multimedia.* Englewood Cliffs, NJ: Prentice-Hall.

Lowe, D. G. (2004). Distinctive Image Features from Scale-Invariant Keypoints. *International Journal of Computer Vision, 60*(2), 91–110. doi:10.1023/B:VISI.0000029664.99615.94

Lu, Y., Gao, W., & Wu, F. (2003, May). Efficient background video coding with static sprite generation and arbitrary-shape spatial prediction techniques. In *Proceedings of the Circuits and Systems for Video Technology, IEEE Transactions* (Vol. 13, No. 5, pp. 394-405).

Lu, J., Yu, C. S., Liu, C., & Yao, J. E. (2003). Technology acceptance model for wireless internet. *Internet Research: Electronic Networking Applications and Policy, 13*(3), 206–222. doi:10.1108/10662240310478222

Ma, A., Sethi, I. K., & Patel, N. (2009). Multimedia content tagging using multilabel decision tree. In *Proceedings of the IEEE Intl. Workshop on Multimedia Information Processing and Retrieval (MIPR)*.

MacQueen, J. B. (1967). Some Methods for classification and Analysis of Multivariate Observations. In *Proceedings of 5th Berkeley Symposium on Mathematical Statistics and Probability* (pp. 281-297).

Makansi, J., & Reactorland. (2001). A board game. *IEEE, 38*(11), 42-43.

Mandelbrot, B. B. (1982). *The Fractal Geometry of Nature*. New York: W. H. Freeman and Company.

Manjunath, B., Ohm, J.-R., Vasudevan, V., & Yamada, A. (2001). Color and texture descriptors. *IEEE Transactions on Circuits and Systems for Video Technology, 11*(6), 703–715. doi:10.1109/76.927424

Manjunath, B., Salembier, P., & Sikora, T. (2002). *Introduction to MPEG-7: Multimedia Content Description Interface*. New York: Wiley.

Maree, R., Geurts, P., Piater, J., & Wehenkel, L. (2005). Biomedical Image Classification with Random Subwindows and Decision Trees. In *Proceedings of the ICCV workshop on Computer Vision for Biomedical Image Applications (CVIBA 2005)* (Vol. 3765, pp. 220-229).

Martone, A. F., Taskiran, C. M., & Delp, E. J. (2004). Automated closed-captioning using text alignment. *Proceedings of the Society for Photo-Instrumentation Engineers, 5307*, 108–116.

McCallum, A. (1999). Multi-label text classification with a mixture model trained by EM. In *Proceedings of the AAAI99 Workshop on Text Learning*.

McGuinness, D., & van Harmelen, F. (2004). *OWL Web Ontology Language Overview*. Retrieved from http://www.w3.org/TR/owl-features/

McLean, S. (2007). University Extension and Social Change: Positioning a University of the People in Saskatchewan. *Adult Education Quarterly, 58*(3), 3–21. doi:10.1177/0741713607305945

Megalou, E., & Hadzilacos, T. (2003). Semantic abstractions in the multimedia domain. *IEEE Transactions on Knowledge and Data Engineering, 15*(1), 136–160. doi:10.1109/TKDE.2003.1161587

Menzies, T., & Hu, Y. (2003). Data Mining for Very Busy People. *Computer, 36*(11), 22–29. doi:10.1109/MC.2003.1244531

Merler, M., Rong, Y., & Smith, J. R. (2009). Imbalanced RankBoost for efficiently ranking large-scale image/video collections. In *Proceedings of the IEEE International Conference on Computer Vision and Pattern Recognition (CVPR09)* (pp. 2607-2614).

Merrill, J. Merrienboer, & M. Driscoll (Eds.), *Handbook of Research on Educational Communications and Technology* (pp. 659-670). New York: Routledge.

Mikolajczyk, K., & Schmid, D. (2002). An affine invariant interest point detector. In *Proceedings of the 7th European Conference on Computer Vision*, Copenhagen, Denmark (pp. 128-142). New York: Springer.

Mikolajczyk, K., Tuytelaars, T., Schmid, C., Zisserman, A., Matas, J., & Schaffalitzky, F. (2005). A comparison of affine region detectors. *International Journal of Computer Vision, 65*, 43–72. doi:10.1007/s11263-005-3848-x

Mitschick, A., Nagel, R., & Meissner, K. (2008). Semantic Metadata Instantiation and Consolidation within an Ontology-based Multimedia Document Management System. In *Proceedings of the 5th European Semantic Web Conference ESWC*, Tenerife, Spain.

Moreno, P. J., Joerg, C., Thong, J. M., & Van Glickman, O. (1998). A recursive algorithm for the forced alignment of very long audio segments. In *Proceedings of the International Conference on Spoken Language Processing*.

MPEG-4. (n.d.) Retrieved from http://www.chiariglione.org/mpeg/standards/MPEG-4/MPEG-4.htm

Multimedia and Expo. 2002. In *Proceedings of the IEEE International Conference (ICME '02)* (Vol. 2, pp. 537-540).

Munoz-Diosdado, A. (2005). A non linear analysis of human gait time series based on multi-fractal analysis and cross correlations. *Journal of Physics: Conference Series, 23*, 87–95. doi:10.1088/1742-6596/23/1/010

Musgrave, F. K. (2004). Fractal Forgeries of Nature. *Symposia Pure Mathematics, 72*(2).

Myers, R. H., & Montgomery, D. C. (2002). *Response surface methodology: Process and product optimization using designed experiments.* New York: John Wiley & Sons.

Nack, F., & Lindsay, A. (1999). Everything you wanted to know about MPEG-7 (Part I). *IEEE MultiMedia, 6*(3), 65–77. doi:10.1109/93.790612

Nack, F., & Lindsay, A., & GMD-IPSI, D. (1999). Everything you wanted to know about MPEG-7 (Part 2). *IEEE MultiMedia, 6*(4), 64–73. doi:10.1109/93.809235

Nack, F., Van Ossenbruggen, J., & Hardman, L. (2005). That Obscure Object of Desire: Multimedia Metadata on the Web (part 2). *IEEE MultiMedia, 12*(1), 54–63. doi:10.1109/MMUL.2005.12

Nascimento, J.-C., & Marques, J.-S. (2006). Performance evaluation of object detection algorithms for video surveillance. In *Proceedings from ICPR'02: 16th International Conference on Pattern Recognition* (Vol. 3, p. 30965).

Natsev, A., Haubold, A., Tevsic, J., Xie, L., & Yan, R. (2007). Semantic concept-based query expansion and re-ranking for multimedia retrieval. In *Proceedings of the ACM International Conference on Multimedia (MM07)* (pp. 991-1000).

Natvig, L., & Line, S. (2004). Age of Computers: An Innovative Combination of History and Computer Game Elements for Teaching Computer Fundamentals. In *Proceedings of FIE 2004, Lasse Natvig, Steinar Line and Djupdal.*

Neubeck, A., & Van Gool, L. (2006). Efficient non-maximum suppression. In *Proceedings of the International Conference on Pattern Recognition* (pp. 850-855).

Neuhaus, M., & Bunke, H. (2006). Edit distance based kernel functions for structural pattern classification. *Pattern Recognition, 39*, 1852–1863. doi:10.1016/j.patcog.2006.04.012

Ng, C. W., King, I., & Lyu, M. R. (2001). Video comparison using tree matching algorithm. In *Proceedings of the International Conference on Imaging Science, Systems and Technology* (pp. 184-190).

Nielsen, J., Clemmensen, T., & Yssing, C. (2002). Getting access to what goes on in people's heads? In *Proceedings of the Reflections on the think-aloud technique (NordiCHI).*

Nielsen, J. (1994). Heuristic evaluation. In Nielsen, J., & Mack, R. (Eds.), *Usability Inspection Methods.* New York: John Wiley & Sons.

Nister, D., & Stewenius, H. (2006). Robust scalable recognition with a vocabulary tree. In *Proceedings of the IEEE Computer Society Conference on Computer Vision and Pattern Recognition* (pp. 2161-2168).

O'Neil, H. F. Jr. (1999). Perspectives on computer-based performance assessment of problem-solving. *Computers in Human Behavior, 15*, 225–268.

O'Neil, H. F. Jr, & Herl, H. E. (1998). *Reliability and validity of a trait measure of self-regulation. Center for Research on Evaluation, Standards, and Student Testing.* CRESST.

Orazio, D.-T., Leo, M., Mosca, N., Spagnolo, P., & Mazzeo, P. L. (2009). A semi-automatic system for ground-truth generation of soccer video sequences. In *Proceedings from AVSS '09: the 2009 Sixth IEEE International Conference on Advanced Video and Signal Based Surveillance* (pp. 559-564).

Oria, V., Özsu, M. T., & Iglinski, P. (2004). Visual-MOQL, the DISIMA visual query language. *Multimedia Tools and Applications, 23*, 185–201. doi:10.1023/B:MTAP.0000031756.10332.9d

Ortiz, F., Simpson, J. R., Pignatiello, J. J., & Heredia-Langner, A. (2004). A genetic algorithm approach to multiple-response optimization. *Journal of Quality Technology, 36*(4), 432–450.

Pampalk, E. (2001). *Islands of Music: Analysis, Organization and Visualizations of Music Archives.* Unpublished master thesis, Vienna University of Technology, Vienna, Austria.

Panasonic. (n.d.). *Color OCR Library.* Retrieved November 10, 2008, from http://panasonic.co.jp/pss/pstc/products/colorocrlib/

Parlangeli, O., Marchigiani, E., & Bagnara, S. (1999). Multimedia systems in distance education: effects of usability on learning. *Interacting with Computers, 12*(1), 37–49. doi:10.1016/S0953-5438(98)00054-X

Patton, M. Q. (2002). *Qualitative Research and Evaluation Methods*. Thousand Oaks, CA: Sage.

Peitz, J., Björk, S., & Jäppinen, A. (2006). Wizard's apprentice gameplay-oriented design of a computer-augmented board game. In *Proceedings of the ACM SIG-CHI international conference on Advances in computer entertainment technology.*

Pekar, V., Krkoska, M., & Staab, S. (2004). Feature weighting for co-occurrence-based classification of words. In *Proceedings of the International Conference on Computational Linguistics (COLING04)* (no. 799).

Peters, L. H., & O'Connor, E. J. (1980). Situational constraints and work outcomes: The influences of a frequently overlooked construct. *Academy of Management Review, 5*(3), 391–397. doi:10.2307/257114

Peterson, T., & Arnn, R. (2005). Self-efficacy: The foundation of Human Performance. *Performance Improvement Quarterly, 18*(2), 5–18. doi:10.1111/j.1937-8327.2005.tb00330.x

Philbin, J., Chum, O., Isard, M., Sivic, J., & Zisserman, A. (2007). Object retrieval with large vocabularies and fast spatial matching. In *Proceedings of the IEEE Conference on Computer Vision and Pattern Recognition.*

Placeway, P., & Lafferty, J. (1996). Cheating with imperfect transcripts. In *Proceedings of the International Conference on Spoken Language Processing* (pp. 2115-2118).

Prensky, M. (2003). Digital game-based learning. *ACM Computers in Entertainment, 1*(1), 1–4.

Pullen, J., & McAndrews, P. (2004). A web portal for open-source synchronous distance education. In *Proceedings of the Seventh IASTED International Conference on Computers and Advanced Technology in Education* (pp. 428-037).

Qi, D., & Yu, L. (2008). Multi-fractal Spectrum theory used to medical image from CT testing. In *Proceedings IEEE International Conference on Advanced Intelligent Mechatronics* (pp. 68-73).

Quinlan, J. (1993). *C4.5: Programs for Machine Learning*. San Francisco, CA: Morgan Kaufmann Publishers.

Quintana Y. O'Brien R. Patel A. Becksfort J. Shuler A. Nambayan A. (2008).

Rajaravivarma, R. (2005). A Games-Based Approach for Teaching the Introductory Programming Course. *ACM SIGCSE 2005 Bulletin archive, 37*(4).

Rander, P. (1998). *A Multi-Camera Method for 3D Digitization of Dynamic, Real-World Events* (Tech. Rep. CMU-RI-TR-98-12). Pittsburgh, PA: Robotics Institute, Carnegie Mellon University.

Reljin, I., & Reljin, B. (2002). Fractal Geometry and Multi-fractals in Analyzing and Processing Medical Data and Images. *Archive of Oncology, 10*(4), 283–293. doi:10.2298/AOO0204283R

Reljin, I., Reljin, B., & Pavlovic, I. (2000). Multi-fractal analysis of grayscale images. In *Proceedings of the Mediterranean Electro-technical Conference, 2*, 490–493.

Remidez, H., Stam, A., & Laffey, J. (2007). Web-based template-driven communication support systems: Using Shadow netWorkspace to support trust development in virtual teams. *International Journal of e-Collaboration, 3*(1), 65–83.

Renyi, A. (1970). *Probability Theory*. New York: North-Holland.

Richardson, J. C., & Swan, K. (2003). Examine social presence in online course in relation to students' perceived learning and satisfaction. *Journal of Asynchronous Learning Networks*, 68–88.

Riedi, R. H. (1999). *Introduction to Multi-fractals*. Houston, Texas: Rice University, Department of ECE.

Robert-Ribes, J., & Mukhtar, R. G. (1997). Automatic generation of hyperlinks between audio and transcript. In *Proceedings of the Conference on Speech Communication and Technology – Eurospeech* (pp. 903-906).

Rothganger, F., Lazebnik, S., Schmid, C., & Ponce, J. (2004). Segmenting, modeling, and matching video clips containing multiple moving objects. In *Proceedings of the Conference on Computer Vision and Pattern Recognition* (pp. 914-921).

Rothganger, F., Lazebnik, S., Schmid, C., & Ponce, J. (2004). 3D Object Modeling and Recognition Using Local Affine-Invariant Image Descriptors and Multi-View Spatial Constraints. *International Journal of Computer Vision, 66*(3), 231–259. doi:10.1007/s11263-005-3674-1

Roussou, M. (2004). Learning by Doing and Learning Through Play: An Exploration of Interactivity in Virtual Environments for Children. *ACM Computers in Entertainment, 2*(1).

Rousu, J., Saunders, C., Szedmak, S., & Shawe-Taylor, J. (2004). On maximum margin hierarchical classification. In *Proceedings of the NIPS 2004 Workshop on Learning With Structured Outputs*.

Rousu, J., Saunders, C., Szedmak, S., & Shawe-Taylor, J. (2005). Learning hierarchical multicategory text classification models. In *Proceedings of the International Conference on Machine Learning*.

Rousu, J., Saunders, C., Szedmak, S., & Shawe-Taylor, J. (2006). Kernel-based learning of hierarchical multilabel classification models. *Journal of Machine Learning Research, 7*, 1601–1626.

Ruan, S., & Bloyet, D. (2000). MRF models and multifractal analysis for MRI segmentation. In *Proceedings IEEE International Conference on Signal Processing* (Vol. 2, pp. 1259-1262).

Rubin, J. (1994). *Handbook of Usability Testing: How to plan, design, and conduct effective tests*. New York: John Wiley & Sons.

Rui, Y., Huang, T. S., & Mehrotra, S. (1999). Constructing table-of-content for videos. *Multimedia Systems, 7*(5), 359–368. doi:10.1007/s005300050138

Saadé, R., & Bahli, B. (2005). The impact of cognitive absorption on perceived usefulness and perceived ease of use in on-line learning: An extension of the technology acceptance model. *Information & Management, 42*(2), 317–327. doi:10.1016/j.im.2003.12.013

Saleh, H. (2008). Computer self-efficacy of university faculty in Lebanon. *Educational Technology Research and Development, 56*(2), 229–240. doi:10.1007/s11423-007-9084-z

Salembier, P., & Smith, J. (2002). Overview of Multimedia Description Schemes and Schema Tools. In Manjunath, B., Salembier, P., & Sikora, T. (Eds.), *Introduction to MPEG-7: Multimedia Content Description Interface*. New York: John Wiley & Sons.

Salkind, N. J. (Ed.). (2007). *Encyclopedia of measurement and statistics*. Newbury Park, CA: SAGE Publications.

Salomon, G., & Perkins, D. (1996). Learning in wonderland: What do computers really offer education? In Kerr, S. (Ed.), *Technology and the future of schooling in America: The ninety-fifth yearbook of the national society for the study of education*. Chicago: The University Press of Chicago.

Sand, P., & Teller, S. (2004). Video matching. *ACM Transactions on Graphics*, 592–599. doi:10.1145/1015706.1015765

Scardamalia, M., & Bereiter, C. (1994). Computer Support for Knowledge-Building Communities. *Journal of the Learning Sciences, 3*(3), 265–283. doi:10.1207/s15327809jls0303_3

Schapire, R. E., & Singer, Y. (2000). Boostexter: A boosting-based system for text categorization. *Machine Learning, 39*(2-3), 135–168. doi:10.1023/A:1007649029923

Schneiderman, B. (2005). *Designing the User Interface*. Reading, MA: Addison Wesley.

Schneiderman, H., & Kanade, T. (2004). Object detection using the statistics of parts. *Journal of Computer Vision, 56*, 151–177. doi:10.1023/B:VISI.0000011202.85607.00

Schoenfeld-Tacher, R., & Persichitte, K. (2000). Differential skills and competencies required of faculty teaching distance education courses. *International Journal of Educational Technology, 2*(1).

Schölkopf, B., Platt, J. C., Shawe-Taylor, J., Smola, A. J., & Williamson, R. C. (2001). Estimating the Support of a High-Dimensional Distribution. *Neural Computation, 13*, 1443–1471. doi:10.1162/089976601750264965

Searle, J. R. (1969). *Speech Acts, an Essay in the Philosophy of Language*. New York: Cambridge University Press.

Seddiqui, M. H., & Aono, M. (2008). Alignment Results of Anchor-Flood Algorithm for OAEI-2008. In *Proceedings of Ontology Matching Workshop of the 7th International Semantic Web Conference*, Karlsruhe, Germany (pp. 120-127).

Seddiqui, M. H., & Aono, M. (2009). An Efficient and Scalable Algorithm for Segmented Alignment of Ontologies of Arbitrary Size. In *Proceedings of the Web Semantics: Science, Services and Agents on the World Wide Web* (2008). doi:10.1016/j.websem.2009.09.001

Seddiqui, M. H., Seki, Y., & Aono, M. (2006). Automatic Alignment of Ontology Eliminating the Probable Misalignments. In *Proceedings of the 1st Asian Semantic Web Conference (ASWC2006)*, Beijing, China (pp. 212-218). New York: Springer.

Serre, T., Kouh, M., Cadieu, C., Knoblich, U., Kreiman, G., & Poggio, T. (2005). *A theory of object recognition: computations and circuits in the feedforward path of the ventral stream in primate visual cortex*. Cambridge, MA: MIT.

Shannon, T., & Shoenfeld, C. (1965). *University Extension*. New York: Center for Applied Research.

Sheikh, H. R., & Bovik, A. C. (2006, February). Image information and visual quality. In Proceedings of *Image Processing IEEE Transactions* (Vol. 15, No. 2, pp.430-444).

Shen, H. T., Zhou, X., Huang, Z., Shao, J., & Zhou, X. (2007). Uqlips: a real-time near-duplicate video clip detection system. In *Proceedings of the International Conference on Very Large Data Bases* (pp. 1374-1377).

Shi, H., Revithis, S., & Chen, S. S. (2002). An agent enabling personalized learning in e-Learning Environments. In *Proceedings of the AAMAS'02*, Bologna, Italy.

Shibata, S. (2007). *Digital Baseball Scoring System Using XML*. Retrieved April 25, 2009, from http://www.ipa.go.jp/SPC/report/01fy-pro/dcaj/techadvn/baseball/baseball.pdf

Shirahama, K., Sugihara, C., Matsuoka, Y., & Uehara, K. (2009). Query-based video event definition using rough set theory. In *Proceedings of the ACM international Workshop on Events in Multimedia* (pp. 9-16).

Shum, H., & Komura, T. (2004). A Spatiotemporal Approach to Extract the 3D Trajectory of the Baseball from a Single View Video Sequence. In Proceedings of the *IEEE International Conference on Multimedia & Expo* (pp. 1583-1586).

Shyu, M.-L., & Chen, S.-C. (2005). Guest editorial: Introduction to the special issue. *Multimedia Tools and Applications*, *26*(2), 151–152. doi:10.1007/s11042-005-0449-1

Shyu, M.-L., & Chen, S.-C. (2006). Guest editorial: Introduction to the special issue on multimedia databases. *Information Systems*, *31*(7), 636–637. doi:10.1016/j.is.2005.12.002

Shyu, M.-L., & Chen, S.-C. (2008). Guest editors' introduction. *International Journal of Semantic Computing*, *2*(2), 161–163. doi:10.1142/S1793351X08000427

Shyu, M.-L., Chen, S.-C., Chen, M., Zhang, C., & Shu, C.-M. (2006). Probabilistic semantic network-based image retrieval using MMM and relevance feedback. *Multimedia Tools and Applications*, *30*, 131–147. doi:10.1007/s11042-006-0023-5

Shyu, M.-L., Chen, S.-C., Sun, Q., & Yu, H. (2007). Overview and future trends of multimedia research for content access and distribution. *International Journal of Semantic Computing*, *1*, 29–66. doi:10.1142/S1793351X07000044

Shyu, M.-L., Xie, Z., Chen, M., & Chen, S.-C. (2008). Video semantic event/concept detection using a subspace-based multimedia data mining framework. *IEEE Transactions on Multimedia. Special Issue on Multimedia Data Mining*, *10*(2), 252–259.

Silvester, I. (2006). *Transcoding: The future of the Video Market Depends on It* (IDC Executive Brief). Retrieved October 15, 2009, from http://www.edchina.com/ARTICLES/2006NOV/2/2006NOV10_HA_AVC_HN_12.PDF

Sirkora, T. (1997). The mpeg-4 video standard verification model. *IEEE Transactions on Circuits and Systems for Video Technology*, *7*, 19–31. doi:10.1109/76.554415

Sivic, J., & Zisserman, A. (2006). Video Google: Efficient visual search of videos. *Toward Category-Level Object Recognition* (LNCS, pp. 127-144). New York: Springer.

Sivic, J., Schaffalitzky, F., & Zisserman, A. (2006). Object level grouping for video shots. *International Journal of Computer Vision, 67*(2), 189–210. doi:10.1007/s11263-005-4264-y

Smeaton, A. F., Over, P., & Kraaij, W. (2006). Evaluation campaigns and TRECVid. In *Proceedings of the ACM International Workshop on Multimedia Information Retrieval (MIR06)* (pp. 321-330).

Smolic, A., Sikora, T., & Ohm, J. R. (1999). Long-term global motion estimation and its application for sprite generation, content description and segmentation. *IEEE Transactions on Circuits and Systems for Video Technology, 9*, 1227–1242. doi:10.1109/76.809158

Snoek, C. G. M., & Worring, M. (2008). Concept-based video retrieval. *Foundations and Trends in Information Retrieval, 2*(4), 215–322. doi:10.1561/1500000014

Song, I. H., et al. (2007). Multi-fractal analysis of sleep EEG dynamics in humans. In *Proceedings of the IEEE/EMBS International Conference on Neural Engineering* (pp. 546-549).

Squire, K., Jenkins, H., & Hinrichs, R. (2002). Games-to-Teach Project: Envisioning the Next Generation of Educational Games. In *Proceedings of the Educational Game Conference*, Edinburgh, Scotland.

Srivastava, A., Joshi, S. H., Mio, W., & Liu, X. (2005). Statistical shape analysis: Clustering, learning, and testing. *IEEE Transactions on Pattern Analysis and Machine Intelligence, 27*, 590–602. doi:10.1109/TPAMI.2005.86

Stadium, D. (n.d.). *Data Stadium Inc*. Retrieved April 25, 2009, from http://www.datastadium.co.jp/

Stanford Tissue Microarray Corsortium Web Portal. (n.d.). Retrieved November 2009, from http://smd.stanford.edu/resources/databases.shtml

Stefan Video. (n.d.). Retrieved from http://media.xiph.org/video/derf/

Stoilos, G., Stamou, G., & Kollias, S. (2005). A String Metric for Ontology Alignment. In *Proceedings of the 4th International Semantic Web Conference (ISWC2005)*, Galway, Ireland (pp. 623-637). New York: Springer.

Stojic, T., Reljin, I., & Reljin, B. (2006). Adaptation of multi-fractal analysis to segmentation of micro-calcifications in digital mammograms. *Physica A, 367*, 494–508. doi:10.1016/j.physa.2005.11.030

Stosic, T., & Stosic, B. D. (2006). Multi-fractal analysis of human retinal vessels. *IEEE Transactions on Medical Imaging, 25*(8), 1101–1107. doi:10.1109/TMI.2006.879316

Struyf, J., Dzeroski, S., Blockeel, H., & Clare, A. (2005). Hierarchical multi-classification with predictive clustering trees in functional genomics. In *Proceedings of the Workshop on Computational Methods in Bioinformatics at the 12th Portuguese Conf. on AI*.

Su, Z., Zhang, H. J., & Ma, S. P. (2000, November 13-15). Using bayesian classifier in relevant feedback of image retrieval. In *Proceedings of the IEEE International Conference on Tools with Artifitial Intelligence*, Vancouver, BC, Canada (pp. 258-261).

Subrahmanian, V. S. (1998). *Principles of multimedia database systems*. San Francisco: Morgan Kaufmann

Sun Microsystems. (2009). *Java SE Downloads*. Retrieved from http://java.sun.com/javase/downloads/index.jsp

Sun Microsystems. (2009). *Java Speech API*. Retrieved from http://java.sun.com/products/java-media/speech/

Sun, B., Song, S.-J., & Wu, C. (2009). A new algorithm of support vector machine based on weighted feature. In *Proceedings of the IEEE International Conference on Machine Learning and Cybernetics* (pp. 1616-1620).

Sun, K., & Bai, F. (2008). Mining weighted association rules without preassigned weights. *IEEE Transactions on Knowledge and Data Engineering, 20*(4), 489–495. doi:10.1109/TKDE.2007.190723

Suzuki, E., Gotoh, M., & Choki, Y. (2001). Bloomy decision tree for multi-objective classification. In *Proceedings of the European Conference on Principles of Data Mining and Knowledge Discovery* (pp. 436-447).

Swain, M. J., & Ballard, D. H. (1991). Color indexing. *International Journal of Computer Vision*.

Symeonidis, P., Ruxanda, M., Nanopoulos, A., & Manolopoulos, Y. (2008). Ternary Semantic Analysis of Social Tags for Personalized Music Recommendation. In *Proceedings of the International Conference on Music Information Retrieval*, Philadelphia (Vol. 8, pp. 219-224).

Szeliski, R. (2002). Video mosaics for virtual environments. *IEEE Computer Graphics and Applications*, *16*(2), 22–30. doi:10.1109/38.486677

Takahashi, M., Misu, T., Tadenuma, M., & Yagi, N. (2005). Real-Time Ball Trajectory Visualization using Object Extraction. In *Proceedings of the Conference on Visual Media Production* (pp. 62-69).

Tang, R. (2008). *Mobile Content Adaptation. Product Marketing Dilithium Networks.* Retrieved October 11, 2009, from http://www.dilithiumnetworks.com/pdfs/white_papers/MKT_ART_MobileContentAdaptation.pdf

Tao, F., Murtagh, F., & Farid, M. (2003). Weighted association rule mining using weighted support and significance framework. In *Proceedings of ACM SIGKDD International Conference on Knowledge Discovery and Data Mining (KDD03)* (pp. 661-666).

Tao, B., & Dickson, B. W. (2000). Texture recognition and image retrieval using gradient indexing. *Journal of Visual Communication and Image Representation*, *11*(3), 327–342. doi:10.1006/jvci.2000.0448

Thatch, E., & Murphy, K. (1995). Competencies for distance education professionals. *Educational Technology Research and Development*, *43*(1), 57–79. doi:10.1007/BF02300482

The MPlayer Project. (2008). *MPlayer*. Retrieved from http://www.mplayerhq.hu/design7/news.html

Theobalt, C., Albrecht, I., Haber, J., Magnor, M., & Seidel, H.-P. (2004). Pitching a Baseball: Tracking High-Speed Motion with Multi-Exposure Images. In *Proceedings of ACM SIGGRAPH* (pp. 540-547). New York: ACM Publishing.

Tian, X., Yang, L., Wang, J., Yang, Y., Wu, X., & Hua, X.-S. (2008). Bayesian video search reranking. In *Proceedings of the ACM International Conference on Multimedia (MM08)* (pp. 131-140).

To detect motion through background subtraction using a PTZ camera. In *Proceedings of the Advanced Video and Signal Based Surveillance (AVSS 2005)* (pp. 511-516). Washington, DC: IEEE.

Tomasi, G., & Bro, R. (2005). PARAFAC and Missing Values. *Chemometrics and Intelligent Laboratory Systems*, *75*(2), 163–180. doi:10.1016/j.chemolab.2004.07.003

Tomassini, M. (1998). A survey of genetic algorithm. *Annual Reviews of Computational. Physics*, *3*, 87–118.

Tricot, C. (1993). *Curves and Fractal Dimension*. Berlin: Springer.

Trohidis, K., Tsoumakas, G., Kalliris, G., & Vlahavas, I. (2008). Multilabel classification of music into emotions. In *Proceedings of the International Conference on Music Information Retrieval*.

Troncy, R., & Carrive, J. (2004). A Reduced yet Extensible Audio-Visual Description Language. In *Proceedings of the 2004 ACM Symposium on Document Engineering* (pp. 87-89). New York: ACM.

Troncy, R., Celma, O., Little, S., Garcia, R., & Tsinaraki, C. (2007). Mpeg-7 based Multimedia Ontologies: Interoperability Support or Interoperability Issue. In *Proceedings of the 1st International Workshop on Multimedia Annotation and Retrieval enabled by Shared Ontologies (MAReSO)*, Genova, Italy.

Troncy, R. (2003). Integrating Structure and Semantics into Audio-Visual Documents. *Lecture Notes in Computer Science*, 566–581.

Truong, B. T., Dorai, C., & Venkatesh, S. (2000). New enhancements to cut, fade, and dissolve detection processes in video segmentation. In *Proceedings of the ACM International Conference on Multimedia* (pp. 219-227).

Tsinaraki, C., Polydoros, P., & Christodoulaki, S. (2004). Interoperability Support for Ontology-based Video Retrieval Applications. *Lecture Notes in Computer Science*, 582–591.

Tsinaraki, C., Polydors, P., & Christodoulakis, S. (2007). Interoperability Support between MPEG-7/21 and OWL in DS-MIRF. *IEEE Transactions on Knowledge and Data Engineering*, *19*(2), 219–232. doi:10.1109/TKDE.2007.33

Tsoumakas, G., & Vlahavas, I. (2007). Random k-labelsets: An ensemble method for multilabel classification. In J. Kok, J. Koronacki, R. de Mantaras, S. Matwin, D. Mladenic, & A. Skowron (Eds.), *Proceedings of the European Conference on Machine Learning* (LNAI 4701, pp. 406-417). Berlin: Springer Verlag.

Tsoumakas, G., & Katakis, I. (2007). Multi label classification: An overview. *International Journal of Data Warehousing and Mining, 3*(3), 1–13.

Ueda, N., & Saito, K. (2003). Parametric mixture models for multi-labeled text. In Becker, S., Thrun, S., & Obermayer, K. (Eds.), *Advances in Neural Information Processing Systems* (*Vol. 15*). Cambridge, MA: MIT Press.

Uma, K., & Ramakrishnan, K. R. (1996). Image analysis using multi-fractals. In *Proceedings of the IEEE International Conference on Acoustics, Speech, and Signal Processing, 4*, 2188–2190.

Urdan, T., & Midgley, C. (2001). Academic self-handicapping: What we know, what more there is to learn. *Educational Psychology Review, 13*, 115–138. doi:10.1023/A:1009061303214

Vadivel, A., Majumdar, A. K., & Sural, S. (2004). Characteristics of weighted feature vector in content-based image retrieval applications. In *Proceedings of the IEEE International Conference on Intelligent Sensing and Information Processing (ICISIP04)* (pp. 127-132).

Vajda, P., Dufaux, F., Minh, T. H., & Ebrahimi, T. (2009). Graph-based approach for 3d object duplicate detection. In *Proceedings of the International Workshop on Image Analysis for Multimedia Interactive Services.*

Van Ossenbruggen, J., Nack, F., & Hardman, L. (2004). That Obscure Object of Desire: Multimedia Metadata on the Web, Part-1. *IEEE MultiMedia, 11*(4), 38–48. doi:10.1109/MMUL.2004.36

Van, E. R. (2006). Digital Game-Based Learning: It's Not Just the Digital Natives Who Are Restless. *EDUCAUSE Review, 41*(2), 16–30.

Van, S., Barnard, Y. F., & Sandberg, J. (1994). *The Think Aloud Method: A Practical Guide to Modelling*. London: Academic Press.

Vens, C., Struyf, J., Schietgat, L., Dˇzeroski, S., & Blockeel, H. (2008). Decision trees for hierarchical multi-label classification. *Machine Learning, 73*(2), 185–214. doi:10.1007/s10994-008-5077-3

Vodanovich, S., & Piotrowski, C. (2005). Faculty Attitudes toward Web-Based Instruction May Not Be Enough: Limited Use and Obstacles to Implementation. *Journal of Educational Technology Systems, 33*(3), 309–318. doi:10.2190/V2N7-DMC4-2JWB-5Q88

W3C. (2003). W3C Device Independence Working Group. *Authoring Challenges for Device Independence. W3C Working Group. Note 1 September 2003*. Retrieved November 5, 2009, from http://www.w3.org/TR/acdi/

Wakabayashi, T., Pal, U., Kimura, F., & Miyake, Y. (2009). F-ratio based weighted feature extraction for similar shape character recognition. In *Proceedings of the IEEE International Conference on Document Analysis and Recognition (ICDAR09)* (pp. 196-200).

Wan, W. (2007). *Semi-parametric techniques for multi-oesponse optimization*. Doctoral dissertation, Virginia Polytechnic Institute and State University.

Wang, W., Yang, J., & Yu, P. S. (2000). Efficient mining of weighted association rules (WAR). In *Proceedings of the ACM SIGKDD International Conference on Knowledge Discovery and Data Mining (KDD00)* (pp. 270-274).

Wang, Y. J., Zheng, X., Coenen, F., & Li, C. Y. (2008). Mining allocating patterns in one-sum weighted items. In *Proceedings of the IEEE International Conference on Data Mining Workshops (ICDMW08)* (pp. 592-598).

Wang, J. Z., Li, J., & Wiederhold, G. (2001). SIMPLIcity: Semantics-sensitive integrated matching for picture libraries. *IEEE Transactions on Pattern Analysis and Machine Intelligence, 23*, 947–963. doi:10.1109/34.955109

Wantanabe, H., & Jinzenji, K. (2001). Sprite coding in object-based video coding standard: MPEG-4. In *Proccedings of World Multiconf, on SCI 2001* (pp. 420-425).

Warshall, S. (1962). A theorem on boolean matrices. *Journal of the ACM, 9*(1), 11–12. doi:10.1145/321105.321107

Wedman, J. (2009). The Performance Pyramid. In R. Watkins & D. Leigh (Eds.), *Handbook of Improving Performance in the Workplace. Volume 2: Selecting and Implementing Performance Interventions.* New York: John Wiley & Sons.

Wei, X.-Y., Jiang, Y.-G., & Ngo, C.-W. (2009). Exploring inter-concept relationship with context space for semantic video indexing. In *Proceedings of the ACM International Conference on Image and Video Retrieval (CIVR09)* (pp. 1-8).

Winkler, W. (1999). *The State of Record Linkage and Current Research Problems (Tech. Rep.).* Washington, DC: U. S. Census Bureau, Statistical Research Division.

Witten, I. H., & Frank, E. (2005). *Data mining: Practical machine learning tools and techniques* (2nd ed.). San Francisco: Morgan Kaufmann.

Wu, X., Zhang, L., & Yu, Y. (2006). Exploring social annotations for the semantic web. In *Proceedings of the international Conference on World Wide Web*, New York (Vol. 15, pp. 417-426).

Wu, P. (2000). A texture descriptor for browsing and similarity retrieval. *Signal Processing Image Communication, 16*(1-2), 33–43. doi:10.1016/S0923-5965(00)00016-3

Yamauchi, Y., Fujiyoshi, H., Hwang, B.-W., & Kanade, T. (2008). People Detection Based on Co-Occurrence of Appearance and Spatiotemporal Features. In *Proceedings of the International Conference on Pattern Recognition* (pp. 1-4).

Yan, R., Tesic, J., & Smith, J. R. (2007). Model-shared subspace boosting for multi-label classification. In *Proceedings of the ACM SIGKDD International Conference on Knowledge Discovery and Data Mining* (pp. 834-843). New York: ACM Press.

Yanagawa, A., Chang, S.-F., Kennedy, L., & Hsu, W. (2007). *Columbia University's baseline detectors for 374 LSCOM semantic visual concepts* (Tech. Rep. No. 222-2006-8). New York: Columbia University, ADVENT.

Yang, C., & Lozano-Prez, T. (2000, February 28-March 3). Image database retrieval with multiple-instance learning techniques. In *Proceedings of the 16th International Conference on Data Engineering,* San Diego, CA (pp. 233-243).

Yang, Y.-H., & Hsu, W. H. (2008). Video search reranking via online ordinal reranking. In *Proceedings of the IEEE International Conference on Multimedia and Expo (ICME08)* (pp. 285-288).

Yang, Y. (1999). An evaluation of statistical approaches to text categorization. *Information Retrieval, 1*(1-2), 69–90. doi:10.1023/A:1009982220290

Yap, M. H., et al. (2009). A short review of methods for face detection and multi-fractal analysis. In *Proceedings of the IEEE International Conference on Cyber Worlds* (pp. 231-236).

Yeh, M.-C., & Cheng, K.-T. (2009). Video copy detection by fast sequence matching. In *Proceedings of the ACM International Conference on Image and Video Retrieval* (pp. 1-7).

Yu, K., Yu, S., & Tresp, V. (2005). Multi-label informed latent semantic indexing. In *Proceedings of the International ACM SIGIR Conference on Research and Development in Information Retrieval* (pp. 258-265). New York: ACM Press.

Yuan, J., Duan, L.-Y., Tian, Q., & Xu, C. (2004). Fast and robust short search using an index structure. In *Proceedings of the ACM SIGMM International Workshop on Multimedia Information Retrieval* (pp. 61-68).

Yu, X., Xu, C., Tian, Q., & Leong, H. W. (2003). A Ball Tracking Framework for Broadcast Soccer Video. In *Proceedings of the IEEE International Conference on Multimedia & Expo, II,* 273–276.

Zabih, R., Miller, J., & Mai, K. (1995). A feature-based algorithm for detecting and classifying scene breaks. In *Proceedings of the ACM International Conference on Multimedia* (pp. 189-200).

Zaharieva, M., Zeppelzauer, M., Mitrović, D., & Breiteneder, C. (2009). Finding the missing piece: Content-based video comparison. In *Proceedings of the IEEE International Symposium on Multimedia* (pp. 330-335).

Zeppelzauer, M., Mitrović, D., & Breiteneder, C. (2008). Analysis of historical artistic documentaries. In *Proceedings of the International Workshop on Image Analysis for Multimedia Interactive Services* (pp. 201-206).

Zhang, C., & Chen, X. (2005, August 21-24). OCRS: An interactive object-based image clustering and retrieval system. In *Proceedings of the 4th International Workshop on Multimedia Data Mining (MDM/KDD2005), ACM SIGKDD International Conference on Knowledge Discovery & Data Mining,* Chicago (pp. 71-78).

Zhang, C., & Chen, X. (2005, July 20-22). Region-based image clustering and retrieval using multiple instance learning. In *Proceedings of the International Conference on Image and Video Retrieval,* Singapore (pp. 194-204).

Zhang, C., Chen, S.-C., Shyu, M.-L., & Peeta, S. (2003, December 15-18). Adaptive background learning for vehicle detection and spatio-temporal tracking. In *Proceedings of the 4th IEEE Pacific-Rim Conference on Multimedia,* Singapore (pp. 1-5).

Zhang, D., & Chang, S.-F. (2006). A generative-discriminative hybrid method for multi-view object detection. In *Proceedings of the IEEE International Conference on Computer Vision and Pattern Recognition.*

Zhang, D.-Q., & Chang, S.-F. (2004). Detecting image near-duplicate by stochastic attributed relational graph matching with learning. In *Proceedings of the ACM International Conference on Multimedia* (pp. 877-884).

Zhang, M.-L., & Zhou, Z.-H. (2007b). Multi-label learning by instance differentiation. In *Proceedings of the AAAI Conference on Artificial Intelligence* (p. 669).

Zhang, J., Marszalek, M., Lazebnik, S., & Schmid, C. (2007). Local features and kernels for classification of texture and object categories: A comprehensive study. *International Journal of Computer Vision, 73*(2), 213–238. doi:10.1007/s11263-006-9794-4

Zhang, M.-L., & Zhou, Z.-H. (2007a). ML-KNN: A lazy learning approach to multi-label learning. *Pattern Recognition, 40*(7), 2038–2048. doi:10.1016/j.patcog.2006.12.019

Zhang, T. (2004). Convex risk Minimization. *Annals of Statistics, 32,* 56–85. doi:10.1214/aos/1079120130

Zhou, J., & Zhang, X.-P. (2005). Automatic identification of digital video based on shot-level sequence matching. In *Proceedings of the ACM International Conference on Multimedia* (pp. 515-518).

Zhu, Q., Lin, L., Shyu, M.-L., & Chen, S.-C. (2010). A novel metric integrating correlation and reliability for feature selection. In *Proceedings of the IEEE International Conference on Semantic Computing (ICSC10).*

Zhu, S., Ji, X., Xu, W., & Gong, Y. (2005). Multi-labelled classification using maximum entropy method. In *Proceedings of the International ACM SIGIR Conference on Research and Development in Information Retrieval* (pp. 274-281). New York: ACM Press.

Zhu, Z., & Hanson, A. R. (2005, September 11-14). Mosaic-based 3D scene representation and rendering. In Proceedings of the IEEE International Conference on *Image Processing (ICIP 2005)* (Vol. 1, p. 633).

Ziegler, A., & Heller, K. A. (2000). Approach and avoidance motivation as predictors of achievement behavior in physics instructions among mildly and highly gifted eight-grade students. *Journal for the Education of the Gifted, 23*(4), 343–359.

Zimmerman, B. J. (2000). Self-efficacy. An essential motive to learn. *Contemporary Educational Psychology, 25*(1), 82–91. doi:10.1006/ceps.1999.1016

Ziou, D., Hamria, T., & Boutemedjeta, S. (2009). A hybrid probabilistic framework for content-based image retrieval with feature weighting. *Pattern Recognition, 42*(7), 1511–1519. doi:10.1016/j.patcog.2008.11.025

Zomet, A., Levin, A., Peleg, S., & Weiss, Y. (2006). Seamless image stitching by minimizing false edges. *IEEE Transactions on Image Processing, 15*(4), 969–977. doi:10.1109/TIP.2005.863958

About the Contributors

Shu-Ching Chen is a Full Professor at School of Computing and Information Sciences (SCIS), Florida International University (FIU), Miami since August 2009. Prior to that, he was an Assistant/ Associate Professor in SCIS at FIU from 1999. He received Ph.D. degree in Electrical and Computer Engineering in 1998, and Master's degrees in Computer Science, Electrical Engineering, and Civil Engineering, all from Purdue University, West Lafayette, IN, USA. His main research interests include distributed multimedia database management systems and multimedia data mining. He is the Editor-in-Chief of *International Journal of Multimedia Data Engineering and Management.* He is a Fellow of SIRI.

Mei-Ling Shyu has been an Associate Professor at Department of Electrical and Computer Engineering (ECE), University of Miami (UM) since June 2005. Prior to that, she was an Assistant Professor in ECE at UM from 2000. She received her Ph.D. degree from Electrical and Computer Engineering in 1999, and her Master's degrees from Computer Science, Electrical Engineering, and Restaurant, Hotel, Institutional, and Tourism Management, all from Purdue University, West Lafayette, IN, USA. Her research interests include multimedia data mining, management & retrieval, and security. She has authored/co-authored more than 200 technical papers. She is a Fellow of SIRI.

* * *

DeeAnna Adkins is the information architect and Web Team coordinator for MU Extension at the University of Missouri-Columbia. She is a master's student in journalism and has a bachelor's of science in agricultural journalism from the University of Missouri.

Kevin C. Almeroth is currently a Professor in the Department of Computer Science at the University of California in Santa Barbara where his main research interests include computer networks and protocols, wireless networking, multicast communication, large-scale multimedia systems, and mobile applications. He has published extensively with more than 150 journal and conference papers. He is also heavily engaged in stewardship activities for a variety of research outlets including journal editorial boards, conference steering committees, new workshops, and the IETF. He is a Member of the ACM and a Senior Member of the IEEE.

Masaki Aono received Bachelors and Masters in Science degrees in Information Science from the University of Tokyo, Japan and a Ph.D. in Computer Science from Rensselaer Polytechnic Institute, USA. He worked for IBM Research, Tokyo Research Laboratory from 1984 to 2003. Since 2003, he has been a Professor in the Information and Computer Sciences Department at Toyohashi University of Technology. His current research interests include text and data mining, information retrieval, semantic web, and machine learning. He has been a Japanese delegate of the ISO/IEC JTC1 SC24 Standard Committee since 1996, and has been serving as a Japanese chair since 2007.

Gerardo Ayala received the BE. in Computer Engineering from the National Autonomous University of México and his ME. degree in Computer Science from the Muroran Institute of Technology, Japan. Obtained the Ph.D. from The University of Tokushima, Japan, doing research on the modelling of intelligent agents for Computer Supported Collaborative Learning (CSCL) environments. His research interest are: answer set programming models for the personalization of learning applications, mobile learning, software agents and the design and development of environments for the social construction of knowledge. Currently he is a researcher at the Universidad de las Américas Puebla, Mexico.

Ramazan S. Aygün received the B.S. degree in computer engineering from Bilkent University, Ankara, Turkey in 1996, the M.S. degree from Middle East Technical University, Ankara in 1998, and the Ph.D. degree in computer science and engineering from State University of New York at Buffalo in 2003. He is currently an Associate Professor in Computer Science Department, University of Alabama in Huntsville. Dr. Aygun has served on organizing committees of conferences as a co-chair of sessions including IEEE International Conference on Semantic Computing (2007-2009), IEEE International Symposium on Multimedia (2006, 2008). Dr. Aygun has also served on the program committees of around 20 conferences and workshops including ACM Multimedia, MIR Workshop, DEXA, IEEE Int. symposium on Multimedia, and AxMedis. His research interests include multimedia databases, P2P systems, semantic computing, multimedia networking, multimedia synchronization, and video processing.

Jeffrey B. Birch is professor of statistics and director of graduate programs at Virginia Tech, where he has been a faculty member since 1977. Dr. Birch received his MSc (1970) and PhD (1977) degrees in biostatistics from the University of Washington. His area of primary research includes most aspects of regression analysis including robust regression, nonparametric and semiparametric regression, and profile monitoring. Birch is a former associate editor of *Biometrics* (1989-1993).

Christian Breiteneder is a full professor for Interactive Systems with the Institute of Software Technology and Interactive Systems at the Vienna University of Technology. Christian Breiteneder received the Diploma Engineer degree in computer science from the Johannes Kepler University in Linz in 1978 and a PhD in computer science from the University of Technology in Vienna in 1991. Before joining the institute he was associate professor at the University of Vienna and had post-doc positions at the University of Geneva, Switzerland, and GMD (now Frauenhofer) in Birlinghoven, Germany. His current research interests include interactive media systems, media processing systems, content-based multimodal information retrieval, 3D user interaction, and augmented and mixed reality systems.

Sergio Castillo is Full Time Professor at the Engineering School of Universidad Anahuac Xalapa. He is the co-author of several papers at international congress like WMUTE 2008, ICCE2008 and LACLO 2008, and a PhD Candidate in the Universidad de las Américas Puebla. His areas of interest are mobile learning, computational models for learning objects in mobile learning environments, learner modeling, content adaptation, personalized learning, collaborative learning and situated learning.

Chiung-Sui Chang is an associate professor of educational technology at Tamkang University, Taipei, Taiwan. She received Ph.D. degree from University of Kansas, U.S.A. in 2000. Her research interests include information and communication technology (ICT) adoption, e-Learning, and game-based learning.

Wen-Chih Chang is an assistant professor in the Department of Information Management at Chung-Hua University, Taiwan. His research interests include e-learning and game-based learning. He received the B.S.B., M.S., and Ph.D. degrees from the Department of Computer Science and Information Engineering of Tamkang University in 1999, 2001 and 2005. From 2001 to 2005, he focused on SCORM and e-learning at MINELAB. His research interests include game-based learning, mobile learning, distance learning, cooperative learning, petri net, web technology and e-learning specifications (ADL SCORM, IMS SS and IMS QTI).

Wei-Bang Chen is a PhD candidate in the Department of Computer and Information Sciences at the University of Alabama at Birmingham. He received a master's degree in genetics from National Yang-Ming University in Taipei, Taiwan and a master's degree in computer sciences from UAB. His main research area is bioinformatics. His current research involves microarray image and data analysis, biological sequence clustering, and biomedical video and image mining.

Yi Chen received the B.S degree in Information System and Information Management from Shanghai Ocean University (Shanghai Fisheries University), Shanghai, P. R. China in 2006, the M.S degree from Georgia Southwestern State University, USA in 2007. Ms. Chen is a PhD candidate student in University of Alabama in Huntsville now. Her research interests include video processing, mosaic generation, and artificial intelligence.

Yan-Da Chiu just leave the army in 2010 March. He received his Master degree in 2009 from the Department of Information Management at Chung Hua University, Taiwan. In the past two years, he dedicated to board game in game-based learning.

Touradj Ebrahimi is Professor at EPFL heading its Multimedia Signal Processing Group. He is also adjunct Professor with the Center of Quantifiable Quality of Service at Norwegian University of Science and Technology (NTNU). Prof. Ebrahimi has been the recipient of various distinctions and awards, such as the IEEE and Swiss national ASE award, the SNF-PROFILE grant for advanced researchers, Four ISO-Certificates for key contributions to MPEG-4 and JPEG 2000, and the best paper award of IEEE Trans. on Consumer Electronics . He became a Fellow of the international society for optical engineering (SPIE) in 2003. His research interests include still, moving, and 3D image processing and coding, visual information security (rights protection, watermarking, authentication, data integrity, steganography), new media, and human computer interfaces (smart vision, brain computer interface). He is the author or the co-author of more than 200 research publications, and holds 14 patents.

Sanda Erdelez is an Associate Professor at the University of Missouri, U.S.A., School of Information Science and Learning Technologies and the founder of the Information Experience Laboratory (http:// ielab.missouri.edu). She obtained bachelors and masters degrees from the University of Osijek, Croatia; and a Ph.D. from Syracuse University, where she studied as a Fulbright Scholar. Dr Erdelez conducts research, teaching, and consulting in human information behavior, Internet search behavior, and usability evaluation. Her research in accidental aspects of information behavior (information encountering) has been funded by SBC Communication and Dell Inc and she also served as a research team member and a co-PI on research projects funded by the U.S. Department of Education and the National Science Foundation. Dr. Erdelez co-edited (with K. Fisher and L. McKechnie) the Theories of Information Behavior (Information Today, 2005) and authored more than 80 research papers and presentations.

Mahito Fujii is a senior research engineer at the human and information science research division of the Science and Technology Research Laboratories of NHK (Japan Broadcasting Corporation). He received BE, ME, and PhD degrees from Nagoya University, Japan, in 1981, 1983, and 2008. He joined NHK in 1983, and he has been working at the Science and Technology Research Laboratories since 1987. He has mainly engaged in research on visual bio-cybernetics, image and video recognition, and 3D image processing. He was a visiting scientist at the Carnegie Mellon University from August 1991 to February 1992. He worked at the Advanced Telecommunications Research Institute International, ATR, from 1998 to 2000.

Lutz Goldmann is a research scientist in the Multimedia Signal Processing Group (MMSPG), EPFL, Lausanne, Switzerland. He received his Dipl.-Ing. (M.Sc.) degree in Electrical Engineering from the Technical University of Dresden (TUD), Germany in 2002. and the Dr.-Ing. (Ph.D) degree in Electrical Engineering from the Technical University of Berlin (TUB), Germany in 2009. In 2002 he joined Siemens CT IC2, Munich, Germany as a research student where he developed image enhancement techniques for video coding artifact removal. Between 2003 and 2008 he worked as a research assistant at the Technical University of Berlin (TUB), Germany on the detection and recognition of humans within images and videos. He was actively involved in several national and European projects, such as GraVis, VISNET, 3DTV, K-Space and VISNET II. He is the author or co-author of more than 20 research publications. His research interests include 2D and 3D image and video analysis, multimedia quality assessment, and machine learning.

Anna Hemsley is an undergraduate student at the University of Canterbury, New Zealand, studying Computer Science and Mathematics. Her interests include 3D computer graphics, computer vision, medical imaging, algorithms and fractal geometry. She is considering continuing her studies at postgraduate level as she finds research enjoyable and interesting.

Ivan Ivanov is a research assistant and PhD student in Multimedia Signal Processing Group at the Swiss Federal Institute of Technology (EPFL), Lausanne, Switzerland. His research interests include multimedia content annotation and tag propagation by merging textual tags and visually similar objects in social network collections of images and videos. He received Dipl.-Ing. (M.Sc.) degree in Electrical

Engineering from the University of Belgrade, Serbia, in 2006. He worked as a Hardware Design Engineer for Texas Instruments, France, where he participated in the development of low-power VLSI multimedia applications for portable devices. After that, he worked as a Radio Access Network Conceptual Planning Expert in Vip mobile, Serbia, focusing on the definition of national 2G & 3G radio access network parameters and the implementation of new radio access technologies. He is a student member of IEEE.

Allan Knight resides with his wife and son in Santa Barbara, CA where he recently completed his Ph.D. in Computer Science at the University of California, Santa Barbara in 2009. His dissertation explored how computer algorithms and systems can be applied to educational technology to better integrate them into learning environments and study their impact on learning outcomes. He currently works at Citrix Online where his areas of research include distributed systems, multicore programming, massively parallel processing, and VoIP.

George Laur is director of publishing and Web development for University of Missouri Extension and has a bachelor's of science in agricultural journalism from the University of Missouri.

Jong-Seok Lee is a research scientist in the Multimedia Signal Processing Group (MMSPG), EPFL, Lausanne, Switzerland. He received the Ph.D. degree in electrical engineering and computer science in 2006, from KAIST, Daejeon, Korea. He was an adjunct professor at the School of Electrical Engineering and Computer Science, KAIST, in 2007. He is the author or co-author of more than 30 research publications. His research interests include multimedia signal processing, multimedia quality assessment, human-computer interaction, and machine learning.

Lin Lin received the bachelor's degree in electronics engineering from Beijing Institute of Technology, Beijing, P. R. China in 2003 and master's degree in electrical and systems engineering from University of Pennsylvania, Philadelphia, Pennsylvania, USA in 2006. She is currently pursuing the PhD degree at Department of Electrical and Computing Engineering from University of Miami, Coral Gables, Florida, USA. Her research interests include multimedia retrieval, multimedia database, and data mining. She received the *Best Student Paper Award* from the Third IEEE International Conference on Semantic Computing (ICSC) in September 2009.

Aiyesha Ma is a Ph.D. student at Oakland University. She received her B.S. from Eastern Michigan University in both Computer Science and Mathematics, and an M.S. from Oakland University in Computer Science. Her research interests are in the area of pattern recognition, image processing, and data mining. Within these broad topics, she has published papers pertaining to image segmentation, image clustering, shape based image retrieval, and surgery outcome prediction.

Yannis Manolopoulos received the BEng degree (1981) in electrical engineering and the PhD degree (1986) in computer engineering, both from the Aristotle University of Thessaloniki. Currently, he is a professor in the Department of Informatics at the same university. He has been with the Department of Computer Science at the University of Toronto, the Department of Computer Science at the University of Maryland at College Park, and the University of Cyprus. He has published more than 200 papers in journals and conference proceedings. He is coauthor of four monographs: "Advanced Database Indexing", "Advanced Signature Indexing for Multimedia and Web Applications" (both by Kluwer), "R-Trees: Theory and Applications", "Nearest Neighbor Search: A Database Perspective" (both by Springer). He has coorganized several conferences (among others ADBIS'02, SSTD'03, SSDBM'04, ICEIS'06, ADBIS'06, and EANN'07). His research interests include databases, data mining, Web information systems, sensor networks, and informetrics.

Dalibor Mitrović is a teaching and research associate with the Institute of Software Technology and Interactive Systems at the Vienna University of Technology. He received a Master of Science degree in Computer Science in 2005 and a Master of Science degree in Computer Science Management in 2008 both from the Vienna University of Technology, Austria. He participated in the high potential program of the Vienna University of Technology in the year 2007. Dalibor Mitrović currently pursues a PhD in computer science focusing on multi-modal information retrieval. His research interests include audio and multi-modal information retrieval, real-time feature extraction, and computer vision.

Ramakrishnan Mukundan received his Ph.D degree from the Indian Institute of Science, Bangalore, India, in 1996 for his thesis on "Image Based Attitude and Position Estimation Using Moment Functions". Currently, he is an Associate Professor in the Department of Computer Science and Software Engineering, at University of Canterbury in Christchurch, New Zealand. His research interests are in the areas of pattern recognition, image classification, image and video compression, facial expression representation and real-time rendering. Mukundan is a senior member of the IEEE.

Alexandros Nanopoulos is a Professor of Machine Learning in Hildesheim University, Germany. He obtained his PhD from the Aristotle University of Thessaloniki, Greece. The tile of his dissertation was "Techniques for Non Relational Data Mining". From 2004 to 2008 he has been a Lecturer in Aristotle University teaching data mining. Alexandros Nanopoulos is co-author of more than 70 articles in international journals and conferences. He has also co-authored the monograph "Advanced Signature Techniques for Multimedia and Web Applications" and "R-trees: Theory and Applications". His research interests include data mining, machine learning, information retrieval and databases.

Nilesh Patel is Assistant Professor in the department of Computer Science and Engineering at Oakland University, MI. He received his PhD and MS in Computer Science from Wayne State University, MI in 1997 and 1993. Dr. Patel is a proven researcher and educator who has also acquired broad industry experience. Prior to starting his academic career, Dr. Patel worked as a Systems Architect and later as a Software Engineering Manager at Ford Motors Co / Visteon Corporation. He was instrumental in launch of first in-vehicle voice recognition system as well as design and development of first Information and Navigational System at Visteon Corporation. He is interested in Multimedia Information Processing – specifically audio and video processing for indexing, retrieval and event detection; Pattern Recognition and Distributed Data Mining from a distributed heterogeneous data sources; Computer Vision with special interest in medical imaging and diagnostics assistance systems and Mobile Computing – with focus on vehicle computing, collaborative vehicular networks, vehicle data stream processing and its applications.

Anindita Paul is a user experience specialist in the Information Experience Lab at the University of Missouri. She received her PhD from the School of Information Science and Learning Technologies, University of Missouri in 2009. Her primary research is in the area of Human-Computer Interaction that involves Human Information Behavior. She does research and practice to understand usability techniques, assess and evaluate the efficacy of user-centric websites, use of Web Analytics in user behavior studies.

Dimitrios Rafailidis received a B.Sc. (2005), and a M.Sc. (2007) in Information Systems in Computer Science Department of the Aristotle University of Thessaloniki. Currently he is a PhD student in the same institute. His research interests include databases, data mining and Web information systems.

Shin'ichi Satoh is a professor at National Institute of Informatics (NII), Japan. He received his BE degree in 1987 and his ME and PhD degrees in information engineering from the University of Tokyo, Japan, in 1989 and 1992. He was a visiting scientist at the Robotics Institute, Carnegie Mellon University, from 1995 to 1997, and he engaged in research on the Informedia digital video library. He joined NII in 2000. He served as program co-chairs of Pacific-Rim Conference on Multimedia in 2004 and the International Conference on Multimedia Modeling in 2008. He served on program committees of ACM Multimedia, IEEE ICME, IEEE ICCV, ICPR, ACM SIGIR, and WWW among others. His research interests include video semantic analysis, multimedia database, video indexing and understanding, high-dimensional data structure, and image similarity matching. He is a member of IEEE CS and ACM.

Hanif Seddiqui received a Bachelors in Engineering degree in Electronics and Computer Science from Shahjalal University of Science and Technology, Bangladesh and Masters in Information Sciences from Toyohashi University of Technology (TUT), Japan. He is now pursuing Ph.D. in Electronics and Information Sciences at TUT and the degree would be finished by the end of March 2010. He has been studying as a Japanese Government Scholar since 2004. His current research interests include ontology engineering, ontology alignment, semantic knowledge management, text and data mining and information retrieval. He has been working as an Assistant Professor in the department of Computer Science and Engineering at the University of Chittagong, Bangladesh (currently on leave) since 2003.

Ishwar K. Sethi received the PhD degree from Indian Institute of Technology, Kharagpur, India in 1977. Before joining the Oakland University in 1999 as chair of the Computer Science and Engineering Department, he was with Wayne State University for seventeen years. He has published over 150 journal and conference articles. He has served on the editorial boards of *IEEE Multimedia*, *IEEE Trans. PAMI*, *Machine Vision and Applications*, *Pattern Recognition*, and *Pattern Recognition Letters*. He was made IEEE Fellow in 2001 for his contributions to artificial neural networks and statistical pattern recognition.

Chun-Yi Shen is an Assistant Professor of Department of Educational Technology at Tamkang University in Taiwan. He received the B.S. in Psychology at National Taiwan University in 1998, the M.S. in Educational Administration, Leadership, and Policy, and the Ed.D. in Educational Psychology and Technology at University of Southern California in 2002 and 2005. From 2005 to 2006, he has been working as a postdoctoral researcher at the Center for Educational Research and Evaluation in National Tsing Hua University and National Taiwan Normal University. His research interests are in game-based learning, interface design, and the methodologies and tools of usability evaluation for different e-learning environments.

Masahiro Shibata is the director of the Human and Information Science research division of the Science and Technology Research Laboratories of NHK (Japan Broadcasting Corporation). He graduated in 1979 from the Electronics Department, Faculty of Engineering, Kyoto University, from which he also received his Masters in 1981 and PhD in 2003. He joined NHK in 1981 and has been engaged in research and development on information retrieval technology, image database, and contents handling systems. He also contributed to standardization activities of MPEG (ISO/IEC JTC1/SC29/WG11), the Society of Motion Picture and Television Engineers (SMPTE), the Foundation for Intelligent Physical Agents (FIPA), and the Association of Radio Industries and Broadcast (ARIB).

Masaki Takahashi is a researcher at the human and information science research division of the Science and Technology Research Laboratories of NHK (Japan Broadcasting Corporation). He received BS and MS degrees in Ergonomics from Keio University, Japan, in 1997 and 1999. He joined NHK in 1999 and worked at the Yamagata Broadcasting Station. He has been working at the Science and Technology Research Laboratories from 2002. He has been engaged in image and video processing, and his research interests include pattern recognition, object extraction and tracking, sports video analysis, and content production technology. He is also a PhD candidate of the Graduate University for Advanced Studies, Japan.

Andrew Tawfik is a PhD candidate in the School of Information Science & Learning Technologies at the University of Missouri. He received his master's degree in Information Science from the Indiana University. His research interests include human-computer interaction, computer supported collaborative learning, and case based learning.

Péter Vajda received his M.Sc. degree in Computer Science from the Vrije Universiteit, Amsterdam, Netherlands, in July 2006 and in Program Designer Mathematician from Eötvös Loránd University, Budapest, Hungary, in July 2007. He performed his diploma work on selection mechanisms in evolution computing and on using prediction algorithms in human-computer interaction. Since September 2007, he is research assistant and PhD student in Professor Ebrahimi's group at Ecole Polytechnique Fédéral de Lausanne (EPFL), Lausanne, Switzerland. He is involved in several European projects such as, Visnet II Network of Excellence, K-Space and PetaMedia. His research interests include mobile visual search and multimedia content analysis in still image and video. He is a student member of IEEE.

Wen Wan received her PhD in statistics from the Virginia Polytechnic Institute and State University. She is an assistant professor in biostatistics and bioinformatics unit in the Division of Preventive Medicine at the University of Alabama at Birmingham.

Te-Hua Wang is an Assistant Professor of Department of Information Management at Chihlee Institute of Technology, Taiwan. His current research interests are in the scope of E-Learning technologies, Web Computing, and RFID. He received his Ph.D. degree in 2007 from the Department of Computer Science and Information Engineering at Tamkang University, Taiwan. He was the chief researcher of the SCORM research team in the Multimedia Information Networking Lab (MINE Lab.) at Tamkang

University. In the past few years, he joined several E-learning related projects, including SCORM-related projects, game-based learning projects, ubiquitous learning projects, etc. In addition, he is now involved with a jointed project of Ministry of Economic Affairs, Taiwan, to construct a RFID-based smart campus.

Xin Wang is a PhD candidate in the School of Information Science & Learning Technologies at the University of Missouri. She received a master's degree in Communication and a master's degree in English from the University of Wisconsin –Stevens Point. Her research interests include Human-Computer Interaction, Human Information Behavior, user studies, methodological studies in usability, image indexing and retrieval, and digital libraries.

Borchuluun Yadamsuren is a doctoral candidate at the School of Information Science and Learning Technologies of the University of Missouri. She received her M.A. degree in Journalism from the University of Missouri, M.S. degree in computer science from the Mongolian Technical University. Her research focuses on information behavior of different user groups, human computer interaction, and usability studies.

Nobuyuki Yagi is the director of the planning and coordination division at the Science and Technology Research Laboratories of NHK (Japan Broadcasting Corporation). His research interests include image and video signal processing, multimedia processing, content production technology, computer architecture, and digital broadcasting. He received BE, ME, and PhD degrees in electronic engineering from Kyoto University, Japan, in 1978, 1980, and 1992. He joined NHK in 1980 and worked at the Kofu Broadcasting Station, the Science and Technology Research Laboratories, and in the Engineering Administration Department and Programming Department of NHK. He was also an affiliate professor of the Tokyo Institute of Technology from 2005 to 2008. He has contributed to standardization activities at ITU, SMPTE, EBU, and ARIB. He is a member of IEEE, IEICE, IPSJ, and ITEJ.

Maia Zaharieva is a research assistant at the Interactive Media Systems Group at the Institute of Software Technology and Interactive Systems at the Vienna University of Technology. She received her Master of Science degree in Business Informatics from the University of Vienna in 2003. From 2003 to 2007 she was a member of the scientific staff of the Multimedia Information Systems Group at the University of Vienna. Since 2007 she is working toward the PhD degree at the Vienna University of Technology. She has been active in various national and international research projects ranging from e-learning and digital preservation to image and video analysis. Her current research interests include visual media analysis, processing, and retrieval.

Matthias Zeppelzauer is a PhD student at the Interactive Media Systems Group at the Institute of Software Technology and Interactive Systems at the Vienna University of Technology. He received the Master of Science degree in Computer Science in 2005 and the Master of Science degree in Business Informatics in 2006 from the Vienna University of Technology. He has been employed in different research projects focusing on content-based audio and video retrieval. His research interests include content-based retrieval of video and audio, time series analysis and data mining. A special research focus is multimodal retrieval of events from non-traditional sensor data such as bio signals.

Chengcui Zhang is an assistant professor of computer and information sciences at the University of Alabama at Birmingham (UAB) since August, 2004. She received her PhD from the school of computer science at Florida International University, Miami, FL, USA in 2004. She also received her bachelor and master degrees in computer science from Zhejiang University in China. Her research interests include multimedia databases, multimedia data mining, image and video database retrieval, bioinformatics, and GIS data filtering.

Liping Zhou is a PhD student in the Department of Computer and Information Sciences at the University of Alabama at Birmingham (UAB) and member of Knowledge Discovery and Data Mining (KDDM) Laboratory. Her research interests include data mining, multimedia database systems, information and image retrieval. She received her BSc in computer science from Qiqihar University, China and MSc in computer science from University of Science and Technology Beijing, China. She is a student member of the ACM.

Index

positive and negative weighted association rules
  (PNWAR) 15
PostgreSQL 39
predictive clustering tree (PCT) 46
Prewitt operator 128
Prim algorithm 266-268
principal component analysis (PCA) 230
Problems and Programmers (PnP) 258-259

Q

Query-by-Examples (QBE) 8

R

Random Attributed Relational Graph (RARG) 99
Random Forests 119, 121, 131-132, 137-141
Random K-Labelsets (RAKEL) 46
Receiver Operating Characteristic (ROC) 47, 106,
  109
relational block 149, 152
relevance feedback (RF) 7, 62, 66
research development 291, 293-295
Robust classifiers 85
Rule based JRip classifier (JR) 22

S

scale-invariant feature transform (SIFT) 29
self-efficacy 290-292, 294-298
self organizing maps (SOM) 243
Self-Similarity Matrix (SSM) 193, 196
Semantic Link Cloud (SLC) 143, 150-151
Semantic Multimedia Abstraction Definition and
  Query language (SMA-L) 9
Semantic Multimedia Abstractions (SMA) 5
Sequential Minimal Optimization (SMO) 20
Singular Value Decomposition (SVD) 225
Smalltalk Card Game (SCG) 259

Social Learning Theory 291
Speech Recognition System (SRS) 204
sprite evaluation framework (SEF) 163, 167
Statistical Package for Social Science (SPSS) 266
Steepest Descent (SD) 69
Sum of Absolute Differences (SAD) 84
Support Vector Machine (SVM) 29, 51, 77, 129
systematic usability evaluation (SUE) 274

T

Tag-Aware 221, 223-228, 230-237
Tag clustering 222
tensor spaces 224
TREC Video Retrieval Evaluation (TRECVID) 29
true positive rate (TPR) 106

U

Universal Resource Identifier (URI) 150, 246
Universal Resource Name (URN) 246
User-Centered Design (UCD) 274

V

Video copy detection 188-190, 193-194, 201-202
video-on-demand (VOD) 3
Viterbi paths 212, 217

W

Wap User Agent Profile (UAPROF) 251
Web Ontology Language (OWL) 144
Weighed association rule mining (WARM) 14
Wireless Universal Resource File (WURFL) 251
Word Error Rate (WER) 209

Z

Zoom patterns 165, 170